THE
BAREFOOT
BANDIT

THE BAREFOOT BANDIT

THE TRUE TALE OF
Colton Harris-Moore,
NEW AMERICAN OUTLAW

BOB FRIEL

HYPERION

New York

"The Barefoot Bandit Song," page 355, © George Nowak/Barefoot Records (www.barefootman.com).

For maps of the Barefoot Bandit's run, go to www.bobfriel.com.

Library of Congress Cataloging-in-Publication Data

Friel, Bob.
  The barefoot bandit / Bob Friel.—1st ed.
      p.   cm.
  ISBN 978-1-4013-2416-2
  1. Harris-Moore, Colton.   2. Thieves—United States—Biography.   3. Criminals—United States—Biography.   I. Title.
  HV6653.H37F75 2012
  364.16'2092—dc23

                                                              2011047366

Hyperion books are available for special promotions and premiums. For details contact the HarperCollins Special Markets Department in the New York office at 212-207-7528, fax 212-207-7222, or email spsales@harpercollins.com.

Design by Renato Stanisic

FIRST EDITION

10   9   8   7   6   5   4   3   2   1

SUSTAINABLE FORESTRY INITIATIVE   Certified Fiber Sourcing   www.sfiprogram.org

THIS LABEL APPLIES TO TEXT STOCK

We try to produce the most beautiful books possible, and we are also extremely concerned about the impact of our manufacturing process on the forests of the world and the environment as a whole. Accordingly, we've made sure that all of the paper we use has been certified as coming from forests that are managed, to ensure the protection of the people and wildlife dependent upon them.

To great parents (especially mine), and good kids

And to all those trying to fill in the cracks

For Sandi

Contents

PART 1

REACH FOR THE SKY

1

A round 8:30 a.m. everything went to hell. Swirling 60 mph winds grabbed the little plane, shook it, rolled it, threw it down toward the jagged peaks of the Cascade mountains, then slammed it back up into the darkening skies.

The morning had started out smoothly, according to plan. After a night of lashing rains driven down the runway by gusts blowing from across the Canadian border, the predawn skies cleared and fleecy air gently blanketed Orcas Island. The barometer rose and the temperature climbed to 57 degrees, about 15 warmer than expected for a mid-November morning in the far corner of the Pacific Northwest. It looked like fine flying weather—unless you'd checked the reports and saw the obvious shit-storm coming.

Pilots of small aircraft obsess about the weather. Ill winds, icing, poor visibility—all can bring your flight to a terminal, smoldering conclusion. Before the FAA considers a pilot minimally safe to solo, he must study and train intensively, racking up forty or more hours of air time sitting along-side a calm, cool flight instructor ready to instantly take over and recover from blunders that could otherwise kill them both. During ground school, student pilots learn the one surefire way to avoid trouble with dangerous weather: don't fly in it. However, when you're a seventeen-year-old with zero hours of official flight training strapped into a stolen airplane try-ing to make a quick getaway from a whole lotta law enforcement on your tail . . . Well, you have other things on your mind besides the weather forecast.

As the sky began to glow, teasing misty details from the island's steep, evergreen hillsides, the teen had busied himself with final preflight preparations inside one of Orcas airport's private hangars. More than seventy small aircraft bed down on the island, and its single runway averages nearly 150 takeoffs and landings per day. You can watch the airplane action from the parking lot, the adjacent dog park, a spot just north called Smuggler's, or from the woods behind the airport's flimsy deer fence. You can also spy on the comings and goings from Orcas Island's small sheriff station—known to locals as the cop shop—that lies within badge-tossing range of the runway's south end.

A few days earlier, one of the landings was made by a 1999 Cessna 182 Skylane, tail number N24658. The would-be thief recognized that model on sight, just as he knew every Cessna, Piper, Beech, Cirrus, and other small plane. Regardless of its challenges with impulse control and social norms, the kid's brain functioned as an aircraft encyclopedia crammed with engine ratings, performance stats, and avionics capabilities. Flying had been his one constant dream, one soaring aspiration in an otherwise bottom-of-the-barrel life, and he'd been teaching himself about flight since childhood, obsessively paging through airplane books until their bindings disintegrated. Now, at an age when most kids spent all their feverish energy trying to wangle a sweaty hour or two with another teen in a backseat or on a basement couch, Colton Harris-Moore's one overwhelming desire was to spend illicit time in the privacy of a hangar with a plane he planned to make his own.

This particular Cessna, he knew, offered fuel-injected reliability and a rugged, easy-to-fly airframe. It was an airborne SUV, the Ford Bronco of the skies, and he could close his eyes, project an image of the cockpit, and reach out to virtually touch every control, switch, and gauge.

The Cessna had landed, rolled out, and taxied to its home in the airport's hangar farm. Other planes slept under the stars, tied down out on the tarmac, but Colton wanted one stored out of sight. After sundown—after the daily FedEx flight and the last of the commuter runs had taken off for Seattle and Bellingham, and the airport's provincial terminal went dark for the night—he simply walked through the open fence.

A typical small-plane hangar features a large door for the aircraft along with one or more regular-size entrances called man doors. Plane theft is practically unheard of and few private hangars have alarm systems despite housing planes worth hundreds of thousands or millions of dollars. It took just a few seconds to jimmy open the man door. Inside, Colton switched on his headlamp and illuminated his dream.

FLIERS LOVE THEIR AIRPLANES. Passionately. During preflight inspection, a pilot caresses the frame. He runs his hands along the ship's smooth skin, probing her flaps, stroking every inch of her propeller blades, even gently lifting her tail. It seems to go well beyond a simple safety check.

An intimate relationship with an airplane offers its pilot superhuman ability, harnessing simple physics to magical effect. Pull back on the yoke and zoom to ten thousand feet, laughing in the oppressive face of gravity that back on earth remains ready to ruin you just for tripping on the stairs or leaning too far back on a bar stool. For aficionados, planes elicit fanatical devotion.

As Colton scanned the inside of the hangar, he saw the Cessna owner's face watching his every move. The plane belonged to Bob Rivers, a popular radio personality who lived down in Seattle and lived *for* flying his plane up to the San Juan Islands on the weekends. Promotion posters featuring Rivers's smiling, silver-maned mug decorated the hangar walls.

The idea that Rivers owned and flew a small plane had been the subject of much banter on his morning radio show. He'd first had to overcome a deathly "medicate me and wake me when it's over" fear of flying. Pilot friends and the interminable lines for the ferries heading out to the San Juans during the summer tourist season finally convinced him to reconsider the power of flight. Now he loved it, and especially loved his immaculately kept $175,000 Cessna Skylane.

Colton foraged around the hangar until he found the plane's key inside a tackle box sitting amid a pile of stored boating gear. He climbed inside the cockpit, powered up the gauges, and saw that the tanks held enough fuel. As he expected, the Skylane's POH sat inside the plane. The Pilot's Operating Handbook is a detailed manual specific to every aircraft, and includes step-by-step checklists for prepping, starting, taking off, flying, and landing. It's the plane's Rosetta Stone.

Colton had all night to pore over the POH as well as manuals for the avionics, radio, autopilot, and GPS navigation equipment. Out of the small flock of Cessnas roosting at Orcas airport, Rivers's was the only one outfitted with a Garmin MX200, an $8,000 add-on GPS "situational awareness" system that makes navigating similar to a video game. One of these modern GPS chartplotters linked to a plane's mechanical and autopilot systems simplifies much of the flier's in-flight calculations and workload. Click a cursor anywhere on the chart and the computer instantly tells a pilot how to get to his destination. It won't get a plane up in the air, though.

Airplanes want to fly. Pick the right one, like the Skylane—not too complicated, not too powerful, stable high-wing design, built to operate at relatively slow speeds—then meticulously follow the POH checklists, and there's a very good chance that even without taking a single flight class, you could get it up in the air. Then, however, you're royally screwed.

Flying is full of old adages, most of them with at least a touch of dark humor. One of the most famous is: "Takeoffs are optional, but landings are mandatory."

Inside the hangar, Colton also had all night to think about what he was about to attempt—something any rational observer would consider almost certain suicide.

At first light, during the blue hour before actual sunrise, Colton pressed the button to raise the hangar's wide metal door. He unplugged the Tow Buddy from its charger and attached its beetlelike mandibles to the Cessna's nose wheel. Using the little low-geared electric tug, he slowly rolled the one-ton plane out of its hangar. Once clear of the building, he not only walked the tug back inside the hangar, but put it in the exact spot he'd found it. Colton didn't plug its charger back in, but that wouldn't inconvenience Bob Rivers much considering he'd soon have no plane to use it on.

After closing the hangar door behind him, Colton climbed up into the Cessna's left-hand seat. Like every aviation procedure, whether it's a pilot's first Cessna solo or thousandth sortie in a 747, starting a plane is done by checklist. The challenge, at first, is just learning where all the switches and gauges are located. For Colton, though, that wasn't a problem. He'd spent many hours looking at this dashboard exactingly reproduced on computer simulations. Even the walls of his bedroom, instead of being hung with scantily clad pop stars, displayed posters of airplane cockpits.

He checked that the fuel tank selector, throttle, prop, and mixture were all set to their correct positions. Normally, a pilot then yells "Clear!" out the side window to warn anyone near the prop to move or risk being sliced and diced. As this was grand theft, it made sense to skip that step. Master switch on, auxiliary fuel pump on just until fuel flows, throttle back to idle. Hit the starter and feel the tingle in your privates as the 235-horsepower Lycoming whines up and the propeller begins to turn, then suddenly the pistons catch with a distinctive throaty flutter. Go rich on the mixture, throttle to 1,000 rpms. Oil pressure? Check. Lean the mixture, avionics on, navigation lights on. Ready to roll.

Taxiing presents a challenge for first-time Skylane fliers since instinctually everyone used to driving a car tries to steer with the wheel instead of the foot pedals. But Colton knew that. (And hell, he didn't have a driver's license either.) In fact, with all his previous study and experience, the most complex part of the entire episode to this point was adjusting the pilot's seat to his gangly six-foot-five frame.

With so many private planes based on Orcas, none of the neighbors took special notice of the Cessna's early-morning growls. Colton released the parking brake, taxied out of the hangar farm, and turned south toward the still-sleeping town of Eastsound. He then spun the thirty-foot-long plane until its nose aimed straight down runway 34. Blue lights focused his view down the black strip, which ended abruptly in the cold, dark waters of the Salish Sea.

Colton Harris-Moore knew more than enough to fly a small plane—in theory. Reality reared up when he pushed the throttle to the firewall. The engine roared, his heart raced, and the Cessna began to roll forward down the narrow airstrip. Lightly loaded, the plane picked up speed quickly, the blue lights flashing by faster and faster. Colton's eyes darted back and forth between the airspeed indicator—watching it climb toward the magic number—and the end of the runway, which came closer and closer.

This was a kid, an outcast, who'd been bullied and beaten, forgotten and failed, expelled, medicated, incarcerated, and seemingly doomed to society's lowest rung. He'd already blown a number of chances in his young life, but he wasn't going to blow this one.

Colton kept his cool, hit his airspeed number, and pulled back on the yoke. After a breathless moment, the plane's rumbling wheels suddenly went silent. The runway disappeared beneath him, replaced with an epic rush of euphoria.

The white plane rose to the sunrise like a phoenix, an image and reference not lost on its pilot despite his failure at formal education. Colton's flight from the ashes of a wretched childhood, though, had taken a crooked path. He was a wanted outlaw, a wily one-kid crime wave that had swept across two tranquil islands, damaging their small communities' sense of security. His illegal deeds had been escalating for years as he studied crime with the same intensity he brought to teaching himself how to fly. Colton had graduated from stealing food to identities, from skipping school to escaping a prison home, from assaulting a soda machine to macing a cop. He often carried a gun, and he was determined not to go back to jail.

Colton Harris-Moore had also just pulled off one of the most audacious thefts in American history—and he was only getting started.

2

With the sky brightening behind snow-capped Mount Baker on the Washington State mainland, the stolen Cessna turned south, its pilot gaining confidence as the plane gained altitude. After just a few minutes, Colton crossed the border from San Juan County to Island County, and his home, Camano Island, came into view. A small airport lies at the north end of Camano, but that wasn't an option. He already had a price on his head there and his face adorned wanted posters all over the island. Colton continued on, flying unchallenged past Naval Air Station Whidbey Island, Boeing Field, and the region's largest commercial airport, Seattle-Tacoma.

He flew along the flat lip of the continent, where, after dropping precipitously from the Cascades, bottomland spills into Puget Sound. It's a spectacular sightseeing route with a series of volcanoes as waypoints—whenever the weather allows you to see them. The safest course to where Colton was headed called for banking east once he was south of Seattle, putting the icy, awe-inspiring bulk of Mount Rainier in his right window and following I-90 as it cut through Snoqualmie Pass past many of the locations used in David Lynch's eerie Northwest mystery *Twin Peaks*.

Of course "safest" is a relative term.

Soon after takeoff, the rain had started back in. The skies closed and winds reared, gusting to 30 mph at sea level, even higher at altitude. According to the Air Safety Institute at the Aircraft Owners and Pilots Association (AOPA), 80 percent of all accidents in a Cessna Skylane—considered a very safe plane—result from pilot error. Of those, the greatest number of serious accidents occur because the pilot flies into bad weather. The statistics also reveal who is most likely to fly himself to death: a new pilot.

THE CASCADES ACT AS a weather wall, giving eastern and western Washington such disparate climates that you'd think you were on different continents. Air sweeping east across the coast tries to climb these steep mountains carrying heavy burdens of Pacific moisture. Like overconfident hikers, though, they can't make it to the top without casting off much of their load. As a result, the environment changes from near–rain forest to desert in a remarkably short distance from one side of the mountains to the other. The air doesn't give up its moisture without a fight, though.

As weather systems storm across the Cascades, wind shear between temperature gradients creates air waves shaped like ocean rollers, with the same effect on small planes as a Jet Ski feels running through a surf zone. November in the Northwest also brings tempestuous surface flows racing through sharp valleys that concentrate the winds and fire them into the sky like an antiaircraft gun. And turbulence exists even on calm days over the Cascades simply because of the push and pull of gravity reacting to the mass of the mountains. Jumbo jets at high altitude feel all these forces as sharp speed bumps and deep potholes, but their effect on a small plane skimming just above the peaks can be catastrophic. Add the rain, snow, sleet, and fog that can suddenly pounce out of the hills to swallow a plane, and you've got conditions that cause even experienced pilots to pucker at the thought of crossing the mountains when there's a hint of bad weather.

On a good day, a trip across the Cascades means lively turbulence. On November 12, 2008, the atmosphere over the mountains was a frightening world of invisible whirlpools and breaking waves, with wind gusts exploding against the little Cessna like aerial depth charges. Colton later told a friend that as he flew into the mountains, the clouds closed around him, describing conditions as a whiteout. A full-on flush of fear replaced his euphoric buzz and screamed at him to either panic or freeze up—two decidedly fatal options for a pilot. One miscalculation on this already remarkably reckless flight would likely be Colton's last. Turning around at the first hint of weather trouble would have been the only smart option, but also meant a much greater chance he'd go back to prison—and that's not how he'd planned to play this game. In his mind, it was all or nothing. So he kept going.

Colton claims that at one point the Cessna fell into a stomach-churning nosedive toward the ground, plummeting from thirteen thousand to six thousand feet. His fright took physical form as his last meal splattered across the cockpit while he fought to keep the plane in the air.

He says he believes it took the intervention of a higher power, but he finally regained control. After what surely seemed like an eternity, the skies began to clear. Colton made it across the highest part of the Cascades and into the drier air east of the mountain range. The winds remained deadly strong, but the turbulence grew less violent. There hadn't been any question of the plane holding together, just the pilot. But he'd made it this far. Gravity now guaranteed the plane would come back to earth—in how many pieces was up to Colton.

Around 9 a.m., the Cessna left the state of Washington and crossed into the sovereign Yakama Nation, a 1.3-million-acre reservation east of Mount Saint Helens belonging to the Palouse, Sk'in-pah, and twelve other tribes of the Columbia River plateau. It's an area famous for having one of the world's highest number of UFO sightings, with local aliens reportedly fond of appearing as hovering, "inquisitive" balls of light that sometimes follow motorists. In the 1960s, the reservation was also ground zero for Bigfoot sightings.

It's good country for wildlife—regular earth animals as well as the mythical. Stands of cedar, ponderosa pine, and tamarack thin out to sagebrush as the hills climb into bald mountains. The land supports large herds of elk and black-tailed deer, along with mountain goats and lots of black bears. Thousands of wild horses also roam free on the reservation. Whether the outlaw who'd rustled the bucking Cessna in order to escape the angry sheriff acknowledged the Wild West symbolism or not didn't matter. Colton was just searching for a place to put the plane down.

At 9:15, a small band of Yakama hunters stalking elk looked up and saw a plane circling over Mill Creek Ridge, sacred tribal ground in the shadow of 4,710-foot Satus Peak. Totally off-limits to outsiders, it's an area the Yakama call the Place Where the Wind Lives.

To a pilot, it doesn't matter much where the wind lives, but knowing its direction and strength is absolutely critical. Airfields have windsocks and weather instruments. Someone attempting to land out in the wild, though, has to gauge wind speed by reading natural signs: bending grasses, rippling ponds, blowing leaves. On this day, with gale force winds howling around Satus Peak, you were just as likely to see flying coyotes.

The Cessna continued to buzz the area for nearly a half hour as Colton scouted a flatish spot, tried to read the wind sign, double-checklisted landing procedures, and double-gut-checked himself. He had to mentally prepare for what pilots call an off-airport landing, which translates into English as, "Oh shit, I'm about to crash on a hillside."

Landings—even on a perfectly level runway—are where the experience gained by repeated, supervised practice combines with a gradually earned seat-of-the-pants feel for the uneasy interface between air and ground to make an art out of the science of flight.

THE PREFERRED EMERGENCY LANDING—exactly like the preferred non-emergency landing—takes place into the wind for the simple reason that the plane will be moving slower in relation to the ground. The tyrannical side of physics says that the energy of an impact rises as a square of speed. Where the guts hit the ground, that means the faster you're moving the greater the likelihood of crumpling, cartwheeling, fracturing, and bleeding.

The tribal police chief who rushed to the site said the wind sweeping across the ridge that morning was blowing so strong, "it was hard for a man to stand up." Converted to mph, that's about 50, which meant a 100 mph speed difference between landing into or with the wind.

In a steady 50, an experienced pilot could walk the plane in and gently touch down moving at only 10 or 15 mph over the ground. Complications arise, however, when the wind and runway don't line up—like at Mill Creek that day. Loads of wildly popular YouTube clips keyworded to "crosswind landing" show the spine-chilling final approaches forced on pilots when the wind blows across the runway. In a maneuver called crabbing, the plane flies straight toward the landing spot while its nose remains pointing into the wind like a big-haired woman crossing the street facing the wrong way just so her bouffant doesn't get blown out of place. The plane literally flies sideways until it's very close to the ground, where the wind generally calms and where, if all goes well, the pilot can bring the nose around at the last second to face forward.

The spot Colton finally chose to put down was a small clearing at the top of a rugged switchback road where tribal hunters park their 4×4s before hiking into the surrounding hills. Adjacent to the clearing was another thousand feet or so of relatively flat ground covered in scrub.

He almost made it.

Evidence on the ground showed that Colton apparently crabbed the plane toward the clearing but, possibly due to the unpredictable gusts, he hit short. The impact wasn't very violent, leaving only a small gouge in the hard-packed dirt, but the landing wasn't over. The Cessna bounced back into the air and leapt forward, flying over the clearing and up a slight hill, then crunched back to earth, its landing gear bending and metal skeleton twisting from the force of the crash. The plane shuddered across the ground, propeller slicing through sagebrush, until it nosed over into a ditch and finally came to an abrupt stop.

After nearly four hours, the alternately thrilling and terrifying flight was over and the pilot's heart was still beating. He'd started the morning as Colton Harris-Moore, trailer-bred juvenile delinquent and petty thief. When he popped open the door of that stolen Cessna, though, and stepped into the wilds of Washington State haunted by the legends of Sasquatch, D. B. Cooper, *Twin Peaks,* and *Twilight,* he became Colt, the new millennium's ballsiest outlaw.

Move over Bigfoot, meet Barefoot.

3

The hunters had seen the Cessna circle behind the ridge once again, but it didn't reappear. They dialed the Yakama Tribal Police and told them a plane had gone down. The police chief himself, Jimmy Shike, jumped into his SUV and raced for the road that led up into the mountains.

They say "Any landing you can walk away from is a good one." Colt ran away from his first solo landing. He headed for the trees and had barely gotten out of sight before Chief Shike drove up to the clearing.

The chief braced himself against the wind and strode up to the Cessna, which lay nose down, ass in the air, like a paper airplane stuck in the grass. The damage didn't look too extensive at first glance, certainly survivable, but when he didn't see a forlorn pilot sitting beside the pranged plane, Shike expected to find someone inside the cockpit, unconscious or worse.

He peered in . . . no body, no blood. The chief's first thought was that the pilot was injured and either stumbling around incoherent or trying to walk his way off the ridge to find help. The idea that this was a stolen plane never entered his mind. He got on the radio and ordered a search-and-rescue mission, calling in tracking dogs and teams from his force and the Yakima County Sheriff's Office, along with volunteers. Then he called in the tail number of the plane to the Washington State Patrol so they could pull up the registration and find out whom he was searching for.

Bob Rivers had just gotten off the air at 10 a.m. after a typically entertaining four hours of commentary, interviews, and repartee with his radio team when his boss walked into the studio holding a cordless phone. He said there was a state policeman from Yakima who wanted to speak to Bob . . . because his plane had just crashed on the Indian reservation.

Rivers's first thought was that it was a prank call, an occupational hazard when you've spent twenty-plus years doing comedy bits and song parodies like "Cheeseburger with Parasites" and the Christmas favorite "Buttcracker Suite."

The cop asked if he was really speaking to Bob Rivers. "I answered yes, and waited for the punch line," says Rivers. "But he said, 'Oh, I'm very glad to hear your voice because, obviously, that means it wasn't you in your plane.'"

Rivers suddenly realized the guy was serious. There must be a mistake, he told the officer. "My plane is in its hangar on Orcas Island." No way his Cessna could have been in the air that day. He certainly hadn't flown it, and even though friends sometimes took the plane up, they always asked first. Besides, this was definitely a no-fly day. Just an hour before, as their newswoman read the local weather, the thought that shot through pilot Bob's weather-obsessed mind was, Boy am I glad I'm not flying in that!

The statie read out the plane's tail number: November 2-4-6-5-8.

"Yes, that's my number," Rivers told him. "But a lot of people confuse the 8 with a B because tail numbers usually end with a letter." He heard the cop relay the message to the tribal police chief who was standing next to the plane. After a moment he came back on the phone: "Nope, he says it's definitely an 8, not a B. It's your plane."

RIVERS'S PHONE BEGAN RINGING off the hook: the National Transportation Safety Board (NTSB), FAA, San Juan County Sheriff's Office, Bureau of Indian Affairs, and FBI. The realization that his plane had been stolen began to sink in. They had no suspects, but at least, thought Rivers, with all these organizations involved and the search teams scouring the landing site, they'd be sure to catch the crook and solve the case instantly. The thief had a forty-five-minute head start, but he was outnumbered and had experienced Yakama hunters and tracking dogs on his trail.

Then Rivers received a disheartening call. "They told me that since it was now a law enforcement matter and not a rescue that they'd called off the search so no volunteers would be endangered."

Rivers's hopes sank, only to be lifted again by a call from Chief Shike telling him not to worry, that there were only two ways out of the area and one of those would mean a thirty-mile hike. The chief told Rivers that his officers were keeping close watch on the only sensible route anyone would use to get off the mountain on foot.

Colt watched the searchers from his hiding place in the woods, then struck out east, taking the long route no one expected.

THE NEXT MORNING, THE thirteenth, the chief called Bob Rivers again. Bad news, he said, a logging truck driver reported seeing a white male, soaked to the skin, walking out of the Place Where the Wind Lives sometime around 5 a.m.

"I asked him about the status of the investigation, the FAA, the FBI, all the boys," says Rivers. "He told me, 'The investigation has been turned over to me . . . and I have concluded the investigation. Your insurance company may take the plane.' "

In fact, the chief insisted that Rivers remove the plane as quickly as possible because he was forced to keep one of his men up in the hills baby-sitting its carcass twenty-four hours a day or else, he said, the boys on the rez would shoot it to pieces just for target practice.

Tribal police collected a vomit sample but no other forensics from the plane. (Questions arose later as to the handling of the sample and delays in testing. Ultimately, it was tested three times but never came back with usable DNA.)

Rivers was crestfallen. "So that was it: white suspect, property crime, some rich guy's toy . . . No one really cared and they'd never find out who took my plane."

The one person who did know kept moving.

Dressed in just shorts, a sweatshirt, and shoes he says were two sizes too small, Colt claims he hiked for four days with no food, subsisting on two bottles of Gatorade. Toppenish Mountain east of the landing site resembles parts of the Afghan Central Highlands. Instead of the Khyber Pass, though, Colt had access to roadways cut by the Bureau of Indian Affairs. For the first day and a half even the weather cooperated, offering him unseasonably warm temperatures 20 degrees above average. After that, it stayed a balmy 60 during daylight, but fell to below freezing at night. Colt says he hiked thirty miles to the tracks of the Northern Pacific Railway, where he hopped a freight to Oregon, jumped off, stole a car, and drove it to Reno, Nevada. Colt says he spent most of the winter in Reno, staying with a friend.

4

Meanwhile, back on the Wild West's watery frontier, the residents of Orcas Island woke on November 12 to a big breakfast of WTF?

As soon as he'd gotten the call from the state police, Bob Rivers phoned his friend and plane mechanic, Geoff Schussler, and asked him to go check the hangar. Schussler found a whole lot of empty where the Cessna should have been.

Two San Juan County sheriff's deputies responded to the call. Schussler had taken great pains not to touch anything, but he says the deputies shrugged it off, giving a cursory look and telling him that "there weren't any good surfaces" to check for prints. Schussler looked around at a lot of smooth metal and hard plastic that the thief had to touch to break in, find the key, and get the plane out of the hangar. "This was an airplane," he says, "not a stolen bike . . . I thought they'd take it more seriously."

If they had successfully lifted a print, the San Juan County Sheriff's Office would have instantly found that their suspect had been in the system for a very long time considering his age. They would have gotten an earful about him and his MO from their law enforcement brethren down in Island County. With that information, they might have figured out that this wasn't Colt's first Orcas crime by a long shot. As it was, though, it'd be nine months and many more local crime scenes and victims before they even knew whom they were dealing with.

Word of the plane theft spread at small-island gossip speed—a startling velocity equaled only by the rate at which facts twist. Orcas has just five thousand full-time residents, and each exists within one degree of separation from everyone else on the fifty-seven-square-mile island. Like in any small community, but especially a small-island community, anybody's business is everybody's.

No one had ever heard of a plane theft before, certainly not one in a place where a puppy caught chasing chickens makes the newspaper's police report. This was the kind of crime, though, that locals could relish. It was extremely rare, which appealed to our sense of exceptionalism. It was bizarre, which fit the eccentric nature of the island. And hardly anyone felt threatened because it wasn't random and it was hard to identify with. Very few people are lucky enough to even have an airplane to steal, so it was like hearing that someone's pet koala had run away. "Gee, that's a shame . . . I wish I had a koala."

No one had gotten hurt during the crime, but that wasn't necessarily a factor for a juicy San Juans–style sin story. The county's most famous misdeed to date had occurred in 1980, when a "kindly" old woman popped two .38 caps in her husband's head, then had her simpleminded brother chop him up in a bathtub using a decorative battle ax before burning all the bits in a barrel.

In the spring of 2007, a body washed ashore on Orcas with its hands and feet missing. Since then, nine feet—all sans bodies—have shown up in the area's waters from British Columbia down to Island County, making national headlines and prompting speculation of foot-fetish serial killers. The mordantly mundane reality is that people who jump off bridges or fall from boats or otherwise end up in the region's rivers flow to the sea just like the trees that turn into the driftwood piled high on Northwest beaches. Hands and feet, like smaller branches on a floating tree, eventually come loose and the feet—usually shod in buoyant sneakers—sail off on their own journeys, eventually stepping back ashore to freak out beachcombers.

Our most recent headline-making incident occurred in March 2008, when we were treated to the electrifying work of a performance artist/eco-avenger named Gabriel Mondragon, who pulled on Playtex kitchen gloves and tried to cut one of Orcas's power lines with a metal pole saw. His stated goal had been to wreak revenge on "rich white people" because a young orca whale had swum into a tugboat's propeller 170 miles away in Canada. When the first lineman arrived, the anarchist's pants were still smoking. He lost an arm, but survived.

While the occasional titillating crime or wayward body part added to island lore, the core belief on Orcas was that our wide moat of chilly Salish seawater stocked with giant Pacific octopuses and killer whales protected us from the horrifyingly random rapes, home invasions, and murders of the mainland. Bad guys knew it'd be stupid to commit a serious crime on a small island with very limited means of escape. Orcas residents enjoyed such a low crime rate and had such a comforting sense of security ingrained into their island identity that most of us never locked our doors—not cars, not homes, often not even businesses. When local sheriff's deputies did shop-by-shop checks in Eastsound, our one little town, they regularly found open doors and windows.

A deputy once asked a young woman whose car had been taken (and quickly recovered) whether she'd left the keys inside. She replied, "Of course I did: I'm an island girl."

There was crime on Orcas, but it occurred at such a remarkably low level that anyone who wanted to could easily persuade himself that he lived on an island embraced by only peace and serenity. Bobbing in a sea of denial.

HIGH CITY CRIME RATES didn't drive my wife, Sandi, and I to Orcas, but as the little SUV that did slipped sideways down an icy road toward the Anacortes Ferry Terminal one cold January morning in 2007, a sense of safety and security was part of the overall flush of warmth that came when the calm sea and the islands appeared and we knew we were here for good.

We'd been living in Orlando ("Place Where Humidity Lives"), where I worked as the editor of *Caribbean Travel & Life* magazine. The position was intended as a short cash-replenishing pit stop in an otherwise freelance writing and photography career. Meeting Sandi convinced me to stay longer and buy a house on an oak-lined brick street in the downtown historic district. The 1917 bungalow had been listed as a unique fixer-upper opportunity. Its brass historic plaque was the only solid part of the structure, which remained standing despite the millions of termites that found its Craftsman architecture charming and its floor joists delicious.

It took more than a year to make the house livable. The night before we were to finally move in, I began to load up all my tools. I'd been hauling gear back and forth every day to a dingy garage apartment, just in case. But now why bother? We were going to be living in the house in eight hours. I left the tools in the bedroom.

When I showed up the next morning, everything was gone. Saber saw, circular saw, Sawzall, all gone. More tools, equipment, and a couple of bikes were missing from the garage. As I was calling the police, two guys inside a beater car pulled up the driveway, then immediately reversed out when they saw my truck behind the house. They'd come back to load up the rest of our stuff. I ran out of the house and into the street, but couldn't get the plate number.

Two Orlando cops showed up four minutes after I called. They were very nice, and listened politely while I described the car and one of the guys I knew had ripped us off. He was a thirtyish downtown street stain who'd snuffled around whenever I was outside working on the house, giving me sob stories and asking if I had anything for him to do. A week before the burglary, I finally gave in and offered the guy ten bucks to help me haul a load of drywall into the garage.

He groaned like every piece he lifted was his last, then suddenly developed a limp and, when that didn't faze me, a hacking cough. Inside the garage, he eyed the bikes and asked how much work it'd take for him to get one. Not for sale or trade, I said. Then he looked at the extension cords I had snaking around the yard and asked if I had any power tools. I gave him his ten and told him good-bye.

The cops *hmmm*'d and *ahhhh*'d at all the right spots during my tale, and even walked around the porch to look at the window the guy jimmied to get inside. When I bent down to show them the fingerprints clearly visible on the sill and asked if they were going to pull them, they both gave me pitying looks. One tore off a copy of the report, told me that's what my insurance company wanted, and they left.

Ours was a relatively minor burglary, but it still cost thousands out-of-pocket to replace our stuff. I learned that one of the biggest aggravations is that if you're not totally anal and haven't itemized, cataloged, and place-mapped every single possession, you never know all that's missing until you have reason to miss it. Where's that antique drill my grandfather gave me? Did you see my college ring? That, though, was nothing compared to what that worthless hairbag did to our sense of security.

From the first night on, every creak of that very creaky old house might be him or one of his buddies coming back for more, or for worse. Obviously the crooks had been keeping tabs during the renovation and just waiting until there was enough loot to make breaking in worthwhile.

I made my living traveling, leaving town for about one week every month, seven nights when Sandi would have to come home to an empty house on a dark downtown lot where she could never be sure there wasn't someone lurking. The thought of that pissed me off so much that every evening for two weeks after the burglary I walked the downtown streets with a pair of heavy work gloves in my back pocket—I didn't want his blood literally on my hands when I beat the bogus tuberculosis out of him.

I never found him, but there wasn't a single night spent in that house over the following six years when he wasn't there in spirit, as the outside lights were turned on, the windows and doors double-checked, the new alarm armed, and the big dog put on duty.

WE BOUGHT PROPERTY ON Orcas Island after a single hearts-and-minds-winning visit in 2002. Each subsequent summer vacation was filled with our ideal outdoor lifestyle—kayaking, boating, scuba diving, hiking—and an expanding circle of local friends. Orcas became our sanctuary.

We'd wrap up last-minute job details, hassle through airports and across 2,600 cramped sky miles, battle the traffic up I-5 out of Seattle to the ferry terminal . . . and then exhale. The ferry ride offered a leisurely segue from mainland madness to the evergreen air of the San Juan Islands that demanded you take deep breaths. Some 750 islands, rocks, and reefs make up the San Juans. Ninety-seven of them have names, and Orcas has most of the superlatives: largest island, tallest mountain, deepest fjords. It's a place where green meets blue, forests flow into the sea, and mountains climb into the sky, all within the intimate embrace of an island.

Jeremy Trumble, who owns the Inn on Orcas Island and whose parents began bringing him here when he was a child in the fifties, describes arriving like this: "When we got here, my dad suddenly started driving more calmly and us kids started behaving better. You were friendlier to people because the island just invited that—it had this aura. Somehow, Orcas made you a better person. You just wanted to enjoy every moment that you had on the island because it was such a special place."

Sandi and I were determined to live within that Orcas aura for more than two weeks each summer. We spent every spare moment figuring out how to knock years off what was first a retirement plan, then a fifteen-, ten-, and finally five-year plan to move to Orcas full-time.

We'd been able to buy island property only because, after a life spent as a hand-to-mouth freelancer, I had a steady magazine paycheck at a time when bankers were flinging mortgage money at anyone with a pulse. Creatively maxing out our finances still bought only a small, drafty cabin with floors that flexed so much you could knock a cup off the kitchen shelf by stomping on the bedroom floor at the other end of the house. A natural history museum's worth of dead critters clung to the fouled insulation in the crawlspace, and the plumbing sounded as if flushing the toilet angered a clan of badgers living inside the walls.

The original owners had collected rainwater to bathe in and wash their clothes, and they used an outhouse for much of their time on the property, which they named Raven Ridge. When we moved in, the outhouse remained amid a copse of young cedars, standing by with a wonderful view of the water and a fresh roll of TP.

A contractor who came out to bid on bringing the septic system up to snuff brought along an old-timer who didn't say a word while we poked at pipes and walked off distances that'd have to be dredged down our roller coaster of a driveway. Something about the quiet islander's thoughtful manner said "common sense," and at the end of the tour I sidled up and asked: "If this was your property, what would you do?" He looked me up and down, gave me a slight nod, and said simply, "I'd paint the outhouse."

Our cabin windows looked out over nothing but woods and water without a neighbor in sight. The closest lights we could see were on a Canadian island. We never even considered putting up curtains. If voyeuristic eagles and raccoons wanted revenge for all my years of watching National Geographic, so be it. At night, those bare windows turned the darkest black. On Orcas, though, the darkness was never threatening.

From Orcas you can see Vancouver Island—which has North America's highest concentration of mountain lions. You can also see a big chunk of mainland British Columbia, which has the most black bears. Not far up the Inside Passage are islands lousy with gigantic *Ursus arctos horribilus*— grizzly bears. However, the most dangerous wild animal on Orcas other than our overpopulated kamikaze deer is the river otter. Each evening, our dog, Murphy, and I walked the shadowy woods. There were plenty of noises to spark primordial tingles, but you always knew that nothing lurking in the Orcas forest had any intent more nefarious than gathering nuts and nibbling leaves.

I continued traveling frequently for assignments, but now I never worried about Sandi. She was perfectly safe at home, and if she broke down on the road, the next person along would stop and either fix her car or drive her to town. Teenage girls hitchhike around the San Juan Islands without a worry, and getting a ride is so easy that longtime residents think nothing of even counting on their thumbs to get them to the ferry on time.

So we settled in happily, having only the same great concern as every other working person on Orcas: Now that we found this wonderful place, how the hell do we afford to stay here? A good number of wealthy people live on the island, and many more have summer homes. The guy in front of you in line at the hardware store may be the ex-CEO of a huge multinational, a Hollywood producer, or a sickeningly young Internet retiree who optioned out of lastbubble.com just in time. At the other end of the scale, nearly 9 percent of San Juan County residents lived below the poverty line in 2008. There are people who are homeless and there are people who squat in illegal campsites, jetsam shacks, and barely floating boats. There are tarp-topped trailers and threadbare yurts, and a number of people you regularly see around the island look like they've escaped from somewhere.

In between the lost souls and CEOs lay the rest of us: retirees getting by and a working middle class of small-business owners, organic farmers, county workers, carpenters and other tradesfolk, plus an eclectic mix of sculptors, potters, painters, musicians, and writers—many of whom wish they knew carpentry or some other skill that might earn them a steadier income.

The island has no industries other than real estate, construction, and seasonal tourism, so there are very few jobs that pay enough to keep you alive in a place where the price of necessities like groceries and gas are 30 percent higher than the mainland. San Juan County has the second-highest income per capita in Washington State, but its average wage is ranked thirty-fifth out of thirty-nine counties. This means that while there's a lot of money floating around the islands, very little of it is being made by residents who have to work for a living. Most of it comes via investment income of the rich and retired (one-fifth of Orcas's population is over sixty-five). Property costs—which are bid up by the wealthy from all over the world who discover Orcas and want to own a piece as a part-time getaway—coupled with the few jobs and low wages make it especially hard for kids born here. They grow up in this fabulous, desirable place, but then many of them find they can't afford to stay if they ever want to own a home of their own.

While I took on every assignment I could wrangle, Sandi went to work in real estate, because if there's one thing in this world you can count on, it's the real estate market.

As the crash began, Sandi picked up a second and then a third job, becoming one of many, many Orcas residents who work multiple jobs in order to help their family cling to what they think is the most wonderful rock on the planet. Orcas or bust.

5

___

I was drinking a late-morning cup of tea when the news reached me about Bob Rivers's plane.

With some 230,000 general aviation aircraft based in the United States, there have been, on average, only eight stolen each year of the last decade. Nearly all of those thefts happen near or across the Mexican border, especially in Baja, where authorities say cartel lookouts keep watch for the right kinds of planes—primarily Cessnas—then call in trained air pirates to fly them off to join drug-carrying fleets. American private pilots even refer to certain antitheft devices that fit over throttles and props as "Mexican locks."

Of course there's another border to the north. Ever since it became part of the United States, Orcas Island, with its scalloped shoreline, deep fjords, and dark, secluded coves, has enjoyed a storied history as a transshipment point for whatever products the era's taxes and laws made profitable to move from Canada into the lower forty-eight. Silk, wool clothing, Chinese laborers, opium for the Chinese laborers, Prohibition whiskey, and so on came through with a wink and a nod. At its closest point, the Canadian border lies less than a five-mile boat run from Orcas's northwest tip. The beach at the top of the island isn't called Smuggler's for nothing.

Today, the most popular hooch flowing south from Canada is the mind-bendingly potent wacky weed called BC Bud that, according to our local Customs and Border Protection (CBP) officers, trades pound for pound with the cocaine headed north. The vast majority of drugs drive across the line hidden in trucks, but CBP has found weed, coke, and hockey bags filled with cash aboard boats crossing the 165-mile-long watery border that runs a zigzag course from the shore of the mainland, around the San Juan Islands, and out the Juan de Fuca Strait to the Pacific Ocean. The CBP's Air and Marine base in Bellingham, just thirteen miles from Orcas, operates blistering-fast nine-hundred-horsepower patrol boats along with a Black Hawk helicopter loaded with all the high-tech surveillance goodies to keep watch on the sea border. Still, it's the thinnest of thin blue lines.

Orcas residents who live near the airport have grown accustomed to hearing planes taking off and landing at all hours of the night. "There are a lot of legitimate reasons for planes to be operating then, especially medical evacuations," says Bea Von Tobel, the airport manager. "But it's also not too hard to imagine a plane coming in to drop off a bag of something and then taking off again."

Once a bale, bag, or bad guy smuggled out of Canada made it onto Orcas Island, it or he would be close to home free. The San Juans may mentally, culturally, and psychically feel like its own independent, far-out archipelago, but it's part of the United States. Orcas is one of four islands in the group served by Washington State Ferries, the largest ferry system in the country, third largest in the world. There are no passport checks, no Customs, and no security screenings to walk or drive onto a ferry at Orcas, and there'd only recently been some random stops at Anacortes on the mainland, where cars rolled off to drive to Anywhere, U.S.A.

"My first thought, after checking to make sure any of my pilot friends who might have borrowed the plane were okay, was that it obviously had to be taken for a drug run," says Bob Rivers. "Everything fit. The random stops were happening. Somebody must have had a load they needed to get off Orcas, so they brought in a pilot to fly it out. Where does the plane end up? The Yakama reservation, where they have plenty of problems with drugs and gangs. Even the spot my plane landed was at the top of a road where they could have had an SUV waiting. And they weren't worried about getting the plane out, just transporting the load. It all made sense; it had to be drugs. My plane stolen to take a joyride? Never. Especially not on a day like that!"

Rivers's insurance agent had other ideas. "I started feeling like a suspect because all the insurance guy ever said was, 'We're sure it was someone you know. Who do you know who could have done this?'"

In one of many fateful connections and coincidences to emerge as Colton Harris-Moore stole his way around the Northwest, his theft of Bob Rivers's plane actually saved a life. One of Rivers's pilot friends had been suffering through devastating health and work problems. Things looked hopeless, so he came up with a plot to kill himself by flying a small plane up into the Cascades until the wings iced over and it fell out of the sky. When he heard about Rivers's plane, though, he had to cancel his suicide because he knew the insurance company would never believe the coincidence of two aircraft connected to two friends going down in the same mountains, both under suspicious circumstances. He feared that his family would never collect the life insurance. So he kept living, and things ultimately turned around and got better for him.

While the insurance company grilled Bob Rivers over his crashed Cessna, the residents of Orcas went back to their lives, the theft just another twisted footnote to add to local history.

6

The fire blazing in their outdoor woodstove made it feel like our friends Jay Fowler and Teri Williams were telling ghost stories that cool summer evening in 2008, several months before Bob Rivers's plane was stolen. Teri, a real estate and building permit pro, had found our home for us. Jay works as a lineman for OPALCO, which is officially called Orcas Power and Light Cooperative when things are operating okay, but is locally known as Occasional Power and Light because the electricity goes out whenever a seal farts near the underwater cable that feeds the island.

Between the two of them, they knew the island, its people, and its goings-on as well as anybody. They'd been instrumental in helping us rush our plans to move to Orcas full-time, and now, when the wine and beer were flowing after we'd just finished off a wonderful Northwest potluck of fresh-caught salmon and Dungeness crab, they were telling us there might be a crime problem.

Teri said that the top cop on Orcas had passed along a private warning about a series of strange break-ins on the island. "He said, 'If you knew the shit that I did, you'd start locking your doors.'"

I was incredulous. We'd been living on the island full-time for over a year and a half and nothing had occurred that might cloud the idyllic image of our new home. Sandi and I discussed it on the way home and weren't concerned enough to change anything. Besides, neither of us had even seen a house key since Christmas.

The details were sketchy anyway—just jungle-drum rumors. I figured I'd check out some of the stories floating around to see if there was anything to them. Little did I realize that what we didn't know—including some un-nerving incidents that our sheriff's office was trying hard to keep quiet—was enough to fill a book. Our untouchable little island had already become the happy hunting ground of the twenty-first century's first out-law legend.

THOUGH JUST A BIT over thirteen miles wide, it can take an hour to drive from one side of Orcas to the other, as roads skirt mountains and coast around the three inlets that cut deeply into the island from the south. A seven-mile-long fjord, East Sound, nearly cuts Orcas Island in two. At the top of the waterway lies the island's only town, creatively named Eastsound.

The town wanders back from its waterfront Main Street and climbs a slight rise. On the other side of the hill, which runs down to the ocean, lies a pocket of schools and churches and the small airport. From shore to shore—fjord to sea—Orcas is barely 1.3 miles wide at Eastsound, with the great bulk of the island hanging down to either side of town. A big-idea guy once tried to dig a canal across that narrow span so trading ships wouldn't have to sail clear around the island and up the long sound. For-tunately he gave up after dredging only about four hundred yards, leaving what's known as the Ditch, now used as a marina, between the airport runway and Smuggler's Villa Resort.

Behind town on Mount Baker Road—named for its spectacular view of the closest snow-capped volcano on the mainland—lies Orcas Center, the cultural core of an island that hosts a tremendous amount of artistic and musical talent in relation to its size.

From Main, Eastsound's shopping district runs up two streets: North Beach Road and Prune Alley, which contrary to popular belief was not named by the island's retirees in homage to their favorite fiber. It got its name because, along with apples, pears, and strawberries, Orcas farmers once grew and exported large harvests of Italian plums.

There are no stoplights in Eastsound—or anywhere else on the island. It's a one-horse town, though instead of a horse, there's a cow. Her name is April, she's twenty-three, lovably homely, and lives in a field at the end of Enchanted Forest Road. April the cow is also a perennial candidate for mayor. Since the town remains unincorporated, it has no actual government. Each year we elect an animal as honorary mayor. It costs $1 a vote, and all proceeds go to support Orcas Island Children's House, a facility that helps local working-class families with educational day care and preschool. The fund-raising pitch for Children's House reads in part: "money not invested in a child during this early phase may cost the emerging community member, and society, enormously in the form of a socially disruptive adulthood."

From an adult's perspective, the island seems an idyllic place to grow up. For some tweens and teens, though, once their hormones tell them that climbing trees and catching fish can't possibly be the end-alls of excitement, the island becomes a big ball of boring. With nothing much to do—not to mention a very limited dating pool—kids begin looking for trouble. Some manage to limit themselves to high jinks such as Yogi Bearing picnic baskets and beer from tourists in Moran State Park. Others go further, venturing into more felonious behavior. No matter what they do, though, there's a good chance they'll get caught. Kids call the island Orcatraz because everywhere they turn there's a prison guard in the form of someone who knows their parents and won't hesitate to call them.

In the early nineties, there suddenly seemed to be a flood of serious trouble with local island kids. Orcas residents looked around and realized they had a big problem.

The single mother of one troublemaker asked Mike Stolmeier, manager of Smuggler's Villa Resort, to accompany her son to the courthouse in Friday Harbor, the county seat, over on San Juan Island.

"There was a dozen other Orcas kids on that ferry, eighth and ninth graders, all going over to get felony charges put on them, and not one parent or even a lawyer with them," says Stolmeier. "I thought, What a bunch of idiot parents we got around here."

Stolmeier had been on Orcas since 1985, was raising his own teen, and saw the storm developing. "Yeah, the kids were screwed up and behaving badly, but it was as if we were eating our young. The community was after them, the cops were after them, and the prosecutor we had at the time was trying to make a reputation so he could move on to someplace else. The community overreacted and really ruined some lives—there was no way those kids would ever get a chance to try and fit back into our society. As a sociological event, it was horrible."

Level heads in the community came up with an alternative to hiring a *Chitty Chitty Bang Bang*-style child catcher. They developed a number of sports, activities, and mentoring programs to give the kids something constructive to do. "These were things that should have been here for them in the first place," says Stolmeier. "It worked for the kids who hadn't already gotten in trouble, and things got a lot better for everybody."

According to stats put together by one of those nonprofit programs, the Orcas Funhouse, over the last decade Orcas kids have grown significantly less drunk, stoned, and pregnant. They've also consistently graded above state average in testing across all subjects. And the latest numbers show that between 2000 and 2006, overall arrests of ten- to fourteen-year-olds fell 63 percent, and property crime arrests of ten- to seventeen-year-olds in San Juan County fell 83 percent.

As FAR AS SPORTS and activities for those over twenty-one, Eastsound has the Lower Tavern. There used to be an Upper Tavern, too, which lives on in stories told whenever visitors ask what the Lower is lower than. Almost all of the stores, restaurants, and inns around Eastsound are mom-and-pops—and many just mom's, as more than a third of all the businesses in the county are owned by women. The largest anything on Orcas is a regulation-size supermarket owned by a longtime island family. Everything else is scaled down. You won't find superstores or fast-food drive-throughs, but you can walk from Darvill's Books to Pawki's for Pets to Rose's Bakery.

Any island business that can't cover its yearly nut by selling essentials to locals has basically a two-month window of heavy tourist traffic in July and August to keep itself afloat. In 2008, every Eastsound business suffered when Orcas's lone large resort, Rosario, shut down for two years, eliminating nearly one hundred jobs from an island with very few to start with. One of the hardest hit was Vern's Bayside Restaurant and Lounge.

THE FRINGE ON FIFTY-SEVEN-YEAR-OLD Belinda Landon's groovy suede boots rarely hangs limp. She could pour drinks behind the bar, take an order from an inside table, check on the action in the little billiards room, then service the tables on the waterfront patio where Vern's patrons soak up the sun—all in the space of about four minutes.

Landon has worked bars and restaurants since she was fourteen, and from her hard-won look and throaty voice, there's no mistaking that she's inhaled some smoky scenes and spent some happy hours in her forty-three years of slinging hash and pulling taps. Plainspoken Belinda is, as they say, one gal who'll tell you whose cow ate the barley. She made her way to Orcas from Idaho twenty-five years ago with two kids and a husband. He left her and she met Vern, who had his own four kids and whose wife left him. There's an old Orcas adage that says, "On this island, you don't lose your spouse, you just lose your turn."

Belinda and Vern and their collective kids hooked up, as she says, "*Brady Bunch*–style." She worked at Rosario Resort back then, as did her daughter, Marion Rathbone, who also started in the food and beverage business at fourteen. Vern was a mason by trade, but ran a little café at the time and always wanted something bigger. A deal came up for what you'd think would be an ideal location for a restaurant: central waterfront, spectacular view, upstairs casual dining room, downstairs bar with space for a couple of pool tables, and a sunny patio just above the lapping waters of East Sound.

The space had a checkered history. "It had dozens of owners over the years and it always went broke," says Belinda. "We were the only ones left stupid enough to take it." No one, however, had tried to keep the restaurant open year-round, and Vern thought that was the secret. They opened in 1993. It was never a gold mine, but they made a go of it.

Vern died in January 2006. Then when Rosario closed in 2008 they lost a lot of regulars who'd clock out of their resort jobs and head to town for drinks. Real estate and construction evaporated in the housing bust, forcing a lot of tradesmen off the island. As the U.S. economy further tanked, everyone—locals and tourists alike—spent less. Belinda had two neck surgeries, two back surgeries, and one on her arm, but she still worked full shifts cooking, waiting tables, and tending bar, trying to keep the business alive. Her daughter, Marion, served as general manager and tried to pull in trade by playing karaoke queen down in the bar.

On August 26, 2008, a package came to Vern's addressed to Belinda. Marion took one look and called up the vendor. Despite their guarantee that her mom would pass all FAA tests or they'd refund her money,

Marion told them Belinda was not interested in Sporty's Complete Recreational Pilot Flight Training Course. Her mom was not, at the moment, tempted to go *Top Gun*.

Sporty's informed Marion that they'd received a valid online order for the six-DVD set from Belinda's credit card. She replied that her mom didn't know how to use a "friggin' computer let alone order something online." Sporty's said they'd be happy to give her a refund.

Marion resealed the package and set it on the desk below the window unit air conditioner that cooled her small, cluttered office adjacent to the restaurant's kitchen. She then went back to handling the hundreds of daily details it takes to keep a restaurant running.

The following morning when Marion arrived at work, her office door was already open. Everything seemed okay at first glance, but then she stepped inside and peeked around the dividing wall that formed a little storage space for office supplies and the restaurant's safe.

"It looked like a bomb had gone off," she says. Powder from the cement used to fill the walls of the metal safe was everywhere. A hammer from Vern's old toolbox lay broken on the floor. Someone had used it and a crowbar to peel back the steel of the safe until the lock gave way. It'd been a major demolition job, very noisy and done on exactly the right night.

Marion felt sick to her stomach. With the rumors of break-ins happening around the island, she'd just convinced her mom to move her personal cash into the office safe instead of keeping it at home. That money was gone, as were two credit cards, Belinda's birth certificate and social security card, and her late husband's passport. To make matters worse, the first thing Marion had planned to do that morning was go to the bank and make her weekly deposit of cash emptied from the bar's pull tab gambling machine. In all, more than $10,000 of uninsurable cash was missing.

The safe wasn't empty, though.

"At the bottom was a single dollar bill and the credit card that had been used to make the online order," says Marion. "It was folded in half, creased as if to say, 'Here ya go, I don't need this anymore.'"

They called the sheriff's department. Vern's had suffered small thefts over its sixteen years, mostly summer employees dipping into the till, but never anything major like this. "We felt violated, raped," says Belinda.

"And then, worse, our police told us we were asking for it . . . just because we didn't have a security system."

In the disorder of deputies coming in and out and still trying to get the restaurant up and running because they couldn't afford to lose a summer day's business—especially now—Marion forgot about the Sporty's package. Then FedEx showed up with another box. This one contained a pair of spy cameras, two tiny, battery-powered, motion-activated cameras designed to be hidden anywhere and record several days' worth of surveillance video. Like the flying course, the cameras had been ordered a few days earlier using Belinda's credit card.

"All kinds of alarm bells started going off," says Marion, who suddenly realized that the Sporty's package had been taken along with everything in the safe. "Learn-to-fly DVDs, surveillance cameras from a company that also sells untraceable cell phones . . . and now whoever ordered all this also had a shitload of cash . . . Hello? Certainly seemed to me like it could have something to do with terrorism."

Beyond general post-9/11 awareness, the Pacific Northwest remains extra sensitive to the potential of terrorism due to Ahmed Rassem, the Millennium Bomber. In December 1999, the Al Qaeda–trained and –funded Rassem filled a car with explosives intending to blow up passengers at an LAX terminal. He successfully drove through U.S. Immigration checks and onto a car ferry in Victoria, B.C.—a city on Vancouver Island less than ten miles from the San Juans across Haro Strait. The bomber's plan failed only because a U.S. Customs agent named Diana Dean at the ferry's destination in Port Angeles, Washington, sensed something wasn't quite right and searched his car.

Marion took the cameras and her hunch to the Orcas cop shop. The deputy shrugged her off.

"I couldn't believe it," she says. "But there was definitely something going on, and I wasn't going to shut up until someone listened." So Marion called the FBI. They did listen and took a report, and an agent phoned a detective at the San Juan County Sheriff's Office headquarters over in Friday Harbor. They decided, though, that there wasn't much to go on.

Marion kept wondering if she was soon going to hear about a crime or terrorist attack involving a small plane. She and Belinda also had another concern: staying in business. "That money was our winter," she says, her soft face taking on a hard glower. "We're not rich. My mom wouldn't have been waiting friggin' tables if she didn't have to." Marion eventually did make that trip to the bank, but instead of a deposit, it was to borrow enough money to keep Vern's open and staffed for what looked to be a lean winter.

"And then we had to borrow another fifteen grand to put in a security system."

7

M ount Constitution rules over the entire east side of Orcas Island as the centerpiece of Moran State Park, a 5,200-acre Northwest wonderland of gigantic old-growth trees where mountain streams and waterfalls feed five blue lakes filled with rainbow trout and landlocked kokanee salmon. The view from the tower atop the 2,407-foot-high mountain (named for USS *Constitution*, aka Old Ironsides) takes in much of the San Juans as well as the Cascades running up into Canada, and, looking south, the Olympic Mountains. It's the highest point in the San Juans, but it's not Orcas's most notable. That honor goes to a smaller but more distinctive geological feature on the west side of the island called Turtleback Mountain. The formation's bulbous head and sloping shell are instantly recognizable from many miles away, and first sight of the friendly turtle is always a comforting welcome home when returning to the island.

In 2006, developers drew up plans to slice Turtleback into housing tracts. Full- and part-time San Juan County residents—including cartoonist Gary Larson, who came out of retirement to draw and donate a *Far Side*–ish frame showing doctors surgically removing the developers from the mountain—worked together with the San Juan Preservation Trust to raise $17 million to buy 1,576 acres and turn it into a preserve. Today Turtleback, along with approximately 20 percent of all the land in the San Juans, is protected in perpetuity.

The day after someone made off with the Sporty's flight manuals and all of Vern's cash, Martin and Ellen Brody (not their real names) returned to their home at the foot of Turtleback Mountain. Wooden stairs, decks, and walkways climb the slope to reach their comfortable single-story that's partially hidden from the road behind a garden. With their back sheltered by the turtle's shell, the Brodys face across Crow Valley, the island's best bottomland. They can even see the small farm they bought when they first moved to Orcas from Seattle back in 1981.

"We'd been to Orcas on vacation and thought it would be the most wonderful place to live and raise a family," says Martin. "And we were right."

He hung out a shingle in financial services and became a gentleman farmer. "The rule was we could have any animals the kids wanted as long as they were small enough for me to chase down and tackle. Cows and horses were out, but we had sheep, goats, pigs, and chickens."

Ellen became a beloved local teacher and spent her free time mastering woodwork. The Brodys kept the farm until their two kids graduated college, then downsized into the home on Turtleback.

"When we sold the farmhouse, the new owners asked for the keys," remembers Ellen. "We said, 'What keys?' We'd never locked the doors in the sixteen years we lived there."

Retired now, Martin and Ellen are big into taking cruises. They had one coming up, but this recent trip was a visit to see their daughter, now a Harvard professor. When they walked into their immaculately kept home, Ellen went through the galley kitchen and nearly stepped into a large puddle of water on the floor outside a bathroom.

"It was right below the skylight and I thought, Uh-oh, we've got a leak," says Martin. They cleaned up the water and he added "fix leak" to his list of things to do before they left in three weeks for a monthlong Pacific cruise. Jet-lagged, they then went to bed.

"The next morning I get up and reach for my box of cereal," says Martin. "But it was gone." He knew he'd opened a fresh box of Honey Bunches of Oats just before they left for Boston. Ellen said she hadn't touched it, so Martin chalked it up to a senior moment. Same thing with the missing carton of milk he was sure he'd left in the fridge.

Ellen took their suitcases into the laundry room to start the wash. When she opened the louvered doors in front of her sparkling white stackables, she instantly knew something wasn't right. "There were two dirty fingerprints, one on the washer and one on the dryer," she says.

Martin had no doubt—"She keeps this place spotless"—but it was Ellen who put words to the unthinkable.

"Someone's been in our house."

Now they went through their home, looking carefully. Ellen called out from her office that her brand-new computer netbook, bought to keep up with emails during their upcoming cruise, was gone. In the kitchen, Martin realized that the leather wallet he'd left on top of their cruise documents was also missing. True to his profession, he knew exactly how much had been in there: "Three twenties."

Martin checked all the doors. Nothing was broken. They had only simple door-handle locks, and it appeared they were easily defeated by some kind of a slender tool like a flathead screwdriver.

They had to accept that a burglar had indeed broken in and taken a wallet and laptop. The head-shaker was that the thief had also taken a shower—leaving the puddle of water—done laundry, and eaten breakfast. Someone had eaten their porridge, sat in their chairs, maybe slept in their bed.

The losses didn't add up to much—at least not enough to deal with the insurance hassles—so at first they decided not to report it. "He could have done anything while he was in here," says Martin. "But nothing was damaged or even disturbed. He didn't take Ellen's jewelry or anything like that; he only took useful stuff."

The following Sunday, though, after Martin went on his weekly bike ride down the valley, he heard that neighbors just up the road had surprised a burglar inside their house. The middle-aged couple had come home around 10 p.m., and as the woman opened the front door, she "startled" a slender young man over six feet tall. The burglar took off through the kitchen, knocked over a chair, and fled out the back door. Her husband chased him down the driveway, but couldn't catch up. On his way back to the house, he found a bicycle that the burglar had apparently brought with him, so he took it inside, locking the door behind him.

They called the sheriff, and as they were waiting for a deputy to arrive, the burglar actually came back; they saw him sneaking around outside and peeking through the window. The bold young burglar disappeared as the police car pulled up. The cop investigated and discovered that the couple's safe had been rifled, but nothing appeared to be missing. He also made a point of checking their liquor cabinet and noting it was intact—something very unusual for this type of crime with a young suspect. The couple showed him the bike and said they suspected it was the thief's. The deputy carried the bike out to his vehicle and drove it back to the East-sound cop shop, where he photographed it, recorded its serial number and identifying details, and then locked it inside the evidence room.

In all their years on the island, the Brodys had never heard of a burglary happening in sparsely populated Crow Valley. They felt two on the same road within such a short period of time must be related, so Martin decided he better report what had happened at their house.

He spoke to the sergeant in charge of Orcas, who had some good news and some bad. He told Martin about the getaway bike they'd confiscated at the neighbors' home. Martin said, "Great, if you got that I'm sure that means you must be able to get fingerprints."

"Well," Martin says the sergeant told him, "funny thing is, we brought the bike to the station, but now it's missing."

Martin could not believe what he was hearing. Then he remembered something strange he'd seen on his last ride. He said, "I think I know where that bike is." Riding along Crow Valley Road, he'd seen a bike tossed into the bushes. It was very unusual, but he didn't stop, thinking maybe its owner was in the thickets picking blackberries. The sergeant asked what kind of bike it was and Martin told him.

"No," said the cop, "the one we had was a black Gary Fisher with red flames painted on it."

Martin felt a strange little buzz. "That's funny . . . I have a Gary Fisher, black with red flames," he said. "But it couldn't have been mine because it's here at the house—I just rode it."

It was an odd enough coincidence that the sergeant drove out to the Brodys. Martin now remembered that his bike had seemed particularly dirty. But it'd been in the exact spot he always kept it—among the tools in their little garden shed attached to the carport—so it didn't register more than an odd feeling. Sure enough, though, when they checked the serial number it was the same bike the police had locked away in their evidence room.

It was almost unbelievable. The only explanation was that the burglar had been staying in the Brodys' house and using Martin's bike to travel around and try to rip off their neighbors. (There'd also been a break-in and attempt to access the computer at a nearby hardware store, Island Supply, where deputies had found a bare footprint.) When the burglar had run off and lost the bike to the police, he followed them the three and a half miles back to Eastsound that same night. Residents near the cop shop later reported that their lawn furniture had been moved into a comfortable arrangement overlooking the station.

The burglar had run a stakeout on the police.

San Juan County doesn't provide Orcas with twenty-four-hour police coverage. There are a couple of hours when a deputy is on call but there's no one actively on duty. Once the cop shop closed down for the night, the incredibly ballsy burglar jimmied open the sergeant's office window, which had no security system protecting it, not even a stick to keep it from being slid open.

Once inside, the thief had enough time to rummage around the sergeant's desk, find the keys to the evidence room, and resteal Martin Brody's bike.

He then rode it back to Crow Valley and returned it to its rightful owner.

THE SERGEANT LEFT THE Brodys' without taking fingerprints off the bike. Martin and Ellen went about their day, but with a different sense of reality setting in about their island home. Was this someone with a vendetta against the police or a twisted sense of decency, or was this just a crook with a sense of humor and big brass pair?

Ellen began cleaning the house and had just wiped one of the fingerprints off the washer and dryer. Oops, she thought. The other print still looked good, though. She could clearly see the swirls with her naked eye. She called the sheriff's office and asked if they wanted to come back out and collect it. They said no.

A couple of days later, Martin was standing at the window when he saw a flash of color in the garden. He reached for the birding binoculars he always kept handy, but came up empty. They were gone, too. The Brodys decided that before they went away again they'd better put in deadbolts. Six hundred dollars later, a locksmith had rekeyed all the knobs and drilled out the jambs and installed new locks. They went about their pleasant Orcas lives for the next several weeks, he puttering in the garden, she in her woodshop. But things weren't quite the same. They each now kept a key with them at all times, and locked up whenever they left the property. They hoped, though, that this had all been just a freak occurrence.

ORCAS'S LOCAL NEWSPAPER, THE *Islands' Sounder*, regularly runs a log from the San Juan County Sheriff's Office. It's a popular feature where you find short, fascinating vignettes such as "An 83-year-old Eastsound woman reported one pair of fur-lined moccasins and three almost-new pair of beige women's underwear stolen from an unlocked old fruit-packing barn." There was also the epic saga of two "friendly" Great Danes that got loose and went llama chasing, and the cautionary tale of a man who fired three rounds from his shotgun aiming for an otter under his porch and instead hit his neighbor in the neck (neither the llamas nor the neighbor were seriously injured). After the follow-the-bouncing-bike incidents at the Brodys' and the cop shop, though, the only thing officially reported by San Juan County sheriff Bill Cumming was that there'd been a "security breach" at the Orcas station.

HEADING SOUTH FROM THE Brodys', Turtleback's shell slopes down to the water, the tip of the turtle's tail splitting Massacre Bay from West Sound. A boaty area, West Sound is filled with bright sails tacking back and forth every summer day. Continuing west on a cliff-clinging road, you come to the tiny hamlet of Deer Harbor. Two marinas and several inns operate on this small picturesque bay. Around the same time as the Crow Valley bike caper, strange things were happening at the Deer Harbor Inn—though no one would suspect a thing until September, when the bills came due.

Deer Harbor Inn was the first resort on Orcas, renting tent cabins in the late 1800s to supplement the income from the owner's apple orchard. A small hotel and restaurant were built after the turn of the century. Since 1982, it's been owned by the Carpenter family, with two brothers, Matt and Ryan, running the restaurant and rental homes. In late August, someone had broken into the inn and gotten hold of Ryan's credit card. The thief had been smart enough to not actually take the card, though, just the numbers and security code, so Ryan didn't have a clue until he opened his statement and saw that he—or at least his identity—had ordered more than $3,000 in spy cameras and other electronics plus a $900 high-tech flight helmet. When Ryan contacted the sellers, they said that their records showed that the gear had all been successfully delivered to Orcas Island. But not, of course, to Ryan.

Back in Eastsound, someone broke through a window at Wildlife Cycles on North Beach Road. He passed over models worth three times as much to snag a particular bike—a Gary Fisher, designed for both street and rugged trail. The burglar raided the cash drawer, spilling bills across the wooden deck as he rolled his new bike out the front door. A computer company in town also suffered a breach of security, with $8,000 worth of software and equipment ordered online using its accounts. The shopping spree included hacking and spyware programs designed for identity theft, along with more infrared spy cameras.

Over at Smuggler's, near the airport, manager Mike Stolmeier opened the door to the resort's sauna at 10 p.m. and found a "big, tall, gangly kid" sitting inside. "We get moochers sometimes," says Stolmeier. "So I said, 'Okay, this isn't working, you gotta go.' I didn't pay much attention to him since he didn't give me any guff and just got up and left."

One odd thing that Stolmeier did notice was that the kid sitting in the sauna with the heat turned up was fully clothed and had a big backpack on the bench next to him.

SEPTEMBER ROLLED AROUND AND it was time for the Brodys to cast off on their long-awaited Pacific cruise. They boarded the ship on September 19. Ellen had lugged along a large laptop since her little netbook had been stolen. As soon as they settled in, she bought a package of onboard Internet minutes, enough, she thought, to cover their entire monthlong vacation.

The first time she signed on, up popped a note from eBay congratulating her on making the winning bid for a smartphone.

"Uh-oh, we've got a problem," she told Martin. The next email was from PayPal: a receipt on her account for the $320 phone. "It was the worst feeling in my life," she says, suddenly realizing that the person who'd eaten their Honey Bunches of Oats had also scanned her home computer and found the document where she kept all her account numbers and passwords. Goldilocks had stolen her identity and was on a shopping spree.

Ellen immediately sent a flurry of emails, trying to cancel the purchase and change all her accounts. The retailer had already shipped the phone and told her to simply refuse the package. When she contacted the San Juan County Sheriff's Office, though, they said not to do that. They asked if she'd agree to have them post a deputy inside their house, using the package as a trap. It sounded like a good plan, and the Brodys agreed.

On September 23, the local courier alerted deputies that the package had arrived on the island. The following day, police set up a stakeout at the Brodys' with the phone left on the front porch. That evening, a retired schoolteacher who serves as a reserve deputy waited alone inside the house. He later told Martin Brody that around 8 p.m.—still twilight in September's long days—he was standing in their kitchen when he heard a key slide into the deadbolt lock. The deputy hadn't locked the door, and was very surprised to hear someone try a key because he knew the locks had just been changed.

The door swung open and in stepped a young man the deputy describes as "NBA big." The cop yelled, "Freeze!" But the kid didn't. Instead, his hand went to his side and then quickly came up holding something metal.

The ex-schoolteacher suddenly found himself in a fiery, choking mist of pepper spray. He staggered forward, but after firing the spray the tall young man had immediately spun and fled back out the door. The deputy chased him outside, and through burning eyes saw him fly off the porch without seeming to touch the stairs. Then, still moving at full speed, the suspect made the ninety-degree turn past the Brodys' koi pond, leaped down another half flight of stairs, vaulted a railing, and scrambled across a large moss-covered boulder before vanishing into the twilight.

(After his capture, Colton Harris-Moore told a similar story, with a few different details: When he went to pick up a package he'd had delivered to a rural Orcas home, he noticed that the inside lights weren't quite the way he'd left them. He crept up to the porch, opened the door, and found himself facing a cop who was sitting in a rocking chair. Colt said the deputy aimed a laser-sighted pistol at his chest and started laughing. Colt never mentioned the pepper spray, but says he turned and ran, escaping by scaling an eight-foot-tall rock "like a vampire.")

The Brodys got the bad news aboard ship. "They could have had him right then and there," says Martin, "but they blew their chance."

He and Ellen had a creepy feeling that was confirmed when they returned to Orcas and discovered that one of their new spare keys had been taken from their cupboard. They also found that one of their window locks had been disabled but made to look like it still worked. The burglar had set it up so he'd always have a way to get into their home.

They wondered why they'd been targeted again, then suddenly understood: Their cruise papers had been on the kitchen counter during his first stay in their home. "He knew exactly when we were going and how long we'd be gone," says Martin. He also knew he had Martin's bike to use—again.

Their phone bill and online charges showed that the burglar moved in, like an uninvited house sitter, on the same day they left. Two calls were made from their phone to the mainland Washington home of a prison buddy of Colton Harris-Moore's.

"He thought he had a safe place to stay for a month," says Martin. "And he would have if Ellen hadn't checked her email."

The Brodys rekeyed again, fixed their window lock, and added sticks to all their windows. Ellen then spent several months trying to clear the charges from their PayPal account. Half a year later they still had eye-burning traces of pepper spray on their furniture, even after multiple cleanings. Martin's Gary Fisher bicycle—which had been stolen for the third time while they were on the cruise—was never returned.

———

On October 2, 2008, the Orcas Island Chamber of Commerce held a meeting to address what the *Islands' Sounder* headlined as a "plague" of sophisticated burglaries. The reporting quotes Orcas deputy sergeant Steve Vierthaler telling the business owners that some of the crimes appeared to be connected and were "very subtle thefts" that included thieves using WiFi scanners to hack into people's home networks and steal their identities.

Vierthaler was asked about the possibility of getting DNA from break-ins. "The reality is not like *CSI* on television," he said. "It is hugely expensive to do lab work and the labs are hugely backlogged." He said that DNA might be used for violent crimes, but not for thefts.

According to the Washington State Patrol, which does all the law enforcement laboratory work for San Juan County, it doesn't cost the county a dime to send DNA samples or other forensics to their lab. The only cost is the time it takes a local deputy to collect the evidence. There are indeed backlogs, and testing is done on a priority basis with murders, rapes, and assaults taking precedence over property crimes, but a WSP lab spokesman says they work with local law enforcement on any kind of crime, especially when it's high profile, highly publicized, or perceived to be an immediate threat to the community. With today's computerized databases of fingerprints and DNA from known criminals (Colt's prints and DNA had been in the system for years by this point), law enforcement experts say that not attempting to collect forensics at crime scenes is the result of poor training, bad policy, or just plain laziness.

Vierthaler told the Chamber members that all the businesses should consider alarm systems. "I would prefer a silent alarm," he said. "But because we are so understaffed, the response time is at least ten minutes, so an audible alarm would be better." He had some simple suggestions, too: "Leave the lights on inside and use motion detector lights outside. These people are like cockroaches: you turn on the lights and they run."

He also suggested that everyone, at their businesses and residences, put wooden dowels in their windows. He didn't report, however, how the sheriff's office had recently learned firsthand the importance of that do-it-yourself tip.

RUMORS FLEW AROUND THE island—as usual—but other than a few unofficial "If you knew the shit that I did" warnings, Orcas residents were never alerted that a burglar brazen enough to break into the cop shop and even pepper spray a deputy had been stalking the island.

There were a couple more break-ins that fall, but both happened at construction operations, typical targets for local kids. Maybe, as the sergeant told the Chamber, "these things happen in cycles and end when [opportunistic burglars] get caught or leave the island."

Then came that surreal November 12, when Bob Rivers's airplane flew away. Burglaries dropped back to their usual low level once the Cessna took off, but the police never connected the plane theft to any of the other crimes that had happened on the island that summer because they had no forensics.

As soon as she heard about the stolen plane, Marion Rathbone went directly to the police and reminded them about the Sporty's Flight Training Course taken from Vern's. She'd been waiting to hear about a crime involving a plane and here it was—she felt it couldn't be a coincidence. She says the sergeant's response was an authoritative "You can't learn to fly from DVDs."

The other person on Orcas who had a clue was Ryan Carpenter, who wondered if the $900 flight helmet ordered with his credit card had just taken off.

8

Airline pilots call the area around the San Juan Islands "the blue hole" because the Olympic Mountains and the Vancouver Island Range hold back the roiling Pacific clouds, often leaving a pocket of clear blue air over the islands when it's raining everywhere else in the region. It's the same rainshadow effect that happens on the east side of the Cascades. Forks, the legendary home of the *Twilight* characters, lies only seventy miles west of the San Juans yet averages over a hundred inches *more* rain per year than falls on the islands—and nothing smells worse than wet werewolf.

The mountain defenses and location in the middle of the inland Salish Sea keep San Juan Islands winters remarkably benign considering how far north they lie. Just to the west, the Pacific coasts of the Olympic Peninsula and Vancouver Island promote "storm watching" vacations where shawl-swaddled folks sip cocoa and watch sixty-foot waves explode against the shore. The Salish Sea, though, is walled off from the open Pacific and its huge swells. In the other direction, rising dramatically in the east and visible from Orcas, Mount Baker holds the world record for highest single-season snowfall: 1999 saw it smothered with ninety-five feet of snow. However, down in the islands the sea moderates temperatures so snow and ice rarely stick around.

If there's one month not to be in the San Juans it's November, when the islands often take hits from major tree-toppling windstorms and the year's hardest rains. The rest of late fall and winter are usually mild, what the Irish call "soft" days of mist and occasional drizzle with cool temperatures.

Still, daylight can be in depressingly short supply this far north, and the low-slung sun seldom rises with enough strength to feel it on your face. Island residents pile Douglas fir into their wood stoves and pull together community potlucks so they can laugh away the darkness with other hardy full-timers. On Orcas, the Giving Tree goes up at Island Market and people buy presents for those local kids who'd otherwise go without at Christmas.

Then winter gives way. The buffleheads and goldeneyes fly off, replaced by spring swarms of rufous hummingbirds returning from their epic Mexican vacations. Spring is also when the San Juans' 125 pairs of bald eagles weave the finishing touches into their massive nests atop waterfront trees, and the three resident pods of killer whales begin spending more of their time around the islands. The real start of summer doesn't depend on the calendar but on whenever the hallowed North Pacific High chases the drizzly Aleutian Low back north. Once this semipermanent air mass takes over around the Fourth of July, the San Juans can see two months of wondrously monotonous blue skies and 72-degree days that seem to go on forever (at this latitude it's dark for only about five hours in midsummer).

Long before any vacationing white man arrived on Orcas, its peaceful, easy summers were enjoyed by the Lummi, one of the Northern Straits Salish-speaking tribes. Lummi Indian clans moved out to the island each June and set up camps where they feasted on the plentiful salmon, crabs, and clams. The only downside to summering in the San Juans back in the day were the occasional murderous raids by Haida and Bella Bella, warlike tribes from up in the Queen Charlotte Islands and the Alaskan coast. The first white settlers in the San Juans married Salish women because they knew the skills to survive in the Pacific Northwest wilderness. However, the native women remained so afraid of the Haida that even in the last decades of the nineteenth century they'd hide themselves under blankets when sailing between islands during the summer raiding season.

From where I live in Deer Harbor, the only road to Eastsound sweeps around Massacre Bay, named for an 1857 raid that wiped out more than one hundred summering Lummi, with the surviving women and children hauled away as slaves in forty-foot-long war canoes. A beautiful little knoll just offshore also takes its name from the slaughter: Skull Island.

When I arrived in town on a brilliantly sunny Thursday, August 6, 2009, the news was that a boat had been found that morning mysteriously abandoned off Eastsound's Waterfront Park. Boats sometimes pull their anchors or slip their knots. They've also been found adrift after their owners leaned across the gunwale to take a leak and disappeared overboard. But not this boat.

The sheriff quickly connected it to the report of a boat stolen from La Conner, a touristy little harbor town on the mainland about nine miles from Camano Island. The trip north to Orcas covered between thirty and thirty-five miles, depending on whether the thief took the protected Swinomish Channel up and around Anacortes, or navigated the wild waters of Deception Pass.

It wasn't quite a forty-foot war canoe, but for the residents of Orcas Island, it was still an ominous sign.

WITHIN DAYS, KYLE ATER, owner of Orcas Homegrown Market and Gourmet Delicatessen, discovered that someone had tried to break into his organic grocery on North Beach Road. The burglar climbed to the second floor, where Ater keeps an office adjacent to a long dining room lined with windows that provide a nearly 360-degree view of downtown. He reported it to the police and asked if it might be related to the previous year's unsolved thefts or the recent stolen boat. The deputy, he says, assured him it was just an isolated incident.

"People had been stealing stuff from Homegrown for years before I bought it," says Ater. "Kids just walking out with beer from the cooler . . . and the police never did anything about it because this was just the stinky barefoot hippie place."

Ater, who'd been on the island for eleven years, sank everything he had into buying Homegrown in 2006. He'd been burglarized shortly after taking over the grocery, and he was determined not to let anyone rip him off again. Like nearly every other Eastsound business after all the mysterious summer of '08 troubles, Homegrown had a security and surveillance system. Ater, though, decided to take it all the way. Each evening after they closed up, he and his girlfriend, Cedra, took their two dogs, Pumpkin and Skyla, plus a loaner Rottweiler named Mattie, and camped out on the floor of the office upstairs. Kyle also bought himself a .44 Magnum revolver.

Serene Orcas Island at the height of its summer season, with tourists in killer whale T-shirts strolling the quaint downtown eating ice cream cones, now had its slender, bespectacled purveyor of natural foods and holistic health supplements patrolling the ramparts packing Dirty Harry heat.

ON AUGUST 18, MEMBERS of a prayer group noticed a short-haired young man acting oddly inside St. Francis Catholic Church, which sits kitty-corner to the airport. The guy awkwardly knelt down at the votive candles and then looked up. He wasn't gazing as far as heaven, though. He had more secular concerns. When he spotted the surveillance cameras, he flipped a hoodie up over his head and left. He unnerved the parishioners enough that one asked for an escort to the parking lot. Two days later, someone broke into the church through a back window, busted open the sacrament room with a hammer and screwdriver, and then climbed up into the ceiling to take four of the security cameras along with the attached DVR. No money or other items were stolen, just the surveillance system. The thief left behind two cameras, but poked them toward the ceiling so they couldn't watch him.

Somebody messing with the church went beyond the pale, and East-sounders held their breath, wondering if St. Francis was just the beginning of another crime spree. The recession was in full swing, tourism down, and local businesses needed to squirrel away every summer dollar to get them through what could be another tough winter.

The previous year's "plague" had briefly reminded residents that, as San Juan County sheriff Bill Cumming told me, "The San Juans do have a dark side." A look through back issues of the *Islands' Sounder* showed occasional flare-ups, with a spate of burglaries occurring every few years on Orcas, San Juan, or Lopez Island. These were almost always attributed to local meth heads.

Learning that there was even such a thing as a local meth head on Orcas rocked my idyllic-island construct. On reflection, though, it made sense. We were a rural, overwhelmingly white community in western Washington State: the perfect formula for growing tweakers. Police officers from the TV shows *Cops* and *Washington's Most Wanted* told speed-fiend stories on Bob Rivers's radio show, saying they'd actually responded to "meth-induced chainsaw fights" in the rustic communities not far from cosmopolitan Seattle. As one officer said: "The reason why *Cops* likes us so much is because we have a lot of crazy white people up here. And crazy white people make for good TV."

Of course, like all the other crime issues, the meth problem on Orcas was at a relatively low level.

Reality took a bit of the bloom off the idyllic Orcas rose, but Sandi and I still weren't locking our doors. We had a big dog, Murphy, a six-foot-from-nose-to-tail Leonberger, which I believe is a cross between a bouncy Tigger and a grizzly bear—at least in Murphy's case. Once we moved to this eminently dog-friendly island, Murphy became a permanent fixture in my pickup truck, going everywhere I went with his massive head hanging out the cab's back window like a trophy mount. With so little crime, we never felt the need to have him stay home to watch over the property. As it was, Murphy's concept of guard-dogging wasn't to prevent anyone from entering the house—leaving, yes, but not entering. Whenever he sensed someone outside our little cabin, instead of barking to warn them off, he silently stalked them, moving from door to door, hackles up, muscles tensed. No amount of prodding could get him to change his strategy. He'd raise a hellhound yowl if someone actually knocked, but if they were just lurking around out there, he waited with a distinct "I'm finally gonna get to eat somebody" excitement.

August 27, 2009, around 3 a.m., Murphy padded heavily into the bedroom, snuffed at the window screen, and raised his hackles. I already had my eyes half open as I'd been lying there with that strange feeling that something had woken me but I didn't know what. The clouded moon bathed the room in just enough dim blue light to see the dog at the window. Then my eyes suddenly opened wider. All manner of deer, raccoons, mink, and other critters rustle around our cabin at night, but none of them had ever moved lumber. Murphy and I both heard the clack of wood against wood in the crawlspace.

The dirt-floor area under the cabin lies open on one end and anything could have wandered in there. It must have been a deer, I thought, because nothing else would be big enough to knock around the 2×4s. We listened for a while but nothing else happened. Yep, had to be a deer stumbling around, maybe drunk on huckleberries. My last thought as I rolled over and went back to sleep was, I hope it didn't knock loose any of the plumbing.

The following night, again around 3 a.m., I woke to the sensation of someone watching me in the darkness. This would have been terrifying if I wasn't used to living with a pony-size dog who thinks he has mind-control powers. Murphy believes if he stares down at me long and hard enough I'll get up and do his bidding—mainly his feeding. He usually waits until after sunrise, though, so this was unusual. When he knew I was awake, he went to the window, again snuffle-snorting like a bear and raising his hackles. I sat up and listened, but couldn't hear anything except a rare summer sprinkling of rain against the metal roof. The thought of pulling on shoes and a rain shell, finding a flashlight, stumbling around under the cabin, and then having to dry off a half acre of wet dog was too much just to chase away some dilettante critter trying to shelter from a shower. The cabin perches atop a hundred-foot cliff, which means there's also no option of simply loosing the hound. In the past, several Orcas dogs tailing hard after deer have Thelma-and-Louised themselves off cliffs.

The drizzle passed after a couple of minutes and everything fell silent again as I slipped back to sleep.

The next morning, Jeremy Trumble woke to find there'd been a B and E at his B and B, the Inn on Orcas Island, one mile away through the woods from our cabin.

Both Jeremy and his partner, John Gibbs, had come from East Los Angeles. "I was a high school teacher in a ghetto school, but I wasn't teaching, I was surviving," says Trumble. "I told John about this place where my mom and dad took me in the fifties, this wonderful, wonderful island with no crime where running a B and B would be the perfect semiretirement lifestyle."

They traveled to Orcas four times a year starting in the mid-eighties to look for just the right property. "Orcas has a drawbridge mentality, not real welcoming for development, but we persevered and in '94 we found this property. We sat here on the grass and it was one of those August days . . ."

Their six acres overlook a tidal wetland attended by stately blue herons. It took five years to get permits to replace the existing double-wide trailer with what is now an exquisite coastal inn. They finally opened in the summer of 2002.

The inn's kitchen faces the wetland and woods beyond, and they never bothered to put curtains on the windows. Gibbs had been sitting in the kitchen working on his laptop until 11:30 the previous evening. Guests filled all the upstairs rooms, every bedroom window wide open to enjoy the cool night air. Nine cars lined the lot, outside lights lit the exterior of the inn and its surroundings.

"The doors were all locked except the French doors on the little deck off the kitchen," says Trumble. "We never thought they needed to be locked when we had a full house and all the windows open. Our suite lies just above that deck."

Sometime between when Gibbs went to bed and 5 a.m., when Trumble got up to start breakfast, someone walked—barefoot—through the landscaped patch around the deck and climbed up and over the railing. Dirty footprints led into the kitchen. The laptop had disappeared. The innkeepers called the police and began a long series of calls to cancel all the accounts that had been on the computer—PayPal, Amazon, credit cards.

"John's wallet was close by and he didn't take that," but because of what had happened across the road at Ryan Carpenter's Deer Harbor Inn they worried about all of their other credit cards, too. The inn represented every dime they had plus twenty years of hard work just to make it a reality. Like most other Orcas tourist-related businesses, it operated on a knife edge of profitability. The computer's value didn't meet their deductible, so the loss was all out-of-pocket.

"It breaks my heart that this happened on Orcas," says Trumble. "Suddenly we had to change our lifestyle and start really watching . . . You're not as safe as you thought you were."

After the break-in, Trumble, one of the most gentle guys on the island, found himself sleeping with a baseball bat next to his bed.

The deputy who responded to the call lived just down the road aboard a boat at the Deer Harbor Marina. The same night as the burglary at the inn, someone walked down the marina's long wooden pier and ducked behind the dockmaster's office. He slid a thin tool between window sashes and opened a latch. Inside, he had access to a computer and the safe—with its key hanging nearby. But he left those alone and instead took only the surveillance cameras and the DVR they were attached to.

Deer Harbor Marina enjoys a brisk trade with visiting boaters. During July and August there's rarely an open slip, with half leased to full-timers and the other half filled with boats from all over Washington and British

Columbia. That night, the place was packed, the docks alive with people wandering up and down, visiting with fellow boaters, barbecuing, boiling up the day's Dungeness crab, cocktailing, telling tall tales, and doing all the other stuff yachties do. Things quiet down in Deer Harbor after 11 p.m., but many boaters remain up on deck chatting under the brilliant stars, their voices and the creak of boats carrying far across the still water.

The marina's showers and bathrooms sit back by the dockmaster's office, forty yards up the pier from the marina store and the boat slips. There's always a trickle of folks heading back and forth to the restrooms. That didn't bother this burglar, though, who strolled from the office to the store and slid open another window. Inside, surrounded by coolers filled with beer, water, and soda, along with racks and racks of snack foods, candy, and wine as well as a complete ice cream shop, the burglar chose to take only the surveillance cameras and DVR.

Word of the break-ins quickly echoed around Deer Harbor. Now *my* hackles went up. There'd be no reason for someone to have gone into our crawlspace unless he was just getting out of the rain. But we're so far at the end of the road surrounded by acres and acres of nothing but woods that even that didn't make sense. I went underneath and found a vent pipe knocked out of place. It still had to be a deer, I thought, but Sandi and I spent an hour digging around for the single house key we owned and went to make a copy. We started taking the keys out of our cars and locking the house overnight, just like back in the city.

That night as we lay in bed with the big black window behind our heads, the woods outside seemed darker.

———

The action moved back to Eastsound just before Labor Day weekend, the last big opportunity for local businesses to rake in summer money. Early morning on September 1, a burglar forced his way into the popular Sunflower Café on the prime corner of Main Street and North Beach. He took $300 out of the till and $3,280 from the ATM before crossing the street to Vern's Bayside.

Belinda and Marion had installed surveillance cameras inside and out after the 2008 hit. Now, one by one, the cameras went dark.

"He WHALED on them with his fist," says Belinda. Then he pried open the side door and went inside the restaurant. A camera in the dining room captured a tall white male wearing a tan T-shirt walking past using a black shirt to cover his face. The burglar went directly to Marion's office, which sits nooked away in a nonobvious spot up a short flight of stairs from the kitchen. A tiny camera mounted on the office ceiling watched as he came through the door and instantly rounded the divider to shine his flashlight at the empty space where the safe had been the year before. He swung his light around quickly, but couldn't figure out where they'd moved it.

At that point, the computer attached to the security cameras began to beep. The burglar bolted full speed out of the office and back out the way he came.

Just down the street, Suzanne Lyons was sleeping in her jewelry store, Orcas Arts and Gifts. Lyons has had some experience with at-risk youth.

"When I lived in California," she says, "I took in five ten-year-old boys as foster kids from really bad families, moms were hookers and everything, but I got them early enough. Four joined the service, and they all turned out okay."

Suzanne's family had been taking turns bunking in their little shop ever since her daughter, Erica, had been woken by a noise in the middle of the night shortly after the stolen boat had shown up. Erica went outside to check and found a very tall young man standing in the private yard between the store and their home. He calmly looked at her for a long moment, then vaulted over the six-foot-high fence and disappeared.

They called the deputies, but they couldn't find the guy. Now, on September 1, it was Suzanne who sensed something was not right. She stepped outside.

"I was in my robe and bunny slippers," she says, laughing. "I saw this big guy running down Main Street away from Vern's. I wasn't really dressed to chase him, though."

The next morning, as word quickly spread, Eastsound's worst fears were realized: the summertime burglar was back.

"This time," says Belinda, "the cops took it seriously." Sergeant Vierthaler came down to Vern's right away and watched the security footage.

He noticed something very strange about the tall young man who'd broken into the restaurant: he was barefoot.

Near the top of North Beach Road stands Orcas Island Hardware, affiliated with Ace Hardware, "The Helpful Place." With so much do-it-yourselfing on the island, Orcas has always had two hardware stores. Scott Lancaster worked at one for fifteen years before buying the other in the spring of 2009. Now, five months later, late in the afternoon on September 4, the Friday of the big Labor Day weekend, Lancaster was straightening up the storage yard when he noticed that part of his chain-link fence was laid over. Odd, but nothing else was out of place, so he heaved it back into position and went home.

"That night," he says, "it started bothering me. I'm wondering if it was pushed over by someone climbing the fence to get onto the roof of the main building. But by that time I'd sat down to a nice dinner with my wife, had a couple glasses of wine . . . I decided not to go back to check it out just based on a gut feeling." Besides, he says, there'd always been a hardware store filled with tools at that spot, the building never had an alarm system, and there'd never been a problem. In fact, long ago when the building first went up, a row of its warehouse windows were installed crooked and had never closed far enough to lock. "It's Orcas," says Scott. "Most of the time we just left them wide open for ventilation."

After dark, someone slipped into the yard behind Orcas Island Hardware. He climbed topsoil bags piled next to the lowest part of the warehouse roof, then pulled himself onto a higher stack of bark mulch sacks that rose another level closer to the edge of the twelve-foot-high roof. Balancing precariously atop the tower of bags, he stretched out one long leg and stepped onto the metal roof, barefoot.

The bandit sneaked around to the row of second-floor windows, slid open the one farthest from the sidewalk, and climbed inside the warehouse loft. He used a ladder to drop down into a corridor, then went into the store's offices. The first thing he saw in the cluttered outer office was the blue glow of a TV monitor. A simple closed circuit, the system transmitted only a live picture of the store—there was no recorder. Still, the burglar switched off its impotent eye. He rummaged through the desks until he found the key to the petty cash drawer, pocketing all the paper money.

Once done with the office, he went downstairs into a B and E man's dream: a fully stocked hardware store. The first tool he wanted was something big and strong enough to open the safe he'd spotted in the warehouse. Ace, the helpful place, had just the thing: a sixteen-pound, six-foot-long forged steel digging bar. The safe gave way. Inside sat two bank bags—one a ten-year-old KeyBank carrier, a distinctive style that isn't used anymore. Both bags were filled with cash organized into neat bundles ready for depositing.

Then the thief went on a shopping spree. Using Ace-logoed five-gallon buckets and a clothes basket to carry the booty, he grabbed a Coleman sleeping bag, two air mattresses (one twin and one full-size), an LED headlamp, a hatchet, two axes, a maul/sledgehammer, two hammers, a crowbar, screwdrivers, six assorted padlocks and cable locks, bolt cutters, a power drill and a cordless drill, along with eight drill bits including two augers used for drilling deep, large-diameter holes—like maybe the kind you could insert a camera into. In all, the burglar took more than $5,000 worth of cash and prizes.

He lugged everything to the store's delivery bay and used his new bolt cutters to snip off the padlock. Up went the big roller door and out he walked. The thief's appetite was bigger than his ability to carry everything, though. He stopped across the street, ducking behind the hedge at Murphy's vet's office to rearrange the load that he must have ferried over in at least two trips. There he left behind the clothes basket with a bunch of the items he'd just taken, and dumped more tools into the landscaping around the real estate office where Sandi works. He kept the necessities, though, and headed off to attempt his most ambitious score. He wanted more cash, and knew the best place to find it.

WHEN ISLAND HARDWARE'S EMPLOYEES arrived the next morning, they found the place had been looted. Scott Lancaster's first priority after seeing that the deputies were on the job scoping out the big bare footprints clearly visible on the metal roof was to make sure he could keep the store running on its busiest day. He couldn't do that without cash, so he went to

Islanders Bank and withdrew $500 from the ATM. Lancaster says that an hour later the police called him to ask if he'd noticed anything strange while he was at the bank.

There's no better example of how little Orcas Islanders worried about crime than Islanders Bank circa that summer of 2009. Not only wasn't there a surveillance camera or alarm inside the ATM/night deposit room, but the room also had a window that wasn't alarmed.

The bottom of the window into the ATM room stood about ten feet off the ground. It was a single long, narrow pane less than two feet tall. The thief broke the glass and scaled the wall by stepping barefoot onto a thin foundation ledge a couple feet off the ground. He then hoisted himself up and through the window. It was a remarkably athletic move considering he did it without cutting himself to ribbons on the jagged glass. Once inside the room, he had plenty of time to attack the cash machine. He tried his new Ace drill, he tried his new crowbar, then his new sledgehammer. He made some marks, but couldn't crack the golden egg. The acrobatic burglar finally gave up and climbed back out, leaving his tools behind.

When San Juan County sheriff Bill Cumming realized he had an attempted bank job on his hands, he called in the Feds. An FBI CSI team arrived on the island and spent some nine hours processing the scene. The first mystery was how the hell someone had gotten through that window. According to bank manager Maggie Vinson, the hole in the glass looked too small for a normal-size man to get through. She said the police looked for ladder marks but found nothing but the smudges of dirt where the burglar put his bare feet against the wall. She also said the cops at the scene theorized that maybe two guys boosted another one up, or maybe, someone joked, two strong guys picked up a little accomplice and heaved him through the window.

OTHER BUSINESSES, INCLUDING BILBO'S Festivo restaurant, were hit over the same couple of nights. Orcas residents went up in arms—many literally. Kyle Ater and his .44 still held the high ground atop Homegrown Grocery, but now it seemed like half the Eastsound business owners joined him, camping out in their stores, locked and loaded in order to protect their livelihoods.

Sheriff Cumming shifted more deputies to Orcas from the other islands and they all started pulling overtime shifts to try to catch what was evidently one big shoeless kid tearing around the island jacking businesses at will. With toe prints found at the scene of at least three break-ins, the local cops began calling their suspect the Barefoot Bandit.

Scott Lancaster walked into Island Market after his burglary and ran into manager Jason Linnes, whose family owns and runs the supermarket. Linnes told him he was sorry to hear about the theft. "That's why we have all of the security at our store," he said, according to Lancaster. "No way the little bastard's going to get into our place."

Two days later, at around 2:20 a.m. on September 8, the woman working night crew at Island Market felt so ill that she had to go home. The person she'd normally call to replace her was on vacation and the stocking was finished anyway, so she decided not to bother waking anyone up. Every day of the year except for a couple of holidays, there's someone inside Island Market twenty-four hours a day. Now, for one short, unforeseeable period, it was left unattended. As soon as the employee left, a burglar tried to get in the back shipping door. He couldn't force it open, so he went around to the front of the building, where on many nights there's a police cruiser loitering in the parking lot. Not that night, though.

He crept along the side of the building until he was underneath the surveillance camera that kept watch over the front door. At 2:35 a.m., he used a crowbar to tilt the camera up, and then retreated into the shadows to make sure no one was monitoring the feed and that he hadn't tripped an alarm. At 2:50, he came back and broke open the sliding doors. He knew there were more security cameras inside, so he held his arm across his face and walked into the store, barefoot, carrying a crowbar and hammer.

The cameras watched the tall white kid head straight to aisle 6—toilet paper, paper towels, Ziplocs—but he didn't stop to pick up any supplies. At the back of the aisle he turned right, walked along a huge display of cold beer without snagging any, then ducked through the swinging doors into the stock area. The burglar knew exactly where he was going. He climbed a metal shelving unit to reach a surveillance camera, and whacked it with his crowbar, knocking off the lens.

There's a big Mosler safe back there, a monolithic old-timer like you'd see Butch and Sundance blow up with a pile of dynamite. The kid didn't even bother to try that one. Instead, he walked back out through the produce department, leaving big bare footprints on the mats, and went through the unmarked door that leads upstairs to the bathrooms and the offices. He pried open each office door until he found the electrical box and, at 3:30 a.m., he turned off the store's lights, which are normally left burning all night. He also broke into the room that housed the security system. Inside, he began pushing buttons on the equipment until the camera feeds went dark. What he didn't know was that he turned off only the monitor. The cameras continued to see and the DVR continued to record as he went back downstairs to his real target.

Island Market's little ATM stands at the front of the store just behind the facade's huge plate-glass windows, near the bird seed and bags of charcoal. The machine is one of those stand-alones, four feet high and about eighteen inches square, with a molded plastic shell covering its steel body. It held about $8,000 that night, and it certainly looked like a breachable target if you had enough time and leverage. The crook went to work with his trusty crowbar and hammer. After many, many whacks, though, he hadn't made much of an impact on anything except the plastic. To be fair, he was hampered a bit by bad visibility: sensing that the cameras might still be recording, he'd hung a T-shirt over his head and had to peek out through its neck hole as he moved around.

The burglar realized the ATM called for more firepower and he had an idea. He jogged back to the loading dock and grabbed the handle of a battery-powered pallet jack, aka a "jigger," a baby forklift that lets its user pick up and move a thousand pounds with little effort. He walked it like a dog on a leash back to the front of the store, then lined it up and rammed it into the ATM . . . over and over and over.

He worked on the ATM for an hour and ten minutes, until the little money machine looked like R2-D2 after being humped by a Transformer. Its plastic housing was pried apart, cracked, and decapitated, and its metal body crumpled. But the money box held. Barely.

"A couple more hits to the door and it would have popped open, but he kept changing angles," says Jason Linnes. What the burglar did succeed in doing, though, was gashing his hand on the sharp plastic. He bled like a stuck pig, on the machine, on the jigger, and all over the floor. At 4:30, he ran to the deli kitchen to wash his cut in the sink. The video then shows that he either saw lights or heard something outside—a police cruiser may have driven through the lot—because he suddenly crouched down by the baguette display and froze for a few moments. This allowed a ceiling camera to get a nice clean shot suitable for framing—or at least for a wanted poster.

The burglar popped back up, showing that he'd wrapped one of his T-shirts around his cut hand. He went directly to the cleaning aisle and picked up a bottle of bleach, which he poured over the blood on the floor, the ATM, and the pallet jack in order to make the blood useless for DNA testing.

At this point he looked at the watch he wore on his right wrist. It was 4:42 a.m., and he knew exactly when he needed to get out of Dodge. He left eighteen minutes before the morning crew arrived.

The staff discovered the assault and battery on their cash machine, but not one thing was missing except the bleach, which added about three bucks to the $12,000 worth of damage done to the store.

When the deputies arrived to take a report, the employees showed them the bare footprints and all the things that'd been touched. Then they walked them over to the deli. The burglar had forgotten about that, and there was very visible, very fresh blood all over the sink. At first, according to the supermarket staff, the cops said they weren't going to bother collecting any of it for evidence. The employees and owner were furious, though—and also all on a first-name basis with the deputies. They demanded that they collect a sample. Finally, a deputy went for a forensics kit and took a DNA swab.

Long before those results came back, though, a San Juan County detective attended a monthly information-sharing meeting with other detectives from around the region. He told the assembled officers about the trouble his county was having with a suspect they'd nicknamed the Barefoot Bandit.

"I remember getting a chuckle out of that," says Island County Sheriff's Office detective Ed Wallace, who was at the meeting. Wallace, however, says the name didn't ring any bells among the Island County contingent. It might have for regular readers of the county's *Stanwood/Camano News*, though, since the paper's front-page headline back in February 2007 had been: "Camano's barefoot bandit caught." The story was about a teenager named Colton Harris-Moore who'd been captured by the Island County

Sheriff's Office (ICSO) after evading them for six months on a small island while continuously breaking into homes to steal everything from food to jewelry. The local paper—as well as the *Seattle Times* and *Everett Herald*— had run quite a few additional Colton stories since then, including a flurry after his escape from detention in April 2008 and resumption of his thieving ways on Camano Island, which lay just thirty miles south of Orcas.

It all finally came together—at least for law enforcement—when a San Juan County detective sent images from the Island Market surveillance camera of the suspect posing by the baguettes. Island County recognized him right away.

"We felt like a doctor giving a patient bad news," says Wallace. "We're afraid you have a Colton Harris-Moore problem."

ICSO gave the San Juan sheriff Colton's file, including a recent portrait taken by Harris-Moore himself. The eighteen-year-old's book-length rap sheet started once upon a time when he was ten. Island County warned Sheriff Bill Cumming that Colton had run their deputies ragged. And said that when they finally caught him and thought they'd rid their island by sentencing him to three years in prison, he'd escaped. The file also included the information that Colton liked to play with guns and often armed himself with pepper spray. Island County had already filed a slew of new felony charges against Colton for crimes he'd committed since going on the lam.

Cumming made the tactical decision not to let Orcas residents know who was tearing up their island. He felt that if Colton didn't know the sheriff's office was on to him, the Barefoot Bandit might step out in public. He sent all the manpower he could spare to Orcas and made sure his deputies had Colton's face burned into their memories. He put more officers in plain clothes and sent them out into Eastsound, especially after dark.

It worked—sort of. The deputies didn't have much trouble spotting Colton, but they soon learned something about him beyond his affinity for going footloose: he was fast. Even those rare few deputies in shape to run after him were easily outdistanced. Every time he was sighted, Colton took off for the woods around town. One cop caught him in the beam of his flashlight and made a positive ID before Colton melted into the trees.

"He virtually vaporized in front of me," said the officer.

Increasing the police patrols may have at least made Eastsound seem like a tougher target. The night following the Island Market ATM fail, the Bandit crept along the Ditch beside Smuggler's Villa Resort. Mike Stolmeier had hosted the usual summer evening campfire for his guests and then gone to bed after making sure there were no tall strangers stretched out in the sauna. Tied up less than forty yards from the occupied villas were whale-watching and fishing boats belonging to a charter operation based at the resort. The Bandit chose a thirty-foot catamaran called *Blackfish*—a traditional name for killer whales. He untied one of its dock lines and jumped in. Starting *Blackfish*'s diesel engines isn't as simple as turning a key; several switches get thrown to power the starters. The thief couldn't figure that out, so he climbed back to the dock and moved to the next boat, a single-engine twenty-six-foot Harborcraft loaded down with fishing gear for the next morning's trip. The keys were in the boat and the engine turned right over. He switched on the GPS unit, slipped the lines, and set off into what Stolmeier called a nasty night to be out boating, "jet black and raining."

The boat thief knew where he wanted to go, though, and the GPS chartplotter offered a video game–like navigation experience as simple as steering a little avatar around the blue screen and avoiding the big beige blocks that signified hard land. Again, very simple in theory. However, Pacific Northwest reality tosses a few challenges into the mix around the San Juans. An enormous amount of water fills and empties the Salish Sea as the tides change. Currents ripping around the islands swirl into whirlpools and, when conditions are right, even pile into standing waves. Just below the surface—and thus not shown as land on charts—lie myriad jagged reefs. A painstaking count of all the islands, islets, seal haulouts, and godforsaken rocks in San Juan County comes to 743. But that's at low tide. At high tide, only 428 of them are visible; the rest lurk beneath a thin film of water. Experienced local boaters look for hints like kelp fronds or patches of calm water that mark rocks, but that helps only during the day. Many of the known reefs are marked on charts as tiny plus signs—as in if you hit one you'll "add" shipwrecker to your résumé. What can't be marked, however, are those Salish Sea specialties aptly named "deadheads."

With logging long one of the Northwest's major industries, innumerable ex-trees have escaped booms and tugs and now roam free in the region's waters. The logs eventually get so soggy that they barely float. Those that bob vertically with an almost invisible sliver of wood above the surface are deadheads. Running into one is like striking an iceberg. The great bulk of the log lies underwater, giving it enough mass to easily splinter a wooden hull or smash a fiberglass one. Open a hole too big for the bilge pumps and you get help fast or go swimming.

Cold water often has the final say in the Salish Sea. Even in summer the water temperature barely gets into the mid-50s. Wind up in the drink and the countdown starts—that is, if it doesn't cause instant cardiac arrest. Depending on body type, it can take one-half to three hours for you to lose consciousness, less if you're treading water or swimming for land.

The Bandit, though, knew how to run a boat at night, or else he was lucky once again. The GPS recorded his track as he rounded the sheer cliffs of Point Doughty and headed down President Channel between the west coast of Orcas and Waldron Island. He skirted the treacherously beautiful Wasp Islands—perennially the most popular place for visiting boaters to come to grief on the San Juans' reefs—and steered southeast between Shaw and San Juan Island until he reached the town of Friday Harbor.

He drove the boat to the University of Washington's Friday Harbor Labs, a marine science center. At U-Dub's dock, he jumped off and let the $100,000 boat float away. The GPS showed the Harborcraft drifting lazily until it grounded off Shaw, where it was found the next morning.

The Barefoot Bandit ran around San Juan Island for two days, hitting a coffee hut in downtown Friday Harbor but otherwise not calling too much attention to himself. Police later discovered a hideaway secreted in a hangar at the airport where he apparently camped out.

Then, at midnight on September 11, 2009, a small plane took off from the San Juan Island airport.

IF BOB RIVERS'S CESSNA was a classic station wagon, this second plane, a sleek, 310-horsepower, composite-bodied Cirrus SR22, was a high-tech hot rod. It featured a low-wing configuration versus the Cessna's high wing. Low wings are trickier for inexperienced pilots to land as they tend to float more near the ground. The SR22 also had a completely different steering system—a side joystick versus the Cessna's classic two-handed wheel.

Considered a safe and popular plane for its class, according to the NTSB the Cirrus SR22 still has twice the rate of fatal accidents as the Cessna 182. And remarkably, for only his second solo flight, Colton decided to fly this one at night.

The $700,000 Cirrus was equipped with two major features not found in Bob Rivers's Cessna. First was the "glass cockpit," a term used not for the plane's windows, but for large dashboard video monitors that gather all the information a pilot needs on-screen rather than split among individual gauges. Fans of the new-style instruments love the amazing amount of data—weather maps, flight info, navigation, and all the plane's mechanical systems—laid on two screens. There are some old-timers, though, who feel the glowing screens might be crowded with too much information, especially for an inexperienced flier.

"I wouldn't recommend a new pilot start out with a glass cockpit in a Cirrus, particularly at night—too distracting, a real handful," says Bill Anders, an Orcas Island resident who owns a Columbia 400 (aka Cessna 400 Corvalis), a slick composite plane that's extremely similar to the Cirrus. And for Bill Anders to call anything related to flying a handful takes a lot.

Anders's first plane ride came in 1946, when he was an eighth grader in Texas. One day as his father drove him to school, they saw a biplane sitting in a cow pasture. "This guy had a sign up, 'Rides $15,'" remembers Anders. "I said to my dad, 'I sure would like to do that.'"

Anders's father had just gotten out of the navy and $15 was big money back then, "but my dad could always make deals and he made one that morning." Anders strapped into the open cockpit of the wood-and-fabric plane and the pilot took off. Whatever his dad paid, young Bill got his money's worth. "He even did a loop, and I thought, Boy, this is fun!"

Anders went off to school with dreams of flying adventures. "Well, on the way home that day, here was the biplane, tail up, in about a three-foot-deep hole . . . The pilot and his paying passenger dead. I didn't fly for quite some time after that."

The pull of the sky was so strong, though, that Anders became an air force fighter pilot and served in an interceptor squadron at the height of the Cold War. One of his claims to fame from that era is intercepting a Soviet Bear bomber over Europe and giving its belligerent pilot an up-close and personal middle-finger salute—decades before Tom Cruise fictitiously flipped one off in *Top Gun*.

Anders then topped that by going on the ultimate flight: strapped atop a huge *Saturn V* rocket for the Apollo 8 mission where he, Frank Borman, and Jim Lovell (of "Houston, we've had a problem" fame) became the first earthlings to leave their planet's orbit and circle the moon. It was on that flight, on Christmas Eve 1968, that Anders snapped *Earthrise*, the shocking first view of our planet existing as just a fragile blue marble adrift in a black void.

Now seventy-eight, Bill lives on Orcas Island for much of the year, cruising aboard his big boat, *Apogee*, scuba diving with the SeaDoc Society, and flying as much as he can, often in service of the Heritage Flight Museum he founded in Bellingham. The museum specializes in warbirds, and we can always tell when Bill is in the neighborhood by the window-rattling grumble of a WWII P-51 Mustang or a 2,700-horsepower Korean War–era A-1 Skyraider as he does a fly-by.

One thing Bill Anders won't do anymore, though, is fly at night in the San Juans. "Not that I'm afraid—I've got lots of night flying time as an interceptor pilot—but I'm always worried about the goddamn geese on the Orcas runway. You can fly over deer because they don't jump very high. But the damn geese, they can take off."

The pilot who took the Cirrus SR22 from San Juan Island wasn't worried about geese or deer. Something compelled Colt back to Orcas Island that night. Once in the airplane, he could have flown away as far as his fuel would have taken him. Instead, he took off, did a short waggling course across the border into the nearby Canadian Gulf Islands, then turned around and headed straight to Orcas, where the entire island was already on high alert.

Apparently all the lights and info on the dashboard monitors didn't bother Colt too much either, because he didn't end up a charred dimple on Turtleback. And he didn't panic, or he might have used the Cirrus's most famous standard feature, a rocket-propelled last-resort parachute that erupts out of the airframe and slows its fall to a survivable speed. Instead, he went for it. One thing on his side was that the San Juans are very dark at night so the runway lights are easy to spot. Scattered home lights pierce the black mountainsides, red beacons flash atop Mount Constitution's cell towers, and a soft yellow glow emanates from Eastsound, but other than that, it's perfect stargazing dark.

The Bandit flew over town, sighted the runway, and touched down to the north—or tried to touch down.

"It's a slippery plane and he lost it a bit," says Bea Von Tobel, herself a longtime pilot. "That's the hardest part of landing: judging how high above the ground you are, especially at night. You really need some time with an instructor who can teach you how to flare and get down comfortably. Instead, he kind of wandered off onto the grass and almost landed on the taxiway."

Von Tobel showed up at the airport Saturday morning for the annual meeting of the Ninety-Nines, a group of women pilots, and saw the Cirrus already surrounded by yellow police tape. "He'd gotten in the plane by breaking the lock out of the door. The second thing I noticed was that he'd hit and broken one of my runway lights. All I remember thinking was that he must have really wanted to get back to Orcas to steal a plane and fly back at night. I guess he didn't want to wait for the ferry."

While the landing hadn't been a thing of beauty, the plane suffered only minor damage and was flyable the next day. "He's very lucky," says Bill Anders. "But given the choice between skill and luck, I'll take luck any day."

Once again, since plane theft is such a rare occurrence, the rumors that quickly spread on the island hinted instead at a partying pilot trying to impress a girl he met at a bar over in "Sin City," the nickname us provincial islanders have for Friday Harbor because there's an incredible number of places where you can get a drink in town . . . like six.

Local police, though, knew the real story.

"August 2008: burglary, commercial burglary, commercial burglary, residential burglary . . . September '08: commercial burglary, commercial burglary, commercial burglary, residential burglary . . . October '08: more commercial burglaries . . . November 2008: airplane theft . . . August 2009: recovered vessel . . ." San Juan County sheriff Bill Cumming tut-tutted as he read down a long list his department compiled once they realized who they were dealing with and had confirmed Colton's MO with Island County detectives.

As tough as it was to believe, Cumming, sixty-one, realized he was up against just one extraordinarily brazen and "pretty darn bright" kid whom he now suspected of at least fifteen burglaries, along with the thefts of two planes and a couple of boats. With half the houses in San Juan County vacant for long stretches during the year, it wasn't unusual to have teen troublemakers breaking in to raid liquor cabinets. However, in his thirty-eight years in law enforcement—thirty-one years with San Juan County, twenty-four as its sheriff—Cumming had never dealt with a suspect like Colton Harris-Moore.

"We've had serial burglars out here before, even people who specialized in unusual things such as entry from the water, but this is unique, this is one person being so prolific. He's easily doubled the number of commercial burglaries we'd normally see. When you have someone that prolific in such a small area, they usually get caught."

Another startling aspect of Colt's spree was, of course, the boats and planes. He was suspected of stealing cars and he'd been convicted years before of taking dinghies on Camano Island, but now he was operating at an entirely different level of sophistication. And it wasn't just the fact that he was stealing the boats and planes that was extraordinary. "We've recovered everything," said Cumming, noting that Colton hadn't tried to sell them. "He's not taking them for joyrides; he's taking them for transportation."

Cumming's job was clear: arrest Colton Harris-Moore. Pressure from the community was growing more intense after every crime. Residents still didn't know who the suspect was; they just wanted him caught.

The evening after the stolen Cirrus showed up on Orcas, September 12, deputies flooded Eastsound determined to catch the Barefoot Bandit. They got lucky: instead of lying low for a while after the plane theft, Colt went out on the town.

The cops spotted him carrying a large bundle. According to a deputy, two officers went after him on foot while another converged by car. When Colt realized the cops were on his tail, he bolted into the street. The deputy in the car tried to sideswipe him, but missed. Colt danced away from the car and ran north through town toward the airport. Police followed, but he lost them by disappearing into a triangular patch of woods that connects the airport with the Ditch and Smuggler's.

During the chase, Colt dropped his bundle. A deputy found it and was checking out its contents when he heard a voice sing out from the dark woods.

"You can't catch me."

He was right. Even though the stretch of forest was only three hundred yards long, there wasn't enough manpower to effectively search it, and the county had no canine to try to sniff out the Barefoot Bandit. Besides, Colt already knew these woods as well as any local. Inside his bundle, the police found the sleeping bag stolen from Orcas Island Hardware, along with blankets he'd taken from an airplane stored inside a private hangar that sat at the edge of the trees where he now hid.

Another chunk of woods Colt knew well covered a peninsula called Madrona Point that dangles into East Sound. He had a campsite there complete with a pup tent, a sleeping bag, and a blanket that had gone missing from the Eastsound fire station. Colt used the camp as a base for raiding the town's shops. Several times, deputies had chased him onto the Point, but he always seemed to vanish into thin air and thick woods.

Lummi Indians used Madrona Point as a burial ground. When the afternoon sun drops low in the sky, the large congregation of orange-barked, red-berried Pacific Madrona trees begins to glow, and it's easy to imagine the area as a place of spirits. In the mid-eighties, a Seattle businessman who also owned much of Turtleback Mountain planned to build condos here on the island's most sacred spot. A grassroots antidevelopment movement sprang up and eventually caught the attention of the U.S. Congress. The land was purchased and given to the Lummi Nation. The tribe managed it as an open park until numbnuts littered the area with beer bottles, used condoms, and other trash. Today, the Lummi section of Madrona Point sits behind a huge NO TRESPASSING sign at the dead end of Haven Road.

Back toward Main Street on Madrona Point lies a small group of homes, some of them the original cabins from a long-defunct resort. Island Market, Islanders Bank, and the rest of downtown Eastsound lie just a few yards away though the trees. One day as a retiree named Annette was working on a cottage she's renovating, a friend mentioned that her old well looked to be about seven feet deep. "How can you tell?" asked Annette. The abandoned well, she knew, had been filled with approximately one ton of rocks the size of babies' heads and sealed with a five-hundred-pound cement lid.

Not anymore, said the friend.

Someone had slid open the lid and painstakingly excavated the rocks. "They were smart enough to not just pile them around the well or I would have noticed," says Annette. Instead, he carried each one at least a hundred feet away. Annette searched around and found the missing rocks on a dead-end gravel road nearby. Emptied to exactly six and a half feet deep, the old-fashioned well made an ideal hidey-hole. The rock walls that show above ground were covered with moss, camouflaging it during the day. Anyone inside would be invisible to infrared cameras, and even if a searcher stumbled across the well, he might not think anyone could be down there with the huge concrete lid in place.

Climb inside, though, and you realize that because the well's stones are smooth, even a six-foot-tall middle-aged writer can reach up and slide the heavy lid back into place. So it would be no problem at all for a six-foot-five athletic teenager.

Annette believes she once even heard Colton. "I was working in the garden and heard what sounded like a big metal bowl drop and bounce— *bump, bump, bump*—inside the house across the road that was supposed to be empty. I thought, Holy shit, it's the Bandit! I didn't do a thing, didn't even turn around, just walked away."

She didn't call the police that time, though she did when she found that her well had been converted into a spider hole. "They were elated," she says, "because they kept chasing him back here and couldn't figure out how he was disappearing." The deputies asked her not to tell anyone about the find, and they noted it as one place to carefully search whenever he ran toward Madrona Point.

The police, however, didn't know exactly where to look for Colt in the woods at the other side of town on the twelfth. It would be two weeks before a resident spotted another of his campsites, this one tucked into the bushes at the edge of the airport near the dog park. Colt had been able to lie back and watch two of his favorite things: planes and pooches.

The cops did at least know that he was just yards away from two previous targets: the airport and all its hangars, and the Ditch with its boats. Somehow, though, Colton slipped past the deputies, went to Brandt's Landing Marina on the Ditch, and climbed aboard a sporty twin-engine cabin cruiser worth about $75,000. The boat he chose belonged to Jason

Linnes, manager of the Island Market, which had been burglarized just four days before. The keys, as with most of the island's boats at the time, were aboard—hidden, but not too hard to find.

"I always left the keys in the boat, and in the car, and left my house unlocked," says Linnes, whose family has been on Orcas since the late 1800s. "I was raised that way."

Once inside, Colton relaxed and stretched out in the berth. Sometime before daylight on the thirteenth, he fired up the engines and pulled out of the slip—no mean feat as there's very little wiggle room at that crowded end of the marina. He managed to drive out of the Ditch without dinging any of the nearby boats, then turned on the GPS and navigated directly to Point Roberts, a geopolitical oddity that hangs off the Canadian coast but remains part of the United States.

Jason could understand his family's market getting hit—"That was just business"—but it seemed like too much of a coincidence that out of all the boats in the Ditch, his was the one Colton picked. "The boat was more personal than the store. And one happening after the other . . . that was creepy. I didn't sleep for days, wondering, Does he know me? Is he after me? Is he really gone? I didn't have shades on my house windows before but now I have ADT installing a security system. That sucks."

According to Linnes, as Colton brought the boat to shore the lower units of both engines hit rocks, damaging their skegs. Later that day, the U.S. Coast Guard found the boat tied to a Point Roberts mooring buoy and they towed it back to Orcas, where a San Juan County deputy found bare footprints on the swim platform.

When residents woke to the news that another of their neighbor's boats had been stolen and found abandoned on the mainland, everyone wondered the same thing: Is it over?

9

We hoped so.

On an island with no industries other than real estate and tourism, the last thing you want are your adjectives changed from "serene" and "scenic" to "paranoid" and "crime-ridden."

The precious image of a calm sea lapping the beach below a cozy-luxe cabin set amid tall firs tarnishes a bit if you have to add barbed wire and light it up like a prison camp. Public relations–wise, the only thing worse for Orcas Island than a serial criminal terrifying the blue hairs would be if our cuddly, iconic killer whales suddenly started crunching on kayaks to get at their soft, chewy insides.

The one bright spot was that word hadn't really gotten out. The *Islands' Sounder* had run its sheriff's logs and the deputy's cautionary tale to the Chamber the year before, but beyond our insular world, there was no story. The name Colton Harris-Moore still meant nothing outside his own Island County, and even there, no one but the police had a clue that they'd exported their troublemaker up to the San Juan Islands or that he'd begun pirating planes and yachts. Colton certainly wasn't on the national radar.

A week after Jason Linnes's boat was found at Point Roberts, I was certain it was all over. Whoever this guy was, he had a plan. You'd have to be defective to keep committing burglaries in the same tiny area—on an island no less—unless you were doing a hit and run. He must have reached his magic number, the dollar amount that would let him kick back on some Baja beach and tip Tecates for a year. Or suck Molsons in Canada. Whatever. It didn't matter. He was somebody else's problem now.

Those somebodies were, for a short while at least, the residents of Point Roberts. Point Bob is a footnote of international politics twenty miles north of Orcas Island as the crow flies—and if you don't have a boat, that's the best way to get there, because the other option is driving through two border crossings. This U.S. exclave illustrates what happens when uninformed bureaucrats attack. The United States and United Kingdom solved a nineteenth-century boundary dispute over the West Coast by agreeing to split the mainland territory along the 49th parallel. Problem was, nobody consulted an accurate chart. The 49 line cuts through a nub of land on what's now called Boundary Bay, south of Vancouver. Instead of simply trading the five square miles for a wagonload of otter pelts and calling it even, the Americans decided to keep the land. It's now a funky little outpost with 1,300 people, a marina, and a small tourist-based economy but very few other services. Point Roberts's kids have to board buses and cross the frontier north into Canada, then loop around for a forty-minute drive to the crossing at Blaine, Washington, where they reenter the United States to get to school.

Life at Point Roberts may be full of inconveniences, but residents consider it worth the hassle for their beautiful location on the Salish Sea and, since their little community is protected by a border guard, for its security.

When Colton landed in Point Roberts, he dialed up the cell phone of his friend Josh, who he'd served time with in Green Hill School, a juvenile prison. Colt had planned a "Hey, look out the window!" kind of surprise for his buddy, but instead got a "Dude, I moved" downer. Josh had relocated to Vancouver. So Colton improvised.

Whatcom County sheriff's deputies stationed in Point Roberts had one of their busiest days in memory when folks who owned vacation homes arrived the following weekend to discover they'd had a visitor. In the couple of days after Colton waded ashore, someone pried open the sliding glass door at one home, took a shower, and then wrapped himself in a blanket while he listened to the radio and enjoyed a can of Coke. Before he left with a stash of canned goods, he refolded the blanket and put it back on the bed. At another home, a burglar jimmied a deadbolted door, raided the fridge, and slept on the bed. At a third, someone tried to force open two deadbolts, gave up, and attempted to reach through the cat door with a barbecue fork to twist the latch, gave that up, and finally broke a window. Inside, he took a nap on the bed. A fourth Goldilocks-style break-in within the same short period qualified the rash as a plague—and potentially a spree. Then the burglaries stopped as suddenly as they had started.

Despite the threat posed by millions of hockey stick– and curling stone–wielding Canadians massed along our borders, the northern U.S. frontier remains loosely guarded. At Point Roberts, it's a simple matter of *not* driving through the checkpoint and instead walking across a road and into the vowel-deprived town of Tsawwassen, British Columbia.

Once Colt reached the Canadian side, he rustled a classy dark gray BMW and drove to see his prison pal.

"He called me on my cell and said, 'I'm right down the street,'" says twenty-three-year-old Josh. "I was pretty surprised."

Colt didn't seem to be nervous about law enforcement chasing him. "No, not at all, totally relaxed. He was enjoying it," says Josh, who cruised with Colt around Vancouver.

Colt had cash—over a grand that Josh saw—and they went to a bar. Colt didn't order alcohol, though. "He's had a drink or two before, but he doesn't like it," says Josh. "No booze or drugs for him."

The two friends who'd bonded in prison when they found out they both lived on Puget Sound had some catching up to do. "He told me about crashing one of the planes in a field and about stealing a boat out in the islands," Josh remembers. "I think he's totally nuts for doing the plane stuff, but he said he doesn't care if he crashes."

Colt had stayed in touch ever since he'd escaped custody in 2008 while Josh was still locked up. He'd called Josh from inside the Brodys' home and from several different stolen cell phones. The calls to Green Hill caught the attention of the prison guards, but little came of it other than getting Josh, when he was released, put on a watch list. "They stopped me once at a border crossing and asked me what I knew about Colt, but that was it."

After a nice, friendly visit, Colt asked Josh to come running with him. Josh said no. He had a good job as a framing carpenter, a beautiful girlfriend, and life was good. He didn't feel the need to risk it all for a rush. He'd served every day of a three-year sentence and had no desire to go back to jail—or worse. Josh says things looked to be headed someplace serious when Colt gave him a peek at some of the gear he was carrying.

"He had a twelve-gauge shotgun and a nine-millimeter pistol," says

Josh. "He said he'd use them . . . said something like, 'They'll never take me alive.' "

———

On September 22, 2009, Sheriff Bill Cumming finally announced that the crook he suspected of causing all the trouble on Orcas over the last thirteen months was eighteen-year-old Colton Harris-Moore. "We wanted to give him a false sense of security," Cumming said as the reason he hadn't let the county's residents in on it earlier.

As Cumming talked to reporters, the cops working Colt's case down in Island County held their breath. "We'd asked Bill not to mention the airplanes."

Island County Sheriff's Office deputies had come across campsites in the Camano Island woods where they found newspaper clippings Colt had snipped out about himself. They were concerned that part of his motivation was a need for attention and that giving it to him would just perpetuate or, worse, escalate his actions. "We always tried to downplay him in the press," says one ICSO officer.

Colt's Orcas spree made the Local section in the region's biggest newspaper, the *Seattle Times*. Jennifer Sullivan of the *Times* and other local reporters had periodically covered the highlights of Colton's criminal career over the previous three years, and they'd spotted the fascinating nugget in Sheriff Cumming's statement that immediately elevated a conventional "prolific teenage thief and burglar, blah blah" story to a higher level. Cumming's information that Colt was a suspect in two airplane thefts made the top 'graph. The *Times* also ran a timeline of Colt's career going back to a 2004 conviction when he was twelve.

Our tormenter had a backstory. He also had a mom.

From the *Seattle Times*:

"Harris-Moore's mother, Pam Koehler (sp) of Camano Island, calls the new allegations against her son 'crap.'

" 'I know for a fact he is not doing all of these crimes,' Koehler said Tuesday. 'Any time the cops can't catch whoever is doing them, they blame it on Colt.'

"Koehler concedes her son has been interested in flying, but insists he has never taken flight lessons."

10

Creston, B.C., lies snuggled into a scenic mountain valley just north of the Idaho line—a 450-mile drive east of Vancouver. South of town, alongside the squiggling run of the Kootenay River, Creston Valley Regional Airport consists of a handful of hangars and a four-thousand-foot runway where the local flying club offers classes on the hazardous art of mountain flying. Colton spent at least two nights and three days there, but didn't sign up for a course.

On September 24, he ditched the stolen BMW at the entrance to a landfill less than half a mile away from the airport and walked across a hayfield to the fence line. Hazards to local pilots had long included a herd of elk that enjoyed the warmth of the asphalt runway on cold nights, so Creston erected an eight-foot fence around the entire 225-acre airport to keep planes from getting gored. Colt climbed the fence and set up camp in the thick woods on the west side of the airport.

Creston was a risky place to try to steal an airplane because its manager, Les Staite, lived on-site with his wife and a "yappy little Shih Tzu" that Les calls a tyrant. "Anybody comes around at all, he's a good alarm system."

That didn't faze Colt, though, just made it more challenging. He staked out a spot where he could keep an eye on all six hangars and the Staites' home. After dark, he slinked across the runway to scope out Creston's airplane inventory.

At the first hangar, Colt leaned against his pry bar until the door lock popped. Inside, his headlamp illuminated a Wild West scene, with saddles and chaps hanging on the walls. Bush pilot Volker Scherm owned the hangar as a base for BearAir, his backcountry guiding business. He'd built a small office in the corner of the hangar, and up top he stored a collection of grizzly bear and mountain goat skins. Colt tried the office door and found it locked. He was in no hurry, though, and didn't force it open. He'd learned long ago that people almost always hid keys nearby. Scherm kept his tucked into one of the saddles.

Skins, saddles . . . made sense there'd be guns close by. Colt left the hangar with Scherm's laptop, a wad of cash, and three guns, including .32 and .22 caliber pistols. He considered BearAir's sixties-era Cessna a dinosaur, so he passed on the plane.

Next door, Colt broke into what eighty-year-old Korean War vet Bill Piper calls his "oasis." Piper's mancave of a hangar features a bedroom, shower, full kitchen, and an airplane. He's piloted everything from jets to choppers, but now flies a Piper Super Cub—a classic bush plane equally at home on wheels, skis, or floats. Again, though, the thirty-plus-year-old plane was ancient to Colt; he was interested only in the most modern models. Instead, he helped himself to a cache of Piper's power bars, bottled water, 7Up, cans of pork and beans, and pudding packets as well as a load of his tools and a portable radio that picked up aviation frequencies.

Colton poked inside all six of Creston's hangars and saw all the planes, but none of them was just right. He'd already spotted the perfect one—a brand-new Cessna 182 Skylane—but it wasn't in a hangar where he could spend time prepping it out of sight. The Cessna was tied down on the main ramp just a few hundred feet in front of Les Staite's kitchen window. Even worse, it sat in a pool of light under a streetlamp.

Despite the risk, Colt stealthed up to the plane and pried open its window to get at the door lock. He climbed inside. As a bonus, the owner had left his satellite phone in the plane. Colt pulled the satphone out of its case and fiddled with it. Everything checked out with the Cessna, so Colt retired to his campsite to wait for the right time.

The next morning, Bill Piper and the other owners discovered they'd been burglarized. The Royal Canadian Mounted Police (RCMP) responded and investigated, after which the hangars were locked back up and Les Staite wired the Cessna 182's window shut as a temporary fix.

Colt sat in the woods, calmly chowing on pudding and power bars and watching all the police activity. He bided his time until nightfall, when everyone else left and Staite and his yappy dog settled down inside their house.

Colt walked back across the runway and, under the streetlight and in full view of Staite's kitchen window, broke into the Cessna again. He took out its tow bar and attached it to the plane's nose wheel. He then muscled the two-thousand-plus-pound plane more than five hundred feet—rolling it up a slight incline—to a dark spot beside the hangars and out of sight of Staite's residence. Somehow, Colt did it all without alerting the tyrannical Shih Tzu.

Colt hadn't found a key to the Cessna, but he knew he didn't need one to start it. The planes aren't equipped with antitheft ignition systems like modern automobiles. Colt followed the checklist procedures, then simply jammed a screwdriver into the ignition switch and wrenched it clockwise to Start. The starter whined and the propeller began to spin slowly . . . but the engine wouldn't catch.

"That plane has a little quirk," explains Staite. "You have to mess with the fuel system and know just how much fuel to give it in order to get it to fire off. You have to know your airplane."

Colt didn't know this particular Cessna's idiosyncrasies, and kept cranking until the starter burned out and the battery drained. Once he realized he was grounded, he went for a vehicle. He chose a GMC Z71 half-ton pickup. There was an antitheft Club on the steering wheel, but it may not have been locked because Colt was able to remove it. His bad luck with batteries continued, though, because the truck belonged to a pilot who only flew in from Alberta every once in a while and it had been sitting so long that the battery was dead. Next Colt tried a Dodge van. He couldn't find a hide-a-key, so he tore the ignition apart trying to hotwire it—so easy in the movies. Not in real life, though.

Colt then went to a 2009 Toyota Corolla that sat next to a hangar. He knew the car probably belonged to a pilot out on a trip, and if so, the keys would be in the hangar. All pilots share the same nightmare of leaving their car keys on a layover and getting back home to a big D'oh!

If Colt had simply cranked on the door with his crowbar like he did at the other hangars, it might have changed the course of his story. This hangar was rigged with an alarm system. Something else Colt had learned early on, though, was to carefully scope out his targets. He'd also studied up on how to defeat alarms. If he triggered this one it would automatically call the police, so he disabled it by cutting the phone line.

Just as he thought, the owner had left the key to the Corolla dangling on a hook inside the hangar. Colt grabbed it, started the car, and headed for the exit sometime before 9:30 p.m. To get in the airport's security gate, a driver needs to punch in a code. Leaving just requires a short pause to wait for the gate to lift when it senses a car. Colt didn't bother waiting. He rammed through the gate and drove off.

The following day a search of the airport grounds turned up soda cans, food containers, water bottles, and—in a hayfield beside the runway—one of the pistols, the .22, still in its holster. Later, Les Staite found Colt's campsite, where he'd left a "practically new" pair of Vans sneakers.

THE U.S. BORDER IS less than a two-mile walk from the Creston airport. A kayaker could also paddle across the frontier, floating down the Kootenay River as it exchanges its Y for an I, becoming the Kootenai on the American side. But Colt was carrying a heavy load and needed a car. Controls along the world's longest border concentrate on vehicle traffic, and Colt didn't have a passport or driver's license, so he ditched the Corolla in Rykerts on the Canadian side near where Canadian Route 21 turns into Idaho Highway 1. On the American side lies a tiny farm community of less than a hundred folks called Porthill ("port" of entry near a "hill"). There's a clearcut shaved through the forest all along the border, with the threat of electronic sensors hidden along this no-go partition, but it's not particularly risky to cross on foot.

On the Idaho side, Colt needed another car to carry his gear and loot. One quickly went missing from Porthill's gas station. The vehicle was later found—minus the camcorder that was inside—twenty miles south, near the little town of Bonners Ferry, which sits very close to Boundary County Airport.

On September 28, a CBP officer who also served on the Boundary County Airport board got wind of the strange goings-on up in Creston that, at this point, were thought to be drug related. He decided to check his airport just in case. He found that a half-dozen hangars had been broken into.

Two days before, Pat Gardiner had put his 2005 Cessna 182 Turbo Skylane to bed after a trip to Redmond, Washington. The meter on Gardiner's immaculate white plane with blue and silver swooshes had ticked nearly 309 hours of flying time in support of his small cattle operation. He provides prime Black Angus seed-stock to ranchers all over the region, and with the few roads that exist up in that chunk of the country forced to skirt mountains and follow river runs, a plane was an essential business tool. Says Gardiner, "It's tough to get anywhere from Bonners Ferry without driving a month of Sundays."

Gardiner came to Idaho ranching the long way—via public lawyering down in Los Angeles. As counsel for L.A. County back in the seventies, he created a specialized child abuse court that became a pilot project for the entire country, and he personally worked more than one thousand child abuse cases. A trip to Spokane, Washington, introduced Gardiner to the Northwest and he fell in love with the area. "The farther north you drive the greener it gets and the less people you find. I liked that." He moved full-time to Bonners Ferry, population 2,500, in 2000 and bought his Cessna the first year the Garmin G1000 glass cockpit option became available.

After his flight to Redmond, Gardiner had checked his fuel gauge. About four and a half hours of flying time remained in the tanks and he decided to fill her up later. He locked the plane and all the hangar doors and took the keys.

Colt got into some of the other Bonners Ferry hangars by finding hidden keys. He worked under cover of darkness and lingered inside, soaking up the airplane ambience and pretending he belonged in that world. In one hangar he even relaxed and put his bare feet up against the wall while he ate a snack. But Colt was really there as a thief. He stole whatever he fancied—a GPS, a digital camera—and then moved on to the next hangar. He found a Cessna, but that one was too old. At another hangar, he came upon a $2 million six-passenger turboprop Piper Meridien, but that one was too big and fast. When he got to Pat Gardiner's plane, though, that was just right.

The late-model 182 even had a turbo and a glass cockpit. Colton padded around the hangar, leaving a trail of bare footprints as he searched everywhere for a key. Not finding one, he jammed a screwdriver into the baggage compartment lock and tried to jimmy it open. Nothing doing, but he kept working the plane until he was finally able to pop open the passenger-side door and climb in. Everything passed inspection, but like his first night up in Creston, this was just a scouting trip. He pocketed Gardiner's Leatherman multitool and a few other items and left, retreating to a makeshift camp where he'd stashed the bank bags from Orcas Island Hardware, the guns, and all his other gear.

When the break-ins were discovered the following morning, calls went out to the police and plane owners. Gardiner arrived at his hangar door and was shocked at what he describes as the "violence" of the break-in. He was almost afraid to see what had been done to his $340,000 airplane. "The baggage door lock was wrecked, you couldn't even get a key in it," he says. Other than that, though, the plane seemed okay.

The initial thought—like over on Orcas and up in Creston—was that drug runners were looking for a transport plane. Some Boundary County folks figured it was maybe some a' them draft-dodgin' old hippie types up in Nelson, B.C. But the thief or thieves hadn't actually taken an aircraft, so the next theory was maybe drifters passing through looking for valuables. The police investigated and got good forensics—fingerprints and footprints were all over the hangars.

Gardiner put his hangar door back together and bolted a thick hasp through the steel wall, topping it off with the most serious padlock he could find. Not that anyone figured on further trouble. "We felt we'd been hit, things taken, a lot of damage done," says Gardiner. "After that, you don't think of a thief having the audacity to come back to the scene of the crime."

Once again, Colt let the police come and do their thing and watched everyone run around patching things up, then he sneaked back after dark. This time he first went to the airport's fixed base operator (FBO), which acts as a combination service station/concierge/rest area for pilots. The FBO is where visiting fliers gas up their planes, check the weather, get a snack, take a nap, arrange a rental car for touring or use the courtesy car for quick runs into town. Some also have bikes. Colt took the FBO's bike, loaded it with all of his gear, and walked it the quarter mile down to Pat Gardiner's hangar, leaving a trail of bare footprints alongside deep tire tracks.

Colt ditched the bike behind the hangar and pulled out his crowbar. He used enough force to rip the bolts through the metal, tearing off the entire hasp. Inside, he again had all night to play pilot with his new plane. He even popped the hood and checked the oil. "It wasn't low," says Gardiner, "but apparently he added some anyway because we found the empty can in the hangar." Colt loaded his stuff into the plane and tossed in one of Gardiner's sleeping bags.

At daybreak on the twenty-ninth, around 5:30 a.m., a Boundary County road crew was already on the job near the airport. Inside the fence, work continued on a new runway, with a water truck wetting the site to keep construction dust down. All the early-morning activity may have surprised Colt and forced him to rush. After he raised the hangar door and muscled the heavy plane out using a manual towbar, he placed the bar back in the hangar but didn't close the door. If he had, his crime would not have been discovered for many hours, if not days.

Colton climbed into the Cessna's cockpit, stuck his screwdriver in the ignition switch, and cranked it to the right. This time the engine caught.

The road guys were used to small planes buzzing in and out of the airport, but they sensed that this one was in trouble. The snarl of the Cessna's engine sounded too high pitched, like it was overrevving. They stopped working and watched the plane accelerate along the ground to the southwest. The runway in that direction is called 2-0, but a couple witnesses said Colt didn't bother with the runway and instead was attempting to take off from the taxiway, a narrow strip of asphalt that ran parallel to 2-0. They watched as the Cessna struggled into the air. It didn't gain altitude nearly as fast as it should have, and was headed straight for a stand of trees.

Gardiner speculates that Colton either set the variable propeller to the wrong pitch, or left the flaps at the neutral setting, which doesn't offer the wing extra lift for takeoff. The witnesses also said he used only half of the runway. Instead of taxiing to the end of the field, pausing to look for traffic, and then taking off, Colt exited the hangar farm at the runway's midpoint, turned left, throttled up, and just went for it.

"That plane should have been at seven hundred feet by the time it reached the trees," says Gardiner. Instead, at the last second and with the turbocharged engine "balls to the wall," the Cessna barely cleared the trees.

AIRBORNE WITH ENOUGH FUEL to carry him at least seven hundred miles, Colt had choices. He'd been heading east, putting plenty of distance between himself and all the recent newspaper, TV, and Internet coverage that had plastered his photo all over northwestern Washington. Regional law enforcement at every level now had a clear bead on his MO. All the real heat, though, was limited to the two small islands where he'd made the biggest impact. If he kept moving away and could stay off the radar for a few weeks, he'd be forgotten everywhere else.

Idaho, Montana, Wyoming, Oregon, Northern California, British Columbia: there was a lot of world-class secluded wilderness within his range. When millionaire adventurer Steve Fossett's plane went down in the Sierra Nevadas it took a full year, and ultimately a lucky break, to find his remains. With Colt's proven fearlessness at off-field landings, he had countless places where he could drop the plane and disappear into the rugged wilds. If he didn't want to play survivalist, he could land closer to civilization and use his technical know-how to steal identities and melt into the fringes of society. He could even head back to Reno, where he'd previously been able to hole up incognito.

At this point, Colt had won. He'd escaped from a prison home. He'd escaped from two small islands where everyone was hunting him. He had a grubstake and a fast, long-range getaway vehicle. Colt had even one-upped D. B. Cooper, because he had control of the plane and could land wherever he wanted to instead of having to jump out with a parachute. In four hours, Colt could touch down more than a thousand miles away from where all his problems began and where he had the greatest chance of getting caught. He'd brought on all his current troubles because he couldn't stomach another year and a half in a laid-back juvenile group home. Now, with more than a dozen felonies already hanging over his head, capture meant facing up to ten years in prison. And, since he'd turned eighteen the previous spring, this time it would be nasty big-boy prison. It made sense for Colt to get lost and stay that way.

Or not.

ONCE IT SAW THE Cessna clear the trees, the Boundary County road crew shrugged and went back to work. An early-bird local pilot, though, arrived at the airport and knew immediately that something was wrong.

"You out flying this morning, Pat?" he asked Gardiner on the phone a little after 7 a.m. "Nope," came the expected answer. "Well, your hangar door is up, the back door is busted again, and your plane's gone." Gardiner told him to dial 911 and said he'd be right down.

After a quick look around the airport, the local police dialed their own 911. Those deep bicycle tire tracks set off alarm bells that, according to what the authorities told Pat Gardiner, rang all the way to Washington, D.C., to Janet Napolitano's office at the Department of Homeland Security. It certainly wasn't some drifter breaking into hangars, and drugs were the most benign explanation for a missing plane carrying a heavy load. The alternate scenario was the stuff of nightmares because there was now a missing plane potentially carrying more than six hundred pounds of anything imaginable with the range to deliver it to Spokane, Sea-Tac Airport, Whidbey Naval Air Station, Naval Base Kitsap—home to a fleet of nuclear submarines and a stockpile of nuclear weapons—or the city of Seattle.

An APB went out on the plane. The Civil Air Patrol was put on alert and missioned to check every small airfield within range. Calls also went out across the border to the Canadians. Air traffic control (ATC) radars blanketed the region and the Cessna's Mode-C Transponder automatically squawked a transponder code that identified the plane to controllers. Surely, they'd get a quick fix.

Colton flew south, over the infamous Ruby Ridge, and down Idaho's panhandle. Above Lake Pend Oreille, he had his chance to turn left and follow the Clark Fork River, which would have led him southeast through the mountains away from Washington. Instead, he continued south another sixty miles and then turned west. Colt added to his troubles by flying the plane across the Idaho-Washington border south of Spokane, another federal offense on top of the one he committed by carrying firearms over the Canadian border.

Colt flew on to Walla Walla, Washington, just north of the Oregon line, then turned northwest and headed for Moses Lake. Moses—named for a Sinkiuse chief—is home to Grant County International (formerly Larson Air Force Base), where Boeing and the U.S. Air Force test and train pilots to fly their heaviest jets. It's one of the largest airports in the country, and it has stood by as an emergency landing strip during every NASA Space Shuttle mission. Grant County's relatively endless 13,500-foot runway wasn't Colt's idea of a safe place to land during the day, though. He continued toward Wennatchee, where he had friends, but didn't look for a landing spot there either. He crossed Lake Chelan, a breathtakingly cold and deep fifty-five-mile-long basin fed by Cascade snows, then once again rock-and-rolled through the turbulence over glacier-topped mountains on his way toward the town of Granite Falls.

Except for his big swing south to avoid the most dangerous sections of the Cascades, Colt now flew on a line that ran direct from Boundary County Airport back to his Camano Island home—the very heart of his problems.

The Cessna's fuel tanks, however, couldn't disregard the big detour. Colt knew he had to get the plane on the ground very soon. But again, he ran into trouble with the weather. As the plane's hour meter ticked over 313, Colt found himself above rugged terrain shrouded in fog and mist. The last minutes of his flight showed some dramatically erratic flying as he desperately tried to find a landing spot before his fuel ran out.

"There's fuel and then there's usable fuel," says Pat Gardiner. The Cessna 182 can run out of fuel with five gallons still in the tanks—and that's if it's flying straight and level. If the pilot puts the plane into an uncoordinated maneuver, such as a turn where the aileron and rudder aren't working together to keep the plane following its nose, the fuel flow can "unport" even though there's enough gas to keep the motor running. "Unporting" is another of those nonchalant aviation code words. In English, it means "Oh shit, why did the engine stop?"

According to investigators, Gardiner's Cessna did some unintentional acrobatics just before landing. Colt later told a friend he was flying upside down at one point. As he got down to his last few gallons of usable fuel, he finally found a break in the mist and what he thought was a decent landing spot. From one thousand feet, it looked okay: an ice cream cone–shaped field of patchwork green and brown, roughly five hundred by nine hundred yards and separated from the banks of the Stillaguamish River by about a hundred yards of trees. Down lower, though, at the point of no return, it became obvious why there was this one treeless spot amid the forested hills: it was a logged clearcut.

The misnomer about the word "clearcut" is that the forest floor is left clear. In fact, the trees are severed several feet up the trunk, leaving behind jagged stumps anchored to the ground by strong roots. At this spot, a summer's worth of fast-growing vegetation camouflaged a minefield. Hundreds of immovable cedar and fir stumps spiked the field, any one of which could totally destroy the plane and its pilot.

The final seconds of this flight were a terrifying blur and by all rights should have been Colt's last. The plane was moving much too fast, faster than would be safe to land even on a perfect runway. Colt fully extended the flaps, which is correct procedure for landing, but that should happen only once the plane has already slowed to a reasonable airspeed. At the Cessna's screaming velocity, extending the flaps was like throwing an anchor. The plane pitched steeply down toward the hillside. If he couldn't pull out of the dive, Colt would end up as the pulpy red bull's-eye in a singed circle of ground.

As a view of the field filled his windshield, Colt fought to pull the plane's nose up. He throttled back to idle, but it was too late. Investigators estimate that the Cessna slammed into the clearcut at more than 115 miles per hour—twice as fast as a normal landing.

The nose wheel crumpled on impact. The plane's two main landing gear are stronger and fairly flexible, designed to withstand hard landings, but they didn't stand a chance against the tree stumps. Both gear were ripped off, leaving just jagged pieces of strut as the plane careened forward, ramming into stumps and logs that hammered and tore into the fuselage. The starboard elevator caught a stump and spun the Cessna, folding the front gear underneath and punching it into the plane's nose. An explosion of dirt and shredded green erupted as the propeller chewed into the field, its blades bending like boomerangs. Bits of soil and plants rained down onto the plane and into its engine compartment as the cowling burst open.

One young tree had been spared by the loggers, but a wing nailed it. The next stump impacted just behind the passenger compartment, buckling and gashing the aluminum alloy as if it were tinfoil.

Once it hit the ground, the Cessna stopped within a snot-flinging distance of ninety feet, a deceleration equal to about seven Gs. It was more than enough force to kill anyone in the plane as he was flung forward into the cockpit controls and dashboard at more than a hundred miles an hour.

Unless . . . In the milliseconds after the plane hit the ground, just as Colt's body flew forward, an airbag built into the pilot's seat belt ignited and shot up in front of him.

"There's no way he would have survived without that airbag," marvels Gardiner.

It still wasn't like falling into a pillow. "I'm sure he had injuries due to the incredible amount of Gs from the impact and from going from high speed to zero in such a short distance," says Brad Hernke, an investigator who specializes in small-plane accidents and who went to the site for U.S. Aviation Underwriters, Inc. "It's incredible that anyone walked away from that crash."

Colt knew he had to get out of the plane fast in case it was about to burst into flames. He pulled the handle of the pilot's-side door, but it wouldn't budge. The impact had been so violent that it torqued the airframe to the point where no amount of pounding would get the door open. During flight instruction, small-plane pilots are trained to open their doors in the air if they're heading for a rough landing. With the door opened, the closed latch prevents it from jamming shut and trapping everyone in the plane. It's on the off-field landing checklist, but Colt hadn't done it.

Expecting an explosion at any second, Colt lurched to the other side of the cockpit and yanked the handle on the passenger-side door. Fortunately, that one opened. He was in such a frenzy to bail out that he forgot he was still wearing the radio headset. As he clambered away from the plane, the cord became taut and ripped it off his head.

Colt retreated to a safe distance and watched. When the plane didn't catch fire, he went back and grabbed his stuff. Knowing how quickly the police had responded way out in the hills of Yakama, Colt must have figured they'd be at the crash site within minutes because he was only four miles outside the town of Granite Falls. The last thing he did was pour motor oil over the inside of the cockpit in an attempt to hide forensic evidence.

Laden with his gear, Colt hiked into the woods. He left behind a plane that looked like a toy broken over the knee of a giant, petulant child.

GARDINER'S CESSNA NOVEMBER-2183-PAPPA HAD taken off at 5:30 a.m. with about four and a half hours of fuel. The police were called at 7 a.m. and the alarm about a possible terrorist incident went off shortly thereafter. Now, at around 10 a.m., Pat Gardiner's plane lay crumpled on top of a clearcut hillside. Gardiner says the Cessna had been crying out, telling everyone that it had crashed. His plane was equipped with an ELT (emergency locator transmitter), a distress signal that activates via an acceleration switch and automatically begins screaming if the plane gets into trouble. Not only does it shout, "Help, I've fallen and I can't get up!" but the ELT transmits the plane's precise location. Pat's ELT used 121.5 megahertz, a frequency that search-and-rescue satellites stopped using in February 2009 because there had been too many false alarms, but that continues to be monitored by ground stations and commercial aircraft, who should have heard the signal.

With all the attention on the stolen plane from various agencies, including Homeland Security, it seems that it would have been easy to find and track the plane during its flight. One would also expect a swarm of activity around the crash site. And there was—but not until thirty-four hours after the Cessna went down, and then only because on Thursday, October 1, a logger drove up a three-mile skid road and stumbled upon the pulverized plane squatting in the middle of his clearcut.

In rare cases (possibly Steve Fossett's) ELTs have failed to go off or haven't been picked up by the satellites, but from what investigators told Pat Gardiner, FAA personnel who responded to the crash site were the ones who switched off his plane's transmitter.

IN THE DAY AND a half before the logger found the plane, the facts of the Boundary County case—bare footprints, scrounged food, the chain of boosted cars leading back to Vancouver, and the fact that this was, after all, a flipping airplane theft—came together and pointed to one suspect: Colton Harris-Moore. When the wreckage was finally discovered, the FAA, FBI, and NTSB all worked the scene along with the local Snohomish County Sheriff's Office and—as proof they had a good idea who was responsible—a detective called in from Island County.

The forensics team took DNA samples that ultimately matched Colt. Bare footprints led from the crash site and trackers attempted to follow, but lost his trail in the woods.

Once investigators gathered all their evidence and wrapped the scene, Gardiner's plane had its wings clipped and a logging truck lifted and slung it aboard a flatbed like a beached whale. Everything went quiet in the

Granite Falls area until 8 p.m. that Sunday, when a couple that lives less than four miles from the crash site came home to find they'd been burglarized, with blankets, a sweatshirt, shoes, their passports, and a cheap .22 caliber semiauto pocket pistol missing.

A Snohomish County deputy responded and, as he and the homeowner were checking out the house, they spotted a light on the hillside behind the property. The officer called for backup, and five deputies, including canine teams, started up the hill around 11 p.m. As the police picked their way through the thick brush, the dogs started going crazy. Then, according to the homeowner, they heard the crack of a gunshot.

Acting on standard procedure, the police pulled back, called in the cavalry, and set up a perimeter. Authorities knew Colt had handled guns, and believed he'd stolen at least five of them over the last several years, but there was no evidence he'd ever threatened anyone with a firearm. However, they knew he had a big attitude problem with cops going way back, and that on Orcas he'd pepper-sprayed a deputy. The year 2009 was also a very bad one for police in western Washington State, with six officers shot dead during a three-month period. Now they believed Colt had fired a gun when cops got close to him. They weren't going to take any chances. The pursuit of Colton Harris-Moore had just taken a deadly serious turn.

COLT TOOK OFF, TRYING get as far away as possible from where the cops thought he was. He'd been chased many times and knew how the police operated. He could move extra fast now because he was traveling lighter: back at the campsite, he'd abandoned the bank bags from Orcas Island Hardware. The money hadn't been touched; it was still banded together. Police also found the .32 caliber handgun stolen from BearAir in Creston, B.C., and a mirror from which the crime lab would lift a nice fingerprint.

Snohomish County deputies set up a cordon, manning roadblocks to control who got in and out of the area. Over the next twenty-four hours, the woods and country roads were flooded with law enforcement. The Marysville Police Department in Sno County sent their specially trained man-tracking squads to join the K9 and SWAT teams in an attempt to run

Colt to ground while the county's MD 500 helicopter and a Department of Homeland Security Black Hawk searched from above.

Colt was close enough to the action that he later told his mom that he heard the helicopters sweeping across the forest canopy over his head.

TV and newspaper images quickly emerged of troopers—some in black, others in camouflage, all armed with assault rifles—along with an armored personnel carrier and ominous black federal government helicopter, all arrayed against a barefoot teenager running through the woods. Now nothing could hold back the story of the boy who stole airplanes. Colton Harris-Moore's tale went nationwide, and then global.

In order to deny Colt a means of escape, the police told everyone in Granite Falls to lock up their homes and cars. Within the small community, though, some people shrugged it off. One woman not only left her keys in her SUV, but also her purse. Searchers never spotted Colt, and the manhunt was called off after a day and a half. They had no idea how he escaped until the woman's SUV showed up ditched in the little city of Stanwood. Her purse was still inside, the contents untouched. Stanwood police also found a passport belonging to the burglarized Granite Falls homeowners sticking in the door of their headquarters. Colt might be able to use her husband's passport, but he had no use for a female identity and wanted to return the wife's. A truck stolen from a nearby thrift store that same night was found across the causeway on Camano Island, at a spot a half mile from the single-wide trailer where Colt grew up and where his mom still lived.

Eighteen-year-old Colton Harris-Moore, now hunted as an armed-and-dangerous fugitive, had gone home.

PART 2

THE CAMANO KID

11

The spark that eventually brought Colton Harris-Moore into the world struck when his mother chose "Crazy."

She was Pam Harris back then, and had gone to a restaurant/cocktail lounge in Lynnwood, Washington, to wait for her oldest sister. After ordering a beer, she punched up the Patsy Cline classic on the jukebox.

There were few patrons in the lounge, but two guys sitting at the bar were talking and laughing so loudly that Pam could barely hear her song. She got up from her table, fed more money into the jukebox, and played it again. The boys kept up the rough chatter, though. Pam drank her beer, lit a cigarette, and did a slow burn. When the song ended, she got up and went for "Crazy" one more time. On the way back to her table, she screeched, "Be quiet so I can hear it this time!"

That got their attention.

"One of them turned around, got up, and came across the room," she says. "He was a big guy, muscular, and I thought, Oh God, I'm going to get hit."

Pam tells the story without any hint that it strikes her as anything but normal that a guy would give a gal a smack in the kisser.

Born Pamela Ann Coaker in the spring of 1951, Pam was the youngest of four—three girls and a boy—spread over nine years. Her father was big in road construction in Kittitas County, Washington, just east of the Cascades, where his family had a sheep farm. According to his oldest grandchild, he was also a big drinker, afflicted with what she calls "the Coaker curse." Pam's mother grew up in the Dakotas as the oldest of fifteen kids in a family with a dash of Sioux blood in their veins—something the entire clan cites to explain their fondness for running around barefoot.

Pam's mom suffered through a couple of bad marriages, lost her voicebox to cancer, and, according to family, used alcohol to help deal with the pain. Both of Pam's parents died in their early sixties.

Pam grew up loving the outdoors, and some of her favorite early memories involve listening to her father play guitar around campfires. She also enjoyed clamming, crabbing, and fishing, even though she's never gotten over a fear of the water. As a teen in the sixties, Pam got into the Beatles and organic gardening, dressed hippie, and wore headbands over long hair that she straightened on an ironing board.

At seventeen, she married an air force mechanic named Harry and moved to San Bernardino, California, where she gave birth to her first son, Paul. Pam loved life in California, but moved back to Washington State and then east to Missouri as Harry followed work. When Chrysler laid him off, the family returned to Washington and settled in for a few happy years. The marriage ended, according to Paul, when Harry left Pam because of her drinking.

Paul, who plans to write a book about his difficult childhood, grew up a latchkey kid, often left alone while Pam worked during the day or was out at night. From the age of six, he'd come home from school to an empty apartment, call one of his cousins, and stay on the phone until his aunt could get there to pick him up. During those years, Pam worked at a dry cleaner and then in Seattle at a series of government jobs in the accounts payable sections of the Department of the Interior, the National Oceanic and Atmospheric Administration, and the U.S. Navy.

The oldest of her batch of nieces and nephews remembers Pam as more of a sibling than as an adult figure. She was the "cool aunt," with a great record collection and even a blurry picture she'd taken of the Beatles running onstage.

"We'd listen to music and go to concerts," her niece says. "We were holding tickets to go see Lynyrd Skynyrd when they died in the plane crash." The niece also remembers Pam telling her who her real father was and helping her get in touch with him—something that pissed off her mother, Pam's oldest sister, to no end. "Pam always did her own thing," she says. "She didn't care what anybody thought about her, what they thought about the men in her life, about her drinking, or smoking 'her weed.' Her attitude was 'I do what I want, when I want, how I want.'"

Another of Pam's notable qualities was her thriftiness. "Tightwad," says her niece. "Her apartment was always freezing in the winter because she refused to turn on the heat and pay for the electric bill." Pam's alcohol budget back then went to a generic econo-brew in a stark white can plainly and boldly labeled BEER.

In June 1985, Pam remarried, this time to Jerry Harris, a guy who'd dated her older sister Sandy for a couple of years. That union didn't last long, though, and soon after it spoiled, Pam found herself in that cocktail lounge faced with the imposing six-foot figure of Gordon "Gordy" Moore bearing down on her while Patsy Cline wondered why she let herself worry.

"He walked over to my table and just said, 'What?' So I said, 'I've been trying to listen to this song three times! Will you shut up?' He laughed, thank God. And then he invited me up to the bar to sit with him and his friend. We had a few drinks—whiskey for him, beer on my side—and then he said, 'Hey, you want to go to the beach tomorrow?' I gave him my phone number and said, 'Call me—at noon.'"

Though she doubted he would, Gordy called—at 11:59. He picked her up and, after a nice day at the beach, said he wanted to introduce her to his folks. "I thought, Well, that's a little quick," says Pam. "My hair was all windblown and I didn't bring a brush, so on the way to his parents' place he stopped and bought me one. I thought that was pretty cool."

Gordy worked as a concrete finisher with full journeyman status and made a good hourly wage. He filled Pam's kitchen with food every time he came over, putting so many cans on her shelves that she couldn't shut the cupboard doors. "He met my son, Paul, and everything was cool there, too," she says.

Gordy liked to smoke turkeys and shared Pam's love of the outdoors, taking her, Paul, and one of Paul's cousins camping several times.

Pam yearned to live someplace more rural than Lynnwood, a Seattle satellite primarily known for its shopping centers and convenient highway access. She was also tired of the long commute to her government job, though she made the best of it. Once during a heavy snowstorm, her bus got stuck in a drift coming home. "I told the driver she should get off and get us all pizza and beer," says Pam. The driver refused, so Pam led a mutiny among the passengers, piloting them to a local Black Angus, where they spent the next few hours warm and toasting.

According to Pam, Gordy worked hard and when the whistle blew he enjoyed the bars. His concept of the ideal home had a pub within walking distance. Pam's woodsy dreams, though, finally persuaded him to pool his money with what she'd raised by cashing in her retirement funds so they could buy a couple of lots on the skinny tail end of an island called Camano.

Shaped like the Pink Panther bound in a straitjacket, forty-square-mile Camano is technically an island, though it's a drive-to. The mainland gateway is the little city of Stanwood, where a conglomeration of superstores and strip malls overwhelms the remnants of a traditional town plopped in the middle of redolently fertilized farmland watered by the Stillaguamish River. A bridge crosses the Stilly just as it deltas into the Salish Sea and offers Camano residents a twenty-four-hour umbilical to civilization— which is good and bad. The good is that people are able to live on a Pacific Northwest island with all its evergreen and coastal beauty, yet still drive to whatever they need instead of being held hostage to a ferry schedule. The bad is that because its residents have relatively easy access to other communities and services, Camano hasn't developed its own resources like Orcas Island has been forced to, with its own kids' programs, performing arts centers, library, museums, and high school.

In many ways, Camano sits in limbo between being a true island community and simply a suburb surrounded by water. About a third of the 13,400 Camano Islanders are retired, and many of the rest roll across the bridge twice a day as they head to and from jobs at Boeing, or in Stanwood or Seattle, or somewhere else along the I-5 corridor. Its accessibility also makes Camano a popular vacation-home market. On summer Fridays, it seems every third car crammed onto the causeway has kayaks on top or a boat on a trailer as weekenders flood the island.

Wherever you are on the island, you're a single turn from one of the four Camano Drives: East, West, North, and South. East Camano heads down island, offering sharp views of the Cascades across Port Susan

Bay. Traffic and commercial buildings peter out to nothing as you pass the Camano Plaza's big IGA. A utilitarian stretch on the west side of East Camano Drive houses a sparse collection of county offices. Island County once encompassed a big chunk of western Washington State but was chipped away over time so that it's now made up of just Camano and Whidbey plus a smattering of smaller islands. Whidbey, with four times the acreage and three times the population of Camano—along with the county seat, Coupeville, and a big military base—overshadows its little sister, which even geologically seems to curl defensively inside the larger island. Camano residents talk of living in Island County's forgotten hinterlands, and since county money follows population and pull, they're right.

It takes ninety minutes to drive the circuitous route from Camano to Coupeville. That's about twenty minutes longer than it takes Camano residents to get to downtown Seattle. It takes that same ninety minutes for Island County police to get from their Whidbey Island headquarters to the dinky prefab that serves as base for Camano's small group of sheriff's deputies.

Around 70 percent of Camano remains forested with thick second-growth. Drooping cedars, showy big-leaf maples, and stately Douglas fir crowd together so tightly along some sections of road that you can't see past the first line into the woods. Outside about a dozen small subdivisions, many of the island's homes are hidden down long tree-lined drives. Houses run the gamut from tarped single-wides to opulent log cabins fit for gentrified Jeremiah Johnsons to modern high-windowed manses facing sweeping ocean views. As you'd expect, plots along the coastline are pricey, with values dropping dramatically as you move inland. Rough-hewn fishing and crab shacks dotted the waterfront back in the day, but most have been torn down over the last few decades, replaced with large homes. As on Orcas, many of Camano's finest homes are seconds—occupied only on weekends or for a couple of weeks each summer.

As you continue south on the island, the houses spread out and the view is mostly wooded acreage—private property along with public land and parks—with plenty of room to roam, or hide.

Mountain View Road, near the top of Elger Bay, serves as Camano's Mason-Dixon Line. Above the line is the bedroom community section of the island where people think nothing of making a daily trip across the causeway to civilization and its jobs. South of Mountain View, though, you hear tell of blue tarps and rednecks, primitive artists and wild-eyed ex-hippies, the cries of coyotes and the strum of banjos. And it's all true. Sort of.

The south end of Camano is more islandy than the north part due to its distance from the bridge. It's about a half-hour drive from the southern tip just out to Stanwood, and there aren't many people willing to make that extra commute. That's left the south less populated and developed. Much of the island's long tail is only a mile wide, and you can walk that in most parts without leaving the woods except to cross the loop road. Other than retirees, many of the full-timers down here tend to be artists and survivors from the back-to-the-land movement of the late sixties and seventies. Like Orcas full-timers, South Enders cobble together a living by doing two or three different jobs. Also similar to Orcas, the south end of Camano illustrates extreme disparity in income and wealth within a remarkably small area.

"The place where time stands still and the stills still stand," says Jack Archibald, the person most responsible for putting the capital letters on the South End. "This is hell and gone. Nobody comes down here for a Sunday drive, and we like it that way."

Archibald moved to Camano in the seventies, "looking to get back to the land." He drove out on a drizzly dark night and told a Realtor he had a life savings of $25,000 and wanted a roof over his head and at least five acres. "He took me to this little cabin surrounded by tall trees, lights on inside so it was glowing, chimney puffing smoke . . . I said, 'I'll take it!'"

Daylight revealed the dream cabin to be just a rickety shack complete with Visqueen windows that did nothing to keep out the winter's cold. Replacing those sheets of plastic turned out to be an act of fate for Archibald, who'd been working as a school bus driver. "I wanted something more interesting than just plain windows, so I took a night class on how to do stained glass." He found he had an affinity for breaking and patching glass back together. Creating spectacular installations for schools, hospitals, libraries, and public buildings became his career.

Archibald and his fellow escapees looked around their section of Camano and decided to embrace the backwoods reputation. Jack created an alter ego, Skeeter Daddle, a rural raconteur, banjo picker, and gentleman nettle farmer who, along with his South End String Band mates, branded the South End as a place frozen in time.

"One of us called the South End 'a poor man's paradise' and that was dead-on because when a lot of us moved in, land was very cheap," says Archibald. "You couldn't believe that you didn't have any money but still got to live in a place like this. Wow, man—utopia!"

That didn't last. "It's harder and harder to live on this island if you're poor, even down here. A lot of struggling folks are kinda grandfathered in, but there are less of them all of the time. More are losing their places now because of the economy hurting real estate, which means the itinerant construction jobs go away and they can't pay their mortgages."

Archibald describes the South End as a mini version of Florida. "It's rich retirees on the coast and rednecky in the middle . . . different worlds within a very short distance. You won't see it on a casual drive, but in the center of the island you find some fairly impoverished people . . . Garbage hasn't been picked up forever, lawn's up, house is falling down."

In December 1985, Pam and Gordy moved out of their mainland apartment and into a twenty-three-year-old, six-hundred-square-foot single-wide trailer set on five inland acres of Camano's South End. The area remained so undeveloped back then that their dirt road didn't even have a name, just a number, 25'55, corresponding to its longitude.

Surrounded by good clamming and crabbing waters but also within easy reach of the Cascade mountains for camping, Camano fit Pam's dream. So did the property, with plenty of room for a big garden, chicken coop, and pigpen. Except for the clearing around the trailer, the acreage remained thickly forested, making it feel like you were in the middle of nowhere with no one else around. To Pam—never one to associate with neighbors or much of anyone else—that was perfect.

Standing at the barbecue with a beer in her hand, screened off from the rest of the world by towering walls of Douglas fir and cedar, Pam was in paradise. Gordy, without a bar within walking distance, was okay—for a while.

"Gordy was a great guy, a lot of fun," remembers Pam's niece, "as long as he wasn't drinking." With a long history of DUIs, Gordy had to pass urine tests to keep his driver's license and get to job sites. "I got pregnant around this time, when Gordy was sober," she says. "Pam was really doting on me, and one day Gordy says to her, 'I don't have any kids—why don't we have a baby?' and Pam said, 'Yeah! I want another one.'"

Pam says she and Gordy tried for about five years to become pregnant, and she had to go in for some plumbing work before finally conceiving in June 1990. "When I finally did get pregnant, Gordy goes, 'I suppose you want to get married now, don't ya?'" she says. "I said, 'No, Gordy, I wouldn't do that to you.' He didn't really want to get married—he liked messing around too much. Gordy does what Gordy wants to do."

Pam, at thirty-nine, became pregnant just as her twenty-year-old first son and his wife, Jacquie, had their own baby girl, Christina. Around the same time, Pam's oldest sister—who'd also moved out to Camano and lived at the end of Road 25'55—was in the terminal stages of emphysema. In January 1991, Pam's granddaughter died of SIDS, which, the family says, had a big effect on her. That March, Pam's oldest sister died.

Pam skipped her sister's funeral because, as she told her niece, she felt she was too close to term. Three weeks later, at 8:38 a.m. on March 22, 1991, at Affiliated Health Services in Mount Vernon, Skagit County, Washington, Pam gave birth to her second son.

"Paul called me and said, 'Oh God, my mother wants to name the baby Colt, after the beer and the gun,'" says Pam's niece. "It was Paul and Jacquie who convinced her to officially make it Colton, since at least that was a real name."

Pam had kept Jerry Harris's surname, and she and Gordy decided to hyphenate. The baby boy became Colton Harris-Moore.

PAM WANTED TO CELEBRATE Colt's birth as an extra special event. "I was working for the navy back then and had a good paycheck," she says. "And Gordy was working steady and everything was cool, so I said, 'We've waited for this baby for five years, how about let's bring him home from the hospital in a white limo?'"

Pam says she'll never forget the limousine driver's name: Dexter. "We had him stop at a little store on the way home. I laid the baby in the backseat and both Gordy and I went inside. When we came back, Dexter was standing outside that limo like a guard. It was cool."

They'd rented the limo for a couple of hours, so little Colt's next stop was the feed store. "We were raising pigs and we had to get our feed," says Pam. "When the owner saw the limo he went in and washed his hands and put on an apron because he wanted to see the baby. He met Colt and then we loaded a couple of bags of pig feed into the trunk of the limo."

After that, they stopped at the market on Camano to show Colt off to some of the cashiers they knew. "God, we had a lineup! People I didn't even know lined up to see that baby," remembers Pam. Pam and Gordy then took Colt home to the little trailer tucked out of sight among the cedar trees.

A Camano resident who was at the market that day when the limo showed up remembers turning to a friend and saying, "That kid doesn't have a chance."

COLT, PAM SAYS, WAS a fat, happy baby. She nicknamed him Tubby and says that from the beginning he always loved to be outside and was fascinated with anything "up." She remembers Colt staring into the night sky as she rocked him, and says that one of his first words was "moon."

Pam went back to work after Colt was born, dropping him off at either her sister Sandy's or her daughter-in-law Jacquie's before heading off for the ninety-minute commute to her job with the navy. (The women in her office had thrown her a baby shower and had given her a novelty frame that said "*Time*'s Baby of the Year," a somewhat prescient gift since eighteen years later, *Time* would name Colt "America's Most Wanted Teen.") Sandy's eighteen-acre spread on the mainland came complete with horses, dogs, cats, and chickens, and Colt showed an immediate affection for animals.

According to Pam, Gordy was "an excellent father for about the first two years. We'd even argue over who got to change the diaper." Then Gordy started to get itchy. "He wanted a bar out his front door," says Pam. "So I said, 'Okay, let's make one. We'll open up all the windows and put a couple of kegs in here.'" That didn't work. Gordy started stepping out on her, which led to increasingly hostile confrontations at home.

"Once he started drinking? Whoa!" says Pam's niece. "Sloppy and mean. He turned evil . . . Dr. Jekyll and Mr. Hyde."

According to court records, the first report to Child Protective Services regarding Colton Harris-Moore's welfare occurred before he turned one.

When he was about eighteen months old, Pam says she began to find Colt sitting on the floor of the trailer banging his head against the wall. Relatives remember him, as an infant, acting out of control, scrambling atop the kitchen counters in the trailer. A former neighbor reported that more than once he saw toddler-aged, diapered Colton wandering down 25'55 alone, "like a wild child."

Before Colt turned three, Gordy was "in and out" of the home. In April 1994, Pam filed a protection order against him.

Colt was enrolled in special education preschool classes at the age of three because testing indicated he'd failed to reach normal developmental milestones. Colt's IEP (Individualized Education Plan) concentrated on helping him with speech and articulation.

Pam also headed to school. She'd been the first in her family to attend college when she took courses in Seattle and St. Louis, and now she enrolled in Skagit Valley College. "I was planning on getting my criminal justice degree," she says. From there she wanted to work toward her law degree and ultimately become a practicing attorney. "I know that at least I'd be an honest one."

When Pam took a psychology class, she suddenly had an insight into what she calls Colt's mental problems. She says that from an early age he never thought through the consequences of his actions. "We learned about brain synapses, and I said, 'That's it! Colt has a broken synapse.'"

With Pam out of work, though, money got tight and she quit school. "Crap just started happening, trucks breaking down, nobody to help me . . . so bag it." Pam and Colt went on welfare. Gordy was supposed to pay child support, and when he didn't, the state's Department of Social and Health Services (DSHS) went after him. Gordy, though, had a way to get around them.

"He knew to work less than a full quarter, which is what it takes for them to find you and take your money," says Pam. "So he just kept moving to another job."

Gordy didn't totally disappear, though, stopping back at the trailer every once in a while over the ensuing years. If he was flush, he'd hand Pam some cash.

Around this time Pam had a falling out with her remaining sister, Sandy, in a continuing round of family feuds. Colton would later remember that event ("when Mom alienated them") as being painful because he was close to Aunt Sandy and loved visiting the animals. According to family members, the feuds were usually about money.

On December 4, 1994, with her sons Paul and Colt in attendance, Pam got married again, this time to forty-one-year-old Seattle native William Kohler. Bill loved fishing, heroin, and raising homing pigeons. He'd served in the army, based overseas in Germany during the sixties, and then, according to Pam, worked as a milker at dairy farms when he came back to Washington. While Colt had already begun to detest Gordy, his biological father, he warmed to Bill. The two, Pam says, did everything together, and especially bonded over taking care of the animals they kept. Colt would later say that one of his best memories of Bill was how he'd walk like a chicken when they went out in the mornings to collect eggs.

Once again, though, his mother's choice of men left Colt with little stability at home. Pam told a counselor that Bill "was not really here much . . . He was a heroin addict, so he was out a lot . . . Colton couldn't count on [him]."

PAM SAYS YOUNG COLT was always more than a handful. "I don't recall ever being able to control him, ever." She found it impossible to discipline him. "I was spanked and I'm okay," she says, though even corporal punishment had little effect on Colt. "He was always so big and strong, even when he was little, that it took more out of me to spank him than what the spanking did to him . . . He just always did what he wanted."

When Colton was four, a witness filed a complaint with Child Protective Services after seeing "a woman" grab Colt "by the hair and beat his head severely." By this time, concerns about Colton Harris-Moore's mental health, education, nutrition, and physical safety had been entered into every part of "the system" possible, with reports to county, state, and federal agencies tasked with child welfare.

Colton continued special ed classes until age six, when he was reassessed and determined eligible for regular grade school. He was an inquisitive kid who could laser focus on things he was interested in—like nature and airplanes—but he never clicked with school. Pam remembers only one teacher who seemed to get through to him, and she moved to another school district after Colton finished second grade. His marks were never good, and they deteriorated as he advanced until at one point he failed every class. Pam says she insisted that the school hold him back, but the controversial policy of "social promotion" kept graduating Colton to the next grade along with his age group.

Outside of school, Colton joined a youth soccer team. Pam drove him to a couple of practices and he got his picture taken with the team. The photo shows an athletic six-year-old—certainly no longer tubby—with a bright, enthusiastic smile. After the team picture and before the first game, though, Colton stopped showing up. Pam said it was because her eyes gave her trouble and she couldn't drive him at night.

With Colton's speed and agility, he likely would have been a star on the playing field. Parents of another boy on the soccer team who also went to grade school with Colton say that Pam never reached out about the transportation problem. "One of the other parents would have been happy to pick him up for practice. That happens all the time with kids' sports and events off the island—people help each other out. We're all in the same boat."

Other than the short stint with soccer, Pam says Colt was never interested in sports. "He'd rather be out playing in the woods."

Colton's main playmate early on was Anne Pitser. Anne's mom worked at the Tyee Grocery, a little market near the very bottom of Camano where Pam bought her cigarettes and beer in those days. She and Pam had babies the same year and lived close, so they brought the kids together at an early age. "I still have a book that Colt and his mom gave me for my second birthday," says Anne. "I just always knew him."

Anne says that all the other kids just wanted to sit around and watch TV. "I thought they were boring. I didn't have TV, so I always had to make my own fun, and Colt was into that."

Every day after school starting in kindergarten, Anne says she and Colt would head to one or the other's home. At Anne's house, they'd play board games or race on her dad's electric slot car track. Over at Colt's, they primarily played outside.

"Inside his house was pretty much trashed . . . You were wading through mountains of things to get anywhere," she says. Instead, they'd spend their time running around with the dogs and playing in the woods. "We used to just love climbing trees. We'd find anything that had a low branch and climb on each other's backs to get to it. We'd climb up to the very top and then be like, 'Oh no, how do we get down?'"

Back then, Camano didn't have its own elementary school and island kids were bused across the bridge to Stanwood. "We were the outcasts there," says Anne. "I was the fat girl with buck teeth, and everyone hated Colt. They made fun of him, they'd throw things at him. They'd pick on him because he dressed different and maybe he didn't bathe regularly . . . He was just a boy. They were mean kids."

Tough times in school brought her and Colt even closer. "We were inseparable. He never wanted to go home when he was at my house, and when I was over there he was like, 'No! You can't go home yet, don't leave!' By the time we were in the third grade, his mom was convinced that we were going to grow up and get married."

Anne says Colt craved attention. "He wanted to be recognized. He wanted people to look at him and say, 'Hey, he's the one who did that!' If he started a science project, he wanted it to be really good so that people would praise him. But I don't think people ever really cared." Anne says Colton once built an elaborate treehouse in the woods by his trailer. "I was like, 'Dude, I can't believe you built this! It's the coolest thing in the world!' That made him feel really good."

The cool fort came down, though, when Pam found out Colton had built it with lumber she'd bought for another project.

"Every once in a while at school he'd be upset," says Anne. "I'd ask him what's wrong and he'd be like, 'Oh, my mom's just stupid.'"

Colt had a really cool dad, though—or so Anne thought. "Colt was always telling me that his dad was a pilot and that there was nothing he wanted more than to grow up and fly planes like him. But I never met the dad that he talked about. I knew his mom had boyfriends, but it didn't sound like Colt liked any of them much."

. . . .

PAM FILED FOR DIVORCE from Bill Kohler in 1998, though it was never finalized. Bill left the family several times, and before Pam would let him come back, she'd search his bags for drugs. Even when she let him stay, he'd eventually leave again. After Bill came Van Jacobsen, a man described in Child Protective Services referrals as "an alcohol or drug abuser," and another questionable role model for Colt. Van drifted in and out of the trailer over many years. Camano locals who know him say Van is "a nice, gentle guy" whose hard living has taken its toll. Pam herself described him as "not playing with a full deck." Neighbors say it sounded like Pam always yelled more than talked to him, but Van kept coming back.

Gordy would also occasionally show up back at the trailer, and Pam says Colt didn't like that. "He was a drunk, and Colt wanted him to leave. They did battle around here almost every day." Colt even argued that Gordy was not his father, insisting to Pam that it was Bill. She says she understood his feelings. "I guess if you have a shitty father you choose the next best thing."

With a growing resentment toward Gordy—and denied Bill, who he did feel close to—Colt clung to a fantasy father, the famous flier.

Other than his lifelong fascination with "up," Pam says she doesn't have a clue where Colton's love of planes originated. None of the men Colt had seen with his mom was an actual pilot. She indulged his interest, though, by buying him balsawood fliers, those featherweight model planes that American boys have been zooming around their yards since World War I. The wafer-thin wings don't stand up to much abuse, and after a few of his rough landings splintered the wood, Pam says Colt would go into meltdown mode. When he kept crashing and breaking every plane he got his hands on, Pam decided that instead of continually buying him new ones, it was smarter to get Colt a big sheet of balsa and let him start designing and building his own aircraft.

Pam says she also took Colton across Saratoga Passage to watch the planes taking off and landing at Whidbey Naval Air Station. Twenty-one active squadrons (the Zappers, Scorpions, Grey Wolves, Fighting Marlins, Black Ravens, and others) are based at Whidbey, with more than enough thundering warbirds in the air to rattle the bedroom windows and fuel flights of fancy for all the kids in Island County.

According to what Colton later told counselors, his relationship with his mom began to deteriorate by the time he started grade school. However, they still shared a love of the outdoors. They bonded over camping trips ("Maybe I shouldn't have taught him all that survival stuff!") and visits to Camano's beaches. One day Pam drove him to the top of the island and dropped him off at Utsalady Beach. "I didn't stay because I had a headache," she says. "When I went back to pick him up at the end of the day, Colt had built hisself a really cool Robinson Crusoe camp using sticks and towels."

He'd also captured what Pam remembers as forty Dungeness crabs (more than six times the legal limit) and had them piled on the beach. "He had a crowd of people watching, so I told him to pick the five biggest to bring home for dinner and let the rest go."

Colton loved Dungeness crab, *Cancer magister*, the Salish Sea's most delicious bottom feeder. These muscle-bound crustaceans make East Coast blue claws look like daddy longlegs, and fresh Dungeness meat comes out in big sweet chunks. Most folks fish Dungeness using pots and traps, with only the hardiest climbing into chest waders and plodding through the frigid shallows armed with dip nets. Young Colt, however, devised a way to catch the big crabs without nets or traps. He used only his bare feet.

Impervious to the cold water as only a true Northwest island boy could be, Colt would splash into the 50-degree sea wearing just his baggies. He'd stalk or swim over the sand and swaying eel grass until he spotted the broad purplish back of a Dungeness, then maneuver behind it. The predatory crabs earn their place in the food chain by cracking rock-hard clam shells with a pair of serrated claws that can also put a serious hurtin' on any errant finger or pinkie toe. Colt, though, would fearlessly poke his toes beneath the crab's belly then quickly flip it up. As the crab frantically flailed the water and snapped its claws, Colt's hand would dart in to snatch it behind the last of its ten legs, safely out of pinching range.

Colt seemed a natural for the Cub Scouts. He joined up and began working his way through the ratings. Pam says he once even won the rain-gutter regatta, a race where the scouts blow through straws to propel little wooden sailboats down water-filled rain gutters. Unfortunately, she didn't make it there to see him win because she says she'd gone back to work and had a night shift. She says Colton ultimately had to quit the scouts because she couldn't take him to the meetings in the winter when it was too dark for her to drive.

Before he left the Cub Scouts, Colton advanced from Bobcat to Wolf Scout. In a childhood recorded by remarkably few photos, Colt's Wolf certificate became one of his few treasured mementos.

12

I n 1999, just after Colton turned eight, an event occurred that Pam says sparked his bad attitude toward the police. Though money was scarce, she'd scraped together $300 to buy him a new bike for his birthday. The bike became Colton's prize possession, a symbol of independence and a vehicle for adventures, real and imaginary.

Pam was up on the trailer's porch when an Island County Sheriff's Office prowler pulled into the driveway with Colton in the backseat. She walked down and asked, "What's up?" She says the deputy just got out, walked around his car, and popped the trunk. "Is this Colt's?" he asked, pointing at the new bike.

"I got pissed!" says Pam. "I said, 'Yeah, I just bought it for him!' They figured 'cause we live in this dumpy trailer and must be dirt poor that how could Colt get a bike like that, well, he must have stole it."

Pam remembers Colton being scared.

The sheriff's office says they have no record of the incident, but don't doubt that it happened. They say Camano-based deputies had already been hearing complaints about Colton from neighbors (nothing made it into official police records until two years later). "Based on his history and what the guys knew about him," says Detective Ed Wallace, "I would not doubt that upon seeing Colton on a new bike that the guys would've wondered, Hey, what's going on? and taken him home. I don't doubt it happened at all. I just doubt whether that was the pivotal dramatizing event of his life."

The police who worked Camano Island in the 1990s and early 2000s considered the South End a trouble spot, and not without reason.

"We had a slog of bad kids around here for a while," says Jack Archibald. "Parents didn't know how to teach them to be students. There were people like Pam, barely hanging on, doing their own thing, letting their kids run wild. The kids naturally looked for trouble and it was easy down here because most of us didn't lock our doors."

"There's a real rugged side to things on the South End," says Bonnie Bryand in her honey-barbecue Texas twang. Bryand moved to Camano in 1994 and raised three kids on the island, including a son named Kory who is the same age as Colton. "A lot of cooking was going on down here until about five years ago." For a while, she says, it wasn't unusual to find meth fixings that had been tossed into the ditches.

According to Bryand, drug and alcohol abuse and a lot of single-parent homes affected an entire group of Camano kids in Colt's generation. "On top of the problems in the households, the kids had nothing constructive to do on the island."

Camano suddenly had its homegrown version of the Dead End Kids as the children living at the bottom of the island became known as the South End Hoodlums. They began to attract a lot of attention from the police. "When I first moved here there was only one cop on duty for the whole island and you were lucky if he'd show up when you called," says Bryand. "Then suddenly it seemed like we had four or five per shift and they were going after these kids real hard."

Bonnie's husband died in a car wreck while intoxicated, and her oldest son began running with the bored kids looking for trouble. She says that once the police identified someone they thought was bad, it was very hard for that kid to break out of the cycle. "If you lived anywhere near here, you got pegged."

Two of the troubled kids Bonnie began to see around the neighborhood appeared to have all the cards stacked against them. One was the son of a meth addict. "His mom . . . I tried to help her out, but she got busted. When she got out of jail you couldn't have her around, you couldn't trust her. They lived in an old trailer house just falling down in the woods, and she had a lot of men in and out of there." The tweaker's son had a friend he ran around looking for trouble with: Colton Harris-Moore.

"Those two young boys, eight or nine years old, basically ran her house, always tearing things up and stealing stuff. Of course, her being a drug addict, she didn't really care what they did."

Though they lived less than two miles apart, Bonnie hadn't met or heard of Pam, but she began to see a lot of Colton. "He was out running the streets on his own from a very young age." Colt, she says, pushed himself into her kids' groups. "He tried to fit in, but he was real aggressive, too rough, so nobody wanted to play with him and that's when it became a problem. He wouldn't take 'No.'"

Bonnie has both a niece and a nephew diagnosed with attention-deficit/hyperactivity disorder (ADHD) and says she recognized a lot of those behaviors in Colton. "I don't think he ever meant to be mean, but every day my daughter would come home crying because Colt had hurt her. I'd always tell her, 'He's just playing with you,' which might have been the wrong thing to say. I didn't see Colt as a demon, though. I liked him and always felt bad for him. The kids didn't like him, but they had no understanding of what he was dealing with. Colt didn't see that he was different."

It wasn't just the kids, though, who had a problem with Colt. "Everybody shunned him," says Bryand. "Most parents didn't want him in their house. The main problem was that he didn't have any manners. They thought he was disrespectful, and he was, but you're talking [about] a really young kid and I don't think he intended to be. It was just all he knew." Bonnie says that Colt would invite himself into her house. "I mean no knocking, no nothing, just walk in. And then he wouldn't be interested in the kids or me. You could be talking to him, but he'd be in his own world looking at the things we had around the house. You had to keep an eye on him because he'd take things, and then he'd wind up breaking them."

Colt also helped himself to her kids' bikes. "He always stole bicycles. He would just go in your yard and take one. He thought he was just borrowing it."

Bryand's son Kory says Camano wasn't a great place to grow up. He had troubles with the same set of kids over in Stanwood as Colt and Anne. "It was hard . . . not a lot of accepting people. Me being half Mexican, they made fun of me."

With his own outcast and South End tinge, Kory seemed a likely friend for Colt. However, he says, "Colt was always difficult to get along with."

He describes Colt as primarily a loner, though says he would get to be friendly with one or another Camano kid for a while. However, the friendships would eventually sour. "Colt's mouth would end it," says Kory. "He loved to argue, usually pointless arguments, and he'd always wind up calling the other kids imbeciles. That was his favorite word." Kory says most of the arguments started because of Colt's tall tales. "He'd make up these unimaginable stories, huge lies about his dad being a pilot and having all these big houses. Everyone already knew what his life was like and that none of it was true. He always had tore-up raggedy clothes, shoes ripped apart . . ."

Colt's longest childhood friendship was with a boy named Joel who also lived on Road 25'55, which eventually got a real name, ironic at least where Colt was concerned: Haven Place.

"Nobody wanted Colt hanging around," Joel says. "None of the kids liked him because he was constantly antagonizing people and he bullshitted so much that it was annoying. He once brought a rusty old key into school and said it was to his helicopter. I was like, 'C'mon, man, I know that you and your mom live in this twenty-two-foot trailer just up the road. You don't need to tell me you have a fucking helicopter.'"

Joel says that because of how Colt acted, "we'd wind up being good friends and then enemies, sometimes in the same day. I never knew what that meant, but from the time Colt was a little kid, my mom always said that he was going to do something crazy in his lifetime."

Colt and Joel roamed the whole of the South End on foot and by bike. They explored the woods, built tree forts, and spent a lot of time playing army. "Colt was really into the Navy SEALs and special forces. He had a mentality like he was some kind of secret agent. He'd talk in code and he was always analyzing and plotting one step ahead."

One of Colt's quirks, says Joel, was the way he moved through the forest. "Whenever he'd run through the woods, he'd always take his shoes off and go barefoot. He said he was able to run better and be more agile that way."

Joel vividly remembers stopping by Pam's trailer when he was nine years old to see if Colt was home. "I knocked on the door and his mom answered with a shotgun in my face. That was pretty intimidating as a kid. After that, my mom was like, 'You don't need to be dealing with those people.'"

Neighbors on Haven tell a story from the same time, in the year 2000, when a Realtor and a contractor were preparing to build a home on the lot that backs up to Pam's. The men were hunting for the property line markers and walked up to the trailer to ask if she knew where the corners were. According to neighbors, Pam's answer was to grab her shotgun, fire it into the air, and chase them off her property à la Granny from *The Beverly Hillbillies*.

When running through the woods pretending to be Navy SEALs lost its edge, Colt and Joel began concocting real secret missions. The first mischief they got into was stealing cigarettes from their mothers. "Then we'd go hide out and smoke them," says Joel. They then progressed to what they called "ninjing," as in ninja-ing, stealthing through the woods and creeping up to neighborhood homes. "We'd go out at night and sneak around trying to find open garages," he says. "We'd take soda pop and stupid stuff like that."

Joel says Colt never worried about getting caught. "He was the same way in school when we'd disrupt the class, or on the bus when we'd start fighting or something. He didn't care if he got into trouble."

By the time Colt, Joel, Anne, and Kory were ready for the fourth grade, Camano's brand-new Elger Bay Elementary was ready, too. They no longer had to bus out to Stanwood, but according to Anne, the kids continued to pick on both her and Colt. At times, she says, the teasing was so relentless that Colt escaped the only way he knew how—"He ran and hid."

From Anne's point of view, Colt had been fine up to this stage in his life. "He'd been a really good kid until the fourth grade. He'd do his homework and was a good student, especially for things he liked. If he took an interest in something he was all over it." But then, she says, things changed. "Suddenly Colt became a troublemaker, a rebel. He'd stand up and start talking in the middle of class and the teacher would be like, 'You need to sit down and pay attention,' and he'd be like, 'Uh, no.' So he'd get sent out into the hall. It weirded me out, the way he just suddenly changed."

PATTY MORGAN TAUGHT COLT in fifth grade at Elger Bay Elementary, though she says that for any discussion about his actual education, you have to look to lower grades because "he'd already checked out by fifth." Morgan says Colt didn't want to contribute and didn't want to do the work in her social studies class (they were studying government that year).

"Mostly he would just kinda slouch in the back and not participate. He was a hard one to read." Morgan says she attempted to engage him because she felt he could do the work if he tried. That led to her most vivid and disturbing memory of Colton. "One time I was trying to encourage him to write his assignment, and I laid my hand on his shoulder. He suddenly jerked really violently and said, 'Don't touch me! Don't ever touch me!'"

"I think there were some teachers that felt bad for him," says Kory, though he sensed that some seemed to care less about the kids they'd identified as troublemakers, including him and Colt. What he and Anne and other students from their class agree on is that Colt seemed to follow the classic arc of the bullied becoming the bully. "He went from being picked on to being the one picking on anyone he could get away with it against," says Kory.

"He wanted to be accepted and he wanted to be just like everyone else," says Anne. Unfortunately for her, being like everyone else at Elger Bay Elementary meant turning on the fat girl with buck teeth. "He'd make fun of me, pull my hair, throw things at me, so the whole class would laugh. No one else liked me, so he thought that if he made fun of me, then people would like him. He turned my life into a living hell . . . I didn't live all of that down until high school."

Colt wasn't able to raise himself too far up the pecking order, though. The kids may have laughed at some of his antics, but very few wanted to hang out with him. Whenever he did reach out and make a connection, it didn't last long.

"He was the black sheep of the school," remembers Mike Bulmer, who was one of Colt's few friends for a while. Also from a broken home and a veteran of mother-son battles, Mike stole his mom's van when he was only nine years old in an attempt to flee to his dad's place on Camano. His father got custody in time for Mike to enter fifth grade at Elger Bay Elementary. As the new kid on the island, he didn't have any friends, so he and Colt gravitated toward each other.

Mike's father's property on Camano was a Shangri-la for little dudes, with BMX bikes and rugged riding trails etched throughout the acreage. Mike and his older brother even had a go-cart and paintball guns. Colt, says Mike, always wanted to be there. "My dad wouldn't let him stay over on weekdays, but every Friday he'd come over and we'd order pizza and hang out for the weekend." Mike says Colt didn't have a bike of his own at the time, so he used to walk the three miles back and forth from his trailer.

Colt never invited Mike to his home. "He said his mom was always yelling at him," remembers Mike. "One time I was at a buddy's house on Haven and you could frikkin' hear her screaming at Colt all the way down the road."

Mike is another one who says his close friendship with Colt began to break down because of the tall tales. One day when Colt was over at their house, Mike's older brother called him out on his stories and drew a circle in the dirt. "He made us fight, full-on fist contact," says Mike. "I was the bigger kid back then and I got Colt on the ground. He looked up at me and I socked him right in the face. That made him really, really angry. I don't know how the hell he did it because I was so much bigger, but he lifted me off and then took a fat tree branch and broke it over my head. Then he went home."

FOR ALL THE REJECTION, Colt continued to seek companionship.

South End sculptor Shannon Kirby first met Colt when he came down her road walking his bike. She looked up from her gardening and saw a cute kid with a flat tire. "He was a little pumpkin."

Shannon called him over and reinflated his tire. "I showed him where I kept my pump and told him it was there if he ever had another flat." It took only five minutes to fix the bike, but then they started talking. "He was very chatty. It was like he was just starving. He just wanted someone to pay attention to him."

Colt stayed for an entire hour. As he was leaving, Shannon told him to come back if he wanted to. A few days later, he did. "I yakked with him for a while, but for less time than before because I was busy. Finally I said, 'Sorry, I've got things to do.' I could just see his face immediately change, with this look of 'Ugh, they always do that to me, they shut me down.'" Colt left. A short while later, Kirby's bike pump was stolen.

The next time Shannon saw Colt was when a bunch of kids came cascading out of the woods onto her property. "They're roughhousing and I'm watching. It was obvious Colt didn't understand boundaries, like nobody had taught him. He was playing way too rough with this one girl. He tripped her and she fell and hurt her ankle, so I went out, helped her up, and gave her a Band-Aid. Colt was like this gangly goonball that didn't know how to behave."

Kirby saw Colton again years later, this time in the Stanwood Library. She said hello, but says he looked away, uncomfortable. By then she'd had another break-in that the police later tied to Colton.

13

___

In 2000, Pam took up with a man we'll call Jimmy, a journeyman mechanic, chain-smoking Caterpillar cowboy, and hard drinker who "could put a hurtin' on a bottle of whiskey before noon by a long shot." Jimmy's the kind of guy who seems to know every road and dirt logging track in the state, and when telling a story will make damn sure you know exactly what byways got you there and where every crossroad leads to. Same thing with machinery details and model numbers. Folks who know him describe Jimmy as "a lost soul," and though in some ways he fit Pam's predilection for bad boys, the then-forty-five-year-old had never been in any real trouble with the law beyond what he calls "some DUI bullshit."

Jimmy hooked up with Pam while doing a land-clearing job down on Haven Place. "It was all happy-go-lucky bullshit for the first while, a good time when you were drunk," he says. So he moved into the trailer, "shacked up, whole shit and caboodle." He says it looked like Pam and Colton had been barely scratching by. "She wasn't working. Nothing in the cupboard and nothing in the fridge but beer," so he filled the trailer with food. Jimmy says he'd cook and Colton would help. He quickly learned the kid's favorite meal. "Crab wouldn't last a day with him in the house."

To add to the Dickens-on-draft scene, Jimmy says that Colt's clothes were rags. "His ass was hanging out of his underwear, so I took him and bought him a couple hundred dollars of new stuff—shoes, jeans, under-wear, everything."

Jimmy says he and Pam rarely went out. "She's not a bar-hopper, not her scene, wouldn't socialize with other people. She just wanted to stay home and lay on the couch drinking her beer." He says he and Colton spent a lot of time outside, playing with Colton's Great Pyrenees named Cody and bonding over heavy equipment. Jimmy taught Colton how to mow the lawn on a tractor, then graduated him to bigger boy's toys. "I put him on my D7 Cat, my 440 articulated skidder, my D2 bulldozer . . . Hell, he could run that within a few minutes. He was a good student, real quick learner."

Some other lessons Colton picked up on real quick were how to hotwire tractors, cars, and boats—skills Jimmy thought might come in handy someday out in the field. "I feel lower than dogshit about that," he says now. "Never thought he'd go and do this stuff."

Colton's fascination with airplanes offered another connection between the two. Jimmy actually had a pilot's license. He'd learned as a kid, hanging around a small airfield, helping out by pumping gas into planes until a friend of the family took him up and taught him to fly. Finally, Colton had met a real pilot.

"Colt was just obsessed with airplanes," says Jimmy. "He had books about them all scattered around and he was always drawing them with crayons and colored pencils. So I started taking him to the hobby shops in Mount Vernon and Burlington and I'd buy him all kinds of plane models— some real fancy with lights that would work off batteries—and then we'd build them together."

Soon Colt had squadrons of model planes in his room, some hanging from the ceiling posed in perpetual dives, others awaiting clearance for takeoff amid the clutter.

Jimmy also had a laptop. "We'd get on the Internet and fart around looking at airplanes. I was thinking about getting a chopper, a small experimental helicopter, two-man job. Pam would be passed out on the couch, and me and the kid would go online to look at the chopper and dream about it."

One of Jimmy's computer programs in particular captured young Colt's attention: Microsoft Flight Simulator. Sitting beside Jimmy, Colt familiarized himself with the sim's aircraft—a Learjet Model 45, a Bell 206 JetRanger helicopter, and a Cessna 182 Skylane featuring an ultrarealistic instrument panel.

Unlike a fantasy video game designed solely to inject adrenaline thrills, Flight Simulator offers an educational experience for those with the flying bug. The screen accurately renders the cockpit gauges, and to successfully get airborne a virtual pilot must learn to operate all of the plane's controls within correct parameters. Forget to release the brakes and the plane won't go anywhere; not enough throttle and it won't lift off; fly too slow or pull the nose too high and the plane will stall and crash unless quickly corrected. With the sim, would-be pilots can learn to navigate between points using instruments or visual landmarks, they can fly day or night or in any kind of virtual weather, and they can practice landing at real, accurately rendered airports around the world (three hundred airports back then; three thousand in the latest version of the program).

Jimmy was impressed by how quickly Colt mastered the highly technical Flight Simulator. "I even had a joystick hooked up so it felt more realistic, and he took to it right away."

While the models and Microsoft had Colt's imagination reaching for the skies, life on the ground, in the trailer, began to more closely approximate hell.

"As time went along . . . man, she was a mean fucking drunk," says Jimmy. "Very moody, just go into raging drunks. Looking into her eyes . . . she had the hate in her. She'd drink and beat up on the kid. I mean she hammered on him—we're talking black and blue. I wouldn't beat my dog that way. Every other day it'd happen. Maybe the kid wouldn't clean up his room or take out the garbage, which was a joke anyway because the whole goddamn place was a hog pen, a total firetrap. She'd be half drunk and start picking on him for one thing or another, nitpick bullshit, then it would escalate and she'd start beating on him."

Jimmy says Colt had his own anger issues, throwing fits when asked to do something he didn't want to do. And together, mother and son brought out the worst in each other. "The poor kid would have enough of his mother nagging and nagging, and then he'd just fucking come unglued. When she got mad she'd break his toys and stuff, so it got to the point where he'd break up his own shit before she could. He'd trash out his room, kick and stomp, bitch and scream and go outside. I'd go out and calm him down and we'd sit out on the picnic table and bullshit. He'd tell me he hated her. I shouldn't have done it, but once in a while he'd be out there crying and I'd have a beer in my hand and give him a sip."

Jimmy never saw Colton fight back. "He was scared of her back then."

Jimmy says the bad scenes inside the little trailer weren't limited to mother and son. "It started to wear down real quick. Then her and I got into it one day and I ended up in Coupeville for a night." He says he and Pam were having a shouting match in the trailer's little living room when Pam went ass over tit behind the woodstove. "She fell over the kindling box," says Jimmy. "But Colt thought I hit her. She yelled for Colt to go call the cops, so he went across the road to the house where a bunch of dopers lived and called the 911."

The Island County deputies and Stanwood police came out. Pam had a shiner coming up, and they arrested Jimmy, who spent the night locked up in the Coupeville county jail. "I took a taxi back the next day and told the driver—a damn good-looking gal, charged me $100 for the ride, though—I told her to turn the cab around and have it facing the main road with the engine running and wait for me just in case. I didn't know what [Pam] might do. I sat in the taxi for a good long time, not knowing whether to shit or go blind . . . then finally grew some hair on my ass, got out, and walked down the driveway. The door was open and she was sitting on the couch, fuckered up. She turned around, big old black eye. I only stayed a few days after that and then decided no way, it's not working out."

Island County records show that the assault charges against Jimmy were dropped.

After Jimmy, Van again became a fixture around the trailer. He and Colt mainly got along. During a later interview with counselors, Colt said that Van was only violent to him twice, while Pam was violent to him "100s of times."

14

With nearly constant trouble and stress at home and at school, Colt increasingly turned inward—maintaining his fantasy life as the secret agent son of a rich pilot—and outdoors, spending as much time as possible in the woods.

Both Pam and Jimmy say they taught him survival skills: how to build fires and set up campsites, which plants were safe to eat and which ones were poisonous. Once inside the evergreens, Colton was home, kicking off his shoes to climb trees or to run full speed through the undergrowth.

"He loved being in there," says Kory. "If you ever chased him, he'd always go for the woods. And once you were in the trees, forget it, because you'd never be able to find him but he'd know exactly where you were. You'd follow him in, but he'd disappear, then suddenly he's behind you throwing rocks, but you still can't see him, so you'd have to back off."

Kory says Colt was equally at home in the woods all over Camano Island. "He knew the woods up by where we lived better than we did, and we were in there all the time."

COLT ALSO KNEW AND loved the waterfront, wandering Camano's coastline from top to bottom, often alone, from a very young age.

"I was out in the water, boogie boarding, just paddling around," says Megan Wagner, "when all of a sudden I see this snorkeler coming toward me. We hardly ever saw strangers down on the beach, and this kid is coming straight at me, closer and closer. I'm thinking, Whoa, that's really, really weird, and I start to swim away. I look back and he's still following me! So finally I stop and turn around. He pops up and says, 'Wow, from underwater, your legs look like Jell-O!' "

It was summer, the ideal time to be a nature-loving boy or girl on a Pacific Northwest island. Megan Wagner, at twelve, was old enough to be offended by someone commenting on her legs. And she was, at first. But looking at this ten-year-old boy* with the buzz cut and the big smile spreading beneath his dive mask without a trace of malice, she couldn't help but start laughing.

He introduced himself as Colton and said, "Want to see something cool?" Megan said yes and followed as he scouted ahead in the shallow water. "Then he bends his knees and suddenly kicks his bare feet up," says Megan. "And this huge crab comes flying off the bottom and Colton just grabs him! I thought that was the coolest thing ever."

Colton thrust the big spidery Dungeness at Megan's face. When she didn't freak, it sealed their friendship. "I was pretty tomboyish, and we definitely hit it off right away," she says. The two played together in the sea until lunchtime, when Megan's mom, Doreen, called her back to the beach to eat. Megan asked if Colton could join them. From that point on, he became part of the Wagners' summertime family.

The beach they picnicked on lay about 150 feet directly below the Wagners' high-bank waterfront property on South Camano Drive, 3.3 miles south of Pam's trailer as the raven flies. Doreen and her husband, Bill, first rented the house for a year when he worked for an aircraft company on the mainland. They loved the spot so much that later, after they moved to California and Bill started his own aeronautical engineering company, they decided to buy it as a vacation home. Along with the main house up on the treed bluff, the property came with a small beach cabin that served as a boat house for kayaks, dinghies, and other water toys.

"You didn't want to have to go up and down that path between houses more than once," said Doreen. "So we'd pack up in the morning and spend the whole day down there." That "we" included Megan and her three

---

*In my interviews with Megan and Doreen Wagner, they said these events happened when Colt was between ten and twelve years old. In a burglary report, the police quote Bill Wagner as saying it was when Colt was between thirteen and fifteen. There is no dispute the events happened, just about the exact years.

younger sisters, along with a revolving guest list of friends and family. And Colton Harris-Moore.

"After that first day, I'd just always make an extra sandwich for him because he was always there," said Doreen. Their Colton was a real island boy, a pint-size Tarzan. "He never had shoes and I don't even remember him even having a shirt, just always showing up in his swim trunks with his mask in his hand."

Every morning when the Wagners hiked down the path to the beach they found Colton waiting for them. "Then after a while," says Doreen, "he started meeting us up at the main house so he could help cart all the stuff down to the beach."

Once down the steep switchback trail that ran through fir, maple, and thickets of blackberries, Megan and Colton would head straight for the water. "We'd splash around, swim, walk along the beach lifting up rocks to see what kinds of animals were under there, like little crabs. At low tide we'd wade around this big rock and see who could find the biggest starfish."

Megan says Colton amazed her with how much he knew about nature, both in and out of the water. "I remember there were these berries grow-ing on the property and I'd always wanted to eat one, but my mom told me not to because they were poisonous. One day I look over and Colton is eating them and I'm like, 'What are you doing?' And he's just, 'Oh, they're good, try one.' He said they were salmonberries."

When Bill Wagner took his summer vacation, he'd fly up to Washington in his twin-engine Westwind business jet with his private pilot, Dan, who'd stay with the Wagners on Camano. The kids had a couple of men around to run the boats, and Colton got to meet more real pilots. Bill would anchor their little cuddy cabin runabout off the beach and every day he or Dan would be out either dragging the kids behind it on inflatable tubes or pulling up pots filled with Dungeness crab. "I really enjoyed having Colt around," says Bill. "And boy was he a spring—he never stopped moving. But he was also just the kindest, most polite little kid . . . and always helpful."

"My youngest sister was six at the time," remembers Megan, "and she freaked every time seaweed touched her leg. She'd scream because she thought a crab was going to get her. So when we waded in or out to the boat, Colton would carry her. He'd even give her piggyback rides, barefoot, up the steep dirt path when we had to go back to the house."

Everyone knew it was time to head up when Doreen let loose one of her ear-piercing whistles. Playtime, though, didn't stop just because they had to leave the beach.

"Colton taught us all how to climb trees," says Megan. "We had a little fort up in a tree that was near a fence and he showed us how to climb the fence first then get into the tree." Colton, the girls, and whatever friends they had visiting would also play tag in the woods along the driveway and the main road. Inside, Doreen set up the home's solarium as what she called the "kids' dormitory" for the summer, with inflatable mattresses on the floor. "It was a place where they could watch TV and play video and board games."

Megan says her and Colton's favorite board game was Life. Doreen remembers that the kids decided that whoever won would have the most babies when he or she grew up.

They also watched movies. The film Megan says they had playing continuously that first summer was *Forrest Gump*, the story of an outcast boy who becomes famous: "Run, Forrest, run."

At dinnertime, Colton always had a place at the table. "We'd have spaghetti or macaroni and cheese," says Megan. "And when Dad or Dan were up and we'd been out on the boat, we'd have a whole bunch of fresh crab and Colton would help clean them." Doreen says he also always offered to help her with the dishes.

Every day, Doreen would tell Colton to call his mom and see if it was okay that he stayed for dinner. She says he'd pick up the phone, talk for a few moments, hang up, and tell her, "Yeah, it's fine." It didn't take her long, though, to realize he was only pretending to call.

After dinner, in the lingering Northwest summer evenings when the sun doesn't hit the horizon until 9 p.m., the kids would head back out to play until bedtime. "It'd get to be eight o'clock, and I'd be, 'Okay, Colton, it's time for you to go home.' He'd say, 'Okay. I'll call my mom.' Well, he was faking that, too, and walking back home." No one saw the friend of his mom's who, Colt said, dropped him off every morning, so they began to suspect that that, too, was a fib.

One evening, time slipped away so smoothly that when Doreen looked up it was 10:30, and Colton was still there. "I said, 'Well, Colton, the girls need to go to bed, where's your mom?' He says, 'Oh . . . she can't pick me up, I'll just walk.' I said, 'No, you're not. Come on, we'll give you a ride home.'" Doreen, Dan the pilot, Megan, and Colton piled into the van. "When we got over to the east side of the island, to the bottom of Haven Place," remembers Doreen, "Colton said, 'This is my road, this is good, just drop me off here!' And I said, 'No, no. I want to make sure you get home okay.'"

Megan says Colton started freaking out. "He tried to open the door and jump out while the car was moving." So *bam!* Dan locked the doors, turned to Colton, and said, "Hey, listen, we don't care what your house looks like or anything like that, we just want to make sure you get home okay."

They pulled into the dark driveway and drove up under the cedars to the clearing. "There's his mom and a couple guys sitting around the campfire, a case of beer on the picnic table," says Doreen. "Colton got out and they all started hollering at him, so he just took off running for the mobile home." Doreen told Megan to stay in the van and she got out and walked up to Pam. "I just said, 'You know your son's been spending a lot of time with us. I thought maybe you would want to meet me.'"

Doreen said she didn't get much of a response from Pam. "She pretty much blew us off." After that, Colt didn't show up for a couple of days.

Doreen, who'd investigated child abuse as a social worker back in the Black Hills of South Dakota, had just always assumed that Colton was a latchkey kid. "Whenever I'd ask why we hadn't seen or met his mom, he'd just say, 'She works,' or 'She's not home.'" Doreen says she hadn't observed any classic warning signs that he came from a troubled home. "He was always clean, his hair was always buzzed neat, there were no obvious signs of physical abuse. He just seemed like a lonely little kid."

"We never saw him with anyone else, no other friends, no other kids," says Megan.

The Wagners were all relieved when, on the third day, they walked outside and there was Colton, waiting for them. "He looked embarrassed," says Megan.

Doreen took him aside and sat him down. "I said, 'Look, I've seen it all, don't be ashamed about anything. I just want to make sure you're safe and that you know you can come to me if there's anything I can do. He said, 'Okay,' and that was it."

After seeing his home, Doreen went out and bought Colt sport sandals and some T-shirts. "I thought it was weird that he was always barefoot," says Megan, laughing, "but I guess that's what he liked because he wasn't too excited to get the sandals. He was just like, 'Oh, thanks,' and I think he only wore them to make my mom happy."

Megan says Colton rarely talked about his home life, "other than one time when I was complaining that I didn't like my mom's smoking, and he said he 'hated!' when his mom smoked. He was all excited one day because he said he'd just bought a remote control tank off eBay and that it shot BBs. He said he hid in the woods and when his mom came out to smoke he'd fire BBs at her. He thought that was great. I was impressed just because I didn't even know what eBay was back then and he was two years younger than me and had it figured out. He seemed really smart and actually really mature for his age."

Colt also never told Megan his dreams for the future, but she says meeting the family's private pilot obviously had an impact on him. "Colt told me that he thought Dan's job was really, really cool," she says. After getting to know Dan, Colt began telling other kids that his father was not only a pilot, but one who flew rich people all around the world. He also began to tell Pam that when he grew up he was going to become a private pilot for people like Bill Gates and Paul Allen, and work for them until he had enough money to start his own aerospace company.

At the end of that first summer, when the Wagners told him they were leaving for California, Colt was visibly disappointed. They wrote his number next to the phone and Megan promised she'd call as soon as they came back the following year. And she did. Colton again became part of the family, spending practically every glorious Pacific Northwest summer's day with them, beaching under the ever-blue skies; swimming, boating, and crabbing in the calm waters of Saratoga Passage; playing games well into the evenings; and eating anything and everything that Doreen put in front of him. By then, Colt had already outgrown the sandals Doreen had bought him and he spent the whole time happily barefoot.

The third summer, the Wagners did more traveling and spent less time at the beach. They lost touch with their island boy. Later, Doreen ran into Colton and Pam at the Elger Bay Store, but she says he acted very uncomfortable, like he didn't want her to talk to Pam. Doreen gave him a hug, and says that was the last time she saw him. That wasn't the end of the Wagners' connection to Colton, though. He'd spend quite a bit more time at their house—not that they'd know about it until they got a call from the police.

15

Colton's summer days with the Wagners were moments of idealized normalcy for him. Back on Haven Place, though, things were growing uglier between him and his mother. In later interviews with counselors, Colton said it was at this age that it became clear to him the extent and damage of his mother's alcoholism. He said that at one point he tried to give her a Bible, and another time an Alcoholics Anonymous pamphlet, but "she burned it." Her drinking, Colton said, led to violence. One day when both Pam and her boyfriend beat him, Colton decided to take off.

AFTER JIMMY MOVED OUT of Pam's trailer, he never expected to see or hear from Colton again. Then one day in 2001, when he was living across the bridge in Stanwood, he got a call.

"It was Colt and he was real upset. He said his mom had been beating on him. I told him, 'If you need to get out of there, get the hell out and walk to the main road.' I called Island Transit [the free bus that loops the island every hour] and told them what was going on. They had a driver go out for him, actually picked the kid up and delivered him right to my door. When he showed up he had bruises all over his arms and legs and a couple on his back."

Jimmy says Colton stayed with him for ten days. Colton spent his time sketching airplanes and rocket ships in a lined notebook. He also practiced with Microsoft Flight Simulator.

"So one day," says Jimmy, "nice day, warmish, good outdoor working weather, I'm watching this kid fly around on the computer . . . man, he just loved airplanes. He was a good kid, you know? He just had issues. So I say, 'Hey, you want to do something different? You want to go *there?*' and I pointed up. Well, when he finally got my drift he started grinning like a monkey eating shit."

Jimmy drove them to a private strip owned by a friend whom he "talked out of a plane." He walked a wide-eyed Colton up to an old Cessna 170, a 145-horsepower tail-dragger that'd been built in the 1950s. Jimmy showed him how to do the walkaround safety check, then buckled Colton into the right seat. "I got in, yelled, 'Clear!' and fired that bitch up. Well, Colt didn't know what to do! He's just going, 'Wow.' I said, 'You ready?' He gave me this funny look, like for a second he didn't quite know . . . and I just said, 'Here we go!' "

After taxiing to the end of the smoothed-dirt strip, Jimmy spun the plane around and opened up the throttle. "I wound her out and yelled, 'Hang on, buddy!' When I got it up to speed and started to pull back, I tell you his guts all but fell out of him!"

Jimmy leaned the little plane into a gentle bank and flew south down the spine of Camano then out over the water, turning east over the top of Hat Island and crossing Possession Sound to the mainland. He says Colt's nervousness drained away as they gained altitude. Jimmy pointed the nose of the Cessna north toward Canada, and set her on a straight and level course at three thousand feet over the town of Marysville. Then he turned to Colton: "Put your hands on the wheel."

Colton stared at the yoke in front of him. "He wasn't expecting that!" says Jimmy. "I said, 'C'mon, this ain't no different than what you been doing on the computer.' So he put his little hands up there and death-gripped that son of a bitch."

Jimmy let go of the wheel on his side of the cockpit and suddenly ten-year-old Colton Harris-Moore was flying an airplane.

"Once he settled down a little, I told him to push the wheel in just a bit . . . The nose dipped and he goes, 'Whoa!' Then I had him pull back . . . 'Whoa!' " Jimmy showed Colton how the trim and the flaps worked and had him reach down and put his feet on the pedals to waggle the tail back and forth. "By this time we're almost the fuck up to Mount Vernon, so

I had him put us into a turn and we came back south." Jimmy took back the controls for the approach and landing on the narrow strip.

"He was just amazed," says Jimmy. Over the following week, he took Colton up twice more, letting him fly the plane longer each time and further familiarizing him with the controls and instruments. Colt was in heaven.

Back on the ground, though . . .

"His mother finally caught up with him. She found out where he was and she'd leave messages, threatening to get me for kidnapping," says Jimmy. "We'd come in and listen to the machine and the kid says, 'Don't send me home.' He was fucking petrified. That's when we did the recording."

Jimmy got out a microcassette and Colton put his story on tape, which, Jimmy says, he gave to the authorities. "We ended up calling the Island County cops and we got a hold of CPS." First to show up was a county deputy. "The kid was terrified when the cop got there, shaking like a leaf, crying and everything—he was scared of the cop," says Jimmy. "I was trying to tell him it was going to be okay. CPS ended up carting him off, but then Pam got him back three or four days later."

Jimmy tells this story teary-eyed. Court documents corroborate the events, referring to a CPS investigation for "negligent treatment or maltreatment" and reports "Colt being afraid to go home after being thrashed by his mother and her boyfriend." It also quotes the police officer saying, "Colton does not want to go home to his mother Pamela . . . and if mother comes to get child tonight I will place him in protective custody."

The CPS risk tag rating for this episode was listed as "high," meaning CPS needed to have a social worker see Colton within twenty-four hours. In Washington State, CPS does not have the authority to actually take a child away from a parent, even temporarily. Only the police—through protective custody—or a judge via a court order can remove a child. In this instance, Colton was placed in protective custody and taken to a foster home. Once a child is under protective custody, DSHS, of which CPS is part, has only seventy-two hours to file a dependency petition or it must return the child to the parent.

In Colton's case, he was returned to Pam, who said that later, when

Colt would get mad at her, she'd tease him about his time in the foster home, asking if "he wanted to go back to his other mother."

FOR HER PART, PAM denies that she was an abusive mother and blames her anger back then on her inability to control Colton. "I talked to his pediatrician about referring us to a hospital to get a brain scan because I knew something was wrong. I couldn't just take him up there because his insurance couldn't of covered it. I wanted to take him because he'd thrown something at me or hit me, my eye and forehead were bruised. She wouldn't do it, and said, 'I don't think we have to go that far.' I said, 'I think we do!'"

Instead, Pam took Colton for an evaluation at Compass Health. Originally a Lutheran orphanage, Compass evolved over the past 110 years into a community-based nonprofit that provides mental health and chemical dependency services to thirteen thousand low-income children and adults—as well as the homeless and incarcerated—in Island, San Juan, Skagit, and Snohomish Counties.

In August 2001, a Compass Health clinician noted instability and sleep disturbances in ten-year-old Colton. They diagnosed him with ADHD, parent-child relational problem, and possible depression.

On September 10, 2001, a Compass clinician described Colton: "Assertive, talkative 10-year-old who can become quite angry—but the situation with mother and her boyfriend drinking, living in a tiny trailer, mother drinking all the time, and the physical abuse Colton has gotten from boyfriend makes his anger easy to understand."

The response was to put Colton on Prozac.

DURING THOSE FIRST INTERVIEWS at Compass Health, Colton told the therapists that he'd gotten into only a few problems so far at school and that he was determined "not to get into trouble this year."

That same month, though, Colton began to find serious trouble outside of school.

"We'd made a path through an undeveloped property on Bretland Road, just east of Haven," says Joel, Colton's friend and fellow ninja. "We even built a ladder to get us down the cliff to the water." Joel says that they were walking along the beach one day when suddenly Colton ran off. "When he comes back, he's got a fishing pole and he tells me he stole it." The boys headed home, and by the time they made it the short distance to Haven Place, Island County deputies were already pulling up to Pam's. "They knew right where to go," says Joel. "Colt gave the fishing rod back to the guy he took it from so he didn't press charges."

Despite the lack of charges, the Island County police made an official report of the incident, naming Colton Harris-Moore as a suspected thief. He was ten and a half years old.

A PSYCHOLOGIST REPORTED THAT Prozac seemed to only increase Colton's "agitation," so doctors prescribed Geodon, a big-league antipsychotic strong enough to chillax a rampaging water buffalo. The drug had just been approved that year by the FDA for schizophrenia, though it was also utilized "off label" for treating mania resulting from bipolar disorder and some cases of severe ADHD. A psychological evaluation of Colton later states: "Records are not clear as to why such a potent medicine was tried, but most likely it was to assist in behavioral control."

Compass Health also sent someone out to the trailer for in-home family counseling. Pam says Colton participated, but that she found "little benefit" from the therapists, who were "well-meaning but ineffective."

WHEN THE CAMANO KIDS moved on to sixth grade, it was back on the bus and across the bridge to Stanwood Middle School, home of the Spartans. That's where, from all accounts including his own, Colton completely lost whatever constructive relationship he'd ever had with school.

"Stanwood had the normal school cliques," says Kory. "Jocks, goths, girlie girlies . . . and Colton couldn't get along with anyone. When people weren't picking on him then he'd start it. He'd argue with everyone."

Christa Postma met Colton that year. "Colt was always getting into trouble. He was like the kid who's always loud in class, not being quiet when he was supposed to, disrupting everything. We'd be learning something and he'd just say his opinion on it. Like he'd say whatever the teacher was saying was 'bogus.'"

The teachers attempted to discipline Colton, but had little success. "Usually you were sent outside the class, and then after a while the teacher would go out and talk to you. If they thought you were going to behave better, then they'd bring you back in. Colt would always get brought back in . . . and then get kicked out again."

Christa, who'd been diagnosed with ADHD and ADD, says she recognized a lot of the symptoms in Colton. "I know I can be really hyper and annoying without realizing it. All through middle school I was on medication for it, but Colt said he wasn't on anything for his ADHD. He'd be hyper and annoying, and then when people called him out for it he'd get pretty upset and then he'd be a jerk to them."

After school, Colton and Christa hung out behind the Stanwood Library. Outside of class, Christa says Colton seemed "really smart" but unable or just unwilling to use those smarts in school. "I'd be like, 'I have to get home and do homework or my mom will kill me,' and he's like, 'Oh, I don't need to.' He kinda resented authority and liked being able to do whatever he wanted. He'd always say how much he hated school."

Reports from clinicians at Compass Health who interviewed Colton around this time state that he told them that his mom was becoming "increasingly angry, does not encourage school." Colton himself estimated that from the time he started middle school he missed about half of his classes and his mom's response was "It's your fault, not mine."

According to Pam, Colton would stay up all night playing video games and then be too tired to go to school the next day. His favorite game at the time was Grand Theft Auto. "Then I got interested in that one!" says Pam. "I said, 'Give me that thing, I want to see what I can do with it.' And then Colt went to bed and I was staying up playing it! He got up a couple hours later and said, 'Are you still playing that?' I said, 'Yeah, I like killing those hookers on the sidewalk!'"

When Colton came home from middle school having failed all of his classes, Pam went to the superintendent to insist that he be held back a grade. "They said, 'Well, we don't do that.'"

Stanwood Middle asked Pam to come in for a crisis meeting about Colton. (Pam claims she went to every meeting they ever asked her to attend: "I was a very involved parent.") Pam says she sat at a big table with a large group of teachers and school counselors who were trying to figure out a way to get Colton engaged in his education. "They said he was being disruptive in class, that he was basically uncontrollable . . . and I tend to believe that about him." A coach suggested sports, and Pam says she pleaded, "Just don't make him stronger! He's strong enough." She says she was frightened of Colt by this point, because he was getting bigger and she felt he had a serious anger problem.

The South End kids who rode Island Transit with Colton on those days he did go to school saw that anger. "He'd get really loud," says Kory. "He'd be arguing with the other kids, and when the drivers tried to settle it down he'd curse at them and sometimes they'd throw him off the bus."

Failing in school, virtually free of supervision at home, and rejected by almost all of his peers due to his antisocial behavior, Colton found acceptance with someone a couple years older, a curly-haired little guy the other kids called the Hobbit.

Harley Davidson Ironwing says he had a rep around Stanwood as a bad guy, and that's why Colton Harris-Moore sought him out.

Born in Loveland, Colorado, Harley wound up in Stanwood via foster care. He and his siblings were taken away from their parents when Harley was four, and he can't remember how many families he went through before ending up in Washington State with Karen Ironwing. Karen changed Harley's middle name to Davidson because . . . well, it was apparently just too tempting.

Harley speaks with a soft drawl when he says that he doesn't do well with authority figures, including cops and teachers. He ran away from home early and often, and told police when they caught him that he'd rather go to juvie than back home because his foster brothers beat him up all the time. Even when he was living on the streets, though, Harley attended school almost regularly and made it to eleventh grade before dropping out. However, he was only halfway through sixth grade at Stanwood Middle School when he was charged with his first felonies.

One of Harley's claims to fame as a young hood happened April 25, 2002. "I was hanging out with my best friend one night and he got hungry," remembers Harley. "We were near an espresso stand, so I broke in and got him a couple of those sugar cookies with the pink frosting." It might've been too much sugar. "After that, we decided it'd be fun to try to blow up the police gas station."

The following morning, the Stanwood police got a call about two kids stuck in a clothing donation drop-off box near the Thrifty Foods. A deputy helped firemen extract Harley and his best buddy from the metal container. Both boys smelled like smoke and their fingers were blackened. There seem to be few times when Harley doesn't fess up to his crimes, and he told the deputies how, after the pink cookie caper, he set out to create a Hollywood-worthy explosion at the gas station "because we were bored."

Harley said he dribbled diesel over the pumps, stretched out the hoses, and then stuffed newspaper in one of the nozzles. Worried it might go up before they'd gotten far enough away, Harley added another piece of paper to lengthen the fuse. He lit it and they jumped on bikes they'd stolen earlier that night. They waited . . . and waited . . . No boom. Harley tried again, but it still didn't quite work like it does in the movies.

After confessing everything, Harley pulled out of his handcuffs and tried to escape. He made it outside, but a female officer ran him down on the street. Harley struggled, and three deputies took him to the ground, then put him in hobble restraints for one of his many rides to the Denny Youth Center.

Harley scoffs at the foster care, school, social services, and juvenile justice systems and whatever help they offered him while he was growing up. "Nothing in the system could have prevented me from becoming a crook."

Harley was in eighth grade when Colton, then in sixth, approached him. "He reminded me a little bit of myself. He was smart, he had a problem with authority. I figured he could be another person I could do crimes with."

As for Colton's motivations, Harley says, "I think he was just looking for somebody that wouldn't put him down. He didn't have any friends, and his mom didn't give a rat's ass about him. He wouldn't have gone for a criminal lifestyle if his mom had been giving him the attention I was giving him."

Harley says there wasn't much to teach Colton about crime. "I gave him some tips on how not to draw attention to himself. Colt used to always want to turn lights on. Bad thing for burglars! That's how you get caught real quick."

Thieving, according to Harley, is not so much about the skill as the will. "It's easy to learn how to break into a house . . . it's whether you can actually do it or not." The big leap, he says, is from thinking about it and

wanting to do it, to actually breaking a window and going inside someone's house to steal their stuff.

Harley calls himself "a drug addict" and counts booze among his addictions along with weed and cocaine. However, he says the rush that comes
from breaking the law goes way beyond the drug high. "It's not the stealing," he says. "It's the adrenaline you get from stealing. Knowing that any
moment the cops can show up!"

Colton had been feeding his adrenaline habit since he was a child, when
Pam says he'd climb to the precarious tops of the hundred-foot-tall trees
around the trailer. Then he found he could score big hits from "ninjing"
around the neighborhood, stealing whatever caught his eye. Just like a
drug, he needed more risk each time in order to achieve the same level of
thrill.

Harley says they got that burglar's buzz even knowing that if they
played it smart there was little chance of getting arrested. "We knew that
the odds of getting caught burglarizing a house are very low," he says. "It's
way better than you can do in a casino." (He's absolutely right: the closure
rate for solving burglaries in the United States is 12 percent.)

And even if they happened to get spotted in the act, there was one simple solution: "Run." According to Harley that was an especially effective
strategy in rural neighborhoods. "No cop in his right mind is going to
chase you through the woods."

As to any moral quandary, Harley says: "It ain't hurtin' nobody else.
Everything I've ever stole is insured, so they'll reimburse them and they
can get something better. These are victimless crimes."

Harley says he and Colton wandered the streets of Stanwood plotting
their future. "Our ultimate plan was to steal a helicopter, land it on the
roof of Costco, and steal a bunch of shit," he says. "Colt always wanted to
fly and he always said how it'd be great to steal an airplane."

16

In August 2002, on his birthday, Bill Kohler died in Oklahoma. When she got the word, Pam says, "I freaked, I started breaking everything that would break, screaming and yelling."

She says she sat eleven-year-old Colton down out at the picnic table and told him that the man he'd been closest to, the man he'd even tried to convince her was really his father, was dead. "He was very upset, and I was crying. I hugged him."

There was no funeral. "They cremated him without even asking me . . . and that's not what Bill wanted." Pam got his ashes but says she doesn't even know how he died. "I never did get the coroner's report because they wanted me to pay for it and that just don't jive with me. Paying to find out how someone died? I mean he's dead, so why pay for it? Not cool."

Even though Bill hadn't been around much, Pam says that his death sent her into a steep downward spiral. "I drank a lot. I listened to Bill's music, this beautiful American Indian music. I went into a deep depression . . . I'm sure it had some kind of an impact on Colt."

Not long after Bill, their Great Pyrenees, Cody, also died. Pam got another Great Pyrenees, but gave it away when it started to suffer from seizures. After that, she took Colt to the pound and picked out Melanie, an energetic beagle, who became Colt's constant companion.

In Pam's narrative of Colton's trouble with the law, she says the two deaths were the turning point when he began having problems. Five months before Bill died, though, Island County deputies responded to a silent alarm at Elger Bay Elementary School. "Myself and another deputy found

Colton hiding in a closet," says Chris Ellis, who commanded the Camano Island precinct. Colt had gathered up a pair of binoculars, a disposable camera, candy, and some change from various school desks and drawers.

"I called his mom, Pam, and said 'This is Lieutenant Ellis from the sheriff's office. I have your son Colton here and . . .' And she jumps in and goes, 'What the fuck did that little asshole do now?'"

Ellis explained they'd caught Colt at the school. "She refused to come pick him up. I had a deputy take him home . . . he was ten years old."

THE NEXT TIME COLTON's name comes up in police records is January 2003, when he and another boy were caught shoplifting at the Camano Plaza Market. That April, Harley once again went outlaw to feed one of his hungry friends: he got nabbed stealing peanut butter and Snapple from Port Susan Middle School.

According to Pam, she and Colton were going hungry, too. "We starved," she says, because money was so tight. She also says that she and Colton now fought constantly.

Colt told friends he was mad because Pam would spend all the money from their assistance check within two weeks, leaving them flat broke for the rest of the month. It was then, he says, that he first began to look at his neighbors' houses as sources of food and money to buy food. He remembers being happy after breaking into one of his first homes, not because of the loot he found, but because he could make pancakes.

Colton continued to receive treatment at Compass Health, but later admitted to a psychologist that he didn't tell the counselors the extent of the physical conflict between him and his mom because he was afraid they would take him away from her. However, he did tell them that Pam had been on two-week drinking binges during which she'd break things. The twelve-year-old told them, "She is in denial about her drinking."

The Compass staff were also aware of the men Pam had coming through the trailer: "Many inappropriate father figures in the home over the time, exposing Colton to domestic violence and drug and alcohol addiction/selling."

The most plaintive words from young Colton come from this period: "I am not happy. I am depressed. I could stay in bed all day. I need help. I am tired of this stuff."

Clinicians reported that "Colton wants mom to stop drinking and smoking, get a job, and have food in the house. Mom refuses."

Colt's pleas, all the interviews, the mounting CPS complaints, the counselors' notes . . . result in two more mental health diagnoses for him: intermittent explosive disorder and depressive disorder. He's prescribed Strattera, an ADHD medication.

IN THE SPRING OF 2003, the original nuclear family had an explosive re-union. Gordy Moore showed up at the trailer on a nice May day. He and Pam started partying out in the yard and decided to fire up the grill and cook burgers.

"Gordy's getting the barbecue-er ready and we told Colt to go inside and get the ketchup and mustard and all that," remembers Pam. "So he does and he brings them out to the picnic table. But then all of a sudden he started taking them back in. He said, 'I don't want to barbecue.' I said, 'I don't care if you want to or not.' So his dad and I brought all the stuff back out and then Colt stood off a ways and threw rocks at us, mainly at his dad, rocks about the size of baseballs. And so they got in a big fight toward the backyard and they're rolling around on the ground toward the sticker bushes."

Colton says he got mad because his parents wouldn't let him fix his food the way he wanted, and in his version he told police that Gordy threw him into stinging nettles, held him down by the throat, and said, "Don't you know I have killed three men because of my anger?" The twelve-year-old took that as a threat. Colton also said he hadn't thrown the rocks until af-ter Gordy throttled him.

According to Colt, Pam was drunk and screaming at him throughout the incident. When he got away from Gordy, Colt ran into the trailer and called 911. That *really* made Pam mad. "Somebody at the school had told all the kids that if anybody hurts you, just dial 911!" she says, indignant. "So Colt did! And here come the cops!"

When Island County deputies showed up, Gordy took off through the woods. He didn't show the same fleet-footedness as his son, though, and they quickly caught him. "Colt had some scratches on his neck," says Pam. "I said, 'So what?!' But they arrested [Gordy]."

Police reported that Pam "harangued and verbally abused the officers during the arrest," and Colt said she kept after him when the deputies left, that she "stumbled around asking, 'What are you going to do now? They've taken your father away.'"

When the police ran a check on Gordy, they found he was already wanted on an outstanding warrant. He was also charged and convicted of assault in the fourth degree for nettling Colt. (Washington police records do not show any accounts of Gordy Moore killing anyone. As of May 2011, though, he is a wanted man, with an active warrant for failing to appear at court for a DUI and driving with a suspended license. His criminal record also shows an arrest in Reno, Nevada.)

Child Protective Services received another referral after the barbecue donnybrook. A case worker came out to the trailer to check and see if Colton was okay.

"I told her, 'He's fine,'" says Pam. But the CPS counselor said she needed to actually see him with her own eyes. "Just then Colt came running around the side of the house and I said, 'There he is, and if you want him, go ahead and take the little bastard, 'cause I'm not jumping through any friggin' hoops!' You know, drug testing or any of that crap. So she said, 'Oh no, we just wanted to make sure he was okay.' And she left."

AT THIS POINT, DSHS recommended Pam get treatment for chemical dependency. She refused. A social worker suggested that Pam see a counselor at Compass Health. She said no thanks. A note in Colton's record states: "Social worker has concerns regarding this child due to mother's possible use of drugs or alcohol; this judgment due to the men and their habits that have been in Colton's life." But no action was taken.

COLTON BEGAN TO STRIKE back. When he got angry at Pam, he smashed the trailer's windows, ultimately breaking most of them. He went into rages at her drinking and her smoking, and for things like playing the TV too loud when he was trying to sleep.

"I even got headphones for my TV and he'd swear he could hear it," says Pam. "I said, 'That is impossible.' So he stuck a screwdriver where my headphones went and he messed it up so I couldn't use it anymore. Yeah, he wasn't very nice to me at times."

Colton scrawled "Pam is a drunk" on the door to the laundry room and began taking full beer cans away from her and putting them out along the road.

IN SEVENTH GRADE AT Stanwood Middle School, Colton once again found some solace and friendship with a girl who was outside the popular cliques.

"Colt was in a few of my classes and it quickly became obvious that there were a lot of issues between him and the other kids," says Brandi Blackford, a blue-eyed blonde with piercings in her eyebrow, tongue, and belly button who'd just moved from Portland to Camano Island. "He argued with people a lot. He'd make little comments at everything they said. He also told everyone that his mom was a lawyer and that they lived in a big, beautiful house, but kids who knew him would call him out on it."

Colton wound up as Brandi's lab partner in science class. He introduced himself to her as Colton Harris, dropping the part of his name that tied him to Gordy Moore.

"Behind the lies and all the drama you could see he just wanted a friend." Brandi became that friend for a while. Her mom would drive over to Stanwood to pick them up from school and remembers having to wait outside in the car because Colton wouldn't leave the building until all the buses had gone—"because of kids picking on him," says Brandi.

On the weekends or anytime school was out, Brandi and Colton went to the beach with Melanie and Cricket, Brandi's Jack Russell terrier. "Colton never wanted to go home."

Colt's time outside the trailer, though, wasn't all spent in such agreeable activities as drawing his name in the sand with Brandi. On October 8, 2003, police caught Colton with a stolen cell phone, resulting in a possession of stolen property (PSP) in the third degree charge to which he pleaded guilty and got sentenced to probation. Then on Thanksgiving of that year, Colton celebrated the harvest festival in a nontraditional way. He and three other boys met up in Stanwood for an evening of mayhem. Armed with a butane torch lighter in the apparent belief that it would work like the plasma cutters crooks use to cut open safes in the movies, Colton went to work on the door of a Stanwood mortgage office. He scorched and melted the plastic frame a bit, but nothing more, so he went old school and pried on the door until a window broke. The boys grabbed a laptop and some blank CDs and moved on to the big Thrifty Foods supermarket, where they set fire to leaflets on the community bulletin board. Then came the big target, that hated bastion of teachers, books, and dirty looks: Stanwood Middle School.

Colton got them in by hammering on the gym doors and breaking a window. Inside, they used the torch on a Pepsi machine, melting the plastic face. On their way out, they set fire to an office window and then vandalized the bus barn before finally calling it a night.

One of the kids' dads figured out the boys had been up to no good and marched his son down to the police station to spill. The cops called Pam, saying they wanted to come out and talk to her son. At the trailer, she pointed down the hall to his room, the first door on the right beyond the little living room. The police found the door not only closed, but padlocked.

Pam said she didn't realize Colton wasn't home. The padlock was no problem, though: she came down the hallway with a hatchet and chopped it off the door.

The deputies stormed into the room looking for the notorious juvenile delinquent and South End bully, but pulled up short: the top of Colton's desk was piled high with stuffed animals. "Are these Colt's?" the surprised officers asked Pam. She assured them that they were. The cops searched the room—no Colton, no laptop—but they spotted a Sony camcorder still in its box and a wallet carrying someone else's identification. Pam told the police that Colton said he bought the video camera at a liquidation store. The cops called bullshit, so she phoned the store—which told her no, they'd never sold Sony camcorders.

The cops finally caught up with Colton at school and he was found guilty of malicious mischief in the third degree and burglary in the third degree. The break-in and vandalism became the sixth and seventh "incident reports" in Colton's rapidly fattening file at Stanwood Middle. They suspended him for twenty-four days and charged him for his part of the damages. "Everybody in school knew him after that," says Mike Bulmer. "They started calling him Klepto Colt."

Colton's legal troubles did nothing to smooth over things at home. He and Pam made it through Christmas, but fireworks erupted on New Year's Eve. Colton now weighed 130 pounds and stood five foot four, big and heavy for a twelve-year-old. He was no longer afraid of Pam, and this time she was the one who dialed 911 and Colton who went running into the woods when the cops arrived. Pam pressed charges, and Colton pleaded guilty to assault 4, receiving a sentence of six months probation, thirty-six hours of community restitution (aka community service), and mandatory counseling, curfew, and urinalysis.

Two weeks later when his probation officer, Aiko Barkdoll, checked to see if Colton was following Pam's "house rules," she told him that he'd bitten her on the forearm and hit her. Pam said that when she tried to call the police about it, Colton had grabbed the phone out of her hand and broken it. She said he'd then chased her around the property with a boat oar, and that she'd escaped only by locking herself in her pickup. When Pam finally managed to call the cops, Colton again ran off into his woods.

When Barkdoll asked Colton about the incident, he admitted that he and Pam often got into physical fights and that his anger came from her "smoking and drinking beer." Colton also showed him scratches where Pam had clawed his arm.

In his report, the probation officer noted: "Colton and his mother share a tumultuous relationship" and have difficulty resolving problems without aggression. He also made a call to Child Protective Services regarding Colton's welfare. He noted that when he contacted CPS, the file on Colton was active (his was at least the ninth referral to CPS for abuse or neglect of Colton so far; there would be a dozen by the time he was fourteen). Still, Barkdoll said that the CPS case worker assigned to Colton Harris-Moore claimed "little recollection of the family."

Two days later, on January 16, 2004, after another fight with Pam, Colton was brought before a judge and had his personal recognizance revoked for "continuing assaultive and threatening behaviors toward his mother." He was placed in juvenile detention for eleven days.

The stretch in juvie appeared to have an impact on Colton. He agreed to more counseling. Pam took him for another mental health assessment in early February, and Barkdoll noted that "Colt has been complying with mental health intervention involving both counseling and medications."

In a later psychological evaluation, it's noted that the one medication that seemed to work for Colton was Strattera, but that he stopped taking it with no reason given. Pam isn't clear on the timing or the particular drug—whether it was the Prozac, Geodon, Strattera, or others—but she remembers taking him off one of them.

"He was seeing a psychiatrist who put him on some medication," she says. "But he got so depressed on it. He sat down in my front yard next to my chair and just hung his head. And God, he would never hardly ever sit down. It scared me. So I stopped giving it to him, and I stopped taking him to that doctor because he wanted to just keep trying different medications. I said, 'Colt's not going to be used as a guinea pig!'"

Testing patients on different ADHD meds and antidepressants and fine-tuning the dosage before finding the most effective ones—"a trial and error process," as the Mayo Clinic refers to it—is extremely common. It often takes as long as eight weeks for the drugs to show results.

SADLY, BY THE TIME his probation officer noted that Colt was cooperating, the adolescent had already set in motion a freight train of additional troubles for himself.

On February 6, Colton was found guilty of another PSP 3, adding six months probation and sixteen hours of community restitution. (In Colton's early sentences, judges allowed hour-for-hour credit toward community service if Colton agreed to attend counseling and mental health treatment.) A week later, felonies were filed for the Thanksgiving tear, and Colton's rap sheet also listed as "still pending" another burglary in the third degree, theft in the third degree, two counts of burglary in the second degree, three counts of malicious mischief, and one count of reckless burning. One week before his thirteenth birthday, Pam called the cops again after she and Colton had a fight. He was hit with assault 4.

On March 16, a walkie-talkie and a video camera disappeared from Stanwood Middle School. Five students fingered Colton. When the principal confronted him, Colton said he "could not stop stealing and did not know why." After several rounds of phone calls from the school administrators, Pam finally admitted that the missing stuff was at the trailer and agreed to return it.

They expelled Colton for the rest of the year. His probation officer tried to use that to get him sent to juvenile prison, but the judge let him stay free with tighter restrictions. Barkdoll believed Colton snowed the judge, writing that Colt "seems to have been somewhat opportunistic in the community though presents as well behaved and remorseful when before the Court."

In April, Colton was charged with trespassing in Stanwood. It was also the month he and Pam got a new next-door neighbor.

CAROL STAR MOVED TO Haven Place so she'd have room for her horses. She bought an existing house and cleared the land for stables and paddocks. She describes Haven as a great place to live—with a couple of exceptions. Instead of stopping by with welcome baskets, the folks along Haven came with warnings about Colt.

"People told me, 'Do not let him in your house because he's going to scope out what you have and come back and get it.' They said he'd been stealing stuff in the neighborhood since he was eight years old. And that he'd even tried to steal the contractor's Caterpillar when my house was under construction."

From the stories, Carol half expected Damien from *The Omen*. She was surprised to meet, literally, the boy next door. "When you talk to him he's a nice kid, very friendly, doesn't look like the bogeyman."

After all the teasing about his raggedy clothes and suspect hygiene when he was a boy, Colton had begun taking responsibility for his appearance. He took charge of the laundry at home and paid careful attention to his grooming. "He dressed well, had the best tennis shoes on, and nice clothes," says Star. Often, though, she says she saw Colton wandering around "looking lost," and started to feel bad for him. "I don't think he had a lot of friends, and it seemed like he just wanted to befriend people."

However, any camaraderie she might have had with Colton got off to a bad start when his best friend tried to eat one of hers. "Colton's dog came into my yard, trapped my cat against a wall, and tried to kill it." Star rushed out and saved the cat just in time. "His dog had a telephone cord around its neck, which I thought was pretty weird, but I grabbed it and tied it to my fence. I figured Colton would come over and get it eventually, and he did. I screamed at him, 'If your dog is over here again trying to kill my cat I'm going to call the Humane Society.' And that opened the vendetta for him . . . A month after that he ripped me off the first time, climbed through an open window and stole my computer, some cameras, and other electronics."

Star says she knows it was Colton even though the police never charged him or anyone else with the crime. "The cops came and said, 'Oh, it looks like dogs were in here running around.' And I said, 'Yeah, they might have because the burglar didn't close the door and it was open all night long. Do you think the dogs stole my computer, too?'"

Even though she lived alone, Star says she was never frightened of Colton. "I don't think he's the type of person that would hurt somebody. The only way he could survive was to break into houses to get food and steal stuff to sell because Pam wouldn't feed him even though she always had money to buy beer."

Just in case, though, Star went out and bought a gun. "And when I got it, I made sure I went out back and shot it just so they knew I had one." She says that was as much about Pam as it was about Colton.

During her six years on Haven Place, Star says she often heard Pam yelling at Colton and Van. "She used to scream at her boyfriend just like she'd scream at Colton." At one point, Star couldn't keep quiet any longer. "She's screaming at Colton, saying all kinds of filthy things, and I was outside in the yard and finally yelled, 'Shut up, Pam, I'm tired of listening to you!' Pam screamed back, 'Fuck you!'"

Star says another neighbor got even more fed up when Colton allegedly broke into her trailer through the skylight and stole a computer she'd been using to write a book, with no backup saved. "She was pissed!" remembers Star. "She drove over into Pam's front yard and just sat there blasting the horn. Pam came running out of the house screaming and calling the police." According to Star, the neighbor yelled back that she just wanted Pam to know what it felt like to be disturbed like she'd been when she was ripped off by her son.

Finally, summer arrived on Camano. Residents and vacation homeowners scraped and repainted their boat bottoms, strung fresh line on their fishing reels, and readied their crab pots and clam rakes. Elger Bay Grocery stocked up on bait and beer, and Friday traffic piled up on the bridge. Skies went blue, seas laid down, and days stretched out. It was a great time to be an island boy with a faithful dog and access to a boat.

It was also a good time to own waterfront property at Utsalady Point, like Glen Kramer and his wife. In 1998, they moved full-time into a home that's been in his family since 1957. Houses on the point stand gable to gable atop narrow lots, but their yards roll straight onto a fine gray sand beach dimpled with white clam shells.

In summertime, boats pass back and forth across the serene blue background of Skagit Bay, providing Utsalady residents an ever-changing view. As if the sunny scene could get more bucolic, Glen Kramer regularly saw a young boy buzzing by aboard a small outboard boat, his beagle up at the bow, its nose in the breeze. In the back of Kramer's mind he thought it unusual that every day the boy and his dog were on a different boat, but he shrugged it off.

On the twenty-second of July, Glen and his wife came home after a short trip to Stanwood. He glanced out the window and instantly noticed that his dinghy was gone. A quick scan with binoculars picked up a strange scene.

"Here's this kid a ways down the beach carrying my outboard—I could tell it was mine because I'd bought it used from a rental outfit and it still had their big silver sticker."

Kramer hurried down and approached the lanky boy he recognized as the same one he'd seen zipping around. Colton was just about to attach his motor to someone else's boat, a Zodiac inflatable.

"I said, 'Hey, that's my outboard! What are you doing?'" says Kramer. "And he instantly started in on a story, saying, 'Some sailboaters found your dinghy drifting offshore and asked me to take the engine off and switch it over to their Zodiac.'"

The kid's obvious gift of gab momentarily stunned Kramer. "He could really think on his feet, but his story made no sense. I asked him where the boaters were and he said they'd gone off sailing for a while. I look around, and here he'd dragged my boat up the beach and hidden it amid the trees. I told him I didn't believe him, and he just walked off."

Not only impressed with the kid's golden tongue but also his strength, Glen had to call his wife to help him muscle their boat back to the water.

He reattached his outboard and then looked at the Zodiac and the gas cans lying beside it. "I knew the boat didn't belong there, so I decided to tow it over to my beach and try to find the owner."

Glen's wife suggested they call the Island County sheriff. Glen simply told them he'd caught a young boy stealing his boat. The deputies knew exactly who to look for. "It wasn't ten minutes later that they came rolling up the driveway with the same kid in the back of the police car. I identified him and they said they'd arrest him, but that he'd be right out again because he was only thirteen."

Not too long after the police left, another vehicle came up to the Kramers' home, this time a battered little pickup. Glen looked out and saw the same kid, now in the passenger seat, with a woman he presumed was his mother or grandmother driving. He figured she'd brought him back to apologize for taking the boat, and went out to meet them.

According to Glen, Pam Kohler got out of the truck and started right in on him, saying: "You stoled our gas cans!"

"What are you talking about?" asked Glen, stunned for the second time that day.

"You stoled our gas cans and we want them back," Pam kept insisting.

Sensing this was not an argument worth having, Glen told Pam, "Well, you tell your son they're back wherever he stole that Zodiac from because I put the gas cans inside it and the owner's already come and taken his boat." Then he walked back into his house.

As the Utsalady neighbors began comparing notes, they found that a number of their boats had been moved around. Several that had older two-cycle outboards had their engines ruined. Glen says they believed that Pam had been bringing Colton up to their neighborhood all summer long. "She was dumping him off at the boat ramp with gas cans." Even though Colton was sophisticated enough to mix and match engines and boats to create just the little cruising package he wanted, he apparently didn't know that the two-cycle outboards needed oil mixed in with the fuel. "He was using plain gas and just running each boat until the engine seized up, and then he'd take another one."

When he got hauled before the judge, Colton was found guilty of theft in the second and third degrees and sentenced to fifty days in juvie plus forty-eight hours community service and six months probation.

. . . .

"COLTON AND I 'DATED' in eighth grade, as eighth graders do," says Brandi. "Holding hands as we walked to class, going to movies . . ." After they'd been dating for a few weeks, though, Colton stopped showing up for school. He'd been sent to juvie, but hadn't told anyone he was going away. "I couldn't get ahold of him and had no idea where he was." Brandi says that when Colton finally returned to school, he was very tan. "He told everyone he'd been in the Bahamas."

Brandi says everything to do with Colton turned even worse in the eighth grade. "Things really got out of control," she says. "The kids got even meaner to Colton." One day, he and Brandi were hanging out at the Stanwood playground when two boys Colton had trouble with walked up. "I said, 'Colton, let's just go,' but he said, 'No, we're fine.' They yelled, 'Hey, fag, you need to leave.' When Colton refused, they grabbed him and pushed him up against the jungle gym. I was begging them to please just leave him alone and they kept asking me why I was hanging out with this 'piece of shit.' Colton tried to get away and one of them pulled out a knife and said he was going to stab him. I was crying and grabbed my phone and told them I was calling the cops. They pushed Colton down, kicked him in the stomach, and walked away."

Brandi called her mom, who rushed across the bridge to pick them up. "She took us back to our house and asked Colton if he wanted to call his mother. He came up with some story that she was out of town. You could see by the look in his eyes that he was on his own. His mom wasn't out of town, but she wasn't going to do anything to help him anyways, so why bother? He didn't act scared, but I know he was."

BACK AT THE TRAILER, the horror show escalated to the point where, in November 2004, it actually appeared that Haven Place was haunted. The tires on Pam's pickup kept inexplicably going flat. Then one night as she sat in her lawn chair having a smoke and a beer, she started hearing things hit the ground all around her. She called the cops, but they couldn't find anyone.

Night after night it happened: batteries, tent stakes, a croquet ball, screwdrivers, all mysteriously fell out of the sky, often hitting the trailer. Pam says that every time she left home, someone went in and took things—a bag of potatoes, socket wrenches, circular saw blades—and then later threw them back at her and the trailer. She says whoever it was threw flour around inside and put human excrement in her freezer. A can of corn came crashing through one of the trailer's few remaining glass windows. The other windows, which Colton had broken and were covered in plastic sheeting, were soon after slashed with a box cutter.

One evening as she and Colton were walking in the door of the trailer, Pam says she heard a bang. When she looked, there was a circular saw blade stuck in the door jamb.

Pam says she called the police every night for a month, but they never found anyone. She fired salvos of buckshot and profanities into the woods, but it kept happening. Then disturbing messages began to show up. The same plywood door where Colton had earlier written "Pam is a drunk" was now covered with spray-painted threats: "I'm sick of you," "Bitch," "Die," and "You Will Die—5 hours." On the floor was written: "Fuck'n Bitch I'll Kill U" and "Die Bitch."

The police kept showing up, but weren't happy about the shotgun. "The cops told me that they would never come here again if I kept the shotgun loaded, and that if I did, I better never come to the door with it or they'd shoot *me,*" Pam said.

Pam thought her neighbors to the east were responsible. They'd accused Colton of stealing a $3,000 car stereo. Pam insisted Colton wouldn't do that because "we already have a radio in every room of the house." The neighbors reported the theft, but said Island County deputies declined to take fingerprints and told them that it was probably Colton who'd taken it.

Pam saw the cops talking to the neighbors a couple of times, but the attacks continued. Desperate, she called Bev and Geof Davis.

RARE ARE THE HARD-LUCK childhood stories with happy endings that do not include a teacher, a coach, a mentor, a local cop, an uncle, a grandmother . . . someone who grabs the kid at the right time—often by the scruff of the neck—and gives him whatever it is he needs to set him on the right path.

For Colton Harris-Moore, Bev and Geof Davis could have been those people.

Bev and Geof moved to Camano in 1977 and live on a seventeen-acre South End family compound that's sort of a down-to-earth mossneck Nirvana, a whimsical backwoods Disneyland, with creeks and woods and quirky yard art and bridges and trolls and fanciful inventions and old gas pumps and summer-camp signs and Wild West memorabilia and guns and trucks and tractors and cool old cars.

They share the acreage with Bev's mom and her sister, and usually at least one person who's in need of a place to stay or a leg up. South Enders know Geof and Bev to be generous, some say to a fault. "Geof, especially," says Chris Ellis, "is a sweeper of lost souls. He sweeps them up and gives them a hand." The Davises have helped people most others consider untouchables, like a guy known locally as Stinky Steve ("You'd understand the name if you ever picked him up hitchhiking"). Bev and Geof, though, understand troubles, having seen more than their share, and those experiences have made them remarkably nonjudgmental.

They both grew up with alcoholic, verbally abusive fathers. Bev herself became an alcoholic, and when she finally saw the damage it was doing to her family, she sucked it up and quit. When she did, Geof stopped drinking, too, out of solidarity, even though he didn't have a problem.

Geof Davis is the kind of guy who makes you feel that if you could just better yourself to a point halfway between what you are and where he's at, then you'd be a good man. Unassuming to an absolute, he also gives you hope by admitting he wasn't always this way.

A genuine Northwest cowboy, Geof grew up on a five-thousand-acre spread along the Yakima River—though he wasn't left a blade of grass when his stepmother died. He competed in rodeos, worked as a Forest Service horseman, and then became a fire watcher when his bronc-busted legs couldn't take riding anymore. He worked a full life doing guy stuff: construction, and driving dump trucks, tractors, and eighteen-wheelers. Geof says that for a long time he had no use for other people—"Hated them, that's how I was raised"—but he got over that in a big way. Common in those kinds of sea-change stories, there's a woman to thank. In Geof's case, it's Bev, who, when she smiles over her reading glasses, looks an awful lot like Mrs. Santa Claus. Which fits . . .

One year as Christmas neared, Geof told Bev he wanted a Santa suit. She did up his eyebrows and rosy cheeks, and Geof went driving around Camano in his 1940 Ford pickup handing out candy canes. That began an entire decade of Geof as the island's Saint Nick. Santa's tour eventually grew to a traffic-stopping parade of Christmas light–covered classic cars that escorted Geof to nursing homes and then to the poorest parts of town to deliver thousands of dollars' worth of donated toys to needy kids.

Geof is as gregarious as Bev is reclusive. He's always out and about and there are very few people on Camano he doesn't know. He first met Pam Kohler when Colton was just a small child, and says she already had a reputation on the island.

"There's some people around here, my God, they'd a shot her if they had the chance," says Geof. "She was drinking a lot more heavily back then . . . she was bad. And crimey sakes, when she drinks she can use more cuss words than Carter has pills." Geof, though, saw her simply as a troubled woman with a young boy, struggling to get by. As he does with many folks he meets in the community, he told Pam to give him a call if she ever needed help. Still, he and Bev were surprised when she did call some time later, asking for a $50 loan. Even more so when she said she'd leave them her shotgun for collateral. "After that we always called her Shotgun Pam," Bev says, laughing.

Whenever Pam called, needing a loan for a new old truck or whatever, "for some stupid reason, I'd always go over and help," says Geof. The reason, though, was Colt.

For anyone who didn't have a dad around, but especially for a rough-and-tumble young boy, Geof would be the guy you'd want to take you under his wing. He's a big man, rugged yet gentle, and plainspoken with a lot of hard-won wisdom. Best, there's still an awful lot of playful boy left in him, even though his seventy-year-old body now has more titanium in it than the Terminator.

Geof has tried to help at least eight at-risk kids on the island. "All the misfits," he says kindly. Some haven't responded. "I've had to kick some of them off, but others are doing okay. They come up to me and now they're married and making it, and they say, 'Thanks for getting me on the right track.'"

Geof remembers coming across eleven-year-old Colton hitchhiking

along the main road because he'd been booted off the Island Transit bus
for cursing at the driver. Geof pulled over and they got to talking. "I knew
Pam's story, and I'd heard about what was going on with Colt in school. It
sounded to me like they'd all just sort of shut their eyes to him when there
were times they could've helped. And CPS . . . they suck, they didn't do
what they should have done. I understand they're understaffed, but that
still doesn't give them the right to not help a kid, especially when they
knew he was troubled. So I'm looking at Colton and thinking here's a kid
that just doesn't have a chance in life."

When Pam told Bev about the mysterious attacks happening at the
trailer, Bev said she and Geof would come out next time. Things started
mysteriously flying around again the very next night, so the Davises put on
dark clothes and drove to Haven. Bev took photos of the damage and graffiti while Geof hunted around the black woods for any sign of intruders. As
Bev went to put her camera away, "BAM! something hit our car, hard. I
turned and saw Colton standing on the lawn with his arms folded."

The next time Bev and Pam were on the phone, Colt yelled out that he
heard something and saw a shadow. He went outside and came back with a
note. Pam couldn't make out the words, so Colt read it: "You have until
Dec 9th." Bev heard Colton tell his mother, "See! That isn't my handwriting, is it?"

Later than night, Pam found another note hanging on a nail: "Death
doesn't hurt, but your dying will." A third note said: "This is the kind of
note that will be sent to your relatives when you die on Dec. 9th."

Bev says Pam was terrified, and understandably so. She was living alone
with just her young teenage son in the middle of thick dark woods and under attack every night. Even though Pam told Bev she trusted "no one!" Bev
hoped that helping her through these night terrors might break through
what she saw as Pam's denial about her drinking and lifestyle. She also
hoped it would give her and Geof a shot at helping Colton. They went as
far as setting up security cameras, alarms, and motion-detecting lights
around the trailer. Within minutes of Colton putting in a tape, the camera
captured a figure running back and forth in front of it. The police, though,
told Bev and Geof that they believed it was Colt on the video and that he
was responsible for all of it. They told them he was "a bad seed."

By early December, someone was setting fires on the trailer's front porch. The police showed up and this time questioned Colton and Pam separately. They told Pam that they'd had the notes analyzed and that it was Colton's handwriting. They also said they'd been hiding in her woods with night vision and had seen him running around throwing things. Pam said, "Bullshit!" and told them that even if Colton *did* write the notes, there was no way he could have thrown saw blades and other things she believed came at her when Colton was standing close by. One cop told her, "Say the word, Pam, and we'll arrest him right now."

"The hell you will," she said, and grabbed Colton, telling him not to say anything more to the deputies.

One positive thing that came from all the drama was that Geof spent time with Colton. After finding Colt walking alone along the main road again, they got to talking about boats. "He really perked up with that," says Geof. "So I said, 'Well, I know some people down there on the water, maybe we can find someone with a cool boat.'" Guys Geof knew had rebuilt a tiny steamboat, and he introduced them to Colton. "Colt went right up and got to talking to these two old-timers, asking them all kinds of questions about the boat. Next thing, he's asking me if he can go for a ride with them. I said, 'Sure, you can.' So I sat and waited for him. Crimey sakes, they had him out there for two hours—he loved it!"

After that, every time Geof found Colton out along the road—which was often—he picked him up and took him along wherever he was going. Geof says he felt Colton wasn't quite normal, "but I disagree with a lot of those initials they saddle kids with, ADD and that . . . I think if they had the right parenting, if the kid got the right response from their family, I don't think you'd have all those initials. Every child has trouble paying attention and acting proper if they haven't been brought up right."

Colton impressed Geof in a lot of ways. "He was a nice kid, polite and smart. Man, he knew the name of every airplane out there. He'd rattle off names right and left, then start describing each one of them for me. I'm thinking, This kid knows more than Boeing!"

DURING ONE OF THE fruitless searches for the invisible tormenters at the trailer, Bev took Colton aside and asked what she could do to help him. "He said that if I could get his mom to quit drinking that would be the best thing," she says. He told her, "She thinks that *I'm* the problem, but she doesn't realize that *she* has the problem . . . When I'm grown and gone she'll see that." Bev told Colton that no matter what his mom did, he was old enough to start making some of his own choices. She said he could start making some new friends, and promised that she and Geof would help him get involved with some constructive activities that would get him out of the house and wouldn't end up with him thrown in juvie. She offered to take him to Alateen and said, "Don't count on your mom to make changes: you do it!

"I talked for quite a while and Colt was silent," says Bev, who wrote everything that transpired during this time in long, detailed letters to her sister. "Then he started, and it was like he couldn't stop, it was like one big sentence. He told me he *never* has friends over because of the dump he lives in and how his mom is mean to him and everyone else, and anybody new that comes over gets met with a shotgun, and that he can tell if she's drunk or not by how she says hello on the phone and how he doesn't feel like going home if he hears her drunk hello, and how she tells him to give her gas money or she won't pick him up, and how he's glad when she runs out of money each month because then she can't buy beer, and that she spends several hundred dollars a month on cigarettes and beer and that money could be used to fix the place up! He said, 'I don't even know what she does all day,' because he does all the cleaning and the laundry. He told me about a friend of his whose mother was so nice, 'if Scott even gets a mosquito bite, his mom is right there looking at it and medicating it!' He said, 'Scott's mom is pretty, and they live in a nice house, and I just wish my mom could be like that. I told my mom how nice Scott's mom was and she said, "Well, goody for her! She's probably in debt up to her eyeballs!" My mom just doesn't understand that they aren't in debt, they work, and I asked her, "Why don't you get a job like a normal person?" and she said, "Why, Colton? So you can have all the pretty little toys you want and be a spoiled rotten brat? You want all that shit, get out and get yourself a job!" ' "

Bev assured Colton that they'd help him if he started to take some responsibility for his life.

The following day, Bev stopped by after delivering Santa Geof to Stanwood for the yearly parade. "Pam was sitting outside in her truck drinking and smoking, but Colton had obviously been working his butt off cleaning the yard and driveway, creating a huge pile of junk. He'd even trimmed a lilac bush and strung Christmas lights on it." Bev praised him effusively, and says he was very proud of his work.

Later, a local deputy Bev knew called her. "He told me I was 'maybe too nice' getting involved with Colton and Pam." The deputy said he thought that out of all the teens he'd ever dealt with in his many years on the island, Colton was "the worst of the worst." He also said he thought it was "way too late for Colton, that he's already gone." Bev's own mother also warned her away because of stories she'd heard from a friend working at the school.

Bev promised everyone that she'd be careful, but told them she still wanted to help Colt and, if possible, even Pam. She said she'd put her trust in God and repeatedly asked her friends and family to pray for all of them.

The next time Bev went over to Pam's, a knife whizzed past her shoulder from Colton's direction and almost hit Melanie. Bev confronted Colt, but he denied everything and told her, "I never want to see you again as long as I live!"

Bev asked Pam to send Colton away for a couple of days to see if the incidents stopped. Pam said she couldn't because last time he went to the one place that would take him he stole the homeowner's bank card. She added that "Colton's dad was a credit card thief." Bev also found that Colton had been rifling through her purse, taking cash.

Bev wrote to her sister that all the notes about the entire episode should eventually go to an author, "for their book about Colton, when he's in prison and when Pam gets drunk and shoots herself or someone else, or when Colton kills her. The only hope for these people is some sort of institution—for both of them!"

BEV AND GEOF DIDN'T give up, though. When Pam called to say Colton brought home his first A in math, Geof picked him up from school, took him go-cart racing, and bought him a remote control Hummer as a reward. Bev and Geof also hauled away mountains of junk—old toilets, car parts, and so on—that Colton had gathered when he cleaned up the property. "We really felt he hated living in a pig sty," so one day while Colton was at school, Bev says she and Geof went to the trailer to "swamp" his room. It'd been so crapped up that Colton was sleeping in with Pam. They spent four hours picking up and sweeping out. They laid down wall-to-wall carpet, installed a new bed, and put up shelves. The final touch was a throw rug with big glow-in-the-dark bare feet on it.

Pam warned them that Colton would freak if anyone touched his stuff, and made Bev and Geof promise to be there when he came home from school because she said she was "tired of the bruises." When they told Colton they'd fixed up his room, he yelled at Pam and ran into the trailer. After a few tense minutes, he came out and walked up to Bev. He handed her a Snickers bar, saying, "For all you've done."

After each promising moment, Bev thought that things would settle down in the trailer. The poltergeist, though, continued to terrorize Haven Place. "Colt called me, laughing," says Bev. "He held up the phone and I can hear the shotgun going off in the background and a drunken Pam screaming, 'That's right, you motherfucker son of a bitch, goddammit you come out, you lily-livered chickenshit!' And Colt's just cracking up."

Pam decided her next strategy to catch the perpetrators would be to lie under the trailer and shoot them with a BB gun. Geof told Colton that he'd come by and do some target practice with him. Colton was excited and repeatedly called Bev, saying, "Mom wants to know when Geof is coming by to shoot BBs with me." When the day came, though, Geof was busy and stopped by to tell Colton he had to postpone. Before Geof could get home, Colton called Bev and told her. Geof was met by an angry Mrs. Claus, or rather Mrs. Claws, who told him in no uncertain terms that this was a kid who'd been disappointed by adults all his life and Geof better get his ass back there. Geof turned right around, and he and Colton shot the BB gun for hours. Colt turned out to be a crack shot, excellent at picking off his mortal enemy: Pam's beer cans. *Plink, plink, plink.*

It felt to Bev and Geof that they were on the verge of a major break-through. Then it all came crashing down.

THE OLD-TIMERS WHO'D taken Colton out on their steamboat told Geof they'd be happy to show him the shop where they'd rebuilt the boat and made the parts. Geof asked Colton if he wanted to go, and got an enthusiastic "Yes!" They planned for Geof to pick Colton up that Saturday.

"A couple of days later," remembers Bev, "I answer the phone. It's Pam and she is mad. I ask her what's up and she says, 'Just put Geof on the phone!' " Geof gets on and has his ears fried.

"She demands to know why I'm taking her son away from her," says Geof. "I told her that's not what I was doing, but she says, 'Well, that's all he talks about, he wants to go everywhere with you and you keep taking him places! I don't know who you think you are. He is my son, not yours! So just back off!' She got vicious, told me off, and threatened to get a restraining order on me. So I said, 'Fine, if you don't want me to see him I won't.' And so I just backed off because . . . wow . . . that's Pam. I didn't want any trouble."

"We just then felt it was all hopeless and we weren't equipped to deal with it," says Bev. "It was very hard on us to realize we couldn't help that poor boy except to be there if he ever called."

The night raids on the trailer eventually stopped. Pam maintains it was neighbors, while the police believe it was Colt. They may both be right. There was a lot of anger toward Pam and Colt in that neighborhood. One of Colt's former friends says he knew a father and son who lived there at the time who "hated" Pam and Colt and wouldn't have hesitated to make their life hell as revenge for thefts they blamed on Colt. The graffiti and many of the coincidences in Bev's exhaustive catalog of events, though, suggest Colt was responsible for much of it. No charges were ever filed against anyone.

17

On March 1, 2005, the employees at the Stanwood Library arrived to find three windows broken. Beneath one of the windows were footprints made by someone hoisting himself up to the eight-foot-high sill. There was also blood splatter from the burglar apparently cutting himself on the glass. Once inside, he took the $61 in the cash box.

The Washington State Police crime lab tested the blood and found there was only a 1-in-150,000,000,000,000,000 chance that it hadn't dripped from Colton Harris-Moore. "I think that one's bullshit," says Pam. "Why would he go in the library? I don't think they even collect fines for overdue books anymore."

On March 7, Colton was sent to Echo Glen Children's Center, a medium/maximum-security juvenile facility in Snoqualmie, Washington, sentenced to six weeks for theft 2 and theft 3. From this point on, there wasn't a single moment in Colton Harris-Moore's life when he wasn't under investigation, wanted on warrant, or actually serving time.

Colt left Echo Glen at the end of April, and in May was again expelled from Stanwood Middle, this time for "continual disruption to the educational process and danger to self and others." The expulsion led to another week in juvie because getting into trouble in school was a violation of his parole. Pam told the court that Colton wasn't following "reasonable household rules," which also violated his parole.

On November 22, another alarm went off at Elger Bay Elementary School. When the deputies arrived, they found Pam's black Mazda pickup in the parking lot, filled with stolen computer equipment. Inside the school, they discovered shoe prints and Colton's fingerprints. They impounded Pam's truck and arrested Colton for the theft of an Apple computer and accessories.

By December 2005, at least twelve referrals to Child Protective Services had been recorded regarding Colton. Whenever there was a big fight at home now, though, Colton ended up going to jail. On Pearl Harbor Day, another domestic disturbance call led to Colton's being arrested again for assault on Pam.

Despite failing grades and multiple suspensions and expulsions, the schools continued to socially promote Colton. He was enrolled in high school and then, in a last-ditch effort to keep him in the educational system, he was transferred to a high school with alternative programs. However, the school reported to the court that Colton didn't attend classes, another parole violation. He also didn't show up for his community service, and then he got hit with another PSP in the first degree.

Colton served another fifteen days, and by the time he got out, the police already had another piping hot arrest warrant ready to serve, this one for the Stanwood Library job. Deputies went to the trailer to collect him, but Colton ran off into his woods. He was now beyond catch-22: he had to go to school or violate his probation, but if he showed up at class the police would nab him on the outstanding warrant. So Colton went on the lam for the first time.

Though the Haven Place trailer was still more like the Thunderdome (Colton told a psychologist that it was during this time in 2006 when "she told me that she wished I would die"), he sometimes stayed with Pam. Other nights, the fugitive camped in the woods. The rest of the time, police believe, he either squatted inside unoccupied homes or crashed with friends, successfully eluding capture for two months. Island County deputies swung by the trailer every so often and noticed a leaning tower of pizza boxes in the bushes. Playing a hunch, they asked the pizza place to let them know the next time they had a delivery to Pam's address. According to the Island County Sheriff's Office, one officer donned the pizza guy's jacket and cap and carried the pie to the door. He saw the silhouette of someone peeking out the window at him, but the disguise worked, because the door opened and there stood Colton expecting some tasty 'za. Instead, the cop gave him a big smile and said, "Hello, Colt."

It was revenge of the Noid. Colton turned to Pam, deflated. She looked up, realized what had happened, and told the officers preparing to cuff her son, "That was a good idea!"

IN JUNE 2006, COLTON began serving a thirty-day sentence at the Denney Juvenile Detention Center for the Stanwood Library burglary. At his hearing, his probation officer offered the court this assessment: "Colton is a fifteen-year-old young man with extensive criminal history with juvenile court. Colton and his mother live alone on Camano Island. She continues to minimize his criminal behavior and make excuses for him. The one positive thing that Colton has going is that he doesn't use drugs or alcohol."

ACCORDING TO KORY BRYAND who was also doing short stints in juvenile detention, Colton had as much trouble getting along with the kids in juvie as he did on the outside. "All the guys in there had problems with him. Colt would just talk crap all the time. The only reason guys weren't beating him up is that nobody wanted to go on lockdown." The threat of being confined to his room without privileges didn't worry Colt, though. "He got put on lockdown for backtalking the COs [corrections officers]."

While Colt was inside, Island County deputies were busy investigating a stolen credit card that was used in May to make ATM withdrawals and to buy a laptop and wireless router—cash and goodies worth $3,708.57. They traced it to Colton.

"Colt always had money from credit cards," says Harley. "That's how you could tell he was smart . . . you have to be pretty smart to get the pin off a credit card."

Mike Bulmer remembers that even back in middle school Colton had a debit card hidden in the woods. "He'd say, 'Don't follow me,' and he'd go off and get the card and then we'd go get the money out of an ATM. He'd give me some and some other guys some, like he was doing it to kinda get friends."

Colton walked out of the detention center on July 7 . . . now *really* determined not to go back.

During Colton's legal limbo, he and Pam headed off island for a family reunion. They arrived at Sandy's spread in Arlington with Pam's little pickup loaded down with bales of hay they'd picked up for a relative's horses.

"I hadn't seen him for a long time," says Colt's oldest cousin. "He gets out of the truck, tall, thin, and barefoot." Colt, she says, visited with Sandy's horses and played croquet with his second cousins while the adults hung out and talked. "When Colt came over to the picnic table where the adults were, he was very polite and quiet." Once he felt comfortable, she says, his sense of humor started to come out. "We're all smart-asses in our family, and he fit in. He also had that typical teenage sarcasm." Colt spoke a lot about Melanie: "He kept saying how much he loved that dog." His other big topic was airplanes.

"It's wide open out there, with a lot of planes flying overhead, and every one that flew by, Colt was 'Oh that's a blah blah blah blah'; he knew every detail about every plane. I was amazed." Someone at the table asked him what he wanted to be. "He said, 'I'm going to be a pilot.' We all knew that he'd been getting into trouble, and Sandy said, 'If you keep out of jail.'"

Colt, says his cousin, was calm and cool "until Pam started needling at him. She told us about his violent rages when he starts running around screaming and tearing things up. She said that one night she was on the computer and Colt wanted to use it. She wouldn't get off, so he picked it up and threw it out the window."

That image, says his cousin, didn't fit the Colt they saw in front of them, who was "quiet and respectful to all the other adults." It was obvious, though, that there were issues between him and Pam. "They just sat there sparring, she'd push his buttons and they'd fight over anything and everything . . . really weird."

She says Pam complained that Colton had stopped taking his meds. Colt said that he stopped because he didn't like them. "She also told us that Colt wouldn't go to therapy anymore 'because he thinks he knows more than they do.'"

His cousin says Colt got madder and madder until he finally ran off to the horse barn. "Pam yelled after him, 'Yeah, run away, that's what you always do, Colt, run away!'"

. . . .

On July 14, 2006, the Island County prosecutor filed two counts for the credit card crime: theft in the first degree and a PSP. Colt was ordered to appear before the court. Knowing there could be only one outcome from the hearing—more jail time—he skipped it. On July 28, a warrant was issued for his arrest and Colton Harris-Moore was once again a kid on the lam.

The fact that he was on a small island with limited room to run didn't faze Colton. He took one of Pam's tents and set up a campsite in the thick brush at the front southwest corner of her Haven Place property. He set up fallback camps at other spots and, according to Harley, he also spent time sheltering with people willing to help him. Colt didn't just lie low and hide out, though; he actually stepped up his criminal activities.

For one thing, he had to feed himself and he'd learned the hard way that it wasn't as simple as waiting for the pizza guy to show up. Fortunately, all of his childhood ramblings around the island came in very handy. He knew every forest path and every backyard in the South End. He also knew the trusting nature of the community, where few people bothered to lock their doors or worried about security.

18

"It was a battle of wits, and I guess I lost," laughs Jack Boyle (not his real name).

Jack certainly didn't come to the battle unarmed. He has a graduate degree in nuclear engineering from MIT and a forty-year career at a prestigious university—nine as dean of the graduate school.

Jack and his wife, Louise, bought a piece of South End Camano back in 1978. Their two acres straddled South Camano Drive, with the building site atop a 140-foot bluff overlooking the waters of Saratoga Passage. The other acre was across the road, a thickly wooded buffer that backed up to an undeveloped patch at the top of Haven Place. The Boyles and their kids camped on the property until 1991, when they built a summer home.

"We'd been told to only use local people when we built or we'd run into all kinds of trouble with permits and things," says Louise. "There's a lot of insider stuff that goes on. The people in the interior of the island are all full-time residents and they kind of own the island, while a lot of people on the coast are just vacation homeowners and are looked on as interlopers." She says the split goes beyond who spends the most time on the island. "Waterfront property is very expensive, interior property very cheap, and that tends to cause a social divide. It's really two cultures."

Still, the Boyles loved the island and their terrific view. In 2002, the now-retired couple decided to give Camano a full-time try. When designing their vacation home, they hadn't bothered planning for all the storage space necessary in a permanent home. Island folks usually even go beyond that and keep a large larder so they don't have to hit the grocery store as often. To rectify the situation, the Boyles enclosed the crawlspace beneath the house, creating a basement. Part was walled off as a little workshop for Jack's tools, and another room served as a wine cellar, which they kept fully stocked with about a hundred bottles. The rest was space for household stuff and, because the kitchen didn't have enough cabinet room, food. The big freezer and shelves were filled with everything from frozen fruit to Frappuccinos.

The Boyles found themselves going down to the basement several times a day and never thought of locking the door. In late 2004, Louise began having little inklings that something was off. "I'd always be saying to myself, 'I could've sworn I bought a case of Coke,' or 'I knew I had this or that in the food reserves.' I'd go down and the shelves were looking empty." This went on for more than a year. "I kept thinking, I'm losing it," she says, laughing.

Then, one evening in the summer of 2006, Louise asked Jack to take a gallon of milk down to the basement fridge. The next morning when he went to get it for breakfast, it was gone. Now they definitely knew they weren't imagining things. Jack went out and bought a lock for the door. "Half the time we'd forget the key and have to come back up," says Jack. So they hid the key on a hook underneath the trellis near the door. "It probably took him three seconds to find that."

Not long after they'd put the lock on, the Boyles were woken at midnight by an alarm going off next door. Someone had stolen Jack's bolt cutters out of the basement and used them to cut a padlock off the neighbor's storage shed. The next morning, they found the bolt cutters on the path that led through their woods to Haven Place.

Jack and Louise began to talk to neighbors and discovered that there were a lot of similar things going on. Then an Island County detective came to their door. He showed them a picture of Colton, saying the department had good reason to believe he was the one breaking into area homes. The cop asked if they'd noticed their front door. "There were pry marks where someone had stuck a crowbar and tried to force the door open," says Jack. In their front garden, Louise's cat statue had been tipped over, "obviously someone looking for a hidden key." Someone had also tried to pry open their locked mailbox.

The Boyles had installed a security system when their home was built, but never used it unless they were going out of town. Now they began to turn it on every night. Knowing that the basement key "hidden" under the trellis was still the weak link, Jack bought an expensive combination lock that didn't use a key but opened with a punch code.

So . . . the Boyles were more than surprised when a neighbor who'd come up for the weekend went into the woods across the road to clear some brush and surprised a burglar in Frappuccino delicto. The perp took off through the trees toward Haven Place before the neighbor got a look at him, but he left behind his partially consumed, highly caffeinated picnic. He'd polished off a can of Diet Coke, four Nature Valley Sweet & Salty bars, a jar of gourmet jelly, and at least two Starbucks Frappuccinos, leaving behind all the empty wrappers and jars, along with nine Fraps out of a twelve-pack and a Ziploc of frozen strawberries.

The neighbor called Jack, who went up the trail and couldn't believe his eyes. "That's our stuff!" He went to his basement and found the door closed and locked. Inside, though, the cupboard was most definitely bare.

They called the sheriff but say they just got a shrug. This kind of thing and worse was happening all over the South End and the deputies didn't have the time or inclination to investigate a minor pantry raid. It was up to Jack to put on his figurative tweed thinking cap, go Sherlock, and try to solve a classic "locked room" mystery.

"I finally remembered that when I first bought the fancy lock I'd spread out the parts and instructions in the basement, but didn't get it installed that first day." On a hunch, Jack went to his filing cabinet and pulled out the paperwork for the lock. "One page was missing," he laughs. "The page with the combination. He'd gotten in, figured it all out, and only taken that one page."

Jack reset the combination, but their stuff continued to walk away: two-thirds of a case of Diet Coke, half a case of classic Coke, more specialty jellies, an eight-pack of tuna, a carton of protein bars . . .

The basement door lies beneath their bedroom window and Louise's superpower is her hearing. A number of times she awoke in the middle of the night to the sound of their neighbor's hot tub going when they weren't on the island, and she's sure Colton was sneaking in for soaks. But she never heard anyone rummaging in the basement. Again and again they'd set their security system—which showed all doors alarmed—then go to bed. No alarms would go off, but they'd get up to find that more stuff was missing—more snack bars, two cans of whipped cream, Dijon mustard, flaxseed meal . . .

It drove Jack crazy. One day he opened the door and it finally struck him. The basement alarm worked via a sensor in the door jamb and a magnet on the door itself. When the door closed, the magnet armed the switch. If the door opened, pulling the magnet away, the alarm went off. Now, staring at the door, something didn't look quite right. Jack suddenly realized what it was. "He'd unscrewed the magnet from the door and glued it to the sensor so it would never go off!"

Jack was impressed. Despite the fact they were always home during the burglaries, they say they never felt threatened. Unlike a "typical" invasion by teens, they also say there was never any malicious damage, nothing else was ever disturbed in the basement, and the wine and hard liquor were never even touched.

To Jack, it was more like trying to outsmart a Mensa-level raccoon. He bought motion detectors and positioned them around the house. Each one went off with a separate custom recording that would alert them: "Someone at basement door," "Someone at front door," and so on. They were very high-tech.

Next to go missing were a box of Kleenex, Ziploc bags, more fancy jam, one of Jack's backpacks, a bunch of drill bits, and two boxes of Christmas lights. "The most poignant," says Louise, who kept a running tally, "were the Christmas lights."

"I couldn't figure out for a long time how he got around the motion detectors," says Jack. "Then I finally pulled down one of the sensors. Here he'd taken the batteries out and then put it back up so I wouldn't know it was disabled."

It got to the absurd state that after each raid Jack would automatically walk up into the woods knowing that he'd find a trail of wrappers, cans, and other litter scattered along the path that lead directly to Haven Place. This raccoon had no compunction about crapping up the forest. After calling the police, Jack would go out to clean up.

It wasn't until months later that the Boyles noticed that the cordless phone they kept in the basement was missing. They found it in their neighbor's dog house, which sat within range of the transmitter. The black Lab never used its dog house and was quickly ruled out as a suspect.

Other homes along Camano Drive were also getting hit multiple times for things like food and bikes, and the police told residents that they suspected Colton in all of it. Across the island from the Boyles' and a mile south of Pam's cabin, Maxine K., a grandmother of eighteen, discovered that someone was foraging in her garage freezer, scarfing up ice cream and frozen pizzas along with whatever canned food was on the shelves. She and her husband would find the empty boxes and containers in the nearby woods, and even found evidence of a fire where she believes the burglar was cooking the food. Knowing that it was Colton—whom she referred to as "Island Boy" and says she felt sorry for—at first she didn't even bother calling the police.

Not everyone was taking the thefts in stride, though. One of the Boyles' neighbors, "summer people," says Louise, made it clear that if he had the opportunity inside his house, he wouldn't hesitate to shoot Colt. "There was a lot of that around the island," she says.

Still, many of the South Enders empathized with a rebellious kid who'd grown up in miserable circumstances and was now forced to hide out in the woods and Yogi Bear his meals. Colton lost some sympathy, though, when people learned he wasn't just taking Frappuccinos and frozen pizzas.

As easily as he could get into the Boyles' basement no matter what the security measures, Colt could get inside almost anyone's house. And while he'd refused to study for school, he did plenty of homework when it came to burglaries.

"Colt would call and say, 'Hey, come on out to Camano, I found some houses," says Harley, who was living in Everett when Colt went on the lam. "I was still on probation and I didn't want to go out there, but he said he'd pay me plus split whatever we got."

Harley says he'd take the bus out to the island and Colt would pick him up at the stop. "He'd already have a stolen car." Harley says he and Colt took cars only for transportation—borrowing them to get from burglary job to job—and never tried to sell them. "One house, we took the car and drove it around and then took it back exactly where we got it. We even cleaned it up and all."

Harley says "you'd be amazed" how many houses they could hit in one night. Usually, he says, Colt had already done the prep work, identifying the houses and sometimes even greasing their way inside. "He had keys to some of them . . ." Harley hints that someone was providing the keys to Colt, but police believe that Colt more likely just sniffed around until he found the emergency keys that people squirrel away under welcome mats, flowerpots, conspicuous rocks, garden gnomes, or on top of door frames—all the obvious places that we homeowners think are so clever. Harley says that if Colt didn't have the key it was still no problem: "We'd just break in."

Harley's criteria for a good target: "Any home where nobody's at."

Once inside, they were primarily looking for jewelry and cash, but didn't limit themselves if something struck their fancy. "I took a couple of pool sticks, two piece, alligator skin case," says Harley. But taking things like that had particular risks. "My mom could tell that I'd stolen them and she confiscated them."

No amount of cash was too little for Harley to pick up, and he was incredulous that Colton passed up change. "He just left that alone, wasn't interested! I was like, 'Cool, I'll take it, I need it for bus fare anyway.' I had about $120 worth of change just from houses out there."

Harley also searched homes for drugs and booze but says Colt never did. "I did enough of that for both of us." And though he says he was never afraid during a job, Harley carried a gun. "I carried it because I could . . . and because I'm not allowed to have 'em, so it was doing what I do best: being rebellious." He says he knew about the serious penalties for carrying a firearm during a crime. "I knew I would never get caught with it. All you gotta do is hit the woods, and I knew plenty of places I could dump it."

At the end of their night shift, Harley would head back to Everett with his share of the loot. He says they fenced what they could, and he'd wait for the next call from Colt to come out and work the island again.

The burglaries with Harley were old-school B and Es: get in and loot the place. Residents came home to find that everything of any value that could be easily carried had been taken. Colt twisted the standard a little because he'd also take things any professional burglar would ignore but that he wanted—not to fence but to play with. Things like remote control toys.

At the same time, though, he began to hone sophisticated skills and to develop his own brand of more delicate crime that mixed ballsy blue-collar burglaries with white-collar computer capers. For these jobs, Colt preferred to work alone.

Colt had always been fascinated with technology, and tech gear was one of his top targets. Friends say that before they knew he was burglarizing local homes, they always wondered how dirt-poor Colt always had the latest iPod and other gadgets. Like every other kid of his generation, Colt was more than proficient at computers. Early on he also discovered the power and possibilities of the Internet, both for benign uses—his Myspace profile under the user name Harris90210 listed his occupation as "pilot"—and as a tool for learning about and committing crimes. The Web, even more than his frontier island, was the real contemporary Wild West. To a budding outlaw, it offered everything from untraceable ways to stay connected with friends and family, to aerial surveillance photos of targets, and complete research on potential victims. It also provided step-by-step instructions on criminal techniques.

Say a wrong-crowd kid lets you in on a secret: you can open almost any door lock using something called a bump key. Google it up, then go to You-Tube and find a helpful selection of how-tos on using bump keys to open locks in two or three seconds without leaving any sign of forced entry. As a bonus, they offer easy instructions on how to make them. Why bother, though, when the sponsored links that pop up along with the search results include several "ask no questions" online shops where for about $30 you can order a full set that will get you into practically any house in the country? Ah, but you need a credit card to order the keys and you don't have one. That calls for identity theft.

There are lots of ways crooks go about ID theft. Colton dabbled in the simplest form: stealing credit card offers out of mailboxes, filling them out, and then intercepting the cards. However, he also realized that if you can ninja yourself in and out of someone's house without them knowing you've been there, forget about it, you've got the keys to the kingdom.

Colt's combination of twenty-first-century tech savviness and nineteenth-century outlaw cojones came together to create a remarkably effective criminal. He wasn't some Cheetos-stained hacker trying to break past software firewalls. This was a guy who would physically break into your home and make himself comfortable while using your computer, Internet connection, and good credit against you.

Boot up the ubiquitous home computer . . . If you're one of the few who actually bother to password protect your system, it takes a few extra minutes to reboot it with an easily available password-breaking program the thief brought on a USB stick. Once he's logged on, chances are you've saved your Amazon, eBay, PayPal, and other account passwords in the Web browser and they'll fill in automatically. If not, they're probably all listed on a document saved on the hard drive, or else sticky noted somewhere close to the computer. The credit card info for payment is either saved as a default for the retailer accounts, or the cards themselves are in the house ready to be entered into the online form. *Click click:* residential burglary at a whole new level.

Traditional thieves are stuck with whatever's lying around the house, hoping for jewelry, electronics, and guns that are easily converted into cash. However, a burglar on the lam determined to remain in the same small area has got to be careful about trusting local fences. He's also not too comfortable walking into retail stores to buy new clothes, the latest music and tech toys, self-defense equipment, and other necessities. What does he do, though, if, when he breaks into your home, you don't have the kind of laptop he wants, or the latest-generation iPod, or your clothes don't fit him? No worries: he just uses your credit cards and computer to order whatever he wants. It's custom burglary with convenient overnight shipping. The challenge is making sure you don't have a clue that he's been in your house—that way you probably won't know what happened until the credit card bill arrives a month later.

Delivery is another tricky part. Colt obviously couldn't have illegal purchases delivered to any address connected to him, his mom, or any known associates because that would give the authorities a paper trail. So that basically left three options: have it delivered to the credit card owner's legitimate address, use an unsuspecting third party, or create a fake address. Colt ultimately used all these methods. Another aspect of the rural, trusting nature that helped him get away with things for so long on Camano and later on Orcas was the unofficial "island rules" used by delivery companies. With homes typically so far apart from one another and from the roads, drivers have little compunction about leaving packages on porches, ripe for the picking.

The innovative crimes, the "subtle" thefts where he sneaked in and out without the homeowner realizing anything was amiss, became one of Colton's identifying MOs. Together with the numerous joint operations with Harley during this period, the Island County Sheriff's Office suspected Colt was involved in dozens of burglaries and car prowls on Camano during a period of just a few months. The *Stanwood/Camano News* listed more burglaries each week, and word quickly got around that it wasn't just food and necessities going missing. Camano residents began to lose sympathy for Colton Harris-Moore, as well as their patience with the Island County Sheriff's Office.

To add to the pressure, it was an election year. One of the new candidates for sheriff, Mark C. Brown, was an ex-navy officer who served thirty-plus years in the Washington State Patrol. Colton's crime spree had become such an issue that one of Brown's campaign pledges was that, if elected, catching Colton Harris-Moore would be one of his department's top priorities.

Not that the deputies weren't already trying. "We had many other things going on in the county that we'd be better off spending our department's time and money on," says Detective Ed Wallace. "But we started setting up special operations to try to catch Colton."

Each time the sheriff's office sent a team out after Colt it meant pulling manpower off much busier Whidbey Island to reinforce the few Camano deputies. Still, they began moving officers and burning up overtime out of an already tight budget. The first place they targeted, naturally, was Haven Place.

"THE POLICE ASKED TO use my property to keep watch for Colt," says Carol Star. "I gave them permission, but they were so obvious! They came in black SUVs and parked in the street. They came up my driveway wearing camouflage makeup and carrying machine guns, and were so loud I could hear them inside my house. They weren't sneaking up on anyone. I told them, 'You guys need to come in an old beat-up van or something, and you're making too much noise.' So one of them says, 'Well, we want him to know that the police are around.' Yeah, then why would you be wearing camouflage uniforms and makeup!?"

The deputies were able to infiltrate Haven Place stealthily enough at least once, though. "Some of us were in the trees at the bottom of the road, others in the bushes closer to Pam's," says Wallace, who was part of the six-person team detailed to try to catch Colton.

Ed Wallace is a cop's cop, in shape and not only a detective but a member of the Hard Entry and Arrest Team (HEAT) that busts into meth houses and does the county's other dangerous dirty work. A second-generation Island County deputy, Wallace, at forty, already had twenty years of policing under his belt plus a stint as an army MP. In a small force (Island County has the smallest sheriff's department, per capita, in Washington State) staff gets spread around. Wallace also serves as the department's computer expert, and he drew the short straw and became its public information officer, tasked with dealing with the media. The Colton Harris-Moore case had Wallace wearing all of his different hats. What he wanted most, though, like all the Island County cops, was to catch him.

"Colt always counted on us playing by the rules," says Wallace, noting that the fugitive banked on officers' professionalism. The deputies did carry Tasers, but Wallace says no one who got within the sixteen-foot range ever felt he had a good enough shot at Colt.

Time after time, deputies waded into the sea of waist-high ferns that filled the understory beneath Camano's tall second-growth trees to search for Colt. Especially in the summer, you can't see fifty feet into the woods. You'd literally have to stumble onto someone or his camp as long as he kept it low profile. But even finding his camp didn't mean cornering Colt. "He'd set up one camp to live in that had several escape routes," says Chris Ellis. "Then he'd have several backup camps stocked with food and water in case he had to run. He always had a plan. Colton Harris-Moore was a thinking criminal by the time he was ten years old. And he wasn't afraid. We searched one of his sites and found out later that he'd been sitting in a tree fifty feet above our heads watching us the whole time."

All year long, Pacific Northwest forest floors remain a maze of fallen branches and slick, moss-covered logs, which made it dangerous, when they did spot him, to give chase. As Colt and Harley knew, the police were reticent to go running into the woods, with reason. One Camano deputy who chased Colt through the trees injured his knee so badly that he was out of work for several weeks.

That night on Haven Place was one of many close encounters the Island County cops had with Colton Harris-Moore during his run. "One of our guys was moving down the road and thought he heard footsteps," says Wallace. "He froze and brought up his night vision, and here's Colt, sauntering right down the middle of the road about twenty feet away. He lit him up with his flashlight and we jumped out, but Colt's a gazelle and off he goes. He makes it to the woods and is running to beat all hell. We tried to chase him down, but frankly, I'm not going to run blindly through the trees and lose an eye or break a leg for a burglary suspect."

ON SEPTEMBER 16, TWO Island County deputies arrived at the trailer. According to Pam's sister Sandy, Pam called 911 three times during this six-and-a-half-month period to tell police that Colt was on the property and for them to come get him.

No one answered the door, but one of the deputies spotted a few items that he recognized as reported stolen—all remote control toys: a boat, a helicopter, and little ZipZap cars. There was obviously a lot more evidence around, so they arranged a search warrant. Pam still wasn't there when the cops returned, so they climbed into the trailer through a window. They didn't find anything inside, and began searching the rest of the property. Colt saw the cops and melted into the woods before they reached his campsite. He didn't go far, though, and watched as the deputies struck the motherlode.

Some items they found were of obvious fenceable value, and others were useful, like the Swiss army knife, six flashlights, and four sets of binoculars—it always helps to have a spare or three. Some things, though, like the toys, seemed to have simply struck Colt's fancy. A partial list of stolen property recovered from his campsite and a couple of caches around Pam's lot showed his omnivorous habits.

Deputies found nine cell phones, two GPS units, four laptops (two PCs and two Macs), a video and two still cameras, an iPod and three other music players, a box of .38 bullets, several watches, eleven jewelry boxes filled with everything from pearl necklaces to pink costume jewelry, a motorcycle helmet, six *Playboy* magazines, a telescope, a Trek mountain bike, fireworks, wire cutters, a motion sensor, a beard trimmer, two calendars, and a commemorative Boeing coin. They found dozens of credit cards and a social security card, a health insurance card, a driver's license, a military ID, a birth certificate, a checkbook, and personal mail, all in the names of various Camano victims. The cops also hauled away Colt's personal items, like his clothes, nail clippers, ChapStick, medications, and size fourteen sneakers. After they'd gathered up all the loot, they added Colt's dog, Melanie, who'd been faithfully guarding the campsite. They drove off, leaving behind a receipt.

Once the coast was clear, Colt came out of the woods and scribbled a note to Pam (spelling intact):

MOM, cops were here everythings on lockdown. I'm leaving 4-Wennachi won't be back est. 2 month. I'll contact you they took Mell. I'm going to have my affiliates take care of that. P.S.—Cops wanna play hu!? Well its not no lil game . . . It's war! & tell them that.

Pam called the sheriff's office and told them about the note. When a deputy came to collect it, she also handed over a stolen laser construction level that had been inside the trailer.

Police say they never followed up on the one clue in the note: "leaving 4-Wennachi." But apparently the sunny town of Wenatchee on the Columbia River east of the Cascades became a safe haven for Colton at least twice when he was on the run over the following years.

CASA, THE CAMANO ANIMAL Shelter Association, is the island's home for homeless dogs and cats. It consists of a compound of metal buildings and fenced yards exactly one-quarter mile from the tiny Island County Sheriff's Office cop shop on East Camano Drive—so close that you can walk or drive between them without leaving the parking lots of various county buildings. CASA has a contract with the county to temporarily house impounded pets, and that's where the deputies took Melanie at least twice while Colt was at large.

"They were chasing Colt through the woods one night," says Pam, "and he called me on his cell phone saying come get his dog because he had to let go of her. So I drove down—it wasn't even half a block away—and this lady officer says, 'You can't have her because she's evidence.' And I said, 'What is she gonna do, get up on the stand and testify?'"

From all available records, it appears Melanie stayed faithful to Colt: the cops were never able to get her to roll over and speak.

At least one of the times they grabbed Melanie, the cops did it specifically to try to lure Colt into coming to rescue her. If this was a war, Melanie was, for a while, a POW.

North and east of CASA lie patches of woods, and that's where a squad of deputies hid to wait for Colt. To ensure their success, they also stationed two deputies inside the animal shelter. Anyone approaching the CASA compound had to cross at least one road and some open ground before getting to the building or the little copse of trees just south of the fenced dog pens. If the officers outside saw someone approaching, they'd radio the inside team. If somehow Colt or an "affiliate" was able to sneak up to the building unseen, the deputies inside would hear him breaking in and would call in the outside troops. They all settled in, daring Colt to try to break Melanie out of the slammer. They waited . . . and waited . . . and waited. Sometime in the night, the ambush went askew. According to a source familiar with the operation, the officers inside CASA left their positions because they got cold. They snuck out stealthily so Colt, if he was watching, wouldn't see them and realize it was a trap. They did such a good job, though, that the cops staked out in the woods didn't know they'd left.

The inside officers eventually returned to their post and once again the trap was set. Only one problem: no bait. Melanie was gone. Someone had gotten past the surveillance, found the right cage, sprang Melanie, and then made it out again—this time with beagle in tow—all without being seen. Or heard, as anyone who's ever walked into a kennel knows the racket the dogs make whenever someone new walks in.

That's the kind of stuff legends are made of.

19

If Colton left the island after the tent raid, he didn't leave for long. In early October, he escalated his war against law enforcement by stealing a digital camera from a Washington State Patrol car. Shortly after, he showed up at the trailer to play paparazzi, taking several pictures of Van. On the twentieth of that month, an Island County deputy taking another swing through the woods around Pam's reported that he heard someone "crashing through the brush" and suspected it was Colton. He gave chase and stumbled onto another campsite. Melanie was there again, tied to a tree. A search recovered two cell phones and a copy of *Flight Training* magazine addressed to Eric Moore at Pam's address. Records show that Colton had been receiving the magazine designed for student pilots for at least six months.

The deputy also found a camera, the Canon Powershot stolen from the WSP police car. A quick scroll through the photos showed a smiling face that the deputies instantly recognized as Van Jacobsen. One of the photos showed Van mugging for the photographer with his finger up his nose. The cops asked Van to come down for a chat and he admitted that Colt had come by and taken pictures.

In the November election, Mark Brown won the Island County sheriff's job and prepared to take over the following January. He would inherit a force with budget issues and the inability to catch a teenage serial burglar running wild on the skinny south end of Camano Island.

With the heat increasing, Colt began to concentrate on the less-invasive custom credit card thefts. Maxine K., the spritely eighty-something grandma who'd been losing ice cream and pizza, received a call from the Kitsap

County Sheriff's Office. Lying just south of Island County, Kitsap is a fragmented peninsula that branches into Puget Sound between the Seattle-Tacoma metro area and the Olympic Peninsula. A Kitsap deputy told Maxine that one of their residents who'd been visiting Camano had an unauthorized online charge on his credit card and that the package was scheduled to be delivered to her house.

When the package arrived, Maxine called the Island County Sheriff's Office. A deputy came out and, according to Maxine, said, "Hmmm," and went back to the office to figure out what to do, leaving the package with her. In the meantime, a power company service truck showed up to deal with an outage next door. Maxine's phone rang.

"It was some fella who said, 'I'm so-and-so and I live at the end of your street . . .'" Maxine, who'd been living there full-time for fifteen years and had island connections going back much longer, replied, "No, you don't. Nobody by that name lives here.

"He asked me why the power company truck was out front . . . I was very suspicious of him." After Maxine hung up with the mystery caller, the Island County deputy phoned back and told Maxine that they couldn't take the package, saying that "it was Kitsap County's problem." Maxine told the deputy about the strange caller. The deputy ran the name and told Maxine that it was the name of a resident, but not anyone living where the caller said he did. And it definitely wasn't someone who lived where he could see the power company truck near Maxine's. It was, said the deputy, the name of one of Pam Kohler's neighbors on Haven Place.

At this moment, Island County had a clear bead on Colton; he'd even baited his own trap. Maxine couldn't believe it when the deputy told her they weren't going to do anything about it.

Maxine had brought the package inside, but when the Island County Sheriff's Office told her and her elderly husband they were on their own, her husband said, "Forget this," and set the box outside. Their house sits a good thirty yards from the main road and isn't visible from the street—no casual passerby could see the package.

"Of course," says Maxine, "the next morning it was gone."

The police still didn't come out, but Maxine and her husband found tracks and figured out where Colt had been hiding. At the top of their driveway, above a sign that reads CAMP RUNAMUCK, is a forest-green plywood treehouse they'd built for their grandkids. It was a pretty luxe structure in its day, accessed by a ladder and featuring a Plexiglas window that provides a nice view of the front of the house—ideal to see deliveries.

LOCAL KIDS LIKE KORY occasionally ran across Colton as he roamed the island. "He always had that dog with him . . . I don't know how he fed it." Kory says that at first, none of the South End kids had any thought of turning Colton in. Most of them were having their own troubles with the deputies. That didn't mean Colton was safe, though. He had a close shave after leaving a house Kory says he'd just burgled. "We saw him head into the woods and one of the guys who lived at the house came out, drunk, with a bottle of booze in one hand and a shotgun in the other. He was pissed because he said Colton had stolen some of his electronics, and he shot at him, trying to hit him. He missed, though, and then Colton was gone into the trees."

Colton himself was seldom without a weapon of some sort, often a knife, but according to Harley and the police, there were also handguns. "Colt had done a burglary in which we knew guns were taken," says Chris Ellis. "He'd escalated to being armed and then graduated to guns. My deputies and I knew from that point on that any interactions with him might be deadly." Colton said he packed a gun because he was associating with some tough guys around this time and he was nervous about them possibly coming after him. Harley—all five feet six inches and 135 pounds—was actually the duo's muscle instead of Colton, who now stood six-foot-two.

"Colt had a couple of kids trying to jack him for money," says Harley. "I stopped them. I may be short, but I grow a couple of inches when I'm mad . . . Colt always said I was like a blowfish that way."

Colton's childhood friend, Anne, had started dating Harley a few months before his and Colt's crime spree became the talk of the town. "He smoked pot and had friends who could get alcohol, so he was cool . . . It was kinda a bad-boy thing," says Anne. "And here Harley turns out to be this perfectly polite, immaculate gentleman. Never said a bad thing about anyone. Even my dad, who hates everyone, was impressed and thought he was a great guy."

Harley, though, didn't tell Anne what he and her old friend Colton were up to, and she only found out when she got into a bit of trouble herself. "I got caught shoplifting, and me and my best friend are in the back of the Stanwood police car talking about how we were going to tell Harley about it. Suddenly the cop slams on the brakes, turns around, and says, 'You don't mean Harley Ironwing, do you?' And I'm like, 'Umm, yes, why?' When we got to the cop shop, he started questioning me about Harley and Colt breaking into places and do I know anything about it. I'm like, 'No, but I'm gonna beat his ass when I see him.'"

In January, Sheriff Mark Brown was sworn in and immediately ordered more resources sent to Camano to catch Colton, saying that the fifteen-year-old was "causing havoc over there." Brown attended a community meeting held on the island to address the increasing anger and frustration. Residents came with questions, including, says Chris Ellis, "Why can't you do your f'n job?" According to the Boyles and others who attended, the sheriff didn't have many answers. "He didn't share any information," says Louise. Instead, he spent most of the time seemingly blaming the victims. "He asked, 'Well, how many of you have a locking mailbox? How many of you have security lights outside?' He just kept slamming us, and when at one point I mentioned that we had been out of town when something happened, he said, 'See, you go out of town all the time.' I was so mad."

Brown said he was giving the community some much-needed straight talk about what was making them such easy targets.

The meeting illustrated growing fractures in the community regarding Colton. "Colt had been driving us crazy for a long time, and we *really* wanted him caught," says Louise. "But we didn't want him harmed and we didn't think he ought to be put in prison for the rest of his life." However, she says that a lot of those who came out were very hostile. "There was a lot of talk of guns, questions for the sheriff on where to buy them and where to go for shooting practice. I think a lot of people were more scared than they needed to be. And not just the old people. There was a young woman, around nineteen, and she was so terrified that when her husband drove in to work at four-thirty in the morning, she'd drag herself out of bed so he could drop her off in Stanwood at a fast-food place until the sun came up and she'd feel safe enough to take a bus back home. She was just shaking, petrified, when she told her story."

Louise says the sheriff and other deputies did nothing to allay those fears. The word that went out was to form neighborhood watches and to be careful if you saw Colton because he could be dangerous. "We got the sense that the deputies were embarrassed because they couldn't catch him and so they wanted to kill him, that's why they were talking so much about him having guns."

Kory says that there was a certain subgroup of "bad-ass cops" on Camano at that time. He'd had some experiences similar to Colton's, including being on the run under an Island County warrant for a year. "Those guys kept showing up at my mom's house basically telling her that they were going to beat me up when they caught me." Kory says the same deputies were letting it be known around the island that it was not going to be pretty when they caught up with Colton. "Part of the reason he kept running was because he didn't want to get hurt."

"What my boys [the Camano deputies] were dealing with at the time was that there were people on the South End who were helping Colt, leaving food out for him," says Chris Ellis. "We could never prove it, but there was no way he was doing what he was without help. On the other extreme, we had people telling us, 'Why don't you just shoot his ass?' I had one guy come in to my office to tell me he'd been out in the woods with his compound bow, looking for Colt. He said, 'Silent death, man!' I told him, 'Thanks for your help, but take your bow home.' Of course, it was an embarrassment to the sheriff's office that we couldn't catch Colt. So I think the actual statement was, 'We need to catch him before somebody gets hurt,' and it was implied that Colt might be that somebody."

Bev and Geof Davis say that the tension on the island had built to an incredible level. They heard the threats and feared Colton would end up beaten or worse, so Bev wrote Colton an email:

Hi Colt,

We'd ask how's it going but we know all is not going well. We are writing to let you know we pray for you daily. We pray that you'll be safe, warm and dry. We are so sorry that we weren't able to do anything to help you Colton! We sure did want to. Geof thinks of you every time he sees the boat show ads on TV or some other function he thinks you'd enjoy going to.

There is nothing that any of us can do now to change the past, but there is your future to look to. It CAN become a GOOD life for you Colton!

You have already won all of the battles with the Camano Cops. They can't catch you and they know it now! Why don't you quit while you're the winner?

Geof and I will go with you ANYTIME you are ready. We will take pictures of you before we go so we have proof that you didn't have any scratches or bruises. We will see to it that you aren't hurt!

We are VERY afraid for you Colton. The cops are making it seem like you are dangerous and that makes it VERY dangerous for you! Homeowners and cops will now be forgiven for shooting you and I'm sure a lot of the cops want to! PLEASE email me and tell me it's NOT true that you are packing! If you are . . . your death will be justified. You are only 15 Colton. That is too young to die. At least in jail you'll be fed, have a bed and be warm. And I'll bet you'll be out in 3 months. PLEASE Colton! Turn yourself in before you get badly hurt or killed. Like I said, Geof and I will do ANYTHING for you that we can. Anytime you're ready!

Please go in now while it's still your choice. Go in a winner!

If you have a gun . . . GET RID OF IT! Bring it to me if it's not stolen . . . I'll buy it!

Love,
Geof and Bev
IF YOU NEED HELP, ASK GOD
IF YOU DON'T NEED HELP, THANK GOD

After the police found several of his camps, Colton developed a group of what he considered safe houses, unattended homes where he hid out. He moved among them, never staying too long. At one of them, on Sea Song Lane one mile south of Pam's trailer, he used the owner's computer to send and receive messages on his 90210 Myspace account and to check emails sent to his mellenie010@hotmail.com address. He also used the home-owner's computer to do some online shopping.

Apparently looking for some last-minute Christmas gifts, Colt ordered three containers of bear mace on December 23. He bought them using the name of a local resident who was away on a three-week vacation with his wife. While they were gone, Colt had been Goldilocksing in their home:

sleeping in their bed, showering in their bathroom, eating in their kitchen, and even motoring around the island in their Mercedes.

On January 17, at 5:58 a.m., the Sea Song computer was booted up again, this time in an attempt to purchase a membership on Barelytwinks .com using the identity of a seventy-two-year-old Camano woman who was battling breast cancer—definitely not the demo of Barelytwinks, a site dedicated to images of slender young gay men, aka Twinkies or Twinks.

A few days later, Colton was online at Sea Song all night, until nearly 6 a.m. He shopped at the designer clothing Web site Raffaello Network, then ordered a computer program called Evidence Eraser. At 5:45 a.m., he read an email from pam@camano.net about buying property on a private island in South America.

On January 22, a deputy on patrol in his black ICSO Dodge Charger spotted a Ford Expedition doing 68 in a 40. The officer U-turned and popped on his lights, expecting the driver to pull over. Nope. Instead, the driver of the big SUV gunned it and took off with the Charger in pursuit. The chase didn't last long, though, as the Ford screeched into a sharp turn onto a side street. The tires had no chance of holding the three-ton truck on track and it skidded off the road, taking out a STOP sign and smashing into a tree. Both doors instantly swung open and two guys bailed. The deputy recognized Harley Davidson Ironwing jumping out of the passenger side before both suspects escaped on foot.

The Expedition turned out to be stolen, and later that week Colton wrote an email that read: "Do I have a story to tell you involving a driver of a 2007 Expedition with Harley as a passenger and a cop." He sent another message to the email address Babygirl that reads: "I can't get into any more trouble, I'm wanted state-wide."

On the twenty-seventh, though, Colton was back shopping for trouble, ordering $33 worth of bump keys and more pepper spray under the name Jim Pettyjohn, a victim who at this point had no clue that a burglar had been in and out of his home more than once while he, his wife, and their dogs had been asleep in the next room.

SHERIFF BROWN DETAILED EVEN more deputies to Camano and put out a request for the public to step up their participation in the capture of

Colton Harris-Moore, asking them to call a tip line with any information. Wanted posters featuring both Colton and Harley were plastered onto nearly every storefront on the island.

Brown also used a system of E-lerts, emails that kept residents apprised of updates in the chase and solicited leads. Tips poured in. "We got them every day and chased them all down," says Chris Ellis. "Some didn't pan out. One caller said, 'I think I saw Colton Harris-Moore, he's got a dog and a backpack on,' so we rolled. It turned out to be a black guy about five-foot-eight tall." Other calls were more promising. On February 1, a tip came in from a housekeeper who suspected Colton had been staying inside a home she took care of on South Camano Drive, about three hundred yards north of the Sea Song house. One deputy responded and entered the home, while a second arrived later, at 6:30 p.m., just as a truck was pulling down the driveway. The officer ducked behind a horse trailer and let the truck pass without challenging it. When he got to the house, the other deputy told him that someone had been inside and "he just stole the truck."

While they were talking, headlights came back up the drive. The cops split up and took cover as Colton and Harley walked into the kitchen. One deputy, positioned in a bedroom, was close enough to hear the burglars talking as well as the chatter from the police scanner one of them was carrying. He heard them mention a credit card, happy that it had a $15,000 limit. One of them, presumably Colt, told the other expansively, "Order anything you want."

One then asked the other if he brought "the bullet." The answer was yes, and the deputy listened to what he described as the sounds of a round inserted into a clip and the clip jacked into a handgun. He then heard Colton tell Harley, "The apple juice is for you." As Harley was about to take a sip, the deputy jumped out of the bedroom and shouted, "Stop! Police!"

Harley says the cop came out with his gun drawn. The officer says Harley froze for a second and dropped the glass of juice, which shattered on the floor. Colt was already out the door.

As the deputy yelled, "On the ground!" Harley snapped out of it and followed Colt. The cop held his fire, and both fugitives got away.

THE FOLLOWING DAY, ANOTHER hot tip came in: it was delivery time for a package that Colton had shipped to the victim of an earlier burglary.

He'd put in a special request that the package be dropped off at the home's gate, a rock-and-wrought-iron affair complete with lion statues protecting a driveway lined with tall cedars. Two deputies fixed up a decoy Express Mail package and, at 5:45 p.m., already dark, dropped it off, then hid in the woods across the street. A half hour later, a vehicle slowly cruised by. The cops then heard footsteps on the gravel drive. Both deputies saw Colton, dressed in a dark sweatshirt and baggy jeans, going for the package. One ran across the street shining his flashlight and yelling, "Stop, Colton! Sheriff's office. You're under arrest!" Colton took off, but not before grabbing the box. The deputies chased him, but Colton vaulted a fence into a horse pasture and then easily outdistanced them. The last they saw of him was as he rounded a barn and ducked into the dark woods. Word had gone out, though, that if there was any chance at all of catching him, pull out the stops and run Colton down. The deputies called it in and Sheriff Brown loosed the hounds.

Island County and Snohomish County deputies responded and set up a containment perimeter. K9 teams loped in from both Everett and Marysville, and followed Colton's trail into the trees. The dogs searched until 8:48, but couldn't track him down. The only thing the police came away with was their fake package, which Colton had dropped in the pasture.

————

With the close calls coming more frequently, Colton decided to head someplace where he felt safe.

On February 8, Dave, a neighbor of the Wagners'—Colton's summer family from a few years back—was out taking a walk when he saw a tall teen near the top of the Wagners' driveway. It was already dark, and the kid had what Dave described as a "miner's lamp," meaning a headlamp, on top of his baseball cap. As they passed, Colton said, "Good evening. Nice night for a walk, huh?" Dave answered, "Yeah," and continued toward his house. Something didn't feel right, though, and he swung around to take another look. The kid had vanished. Like everyone else on the island, Dave knew about all the recent break-ins. He hurried into his yard, where he could see the waterfront side of the Wagners' house. Lights were burning inside, so he called Doreen Wagner.

"I told him we had a couple of lights on timers," remembers Doreen. "But he said there was a bright light on in the back bathroom where I knew we only had a little night-light." Dave told Doreen that they'd been having trouble with a burglar on the island and this could be him. He hung up and called the cops, telling them he thought he had just seen Colton Harris-Moore and knew where he was hiding.

Inside the Wagners' summer house, Colton grabbed a bottle of water and popped a Hungry-Man TV dinner in the oven. He'd already washed his previous night's dishes and placed them neatly in the sink drainer. He'd also made his bed and hung up his bathroom towels. According to Bill Wagner, he'd even vacuumed. Again and again over the course of his time on the run, whenever Colt stole into people's lives by staying in their homes or driving their cars or boats, he seemed to go out of his way to prove, maybe just to himself, that if he had nice things he could take care of them—that it wasn't his fault he grew up in a dumpy trailer.

Colt lifted the television off its stand and put it on the floor so its light wouldn't be as noticeable from the outside. Now he was ready to just chill.

The first Island County cop who arrived at the Wagners' was a plain-clothes detective. He pulled up in an unmarked car shortly after 9 p.m. and quietly approached the house on foot. Other than the glow coming through the trees from a few neighboring homes and the distant twinkle of lights on Whidbey Island, the area was completely dark. The detective inspected the front of the house, found nothing amiss, and then walked around the corner toward the side facing the water.

Inside, Colton took his Hungry-Man out of the oven and forked it onto a plate. He carried the food and water over to the TV and sat down on the floor to eat.

As the detective cautiously stepped along the side of the house, trying to keep silent and out of sight so he could surprise whoever was inside, he was suddenly blasted by a blinding light. He'd walked under a motion detector.

The cop continued around to the back of the house and found the sliding glass door opened slightly. He got on the radio, called for backup, and waited outside until two more deputies showed up. When they entered the home, the first thing they noticed was the smell of food. They cleared the

place room by room, but Colton, of course, was gone; he'd bolted out
the back door the second he saw the lights pop on. What the cops did find,
though, was evidence that Colton had been using the Wagners' home for
quite a while—and taking good care of it.

Nothing was missing except for food. None of the Wagners' belongings was out of place, all the beer was still in the fridge, even a big jar of
change had been left untouched. In a closet they found a sleeping bag with
some of Colton's things rolled up inside. All the beds were made, but one
of the officers noticed a strange lump under the covers in the master bedroom. It was a black can of UDAP Bear Spray, the magnum size.

Down in California, Doreen hadn't connected anything to her little
Tarzan, but asked Megan to look up the *Camano News* online to see if
there was anything about the rash of burglaries. "I Google it and see this
mug shot, and I'm like, 'Oh my God!'" says Megan. "My mom had already gone to bed, and I yell up, 'It's Colt who's breaking into these
houses!'"

The police already knew Colton's fearless affinity for going back to
crime sites, so they asked the Wagners for permission to install a silent
alarm at their home and wired it to the cop shop.

COLTON WENT TWO MILES UP the west side of the island, back to the yellow, lap-sided home with six steep gables on Sea Song Lane. Despite Harley's lesson about nighttime burglaries—Don't turn on the lights!—Colton
flipped on a light in one of the property's outbuildings. A woman who
lives in the farmhouse across the street spotted it and told her husband.
He looked over but the Sea Song house itself—partially screened by tall
evergreens along the fence line—was dark.

The next evening, a cold and clear Friday, February 9, Colton was inside the house and back on the homeowner's computer. Across the street,
the neighbors had been keeping an eye out and suddenly saw a light in the
window. This time they called the police.

At 7:49 p.m., Colton opened his mellenie010 email and saw the letter
from Bev pleading that he turn himself in. If it swayed him in the slightest,
he didn't have a chance to act on it. By coincidence, Geof Davis was a mile
south of Sea Song, over at the Mabana Fire Station, where there was a

meeting going on. The subject: what to do about Colton Harris-Moore. There was a deputy there, and a radio call came in at 8:15 saying that two Island County cops were just up the road and had someone cornered inside a home. They believed it was Colton. Geof and the deputy jumped into a car and drove to Sea Song.

A detective on scene noticed a second-floor gable window was open. He called out, "Colton? Colton?" More police arrived and pulled on tactical gear. Colton peeked out the window and saw he had no chance of escape. He picked up the phone and called his mom.

Colton told Pam where he was and said that a SWAT team had him surrounded. He was in a panic, "What do I do? What do I do?" Pam told him that he was going to turn himself in, but that he should wait until she got there.

"Colton?" The detective continued to call up to the window. Finally, Colt answered, saying he was talking to his mom.

Pam hung up and immediately called Bev. She told her she was scared that the cops were going to hurt Colt and that she wanted to get as many people over there as possible. Bev said she was on her way. "It was easy to find the right place," says Bev. "There were already so many cop cars there with their lights flashing. They'd blocked off the road south of the house and a crowd was starting to gather."

At least a dozen officers from Island and Snohomish Counties arrived on scene. Cops in tactical gear spread out around the home while the others manned the front and kept the civilians back. Even Sheriff Mark Brown showed up.

Bev found Pam, who was with Van. Pam says she asked the police if she could go in and get Colt, but they refused. The homeowner's brother arrived and told the police where they could find a key. "Word started spreading around that Colt might have a gun," says Bev. "It was very melodramatic, and I started wondering maybe they actually were doing it so they could hurt him." She asked Pam and Van to take her hands and said a prayer for Colt's safety.

Another ten minutes went by and Colton still refused to come out. Deputies finally put Pam on the phone and asked her to "talk him out." Pam told Colt that there were plenty of witnesses around and even a couple of TV cameras, which was both good news and bad news as far as

Colton was concerned. They talked for ten minutes and then Pam put Bev on the phone.

"I told him to just come out, that no one's going to hurt him and the cops aren't going to go away . . . He said, 'I know . . . but could you just go home? This is embarrassing, I don't want you to see me like this!' I told him okay, that I'd leave."

A minute or so later, at 9:30 p.m., Colt was outside and in handcuffs, being led to a squad car. His nearly seven-month run was over.

THE COPS MIRANDIZED COLT and transported him to the Island County Juvenile Detention Facility. Colton didn't have a firearm when he was taken into custody, though he was loaded for bear with another pepper spray canister. During questioning by a detective, Colton says he never had a gun on him, just a knife, but the cop asked about three specific handguns—a .45 Ruger, a Glock, and a Walther PPK. "You guys don't need to worry about that," Colton told him. "They're not going to be taken out, you know, shot at people and everything."

When the detective pressed about a .45 caliber slug found in one of the houses he was staying in, Colton told him, "I wasn't the one who shot the gun. I'm the big fish in the pond . . . Well, I'm not the big fish in the pond. That's all I have to say. You can talk to Harley [about the guns] because he'll be more willing to talk than I am because, you know, he doesn't care if people come after him, so let him get chased and shot and everything . . . I don't even know what stole property you're talking about . . . I'm not the connected one here who knows where everything is . . . I'm not going to tell anybody because of my personal safety and my mom's that need to be put into consideration in this . . . They've threatened to dispose of her truck and my dog."

Aside from these shadowy figures, Colton's main worry was the media, which he universally refered to as "the paparazzi." He told the detective, "I just don't want this to be on the news."

The following day, Sheriff Mark Brown held a "We got him!" town hall meeting at the Camano Grange. It wasn't a victory parade. He faced tough questions from the large crowd who wanted to know why it took so long and why he hadn't caught Harley yet. Everyone, though, was happy Colton was finally in custody and most were glad it ended peacefully.

Following Colton's capture, Dave Pinkham wrote an editorial in the *Stanwood/Camano News*: "The Colton Harris story will soon be out of the headlines. Will we then forget to analyze how this boy came to fall between the cracks? Will the larger problem gradually fade from our consciousness? Or will we face the question: Was there something that could have been done differently or better in this case? Did this have to occur?"

A FEW DAYS LATER, Harley saw the writing on the wall—or, more accurately, saw wanted posters on every wall that now featured just his mug on them. He turned himself in. When a detective asked about the night he and Colton were in a home and the deputies jumped out at them, Harley said Colt had a Ruger .45 pistol, but that it wasn't loaded. When the detective asked why he ran when the deputy told him to stop, Harley answered, "Old habits."

In March, Harley pleaded guilty to first-degree criminal trespass and second-degree taking a motor vehicle without permission. He was sentenced to "up to 50 weeks" in a juvenile facility.

Colton had a more complicated path through the juvenile justice system. He was charged with twenty-three crimes against a dozen victims. Counts included theft, obstructing a law enforcement officer, and multiple counts of residential burglary, computer trespass, and possession of stolen property. Colt was held on $10,000 bail, which a judge then raised to $35,000. That didn't matter, though: no one was going to spring him. Pam said, "I don't ever bail anybody, I don't care who it is."

As Colton approached the courtroom for his first hearing—buzz-cut hair and wearing an orange jumpsuit and sandals with white socks, hands cuffed to a waist belt and chains around his ankles—he peeked inside the door and instantly reared back. He'd spotted the photographers and a TV camera. "Paparazzi," he groaned.

Along with what they felt was plenty of evidence—much of it from the stolen property found at his campsite on Pam's property—the prosecutor's office filed impact statements in which victims told of still-missing favorite pieces of jewelry, having to pay large insurance deductibles, feeling insecure in their homes. One mother wrote of having to console her young children for weeks after a fire had been set in their home, allegedly as a diversion when they came home and surprised the burglar, who ran past the kids as he escaped.

One woman, whose property was found at Colton's campsite and whose fifty-five-year-old husband died of a heart attack about a week after the burglary, wrote that he'd "defiled the sanctity of our home. Hopefully the sentence will help and not hurt."

The court appointed Rachel Miyoshi, who'd been in practice for four years, as Colt's defense attorney. Like most adults who spent time with Colton, Rachel immediately liked the teen and found him very smart. Rachel hired Shauna Snyder, a private investigator, to help with the case. Between working as a PI and a paralegal, Shauna had twenty years of experience doing defense research and had worked a lot of juvenile cases. She considered Colton the poster child for someone marked for attention by the local police after getting into trouble at a young age. "I think that Pam gave him some of that bad reputation with the police, too, because she's such a hard-ass." Shauna says she'd never met someone quite like Pam, who showed up with both barrels blazing.

"She wasn't the most receptive to listening," says Shauna. "And she is distrustful, so it was hard to explain to her that they had stuff on him. She had this thing that he's just getting the blame, a scapegoat, that he didn't really do it. Ironically, though, she was the one that turned him in for most of it. She turned him in for the tent that was on the property with all the stolen stuff. They didn't have a clue about that. Had she not, they never would have had any of it. I mean, she hurt him."

Still, Pam was adamant that Colton should not plead guilty to anything. "Pam would come into the office threatening to kick everyone's ass . . . 'Fuck them, blah blah blah.' But then I'd talk to her, and by the time she left she'd be offering to take us all out for beers," says Shauna. "So we got along great. She was engaged in the case and she was genuinely concerned. And it seemed to me like she's the only one Colton gave a shit about. He understood that his mom was like who she was. But you know . . . it's his mom."

Shauna reviewed the police work: "Sloppy . . . and the reports are like illiterate. He probably did all these things, but they just didn't have the evidence." She says the county was also looking for victim restitution of around $36,000. "We whittled that down to something like $600 just by tracking who got their stuff recovered."

When she went to the juvenile detention facility for her first meeting with Colton, Shauna didn't know what to expect. "Some kids are kinda scary. You're sitting locked in the cage with them and who knows if the jailer is around. Or else the kid might put on an attitude—'Fuck the cops,' or 'I can do thirty days standing on my head'—acting rough and tough to cover that they're shaking inside. But Colton wasn't like either of those. He had no pretense. He was unassuming, polite, very calm, and stoic."

The only time Shauna saw Colton react strongly was when partway through that three-hour first meeting a guard brought in his lunch. "He said, 'I'm not going to eat this crap,'" she says. "And it did look like shit, some kind of bean medley. He said, 'I'll drink the juice,' then he put the rest of the cafeteria tray on the ground like dog food."

Shauna says that at first Pam had Colton convinced that the county didn't have much on him. "I told him, 'They don't have you for all of it, but they've nailed you for some of it. Let me walk you through,' and I meticulously showed him page by page." She says Colton sat calmly and didn't say much until she explained how they nailed him for his Web usage. "He wanted to see how they did the IP mapping, and how they'd subpoenaed the email records. Some of the Internet providers refused to give their records to the police, and he was very interested in knowing which ones."

Shauna's overall impression of Colton was that he was "a nice kid" and nothing like the sociopaths she'd dealt with before. "The vandalism stuff like the fire and the shot fired in the house, that only happened when Harley was there, not when Colton was on his own," she says.

In preparing his defense, Rachel Miyoshi reviewed not only Colton's criminal record, but also his school, health, and CPS files. In April, the court approved her request to hire Delton Young, PhD, at county expense. Bellevue-based Dr. Young is a psychologist with thirty years' experience, including nine years at Harvard Medical School. He's also the author of the book *Wayward Kids: Understanding and Treating Antisocial Youth*, in which he makes the argument that the only way to successfully combat juvenile crime is to understand the psychological, social, and biological factors that cause it.

Dr. Young reviewed all the records and then met with Colton for interviews and testing, which included an IQ exam, the Wechsler Intelligence Scale for Children. His report states: "Given that Colton has only superficially participated in school for several years, these scores are reasonably strong and suggest that his intellectual capacities are easily in the average range." He also found the now-sixteen-year-old Colton to be relatively mature.

The full evaluation, filed June 15, referred to the dozen Child Protective Services reports and covered Colton's past mental health diagnoses and treatments, including "a wide range of psychiatric medications including antidepressants, stimulant medications, mood stabilizers, and even an anti-psychotic medication."

Dr. Young recounted the teen's pattern of destructive behavior, and admitted, "On paper, Colton resembles the picture of an emerging antisocial character—violating the rights of others and neglecting his own individual development (e.g., education)." However, he found several factors that he believed showed that Colton was "not a typical antisocial youth."

Colton's violent episodes, Young noted, appeared to be limited to fights with his mother. He didn't use drugs or alcohol, a fact that separated him from the vast majority of antisocial youth. "By Colton's account (and that of numerous available records) Colton's mother has been heavily affected by alcohol abuse throughout Colton's developmental years; and there has been a variety of men in the home who had their own alcohol and drug addictions. Colton understands that both his parents have had severe substance abuse problems, and he wishes to avoid complicating his life further with drugs or alcohol." Young also found that "Colton does not externalize blame and responsibility for his actions. He readily acknowledges his poor choices . . . He holds out some hope of taking up a much healthier developmental track in the future."

During their meeting, Colton told Young about his issues with insomnia, low energy, poor appetite, depression, and anger, but said that even though he knew he was eventually going to be caught and "locked up," he felt better in every aspect when he was out on the run as opposed to when he was at home. "He reports that for many years he has felt depressed when he is around home and his mother."

Dr. Young concluded that Colton's primary issue was "long-term, agitated and self-defeating depression" caused by his upbringing, which "precluded the development of basic trust and psychological health of the child." Young traced Colton's social anxiety, deep resentment, impulsiveness, and lack of focus and interest in schoolwork to that depression. He provided several DSM diagnoses; the most serious was the continuing depression stemming from "many years of stressful, unstable and even abusive home environment." He also reported that Colton still suffered with parent-child relational problem, "a serious psychiatric problem located not within the child, but between the child and his parent." Young reiterated that "a good part of his self-defeating and defiant behaviors can be traced to an accumulation of resentment, hostility and despair in that maternal relationship."

Colton told the psychologist that he understood he needed help from mental health professionals and said that his number-one worry was "his future."

Young wrote that "Colton is the kind of teen whose psychological development could be hardened into an uncaring and unhopeful young man if compelled to spend lengthy periods in JRA [Juvenile Rehabilitation Administration] institutions. What he needs most at this point is to associate with healthier peers, teachers and other adults; and to get to work and school."

Colton was clearly not happy being locked up, but told Young that some times were worse than others. "He was able to relate that his mood drops precipitously after he has a telephone call from his mother. He fears that his mother wants him to get a long sentence."

Looking ahead to Colton's eventual release, Dr. Young's report said that "Colton surely cannot be expected to stay on a positive course living in his mother's home," and mentioned that his aunt Sandy offered to provide him with a home and structure. Sandy wrote a letter to the judge describing her ranch and the animals that Colton had shown interest in and said, "We would play a positive role in his life."

JUVENILE COURTS DON'T WORK the same as the adult court system. There's no trial by jury, just adjudication by a judge. The test for guilt is a preponderance of evidence, not "guilty beyond a reasonable doubt." Despite that, Colton's defense team felt the county had little to go on for many of the charges.

"We whittled it down from the twenty-three to three that they could probably prove," says Shauna Snyder. "There was only one they had absolute proof on and that was the house they caught him in. The other two counts, they had some proof, so we took the deal instead of having to go to trial on all twenty-three. Plus they were threatening to pile on even more charges if we didn't take the deal. It would have been a mess to go to trial."

For the county, a deal that resulted in serious incarceration time made sense. "He'd become known in our office as a frequent flier," says Island County prosecutor Greg Banks. Banks had been serving as prosecutor since 1999, but says Colton stood out among juvenile offenders. "For a young kid, he had been through the system a lot." Each of those previous times, Banks says the system had been more than fair. "With juveniles, rarely do we just bring the hammer down. The idea is to try to rehabilitate them, and the system is designed with more flexibility than the adult justice system." Banks notes that a number of times Colton had been given community service instead of detention, and credit had been given for attending therapy.

"There were services provided to Colton along the way," he says. "Most of the time we have pretty good results, but Colton was a glaring exception. He'd been escalating, really shaking up the community. Now we had evidence that he and Harley were in possession of a gun, so it seemed like the best way to protect the people of Island County was to incarcerate him."

The deal they struck had Colton plead guilty to three charges, each with a sentence of fifty-two weeks, to be served consecutively. On any one of these felony counts, the maximum sentence for a juvenile could have been detention until his twenty-first birthday, which in Colt's case would have meant about five years from the time of his arrest.

Prepared to take the three-year sentence, there was still one more big hurdle for Colton: appearing in a public courtroom. Rachel Miyoshi says Colton begged her to try to get cameras banned. When she couldn't, his next priority was getting a haircut. Says Shauna Snyder, "We had to file a whole motion to get a barber in the jail because Colton didn't want to go to court if his hair wasn't cut."

20

Judges have discretion as to where juveniles serve their time. In Colton's case, the judge looked at his history of successfully eluding the police and punched his ticket for Green Hill School, the highest-security facility in Washington State's JRA. Seventy-five miles south of Seattle in the town of Chehalis, Green Hill accepts only male prisoners, and along with those convicted in JRA it also houses juveniles sentenced as adults under the state's Department of Corrections. Any kid convicted of murder in Washington State goes to Green Hill until he's eighteen and transfers out to adult prison.

Despite its maximum/medium-security designation, Green Hill is no Alcatraz. A fence surrounds the school and shop buildings, a gymnasium, and the housing units. Inside, though, it feels more like a school with extra security—that is, until the occasional hell breaks loose. The kids can't go home at night, but otherwise, Green Hill's general rules—no talking when moving between buildings, but liberal policies on cursing—seem looser than a Catholic grade school.

Colton arrived and, like all prisoners, was assigned to a high-security intake unit for his first thirty days so the staff could get a behavioral assessment. In this unit, called Birch (all housing units are named after trees), kids go to classes, eat, and recreate separately from the general population. Staff look over their records and closely watch how they behave, then send them either to a sex offender unit, drug and alcohol education unit, or general population housing.

During intake, the boys are given their uniforms: white sneakers, navy blue pants, and green T-shirts, sweatshirts, and jackets. They're told the house rules and about honor levels, which offer increased privileges in exchange for good behavior. Honor Level IV can nab a detainee a private room with his own TV and PlayStation. The kids are also instructed from day one that they can get out of Green Hill asap via what's called a CRA, community risk assessment. The CRA is a mandatory report card completed for each juvenile inmate every ninety days. Based on a point system, two consecutive low-score CRAs count as a "get out of jail free" card. Depending on the exact scores, kids can either be sent home if they've served their minimum sentence or to a low-security community facility, aka group home, aka halfway house.

After his thirty days in Birch, Colton was transferred to Maple Living Unit in the general population. Maple had ten rooms per wing, including two special Level IV honor rooms. Staff say that typically they try to limit the number of kids per wing to twelve or thirteen, with a few doubled up and the rest single-bunked. Other than assigned roommates, "the kids are never allowed in each other's rooms." There's a video game console in each wing's common area, and that's also where the guys hang out to play cards and watch TV.

The daily grind at Green Hill means school from 8 a.m. until lunch, then back to the housing unit for a while, then back to school until 4 p.m. Kids work on their high school diplomas, GEDs, or pre-college courses, and get vocational training in computers, metal shop, vehicle maintenance, and landscaping. Along with classes, the kids go to various meetings, like AA and NA (Narcotics Anonymous), depending on their issues. Green Hill staff say that about 95 percent of the kids come in with substance-abuse problems. All the boys also take part in therapy.

Washington's JRA uses the Dialectical Behavior Therapy (DBT) treatment model. "Most of the kids we get don't know how to appropriately interact with people or deal with stress or their own emotions," says one longtime staffer. "DBT offers one-on-one counseling, skills acquisitions groups, and milieu therapy, which is a monitoring of their activities in the environment to see what other interventions and coaching are needed."

After school, the kids get one hour of recreation and then they're sent back to their housing unit, where they can watch TV and play video games until bedtime. Each boy is allowed a ten-minute phone call every night, and can request a second. Parents can call in, and the kids can call out collect. On weekends, they're allowed outside to play baseball, football, and gang war.

MS-13, Surenos, Nortenos, Bloods, Crips . . . according to staff and former inmates, Green Hill has "tons of gang activity." The gangs take part in frequent race-based beat downs, including choreographed events where they'll start numerous fights at the same time in order to overwhelm the guards' abilities to respond. Serious infractions of the rules are punished by a timeout in Intense Management Unit (IMU), where bad boys are put on lockdown twenty-three hours a day. Not every kid coming into Green Hill has to pledge to a gang, though. "There are groups of kids that aren't involved," says a staff member. "It's like high school, there are different cliques . . . like over here you have the cheerleaders, and over here you have the Crips."

"I stayed out of the gangs, and so did Colt," says Josh from Point Roberts. "But there were still a lot of fights and lots of people just running up on guys and beating them up." Josh was sentenced to three years in Green Hill for malicious mischief—"I stole a boat and wrecked it on a beach"—and for intimidating a witness. When Colt arrived at Maple Unit, he and Josh found out they lived not too far away from each other on Puget Sound. "We got pretty tight," says Josh. Colt told him that his dad had been in the army. "And he said his mom used to be a sheriff, but he didn't get along with her."

Josh says Colton stood out among the kids at Green Hill. "Colt was a nice guy and smart, really smart." Proof, he says, was that Colton read books and studied subjects other than what they were forced to for class. "He knows things, uses a lot of big words." Staff at Green Hill say the average reading level inside is about fifth grade, so any book learnin' can come off as smart. According to Josh, Colton had three specific interests he liked to study: "Criminology, psychology, and flying."

One of Colt's favorite books while in Green Hill was a psychology text on how to diagnose various disorders. At one point, says Pam, Colt called and diagnosed her with ADHD and post-traumatic stress disorder.

According to Josh, a lot of Colton's airplane research came from the guards. "He talked about wanting to fly a lot. And you could ask the guards to look up stuff for you online. It was up to them whether they'd give it to you or not, but he asked for a bunch of information on flying, and they downloaded it for him."

The kids don't have Internet access themselves, but staff members say they'd do research for them as a reward, "a motivational tool to stay in treatment." One of Green Hill's computers also had a flight simulator on it, and Colton jumped on that as often as possible.

Another thing about Colt that stood out was his manner. "He didn't swear at all, which was really rare," and it wasn't long before he started having trouble with the other boys. "Guys picked on him a lot in there," says Josh. "They'd punk him, take his stuff, and push him around, smack him. He wouldn't fight back, which made it worse."

In a shark tank milieu like juvie, acting less than tough can get you turned into chum. But it wasn't just Colton's atypical big-word vocabulary and his annoying habit of diagnosing other kids' mental problems that got him punked.

"He made a bad name for himself with his mouth," says Josh. "He'd say some really creepy things, like that when he got out his plan was 'I'm going to take over the world.' Everyone would laugh at him, but he was totally serious about it. It was kind of mad scientist stuff. He didn't quite have the plan together, not many details—he was still plotting—but he was going big, getting a lot of money, and he didn't want to earn it, just wanted to steal it all."

Colt, says Josh, made no secret of his plans—or anything else that popped into his mind—and that's what caused problems. "He just told people all of his thoughts and they'd turn around and tell him he was stupid and should shut up." Colton would back off for a bit, "but then he'd run his mouth back at them. He'd keep at it when they told him to stop, so then when he'd go back to his room, someone would run in right behind him and pound him. This went on the entire time he was in there. He's smart, but he has his mind in the wrong place."

Colt's battles with the other kids stayed below the radar of the guards and counselors, which was important, because getting caught fighting meant a bad mark on his all-important CRA. The one part of his master plan for taking over the world that Colt did already have plotted was getting out of high-security Green Hill and into a fenceless group home as soon as possible. And for that, he needed those consecutive good report cards.

"He always went to school and always did what you told him," says a Green Hill staff member. "In a lot of respects he was a pleasure to deal with. You'd say bedtime is nine p.m. and he'd always be in his room at nine. He was always friendly with the staff . . . but you just had this feeling about him." The staffer says they could sense the wheels turning in Colton's head. "He was pretty quick, bright, but also criminally sophisticated in that he was a planner, a thinker . . . he was heads and shoulders above the other kids in those respects."

The majority of boys at Green Hill had crappy upbringings, coming from broken homes often darkened by neglect, abuse, and substance problems. Many were fighting mental health issues along with their own booze or drug monkeys, and plenty had run wild on the streets from a young age. The programs and therapies in JRA are designed to break through to those kids able and/or willing to be salvaged.

Colton's particular makeup, though, made him difficult to treat. "He was psychologically and intellectually very mature, but emotionally immature," says one staff member who worked with him. "He never took any of our 'shaping the future' stuff seriously. In therapy, he would always have smart answers, never true answers."

They say that Colton wouldn't open up to the counselors, which was an integral part of getting him help. "He'd never truly say this is the kind of home life I had, or this is what I was lacking growing up and so I want to change this, deal with this to move on . . . I think that by the time Colton got to us he was past the point of being able to open those floodgates and tell you what he wanted."

Instead, staffers say Colton put his efforts toward manipulation. "It was as if he had this intense grudge against the system and felt that however he could beat it he'd beat it instead of working within it to better himself."

Beating the juvenile prison system meant one thing for Colton: getting two good CRAs. And the way that's set up, it was a piece of cake for him. The CRA is a simple form asking nine "yes" or "no" questions along with two that have a third option: "moderate." Depending on the question, each answer coincides with a point score—0 for a no and up to 12 points for a yes. Inmates shoot for scores under 20 to go home, under 25 to go to a community facility/group home.

The questions that staff have input on are: In the previous ninety days, has the "client" escaped or attempted escape? Assaulted anyone? Not complied with core requirements (gone to school, etc.)? Not shown appropriate response to problems? Had hostile responses to frustration? Used chemicals or alcohol? Victimized peers? At least moderately participated in specialized programming? Been charged with another crime in prison?

By the CRA scorecard, a "client" could commit multiple assaults, victimize other kids, or get caught using drugs and still score low enough to go home. For Colton, who did none of those things, it was a walk in the park.

"We couldn't give Colt points to keep him here," says a staff member who saw him every shift. "There's no middle ground on any of the questions, and the worst part about that form is that there's no place for subjective comments."

The staff didn't want to keep Colton around just because he was such a pleasure to deal with. "We all knew what was going to happen. We knew he was just acting good so he could get to a group home and escape."

This wasn't just a gut feeling. Colton hadn't kept his escape plan secret, and the information made its way to the guards. "Three or four weeks prior to his release, there were notes in Colt's tracking saying that he should be considered an escape risk because he's making escape plans."

There's no question on the CRA form that asks, "Is the 'client' planning an escape?" However, the tracking notes would have been part of the overall review before Colton was released to a group home. Even if his scores weren't high enough to keep Colton in the secure facility, there was one failsafe built into the form, an "administrative override" that could have denied his release. "There's no way he should have passed," says a staffer, "but they went ahead and released him."

Unfortunately for Colton, his plan worked. At Green Hill, he'd been attending classes and doing relatively well. He was reading college-level psychology books and studying more about flying. He wasn't taking full advantage of the therapy offered, but maybe a little more time would have brought about a breakthrough. His buddy Josh, who'd also been a dropout, walked away after spending a full three years at Green Hill with a GED, a clean slate, and a determination not to get into trouble again.

There's no telling if more time would have rehabilitated Colt—but it might have. What's certain is that releasing him when written records showed he was actively planning an escape set the stage for dozens of additional victims and millions of dollars in damages and costs associated with Colt's next run.

ON VALENTINE'S DAY 2008, just over a year after he was arrested and about seven months after he'd been sent to Green Hill, Colton was transferred to the Griffin Home Residential Treatment Center. Griffin sits on a nicely wooded six acres just across the railroad tracks from the shore of Lake Washington in Renton, a Seattle suburb. He was placed in a home-like setting with eleven other boys and given a routine similar to that at Green Hill, with schooling, therapy, and behavior classes.

The residence's doors are alarmed and kids are supposed to be under twenty-four-hour supervision, but security is low-key by design. Group homes are transitional phases between prison and the community, providing boundaries and structure while easing offenders back into society. For someone like Colton, it could offer a nice, safe place to live, more education, and more counseling to help him overcome his socialization issues. For someone like Colton, though, it was also still a cage.

Colton began grumbling shortly after he got to Griffin. He called Pam to complain about the drug and alcohol classes they made him attend even though he didn't have a substance-abuse problem. "He said, 'Mom, do I have to go?' And I told him just do what they tell you," remembers Pam. Colton also told her that the counselors were trying to "brainwash" him via therapy.

If the brainwashing was to convince Colton that there were more important things in life than money and the trappings of wealth, it didn't work. While in Griffin, he created a remarkably prescient collage from photos, words, and phrases clipped out of magazines. It even has the words "Buyer's Guide" pasted in. Topped with "World of Comfort and Style" and an image of a twin-engine business jet captioned "May I Have Another," the collage has one hopeful self-identifier, "Profession: Pilot." The rest is: "Money, Money," "Wealth," "Dollars," "Keep It," "Get More," "Passion," "Enjoy the Taste," "Live Richly." "Make Money, Not Mistakes."

The artwork includes a stack of gold bars, a Jet Ski, three smartphones, two cruise ships, and a yacht. The largest single image is a Rolex. Fashion-wise, Colton added the logos of Gucci, Chanel, Hugo Boss, DKNY, Guess,

and Armani (whose products appear twice), all adjacent to the word "Sexy."
For his idea of suitable transportation, there were images of a Porsche,
Lexus, Audi, Jaguar, Land Rover, and Lincoln, as well as two Cadillac sym-
bols, and right below a martini (presumably shaken, not stirred), the logo for
Aston Martin, James Bond's favorite getaway car. Dead center is a cruise
ship with a line below it saying "See what you're missing." There are tourism logos for Mexico and the Caribbean. To pay for it all, Colton included a
baker's dozen of credit cards.

The collage, laminated on regal purple construction paper, is shock-
ingly crass-spirational, a two-dimensional episode of MTV *Cribs*.

The only two things that didn't quite fit with all the bling were a large
image of a piece of strawberry cheesecake and a small photo of a border
collie. The artwork screamed of everything Colton felt he'd been denied
and was determined to get. On the back it also showed a quiet protest: he
signed it "Colton Harris-," actually leaving the hyphen but dropping his at-
tachment to Gordy Moore.

Pam says she went to visit Colton "in all the slammers," though the
memories kind of run together for her. At one, she brought him some new
clothes. "Of course he told me exactly what to get . . . and just the shoes
were a hundred dollars!" Another time she carefully packed along a robin's egg that she'd found. "We used to go looking for them in the spring, so
I asked the guard if I could give it to him . . . They said no, so I could only
show it to him through the glass."

Colton told Pam he was having headaches from the lighting in Griffin. She
says they had a doctor see him, but not an optometrist like he wanted. As a
solution, she says, they let him wear sunglasses inside. Then on Monday, April
28, he called home and told Pam they wouldn't let him wear his shades anymore, presumably because it was causing problems with the other kids.

The following evening, after less than eleven weeks at Griffin Home,
Colton pulled on a pair of jeans and a T-shirt, laced up his white Adidas, and
snuck out a window between bed checks. The windows weren't alarmed,
and staff didn't realize he was gone until an hour later. Griffin called the local police at 10:40 p.m. to report the escape. They also phoned Pam.

"A guard called me to say Colt left," she remembers. "I just said, 'Son
of a bitch.'"

PART 3

TAKING FLIGHT

21

Colton's escape from Griffin was a local news item the next day, which is how, Ed Wallace says, the Island County Sheriff's Office first heard about it. As far as anyone knew, he was safely tucked away for another twenty-two months. Sheriff Mark Brown immediately reactivated his E-lert system to tell Camano residents to lock up and keep a lookout. He and other county officials didn't hide their displeasure.

"I couldn't believe it," says prosecutor Greg Banks. "This is a kid who was very good at running away and eluding police . . . Didn't they know how hard it was to catch him the first time? Now we have to do it all over again?" Banks and the sheriff suspected that Colton would head home to Camano. "That's where he was comfortable and that's where he was successful," says Banks. "The woods and all those empty vacation homes were still there."

Josh Flickner, whose family owns the Elger Bay Grocery at the top of the South End, and who served as head of the local chamber of commerce, says the residents were outraged. "It was 'You did *what* with him!?'"

Pam heard from Colt soon after his escape. "I think as soon as he left he was sorry," she says. "The way he was talking it sounded like he regretted it." Pam, for once, found herself in agreement with Sheriff Mark Brown—they even spoke—and they both relayed through the media calls for Colton to turn himself in. If he had, he would have been sent back to Green Hill with another twenty-eight days tacked on to his original sentence. He would also have had a tougher time scoring low enough to be released to another group home before serving his full sentence. But that's all he had hanging over his head at that point: his original time plus a month.

Colton had choices. He could go back to juvenile prison for about two years, pay his dues, and then try to move on with his life. Or he could leave the area and attempt to start over—not easy for a seventeen-year-old with no money, no job skills, not even a driver's license, but kids run off and try it every day. Or he could head back to Camano, where he'd instantly be "most wanted" and be right back playing nonstop hide-and-seek with the cops.

Getting back into the game had to be attractive in some respects. Colt had been successful for a long time and mainlined lots of juicy adrenaline hits along the way. He'd honed and expanded his criminal repertoire, and by examining the evidence from his last arrest, he'd schooled himself on mistakes to avoid. Going back to Camano would be like repeating a level in a video game: it's easy up to the point the Zerg, Slicers, Flood zombies, or po-po got you the last time you played. After that, it gets even more fun, more challenging, and more rewarding adrenaline-wise. Sure the cops would be waiting, sure he'd be back in a place with limited room to run and only one way out, but that's the exact setup for any good video game or action movie—and this was a kid who felt he was equal parts James Bond and Rambo.

Besides, as Colton had told Dr. Young: he slept better, felt better, and was happier when he was on the run.

Colt pressed reset and headed for Camano.

ONE THING COLT WOULDN'T be doing was hooking up with his old riding buddy Harley Davidson Ironwing. Harley had served his time for the Camano spree and made it back out onto the streets. He gave the straight life his best shot. "I worked a steady job for a day," he says. "I worked all Valentine's Day in the flower shop where my mom worked in order to get a bouquet of flowers to give to my friend. It was boring . . . not as much fun as breaking into places . . . but better."

Not long after that, though, "fun" and easier money beat "better." Harley went back to the flower shop after hours. He busted a window and found about $150. "Then I broke in the salon next door because I knew they had two cash registers." Harley got only $20 from the salon. That kinda cash didn't last long. He needed a bigger score, and who has more money than God?

On Sunday, March 30, Harley went to Stanwood's Cedarhome Baptist Church, because he "saw they had money." It was his mom's church, and it did have cash, thousands tucked away in a big safe in the basement. One of the core beliefs at Cedarhome is "We value giving as an act of trust in God," and surely there were people there who would've reached out to help Harley. There's no thrill, though, in receiving charity.

While the faithful were upstairs hearing the Word, Harley crept downstairs to dip into the collection. However, the pastor bore witness and called the cops. When they arrived, Harley took off with police and parishioners in pursuit. And thus the Hobbit was smote.

Harley went to prison just a month before Colton escaped from the group home. His getting pinched, says Harley, ruined their plans for the big helicopter raid on Costco.

THE FIRST PLACE YOU'D figure anyone would look for Colton would be the trailer, and that's just where he went. "It was raining," says Pam. "Colt came in and ran right into his room. I waited out in the living room while he was looking around for something. When he came back out I said, 'Did you find whatever it was?' He said no. I said, 'If you're looking down in the heat vent, I took a whole bunch of papers out of there and burned them.' And he went, 'Oh!' He was heading right back out the door again, and I said, 'Wait a minute.' I hugged him, and he was soaking wet from the rain."

Pam was surprised by how tall Colt had gotten. The green-eyed towhead she'd nicknamed Tubby now towered over her and had to stoop to get inside the door. He'd grown into a slender, brown-haired giant at least six feet four inches tall. "He always seemed to shoot up when he was in the slammers," she says. Colt's height was a surprise. Gordy is six foot. Pam stands five-eight. Pam's mom was five-two, and her father wasn't tall either. Her grandfather, she says, was so small they called him Shorty. Pam can only attribute Colt's height to her well water, saying her vegetables always came up oversized, too.

In the Camano cop shop and over in the Coupeville headquarters, the police expected "the call" any day. "We knew it was coming," says Ed Wallace. "Sooner or later we'd see a crime that fit Colt's MO."

Pam says she called the sheriff's office soon after Colt came home. She says she told them where she thought he was staying and said that if they escorted her, she'd take them there. She says, though, that "they never bothered." The police say that at one point they told her, "Okay, show us," and she then refused.

One of the next calls to the police came from Maxine. On May 8, just two days after her husband passed away, her mailbox was stolen for the second time. "I called the sheriff's office," she says. "But they didn't come out." The grandmother of eighteen says she still wasn't scared of Colton, and in fact she still felt sorry for him. Nonetheless, she started locking her doors for the first time since she moved to Camano. That didn't stop the raids, though, and once again pizza, ice cream, and any money she'd left lying around began to disappear. Most bewildering to her was how Colton was able to do it without alerting her little dog, Emma, who greets strangers who approach the house with teeny but effective barks and growls.

On May 11, Colton played paparazzo. He used an Olympus digital camera to shoot twenty self-portraits, including some sultry poses. He also took a shot of a big pile of crabs he'd caught by hand. The island boy was back in his element, feasting on Dungeness.

Just a third of a mile up Camano Drive from Maxine's, homeowners who had experienced a peckish poltergeist during Colton's previous run found their freezer emptied again, too. Sheriff Mark Brown himself came out and told them that Colt was definitely back on Camano and that they were getting a number of similar complaints. Brown said he didn't want word to get out, though, in order to avoid media attention that would let Colt know they were on to him.

Brown approved overtime for his deputies and once again pulled officers off Whidbey for special Colt duty on Camano. He also ordered his cops to use every trick and technology at their disposal. He didn't want another drawn-out, money-and-morale-sapping chase. In 2006, along with food, the homeowners near Maxine had also lost a bike, which had eventually been recovered. Brown now asked them for permission to install a motion detector that would alert the cop shop if anyone broke in. They said yes . . . and so were pretty surprised to wake up not long afterward to find that the same bike had been stolen again, this time out of a garage equipped with a police-installed alarm system.

The same thing happened on the other side of the island, to the neighbor one house south of Jack and Louise Boyle, just past the far end of Haven Place. A bike stolen from their garage had been recovered, and the owners alarmed the building. Someone came along and took the new security as a challenge. He defeated it by stealthily removing a window without breaking the glass, then reaching in and ripping out the alarm system control box. The thief went to all that trouble simply to resteal the same bike.

Almost every time the Camano deputies recovered a stolen bike and returned it to its owner, it would be retaken. Whoever was doing this seemed to take delight in punking the police. On July 3, Colt re-declared war directly on Island County by breaking into the county annex, stealing a safe and sinking it in a pond.

Over at the Boyles', where Jack had previously lost several rounds and lots of his wife's strawberries, he'd had a full year to add layers of security. It worked. This time not a single Frappuccino or Christmas decoration disappeared out of their basement, even though there was ample evidence that Colton was active all around their neighborhood.

To the north of the Boyles, Sharon and Dan Stevens owned the hot tub that they believed Colton regularly soaked in, as well as the dog house where they'd found the Boyles' phone. Sharon is a volunteer court-appointed special advocate who has represented abused and neglected children for more than twenty years. However, she works in King County (Seattle), not Island County, so never had an opportunity to know Colton.

"I would have loved to have gotten my hands on this kid when he was seven or eight," she says. "It's outrageous . . . between the school, the authorities, CPS investigators . . . somebody should have intervened." Sharon believes the entire system, which in some cases can lead to a parent fighting to keep custody of a child simply for the extra government assistance funds, needs improving. She says she was very disappointed when Colton escaped. "It's sad that instead of taking the help, that Colton came back to the same life and crimes. Some of these kids are lost."

Sharon and her husband, Dan, both in their mid-seventies, came up to Camano for a short stay and were woken by their black Lab's insistent barking. They went out to investigate and found a trail of belongings scattered across their yard. First it looked to them as if someone had approached the house and been scared off by the dog, dropping two very large sneakers and a DVD case as he fled. Then they spotted other droppings that could explain the hurried run: a pile of human excrement squatted near the playhouse. The Lab either scared the crap out of him, or the prowler had been in the middle of relieving himself when the pooch sniffed trouble and started barking. Either way, he left in a hurry when the dog went off and the lights went on. As the shoes were found far apart—one by the playhouse and the other up by the road—it appeared the guy kicked them off as he started running for the woods leading toward Haven Place.

Sharon and Dan began to find a number of other things on their property now that Colton was back on the loose. Most interesting was a note. They discovered the yellow Post-it on the switchback trail that leads from their home down to the beach. It's Colton writing to Colton, thinking things through on paper. He was back to collecting safe houses, potential targets, and credit cards. Part of the note appears to be about a certain name, noting "lost $ moved." Below that are reminders: "#1 of 2," with "2" circled, and "Use $ 4 orig pkg." A guess would be that he used the dollar sign as a symbol for credit cards, and he kept track by numbering them.

The real insight, though, came after his $ figuring.

"Peroll [*sic* of "parole"] 5 months? Think if *otherwise*. I might be out Christmas?—home?"

Colton was considering the kind of deal he'd accept to turn himself in. He didn't know that an escaped felon, even a juvenile, doesn't hold any cards when it comes to making a deal. The last word he wrote was the big question: Where would he go to live whenever he did get out of prison? "Home?"

Colton's decision on the first question about whether to turn himself in was clear by his actions: he never approached anyone looking for a deal. He chose freedom, regardless of the risk.

With the note, a bottle of aftershave, shoes, and other souvenirs of Colton's continual presence on her property, Sharon says she still never became one of those afraid of him. "I don't think he's a scary kid or ever wants to hurt anybody . . . I think he's always been looking for survival."

THE LOSS OF HIS Post-it appeared to be another lesson for Colt. He needed a better place to entrust his important notes and thoughts, and switched to a journal. In it he kept his important digits—some of which happened to be other people's credit card numbers and security codes.

Colton also had to solve a logistical problem. How can someone who's essentially homeless receive all the stuff he ordered online with stolen credit cards? He solved this with a brilliantly simple ploy. In many rural areas, mail carriers don't deliver house to house, especially on a dead-end road like Haven Place. At Haven, residents put all their mailboxes at the bottom of the road where it hits Camano Drive. So Colton added a mailbox near his mom's and made up his own address: 550 Haven Place.

Legitimate addresses on Haven start in the 700s and go up to 1100, so the not-so-bright move was failing to pick a number within that range. An obviously nonexistent address might work with some of the shadier online retailers, but surely big-bank credit card companies would check a little more closely to see if such an address actually existed on the planet.

On June 5, a Seattle couple, Jackie and Paul, arrived at their vacation home on Shady Lane—just behind the Wagners' summer home. They stayed for three and a half days, never leaving the house. They don't store financial records on Camano and don't keep computers there. Still, two days later, Paul's social security number was used to apply for credit cards from seven companies. The address used on all applications was 550 Haven Place. At least one of the cards was approved, delivered to the fake address, collected, and activated.

Mail carriers continued to service the phony mailbox for some time. Chase delivered a credit card to 550 Haven in the name of a Camano resident who'd been burglarized while he was out on a fishing trip. The card was used to pay for $39.95 worth of research on PeopleFinders.com (creepy slogan: "Find anyone, anywhere") and $29.95 on another stalker-friendly identity collection site. Colt also used it to shop for necessities such as police scanners on Amazon.com. Chase Bank records show the same card used at 3:34 a.m. on the sixteenth of June to withdraw $300 from an ATM on Camano. The following morning, four more attempts were made for $200, $300, $300, and $500. When police pulled the bank's security footage, it showed Colton Harris-Moore standing at the ATM punching numbers.

WITH EXTRA POLICE PATROLS detailed specifically to track him down and residents back up in arms, if Colton was worried about anything it didn't show on his face. On July 8, he spread a Hilly brand jacket onto a bed of ferns and lay back to pose for another private photo shoot. Dressed in a black polo sporting the Mercedes-Benz logo, with his iPod earbuds inserted, and a diet green tea bottle and a portable power supply by his side, Colton stretched out his long arm and took a series of eleven photos of himself with a Nikon Coolpix camera that he'd stolen from a Camano resident three days earlier. A number of shots featured different come-hither looks. Another was an eyes-closed fail. And then there was one frame in which he wore an enigmatic, barely perceptible Mona Lisa smile, a look that would come to be both fawned over and ridiculed for the next two years as it was reproduced again and again ad nauseam.

You could speculate that by taking so many pictures of himself Colt was making up for a childhood deprived of snapshots. Or, as the police believed, that he enjoyed a narcissistic personality disorder. Another explanation is that Colt's self-portraiture simply fit his generation's penchant for self-broadcasting and self-dramatizing. His peers were continually taking photos of themselves and posting them on social media. For the millennials, few things happen without a visual record, and sites like Facebook encourage them to broadcast mini reality shows about themselves. Throughout his run, Colt kept in contact with people both by phone and the Internet. It's easy to assume he took photos of himself in various locations to send to friends.

Colton deleted all the photos from the Nikon's capture card. But he didn't format it, which would have permanently gotten rid of them. Instead, the images remained lurking as little digital ones and zeros that would come back to haunt him.

. . . .

ONE OF THE PEOPLE Colt kept in touch with while he was on the lam was Josh, who remained behind the fence at Green Hill. "He started calling here, asking to talk to his buddy," says a staff member at the prison. "We reported it to the administration, but they wouldn't let us call the cops. We wanted to get a trace, but they wouldn't let us do anything. They just told us to monitor the calls, which we did."

Josh says he wasn't too surprised when Colton called. "He told me that his plan worked, that he'd escaped, and that he was back having fun doing what he likes: running around staying one step ahead of everyone." Josh describes Colton's manner as unnaturally calm despite knowing that he was again being hunted. "He was happy, totally relaxed . . . It was kinda weird . . . nuts. But that's what he lives for."

Colton called often just to bullshit, says Josh. "He was just seeing how everything was going. He never said where he was and I didn't want to know details, but sometimes he'd call from places he'd broken into, other times from a cell phone, usually late at night."

Police later recovered stolen cell phones with dozens of calls to Green Hill School, which Colton had programmed into the phones' memories as "Ghs." Each call to the school was monitored by staff who could only sit back and listen while Colton boasted of his escape and his future impact.

"We knew he was doing stuff, and there was nothing we could do about it," says a staff member. "Colton told [Josh]: 'Watch the news because I'm going to be all over it.'"

COLTON'S MAILBOX RUSE CONTINUED to work until one of his victims got word from multiple credit card companies that someone had applied for cards using his name and the 550 Haven Place address. He notified the sheriff, and a deputy found the mailbox. The police left it in place, though, and told the postmaster to contact them if anything came through addressed to 550. It wasn't long before they got a call.

The next package for 550 Haven Place was too large to fit in the box. Working with the police, the mail carrier left a note asking how the addressee would like it delivered. Colton answered and even helpfully provided a plastic bag, telling the mailman to just wrap the package in the bag and leave it.

Before the carrier's next round, Island County deputies and detectives secreted themselves into the woods all around the bottom of Haven Place. The package was delivered and placed on top of the 550 mailbox. Haven residents came and went, picking up their mail, not knowing that an entire squad of cops was watching from behind trees. Then a familiar vehicle approached. Pam Kohler got out of her truck and checked her mailbox. She then looked over at the package on top of 550 and began speaking to someone on a cell phone. Deputies strained to hear what she was saying, but couldn't make it out. Pam left the package alone, got back into her pickup, and drove off.

The cops were totally keyed, suspecting Pam had just let Colton know his package had arrived. They waited . . . and waited . . . "We had that stakeout manned for about forty-eight hours," says Detective Ed Wallace, who took shifts in the woods. Finally, though, they gave up and pulled out, taking the package and the mailbox. The lab successfully pulled Colton's fingerprint off the note to the mail carrier.

———

Born and bred in west Texas with the tarrying twang to prove it, Jimmy Pettyjohn drove through Snoqualamie Pass back in 1989. At its western end, the pass opens up on a stunning view. "I've been a waterman all my life even though I had to drive five hundred miles in any direction to hit wet back in Texas," said seventy-year-old Pettyjohn, who passed away December 2010. "Well, I got that first look at Puget Sound and said, 'Wow, I'm not going back!'"

The Pettyjohns settled on the east side of Camano's South End, in a modern log home kept humming by visiting grandkids. "Doors and windows always open, never take the keys out of cars . . . and we're retired, so we're here all the time. Never worried about crime."

The first hint of trouble was a charge on Jimmy's American Express for $107.90 worth of Pepper Power Bear Spray from UDAP out of Bozeman, Montana. It's a product specially formulated by the survivor of a grizzly attack to blast a fog of pain so nasty it'd force Smokey the Bear to leave a campfire unattended.

Jimmy had never ordered any such thing, so he called AmEx and they absolved the charge. Simple mistake somewhere . . . He hadn't noticed anything amiss in his house, no clue that anyone had broken in, and Jimmy saw no reason to quit the old habit of leaving his billfold in its customary place on a shelf above his computer. Pettyjohn's PC sat in a room off the garage that he used as a workshop/man cave/heavy smoking den— with the smoke provided by both a steady stream of cigarettes and a big stainless-steel barbecue (yes, the barbecue is indoors . . . he was Texan). On the edge of the shelf above his monitor there's a peg. That's where Jimmy always hung his wedding ring and his gold Rolex when he had some puttering to do. Something else he'd come to realize was a bad habit.

On the morning of July 9, Camano's indoor barbecue king ambled into his cave and reached for his Rolex. The watch was gone. Surprisingly, though, his wedding ring still hung on the peg. "I really cherish that ring, been wearing it for fifty years, and if he took that my feelings woulda goddamn sure been hurt . . . But he didn't."

Pettyjohn was so relieved, figuring he'd gotten off easy, that he never even reported the theft. He didn't notice anything else out of place. His wallet sat on its shelf, all the credit cards accounted for and all in exactly the right order he kept them.

Two days after the burglary, a package arrived addressed to Pettyjohn. He'd ordered a book from Amazon, and signed for the FedEx figuring this was it. "Open it up and it was a couple little electronic devices and a tiny CD," he says. "I think, Oh shit, they sent me one of those new electronic books." Jimmy put the gadgets in a Ziploc and wrote the date on it in case he had to return them. He put that on a table in his sanctuary. "I'm thinking the gran'kids would be over on the weekend and show me how to install it." He used the FedEx box to store the nuts and bolts from a swing set he was dismantling out in the yard.

When his clan came over a couple days later, he went to show them the devices. They looked everywhere, but the gadgets were gone. Pettyjohn realized that a thief must have been watching for the delivery and then broken into his home again to steal the package. "He'd paid for overnight . . . I think thieves spare no expense on the shipping." Jimmy couldn't ignore it this time. "I got to callin' the sheriff and told him about it, but they didn't do anything."

He didn't let it drop, though. "I called around on my own and got the outfit in Austin that shipped the package [Scancity] and found out that the electronic things were a couple of credit card–swiping devices. Called the sheriff back and told them that, and that's when they finally got interested."

Jimmy did the legwork and provided the sheriff with a printout of the card reader specs. They were "Mini 123s," tiny 1.2-ounce battery-powered gizmos that fit in your palm and record the numbers off credit cards' magnetic strips. Two of the $230 devices had been ordered, and each could store 2,500 swiped credit cards. The deputy took prints off a window where Pettyjohn's wife noticed the screen had been removed, and asked Jimmy to dump out the nuts and bolts so he could take the FedEx box.

"This is Camano Island . . . I never bothered to think too much about locks, and didn't have any lights outside," said Pettyjohn, who grew up in the oil field construction business and served in the army, taking "a government-paid vacation to Southeast Asia for a year." The idea that someone had been brazen enough to come into his house at least three times, including the 2006 credit card theft, made him start to think about security. A freaky thing about the burglaries was that the Pettyjohns have two dogs, "a yappin' poodle" and a long-haired dachshund, which both make noise at a pin drop. "He had to be pretty damn stealthy."

After Jimmy got back from Vietnam, he'd decided to never pick up another gun. And he didn't—until these break-ins convinced him otherwise. "I didn't want to see him get hurt . . . He wasn't doing near as bad a things as some kids his age . . . But we're retired and here all the time. We were home, just behind that door when he came in here. That concerned us." One of the Pettyjohns' three daughters was worried enough to buy them two guns; another friend gave him a Glock. "And now I've got the place lit up like an all-night liquor store. It is a shame."

Colton Harris-Moore stole some of Camano's charm from Jimmy Pettyjohn, which is tough to forgive, but if things had been just a little bit different, the transplanted Texan and the Barefoot Bandit could have been buds. The two are simpatico on at least one passion.

"When I was growing up in Amarillo, I always used to hang at the local airport . . . even did my homework there. Back then the CAA (precursor to the FAA) would give you your pilot's license at fourteen, same age you could get your driver's license." Jimmy's dad had been an "airplane driver" in World War II, and always owned a plane because he had business all over Texas. "I turned fourteen on a Sunday, but took my check ride on Saturday when I was still thirteen," said Pettyjohn, "which makes me the youngest pilot ever licensed in the United States."

Pettyjohn kept a plane on Camano, "a souped-up Piper Cub." He loved to take off from the island and fly around Mount Baker, giving air tours to his kids, grandkids, friends, and even the deputy who came out to investigate the stolen credit card swipers.

Two weeks after his Rolex disappeared, Pettyjohn's credit card statements started arriving. "The Discover card bill came in and had $485.44 worth of iTunes purchases." The Pettyjohns had about as much use for iTunes as they had for anti–grizzly bear spray. "Then Visa comes in with all these other electronics ordered on it and over $300 on PayPal. That's when I realized he'd gotten every goddamn credit card out of my billfold and copied down the number and the little three-digit code on the back and then put them back just exactly where they were so I never noticed. Pretty clever . . . nitwit kid."

ON JULY 18, 2008, Colton pulled one of his least clever moves. It was a nice evening for a drive, and he tooled around the South End in a shiny black Mercedes. Always mindful of the people who'd teased him about his raggedy clothes and crappy trailer, Colton stopped by at least one home to shout out, "Who's poor now?!"

The Mercedes hadn't been reported stolen, so Colton could have driven forever with little chance of getting spotted—if he'd driven well. Instead, he flew around the island, speeding and swerving along the tree-lined roads. At around 11:30 p.m., he was doing 69 mph in a 50 when he blew by another black car, an ICSO deputy's Charger. The cop watched as the Mercedes crossed both the center and the fog lines. He popped his blue light, but rather than pull over, the Mercedes took off.

The short car chase ended as the Mercedes turned into the parking lot of the Elger Bay Café with the cop car right on its tail. The driver wasn't giving up, though, just trying to put the odds in his favor by switching from a car chase to a foot pursuit. As the officer and a reserve-deputy intern watched in disbelief, Camano's "most wanted" leaped out of the Mercedes while it was still moving and then ran down an embankment toward the woods. The Mercedes continued to roll, heading toward a big propane tank that feeds the restaurant.

The cop slammed his car into park and jumped out, but he was too late to stop the Mercedes. Fortunately, it barely missed the propane tank, though now looked like it was about to drive over the twenty-foot-high drop-off behind the café. Before it reached the edge, however, the car hit a large plastic trash Dumpster and finally came to a stop. With Colton beating feet into the darkness, the deputy began to give chase. Then, however, he realized that the car or the trash can had clipped the gas line where it entered the building. The deputy ran to his patrol car, backed it away from the propane tank, and called in the fire department to handle that potentially explosive situation. Next he radioed for backup to try to corner Colt.

All available Island County officers responded to the call and set a perimeter. A Snohomish County dog team and the Marysville "manhunters" arrived to try to track Colt down. Just a half mile west of the parking lot, though, private woods led directly into the large expanse of Camano Island State Park. Once again, as soon as he hit the trees, Colt was as good as gone.

The cops' disappointment, however, soon turned to cheer when they checked out the Mercedes. A quick run of the plates came back to Carol Star, Colton and Pam's next-door neighbor who was away on a trip. "The cops called and I told them that if the keys were in the car that meant he'd broken into my house," remembers Star. She says Colton had taken down part of a trellis and used it as a ladder to get onto her roof where he tried to get in through the skylight. "It was bolted on too good, though, so he crowbarred open the slider door. I'd just gone to Costco, and he hit my pantry looking for food. He took muffins and a nice fresh mango—didn't touch the beer. My car keys were hanging in the pantry."

Star's car gave Island County a motor vehicle theft charge against Colton, but that was just the tip of the eventual iceberg of an indictment. When Colton bailed out, he left behind a backpack he'd stolen from Star's home. A peek inside revealed digital cameras, cell phones, a GPS, and other recently stolen property including a wallet containing credit cards reported missing just two days before. When a deputy lifted the backpack, underneath lay a $30,000 infrared camera that had been taken from the South End's Mabana

Fire Station. The police applied for a warrant and, when approved, spilled all the backpack's contents onto a table in their evidence room.

The magnetic card readers taken from Jimmy Pettyjohn's place were there—one of the readers had already swiped two Camano residents' credit cards. A compact mirror held Colton's thumbprint. A further bounty of evidence came from a journal that conveniently had the name Colton Harris written on the inside cover. Its pages contained lists of the names and credit card numbers of burglary and identity theft victims.

The cell phones, cameras, and other digital equipment from the backpack were turned over to Detective Ed Wallace, who's also certified as a seized computer evidence recovery specialist. A stolen pink Motorola V3 phone had been used to call Green Hill School twenty-one times. It had also called the residence and work numbers of two different burglary victims, presumably to check if they were home. Another phone had been used to call Pam, Green Hill, and the real estate office where another burglary victim worked. When Wallace got to the cameras, he ran special software that recovered dozens of deleted photos. Another bingo: Colton Harris-Moore was staring right at him in frame after frame.

The Mercedes story instantly flashed across the island—usually told presuming that Colt had purposely tried to blow up the propane tank. Mark Brown decided he had to end the media blackout. With all the evidence he'd left behind in the car, Colton obviously knew they were on to him now anyway. They chose the shot of Colton lying in the ferns and sent it out to the local press, figuring a recent photo and description along with a request for information would lead, once again, to a quick capture. Brown also set up another town hall meeting at the Mabana Fire Station.

Maxine, the Boyles, Jimmy Pettyjohn, and many others went to that meeting on July 23, 2008. Neighbors there began organizing block watches and citizen patrols, and as Pettyjohn remembered, "There were a lot of people there who were buying guns and saying let's get something done here."

––––––––

After the Mercedes crash cost him all his credit card numbers and put an intense amount of heat on his tail, Colt decided to vamoose. They continued to search for him on Camano, burning through the sheriff's office budget on overtime hours, but there were no new reliable sightings. Some burglaries kept occurring on the island and many residents had come to assume that every crime they heard about must be connected to Colton. The police didn't believe that, though, because these didn't fit his MO. After several months with no Colt-like break-ins, Island County authorities started to believe that he'd gone into hibernation. He'd actually just gotten on a ferry.

To the north of Camano, the San Juan Islands were an orchard filled with juicy, low-hanging fruit. One out of every three homes in the county was a vacation property—3,300 houses that lay empty for long stretches of the year. Colton had four main islands to choose from, and he chose well. Orcas offered the thickest woods, most rugged terrain, and windiest roads, making it easy for a kid who liked to run and hide in the forest, and hard for cops chasing him to get anywhere fast. The island is 43 percent larger than Camano yet has only about a third of the population—enough people to provide plenty of prey while at the same time ensuring there'd be only a token police force to protect them. Because their island was considered so incredibly safe, Orcas residents and all the businesses in sleepy little Eastsound were the ideal unsuspecting targets.

The timing couldn't have been better for Colt. It was the height of the summer season, with plenty of strangers on Orcas. His was the best-known face just south of the border in Island County, but he could have walked Eastsound, shopped the shops, and hitchhiked the roads with little fear of being identified that first summer—or most of the second.

For Orcas in 2008, Colton came and went like a phantom—the bike stolen from the cop shop evidence room, the deputy pepper-sprayed, the flight manuals ordered and stolen out of Vern's, and so on—until finally in November Bob Rivers's plane went native and crashed on the reservation. Island County knew who they were chasing, but the connection was never made to the Orcas troubles.

While Colt says he then spent the winter in Reno between jaunts to see his friends in Wenatchee and a side trip down to Sacramento, the Island County prosecutor filed ten charges against him. The warrant included car theft, attempting to elude, malicious mischief, three counts of identity theft, and three counts of possession of stolen property. He'd also been charged as an adult for "flight to avoid prosecution."

With all that hanging over his head in May 2009, Colton left the safety of Nevada and once again went home. Maybe springtime on the Salish Sea was just too beautiful to pass up. Maybe he found the straight life boring and needed to get back in the adrenaline game. Maybe he missed his mom. Whatever the reason, Colt arrived back on Camano and quickly escalated his "war" against the police to a level unprecedented in Island County history.

In the wee hours of June 19, 2009, Colt broke into a car parked outside the house where its driver lay sleeping. The vehicle was a black-and-gold cop car, its driver an ICSO deputy. Colt had previously busted into a statie's patrol car and taken his camera. This time, he took everything: the officer's cell phone, digital camera, Panasonic Toughbook, breathalyzer, even his ticket book. What got Sheriff Mark Brown, his entire force, and all the Camano residents really torqued, though, was that he also took the deputy's Smith and Wesson MP-15 assault rifle and a supply of ammunition.

Colton had his war. Island County Sheriff's Office pulled out all the stops. "We started really leaning on CIs, confidential informants," says Detective Ed Wallace. "We had some pretty heavy stuff over these people's heads to give us leverage, and I believe they would have gladly given us information if they had any. Instead, they told us they hadn't seen this kid and didn't know who he was hanging with."

With Colton living, as Wallace describes it, "off the grid," he was much harder to track than the typical thief. "We had other burglars working Camano at the same time, people responsible for stealing much, much more property than Colton, and we were catching them because they drove cars, they pawned stuff for money, they associated with other people. They had friends. Colt didn't.

"We began to use game cameras in places where we knew he was operating," says Wallace. The camouflaged and motion-activated digital cameras are the same tools used by hunters to study the movements of their prey and by researchers to catch glimpses of the most elusive animals. The police also set out a decoy vehicle hoping Colton would steal it or at least snoop inside. Wallace was among the officers who staked out the bait car along one of Colt's regular routes. Sure enough, says Wallace, late that night he came riding down the road on a bike. Officers gave chase, but once again the speedy teen immediately went for the woods, dropping the bike and losing the cops on foot.

Deputies spent hours combing the South End woods on and off duty. Two weeks after the cop car was ransacked, they found a campsite in thick woods a little over half a mile from Pam's property. A bike and a Ziploc filled with phone cards that were there one day and gone the next told them Colt was actively using the camp. They set up a stakeout, but Colt sniffed this one out, too, and didn't return. When the cops gave up waiting and took apart the site to collect evidence, they found the stolen breathalyzer, an ICSO tag, and the deputy's cell phone with Colt's fingerprints on it. They didn't, however, find the assault rifle.

With too many close calls, and with the anger and fear rising on Camano, Colt bolted back to greener pastures on Orcas in the summer of 2009. It was after that spree—when he hit businesses all across the island and stole a plane and two boats, the last one starting him to Canada and eventually Idaho to take the Cessna he crashed in Granite Falls—that everyone finally knew about the Barefoot Bandit.

———

October 2009, Orcas Island. Like a diesel-drinking tyrannosaurus, the big excavator lunged forward and bit down on a pile of stumps and branches. It reared back with a quarter ton of wood clamped in its jaws and swung back over the top of the bonfire. A huge shower of sparks and flames erupted as the pieces fell. Embers alighted on the branches of a big Doug fir thirty feet above our heads. They glowed momentarily, then slowly blinked out. The intense rush of heat from the massive stoking had us all grabbing our beers and retreating a few yards. Now all eyes turned toward the night sky, curious to see if the trees were going to catch fire. Along with using heavy equipment to feed the blaze, the fact that burning season wasn't open yet made this a fairly typical full-timers backyard party. Summers may see a lot of second-homers hosting garden soirees, but fall and winter are when the rough-hewn and hunkered cut loose.

Enormous homemade barbecues held big slabs of beef and pork plus an entire side-hill salmon—the wink-wink nickname for local deer shot out of season. Out in the driveway, a good percentage of rigs were illegal in one way or another—cracked windshields, expired tags, bad lights . . . This wasn't an outlaw gathering, though, just regular island folks, if not pillars then at least upstanding 2×4s of the community. Islands tend to draw those with strong individualist and antiauthoritarian streaks, creating live-and-let-live communities that are, at the same time, knit tighter than they'd be on the mainland because of the shared experiences and hardships. Orcas is the eighth island I've lived on and it's certainly no exception. The reason no one was concerned about the illicit bonfire was because about half the fire department—including the guy at the controls of the excavator—was crowded around it, drinks in hand.

Colton Harris-Moore had been off the island for more than a month—we hoped—but the topic flared whenever a little more information leaked out. Everyone on the island seemed to have part of the "untold" stories, but fragments from different events melded like an octopus orgy, and to find the truth you had to carefully pry apart all the slippery bits. No wonder the Internet buzzed with misinformation, when fact so quickly morphed into fiction even at ground zero. The police remained tight-lipped. "I'm very cognizant of the fact I don't want to be part of the problem with this young man by giving him notoriety, creating myths behind him that endanger the community and do not bode well for him in the long run," said Sheriff Bill Cumming. The cat burglar was out of the bag, though. The information vacuum quickly filled with rumors that simply added to Colt's growing legend.

Very few details had come out about his childhood, but Colt was engendering sympathy from some on the island, especially women and especially those who'd raised teenagers. At the other extreme, several guys filled with beery bravado stood around the bonfire discussing ways to lure Colt into their homes so they could legally take care of him—with extreme prejudice.

A few folks found some satisfaction in the fact that Colt had run the local deputies ragged. One retired contractor who embodies a definite Orcas archetype—Will Geer-ish with gray beard, long hair, overalls on top of flannel—and who'd dealt with all the deputies during his thirty-plus years on the island, said he was glad Colt was "sticking it to 'em."

There's a delicate balance in policing a place like this where small-town affairs are under an even more powerful microscope because it's an island. The news a couple of years back that two additional deputies had been hired for Orcas and that their salaries would be paid for by the expected increase in revenue from the tickets they'd be writing was not met with a ticker-tape parade. When the new guys arrived and pulled over what seemed like half the island within the first three weeks, there was almost an uprising until they stood down to a tolerable islandlike level of officiousness.

People don't dislike the officers in the islands—they're neighbors, too—but there's a different relationship from that in a large city or any other place that has more police coverage. Here, depending on when you call and what part of the island you live in, a 911 could have a cop to you in five minutes or an hour. No one is under any assumption that they'll be right there when you need them. They can't. It's a tiny department, and unlike almost every other place in the country, there are no overlapping jurisdictions to offer backup. Most rural areas have a sheriff's office plus state police and maybe even a small city police department that can all work together. In San Juan County, it's just one sheriff's office spread out to cover all the islands. If something happens that overwhelms the small contingent on one island, officers need to fly or boat over from another, with the weather and sea conditions coming into play.

So in most cases, folks on Orcas know that the police aren't going to be there in time to save them if the hockey-masked serial killer comes to call. Out on our fringe of the island where there's a much better chance of getting a quick response from a volunteer firefighter than a cop, I've told Sandi that if anyone ever breaks in she should light him on fire. It's another reason people here tend to be more self-reliant—and why many are armed (the seemingly redneck—or mossneck—trappings of guns and chainsaws and "Keep your government ass off my property" rants cross the partisan divide here, a county that votes heavily Democratic).

WITHOUT MUCH OPPORTUNITY FOR cavalry-like heroism, or much success at fighting the obvious problems like the handful of meth heads everyone knows about, the most visible parts of the deputies' jobs are speeding tickets and DUI stops, neither of which is very popular with many residents. Their other main task is handling ugly domestic disputes. It's not an enviable job, and the deputies are not paid well in a place that's very expensive to live. At this point in time, the turnover rate for deputies was high, the training opportunities low. The fact that a kid had now come back two summers in a row and burglarized at will made it easy for some people to bring out the Barney Fife references.

But communities get the police force they want and are willing to pay for. Residents of the San Juan Islands bristle at zero tolerance and won't pay for a cop on every corner. Colt really had chosen well. The department had few deputies, no canine units, no helicopter, no SWAT team, no trained "manhunters." And while Sheriff Cumming, a nationally ranked racquetball player, might have been in good enough shape to chase Colt up Orcas Island's hills, his local deputies weren't.

Bill Cumming says that in his thirty-eight years in policing and criminal justice, he'd never faced someone like Colton Harris-Moore. Colt was a cop's nightmare. He was stone-cold sober, not prone to druggie desperation and mistakes. He kept to himself instead of associating with other known criminals. While he didn't have, as he'd told his mom, an Einstein-level IQ, he was more than smart enough. Despite his history of impulse control problems, he'd become a patient, calculating thief. And he always had an escape strategy: Run! Colt never wavered or hesitated, just ran, and ran for the woods where he'd trained himself to run and hide since he could walk. The cops carried all their gear along with extra pounds and additional years. They never had a chance in a foot race.

They did have chances at stakeouts, though, and Colt still got away. Of course, the San Juan County deputies hadn't done worse than any other department that chased Colt over the previous eighteen months. He'd gotten away from everyone, including all the SWAT teams, manhunters, and helicopters they could throw at him in Granite Falls.

Through it all, the people who spoke with Colt said he was "relaxed," "calm," and "enjoying it." Whether this was pathological, or a sign of hopelessness about his future, or just evidence of a steel sack, Colt's willingness to take ridiculous risks was both what would make him the most famous outlaw of his generation and prove to be his greatest weakness.

WITH A LITTLE EMOTIONAL distance from his end-of-summer tear around Orcas, there was an almost universal acknowledgment among the bonfire-and-barbecue crowd of at least Colt's moxie. Parts of his story resonated with the romanticized character of this frontier island. He was canny and resourceful, able to survive with all the odds stacked against him. Whatever appreciation there was, however, no one wanted to see him on Orcas again. Few doubted he'd be back, though, unless he was killed or captured before then. As one deputy told me, "I just hope he's caught before it's our turn again."

Despite the nods to Colt's abilities, there remained a gulf between what the vast majority of residents on Orcas and Camano were feeling about him and how a growing number of people across the country and around the world saw Colt. In early October, the first Facebook page dedicated to Colt went up and starting collecting members, eventually numbering almost a hundred thousand. An Internet fan club also went live, and T-shirts began flying out of a Seattle shop emblazoned with Colt's face and, ironically, the words "Momma Tried"—from the Merle Haggard tune.

WHEN I LEARNED THAT the crook who turned our open, trusting community into Paranoid Park was a feral kid with a Wild West name who'd come from just downstream to roam our woods barefoot while using high-tech spy tools to steal our identities, I put aside my other writing projects. I felt I had a personal stake in finding out the truth behind this Jesse James Bond. After digging out the reams of records on Colt down at the Island County courthouse, learning about his childhood and finding out that he wasn't a typical drug-addled, violent punk, I was hooked.

22

The beginning of the truth about Colton Harris-Moore lay south, on Camano Island. After the hour-long ferry ride from Orcas to the mainland, the drive between Anacortes and Camano runs through Skagit Valley. It's a great back-road drive at the right times of year. In spring, the valley erupts in an acid trip of colors as millions of tulips bloom. Wintertime brings thousands of snow geese and trumpeter swans that form drifts along the farmland furrows and occasionally lift off in huge honking blizzards of white. Driving through on the day before Halloween, though, there wasn't much to slow down for.

In normal times, talk on Camano tends toward fishing and crabbing. In the fall of 2009, though, it was all about Colt. The wanted posters were back up, rewards were offered by the local chamber of commerce and Crime Stoppers, and Sheriff Mark Brown was trying to keep his cool. After the plane thefts brought the case a higher profile, more law enforcement started pitching in to help catch Colt. Snohomish County's manhunter teams worked the island, and other agencies lent Brown helicopter support whenever there was a solid sighting. Island County deputies began camping out in garages and backyards where Colt was known to forage.

Now "the cops meant business," says Maxine, who had canine teams sniffing around her property trying to pick up Colt's trail. She told police that even after being hit eight times, she still wasn't afraid of Island Boy. "A female deputy said, 'Well, you should be.'"

Local kids ventured into the woods looking for Colt and a piece of the reward money. They found two more of his campsites behind the mailboxes at the east end of Haven Place. The police also found several camps tied to Colt, some with stolen property, others with keepsakes surprising for someone who professed to have such disdain for the press. "Colton was collecting all the news clippings about himself," says Ed Wallace.

Islanders say the cops were embarrassed and getting more pissed every time Colt made news. More off-duty deputies began stalking the woods. Even rangers at the local parks beat the bushes on their lunch hours.

The media repeatedly shorthanded Colt as a *Catch Me If You Can*–style action hero and the Northwest's new Robin Hood. Then they'd thrust cameras in Sheriff Mark Brown's face to get his reaction.

One crew finally got what it wanted. When Canadian CBC TV asked about the fan clubs and Colt's hero status, Brown's round and ruddy face turned a new, threatening hue.

"He's certainly not my hero," he said, then added ominously, "I hope that you and I and everybody else, when he does make that fatal mistake, are not responsible for something other than an arrest being made without an incident."

The tenor of Brown's response heartened those villagers already carrying flaming torches. And it horrified others.

"The mentality here on Camano when all this started was ridiculous," says Maria (not her real name), a local woman who, a few years before, supervised Colt while he did community service at the park where she works. "Not a lot goes on out here, so when something does happen it gets blown out of proportion."

Maria previously worked for years as a crisis worker in Bellingham, counseling at-risk youth who included those she calls "the worst of the worst, extreme cases, kids that were too psychologically wounded to stay in juvie." She saw hundreds run through the system. "I had experience with children that came from some of the most horrific environments you can imagine, and we [society] still had these expectations that they were going to behave and fit in like any other child. I loved my job, but it just became too much for me." That experience, though, gave her the confidence to volunteer to take on Colt even though he already had a reputation as trouble.

Maria says Pam dropped him off the first two days but then stopped. She didn't know how he made the twenty-mile round-trip the rest of the week. "He showed up every day without any food or anything to drink, and he was expected to work all day outdoors. So I fed him, gave him water, and he was just so very grateful."

Despite his reputation, Colt struck her as "a good-hearted kid who'd always been looked at with negative expectations and didn't have a lot of motivation to feel good about his life. Yet give a kid like Colton a chance, some stability, look at them with some possibility, and they tend to shine. Colton took this opportunity and he just worked his butt off, sawing and hauling wood, pulling weeds and cutting brush to create a picnic area."

She said Colton was quiet, a bit shy, that he didn't talk much except about the work at hand. "He had just a ridiculous amount of knowledge about the plants and what would grow here. He struck me as being really smart, so I started to ask his opinion and advice and he instantly perked up and became really engaged. I told him he might have a job here when he graduates and he said, 'You think so? All right, right on.'"

Colton gave her plenty of great ideas for plantings, but Maria explained that she had a very tight budget and couldn't afford to buy new plants.

"When he left, he said, 'Thank you so much,' and he wanted to know if he had any more community service to work out, would I be willing to have him here, and I said, 'Absolutely, in a heartbeat!' It was an absolute pleasure working with him."

Two weeks later, Colton rode his bike ten miles back to the park. "He was kinda shy, handed me three small bags and just said, 'Here.' He'd remembered about the budget and went out and hand-harvested seeds from local flowers that he thought would grow well in the park. I said, 'Oh my God, thank you so much!' And he's like, 'Yeah, all right. Well, I guess I'll go, bye.' He started to walk away but then turned around and said, 'Thank you for being so nice to me.' I was literally teary-eyed."

As I CONTINUED SOUTH on Camano, Maria's take had me thinking of Huck Finn. Huck, whose life's theme was freedom and escape—from rules, schoolin', and his drunk dad who'd locked him in that backwoods cabin. Huck, who did what he had to do to survive, including "borrowing" what he needed, like food, clothing, and canoes. Was Colton just a kid who'd struck out on his own to escape a bad home and then got swept

along in a big current of circumstance? Were our yachts and planes just
fancy rafts transporting him from one test of his relative morality to the
next?

On the way to my first visit to Pam and Colt's home, I stopped at the
little back-country commercial oasis a half mile south of Elger Bay Elementary School. There's a general store and a nice little café that both carry the
Elger Bay name. Together they serve as the dining, grocery-shopping, gas-
and propane-filling, mailing, DVD-renting, fishing, hunting, and banking
center (via an ATM) for the South End. An antique Coca-Cola sign and a
big community bulletin board decorate the outside of the grocery. There's
an elaborate jerky display near the entrance, and the fine wines and crab
bait are just a few steps apart. It is truly a convenience store.

It's also the South End's social and gossip center.

"Local people come in here and when you say, 'How are you today?'
you *really* hear how they are today," laughed Kara Weber, a longtime islander who works at the store. "And when anything happens on the island,
the phone here starts ringing."

Over the past three years, Colton and his mom had kept the phone busy
at Elger Bay, with both talk about them and between them. "She thinks her
phone is tapped, so she comes down here and uses the pay phone to talk
to him."

Chances were decent, said Kara, that the next person walking in would
be a crime victim. "A guy who comes in the store got hit and had just gotten
his insurance in place when that little bugger hit him again! Another local
woman had her credit cards stolen and we caught Colt in here on video using them to take money out of the ATM. I've heard the term 'Robin
Hood' . . . well, this guy isn't stealing from the rich and giving to the poor.
There used to be a feeling around here that if they need it that bad, then
there, take it. But after it just kept happening and happening, then people
got really pissed off. It's certainly hurt the confidence we had in our sheriff's department. When this all started I got a dog, and Joe is the kind to eat
first and ask questions later."

Despite her consistent denials that she ever helped Colt while he was
on the lam, Pam Kohler's involvement is a constant subject of speculation
in the area. Kara said there were rumors of a trap door in the trailer, even
a tunnel so Colton could come and go without the police seeing. Kara

was at the counter one day back in 2008, after Colton had escaped from the prison home and was back committing burglaries on the island. "Pam comes in and pulls out a Ziploc full of money like I've never seen. What really threw me is we're talking about a woman that's on assistance."

Kara can soften a bit talking about Colton. "He didn't stand a chance. He truly went through hell and I think this all boils down to what he went through as a kid." But then she turns angry again when she considers what he did to her community. "He knows right from wrong—if not, why would he run from the cops? He's smart, too; the problem is that he's just using it for the wrong things. He figured out the electricity timing, just like Josh thought he would."

Josh is Josh Flickner, whose family has owned and operated Elger Bay Grocery for eighteen years. The electrical event was when the Washington DOT announced that they were cutting power to Camano overnight as part of the new bridge construction. The warning provided a save the date for would-be thieves who knew exactly when the entire island would go lights out.

With Colton back on the island, Flickner—who was also head of the local chamber of commerce—called Sheriff Brown and suggested that he station deputies at his grocery and other likely targets. Flickner says his idea went nowhere, so his sister and another employee camped out in the store. In the middle of the night, they awoke to someone tearing the deadbolt out of the back door. They saw the silhouette of a man, "about six-five, same build as Colton, carrying a big empty trash bag," says Flickner. "They said, 'Hello?' and he just calmly turned around and left."

Josh had become the voice of local anti-Colt sentiment. "All he's doing is hurting people—financially, psychologically, he's hurting people, yet here we are putting him on a pedestal, glorifying him, idolizing him. He's got a Facebook site . . . I want to vomit, okay?"

Josh disagreed with Sheriff Brown on tactics. "I think we could have caught him two years ago. I know about sixty guys that would've volunteered to comb the woods in the south end of the island—it's not that wide. A sheriff has the power to deputize citizens, but he said no, he'd never do that. People are getting really frustrated when the sheriff says don't take it into your own hands while every day more people are victimized."

Josh said Pam still came into the store regularly. "She buys $2 of gas, cigarettes, and six-packs of Busch Ice. We talk to her and half the time she's in denial and the other half she's talking about how proud she is of Colt. Now she's being quoted in *Time* magazine. Our society is so sad."

Josh remembers Colton coming into the store as a young boy. "There was always something shady about him. I remember looking into his eyes and something did not look right . . . just a look of malicious intent . . . I lean toward saying evil."

I left Elger Bay Grocery wondering whether I was looking for Huckleberry Finn or Michael Myers from *Halloween*. It was the thirtieth of October, and Josh's account of young Colton resembled Donald Pleasence's "child with the devil's eyes" monologue from the horror movie.

The one issue everyone seemed to agree on was Colton's mother, Pam. Kara told me that all the neighbors are scared of her "because of the shotgun . . . They don't know how far she'll go."

From what local reporters and police told me, I was the first writer invited to the trailer. I'd written Pam a letter, telling her a little about my background. I said I felt I could empathize with all sides of the story. I knew a number of the victims, lived in one of the affected communities, and had cops in my close family. By Colton's age, I'd also had a few scrapes with the law, and a few years after that I wound up halfway around the world in the Republic of Maldives working at an island resort with David Friedland, a former New Jersey state senator who'd faked his death in the Bahamas to escape racketeering charges. Friedland ascended to number-one most-wanted fugitive status, hunted ceaselessly by the feds and Interpol. I saw that pressure firsthand. I also belatedly understood what my escapades did to my parents. All they knew was that I was somewhere overseas where my day-to-day life involved charging tourists to watch me stick dead fish in my mouth and feed them to wild sharks—I'd thoughtfully sent them video footage. For nearly two years, my parents spent their nights not knowing whether I'd end up lost at sea, decapitated by a shark, or locked away in some fetid fourth-world prison.

I was also an adrenaline junkie, and had even soloed an amphibious ultralight airplane after the sketchiest of instruction. I told Pam that my experiences might give me some insight into what both she and Colton were going through.

. . . .

On Haven Place, I slowed to a crawl at a low point in the swaybacked road where damper soil encouraged a thick stand of cedars. I first passed by what looked like just a narrow gap between trees but turned out to be a driveway. When I backed up I saw the two big WARNING NO TRESPASSING signs. I turned into the cavelike entrance, branches reaching out to hiss and scratch the length of my truck. I stopped under a large tree beside three other pickups in varying states of decay. Two of them, including a cool 1966 Chevy, were far down entropy road; the other was a typical island clunker rig that still looked drivable. An orange bowling ball lay in tall grass next to the broken tin skeleton of a kiddie pool filled with many summers' worth of browned cedar branchlets.

I ducked under a final, dripping bough and entered a small clearing. A moldering, moss-stained single-wide trailer home slumped across the space. About a hundred feet of flat lawn stretched in front, with a picnic table and rock fire pit. A smaller clearing behind the trailer led to a garden, an animal pen, and a chicken house.

An extra room and a deck had been cobbled onto the narrow trailer at some point over the years. I climbed a wobbly stack of cinder blocks that stood in for steps up to the deck. Looking out from atop the rain-slicked planks, it was a beautiful, tranquil piece of property completely screened by billowing drapes of cedar and Douglas fir, everything a deep evergreen in the misty overcast. The trailer, the junk, the aluminum shed frozen in mid-collapse, the camper decaying under the trees—nothing was really so far out of a certain ordinary for around here.

At the far side of the clearing, in a natural grotto amid the soaring cathedral of hundred-foot trees, stood some kind of statue. It was about four feet high, indistinct, but I could make out a head and outstretched arms. It might be a Virgin Mary.

"That's an armadilla that used to stand outside a liquor store," said Pam Kohler. "The chickens got to it, though, and pecked off some of the Styrofoam." The statue, she said, was on the property when she bought it twenty-four years ago.

Dressed in a sagging gray sweater over white pants and house slippers, fifty-eight-year-old Pam was hunched over and moving slow, as if life had her weighed down. Beneath brown hair her eyes were milky blue and tired. Nicotined fingernails and ashtrays filled with Pall Mall butts floating in a black ooze of ash and rainwater explained the load of gravel in her voice.

She invited me in and the door opened directly into a small living room with a brown couch facing a wood stove and TV. She said her antenna pulls in a few broadcast channels, but mainly she listens to the radio or watches movies—Westerns are her favorites—on the TV in her bedroom. She used to have a DVD player, she said, but had to sell it, so she watches VHS tapes.

Even accounting for the overcast day, it was dim inside. The windows that weren't broken and covered with plywood were obscured by newspapers "to keep the reporters and the cops from looking in." A sallow light filtered through, matching the cloying scent of cigarettes.

Pam calls the trailer "dumpy" and she's not wrong. She said she'd been cleaning for a week in anticipation of a visitor, a childhood friend of her late husband who'd been writing to her every week from prison. Now he was getting out after serving a thirty-seven-year sentence and was going to live at the trailer "to protect me and Colt. Nobody's going to mess with me once he gets here."

Melanie, Colton's dog, greeted me with her tail wagging at 100 rpm. "I think she's some kind of hunting dog," said Pam. "This summer she got one of the biggest snakes I've ever seen, and then some kind of rodent." Melanie also snagged a neighborhood chicken that day, whose fresh carcass I almost stepped in out on the lawn.

According to Pam, Mel also has a nose for money. She told me the story of a couple who moved their travel trailer onto her property for a while. "They stayed one night and never came back, so Colt and I went in. We found hypodermic needles in there . . . Melanie kept scratching at one of the seats, so I said to Colt, 'Let's break in there and see what it is.' There was a hundred and seventy-some dollars in there. Colt grabbed it and the chase was on!" She laughed.

Just last month, Mel found something else unusual on the property. "She was barking out in the yard, so I walk over and it's a SWAT guy hiding in the trees in his full G.I. Joe outfit." Melanie, Mel, or Meeshee, as Colt sometimes calls her, has plenty of experience sniffing the police. "You can always tell when they're around because they all wear foo foo," says Pam, meaning cologne.

All the jurisdictions except the Mounties had been there, including the FBI and officers from an auto theft task force who, Pam said, told her they thought Colt had stolen between forty and sixty cars. "Those guys brought me a plate of chocolate chip cookies," Pam said. "It's all weird." Other cops brought cans of dog food for Melanie. The FBI agents, she said, had been professional so far, but she had a big, long-standing problem with the Island County deputies, who she described as "bumbling idiots."

"Everything that happens on this island they blame on Colt. I'm sure he's done some of these things . . . but he'd have to be sixty or seventy years old to have done all the things Mark Brown says he's done."

We sat at a small kitchen table, Pam drinking coffee. The fridge went bad, so she has only a dorm-size. Plus, she said, "Vacuum broke down, wash machine broke down, my truck broke down, all within forty-eight hours." The ceiling's falling down in patches, too, but there's a new wood laminate floor that Pam told me Colt had installed for her before he last went to "the slammer."

A friend gave her a dishwasher, and she also has plenty of music. While on the lam, Colt had sent her a couple of iPods preloaded with Michael Jackson and Patsy Cline—"Colt thinks she's got a beautiful voice." Colt has wide-ranging taste in music, from the latest rap to Ol' Blue Eyes, and one of Pam's favorite memories is dancing with him out on the deck to Sinatra's "Summer Wind."

She was adamant that Colt wasn't living out in the woods. He'd told her he was staying in a house protected by high-tech surveillance equipment. He had his own room, TV, and computer. The people who own the house were a recently married couple and there were also two men a bit older than Colt living there, one of whom was ex-military. Pam called those guys "Colt's goons." Colt, she said, had free access to the family's big SUV and did computer work for them, getting paid $600 a week. The wife was a chef into organic food, though Colt asked her to stop cooking it for him because he was trying to put on weight. Once, the chef even cooked Pam a gourmet meal that someone delivered to her mailbox at the end of Haven. Pam says the family also gave her a Bose Wave radio. "I had to pawn it once for money, and they ran the serial number to make sure it wasn't stolen—and it wasn't."

Pam said the police knew all these details. "I started thinking maybe they didn't want to find Colt," she said. "That way they could go to the public and say, 'We can't catch this kid because we don't have enough manpower. We need more money.'"

The mystery family had now moved off Camano, but Pam said she didn't know where. Colt still stayed with them, though, proof that he had no reason to be breaking into people's houses or businesses. When I mention that police had found his fingerprints at crime scenes, she said, "I know for a fact that Colt doesn't leave fingerprints. In fact, I have a pair of my gloves that he used to wear . . . those little ones that stretch to any size, real soft."

Pam said the deputies had been following her. "They think I'm hiding him, but I'm not, and I don't know where he is . . . and wouldn't tell them if I did."

Her mail had recently stopped for a week, so she called an FBI agent who'd left his card. "He said, 'We don't do that, but maybe Island County cops were taking it.' The next day all of my mail showed up. There's just too many weird things going on."

Pam was sure they had her phone bugged, and maybe the trailer and her truck. Her prison pen pal, she said, was going to sweep the place for listening devices when he got there. She said she was suspicious and leery of everything. "One of these sheriffs that was here yesterday, he told me he knows a colonel in the army, that he can get Colt in touch with him and go into special forces . . . And I don't believe it. I don't believe anything anybody ever tells me. I never have."

After Granite Falls, a Snohomish County police officer called her. "He said, 'I'm at a crash site and Colt's name has been mentioned.' And I thought he meant a car crash! I said, 'Where are the people?' He said there was nobody there. He wasn't giving me any information . . . I asked if an aid car had taken Colt to the hospital, and he just said nobody's here. So I asked, 'Well, are there like body parts or what?'"

The officer finally told her it was a plane crash.

"I was pretty shocked. I really don't believe Colt flew any planes . . . but if he did, I am very, very proud of him because he woulda had to teach himself. And if he is flying them, then I hope he wears a parachute and works on his landings."

I find that Pam has a sense of humor, albeit a rough one, though it doesn't sound like she gets to exercise it much. And she admitted to being prickly. "Fucking-A right I'm hard to get along with! I don't have any friends, I don't associate with anybody. I only leave the property to go to the store if I have to. I don't like people, I don't like relatives . . ."

Pam wasn't working and said she was now disabled. Social Security denied her benefits, but she was fighting them and hoped the money would kick in before she lost the property for failure to pay taxes (it did after, she says, she was diagnosed with a broken back). She said her widow's benefits stopped when Colt turned eighteen, and she once had to consider selling the Camano land. "Colt just freaked out: 'But Mom, I wanted to show my kids all the trees I've climbed!'"

No friends, no money, no family around . . . Pam was leading an insular life even for an islander. Her older son, Colt's half brother, Paul, fell off a three-story roof twelve years ago and is disabled, living on the mainland. Now the one family member she said she was close to had been on the lam for eighteen months.

Pam asked the FBI to find Colt's father, Gordon Moore. "I think he oughta be out here worrying just as much as me!" She tried to get ahold of Moore herself by calling the last place she knew he was staying. "He was living with this old lady and she told me, 'He's not here and he better never come back!' She had this little tiny rat dog, yippin', and it musta drove him nuts, and I guess he took it outside and killed it . . . That sounds like Gordy."

She said Colt doesn't take after his father. "Colt decided by himself that he didn't like Gordy. I would say that was a good call." Colton, she said, loves animals. He even had a pet spider out by a patch of holly trees. "He fed it for years," Pam said. "He'd get bugs and throw them into its web and it would run over and wrap them up. One time when he called [from out on the run] I said, 'You want me to keep feeding that spider for you?' And he goes, 'Oh, Mom, you don't have ta.' I said 'I will if you want me to.'"

During another of their recent calls, Pam told Colton she was doing some cleaning. He was, she said, very concerned about his stuffed animal collection. "I told him they were fine, that I put them in a Rubbermaid for him." Nonchalant about getting chased through dark woods by SWAT teams and Black Hawk helicopters, the famous Barefoot Bandit was worried about whether his plush puppies were well cared for.

There were no photos and few personal touches on display in the trailer besides a couple of fish and animal knickknacks that Pam said were Colt's. "We didn't take many pictures," she said. Pam thought the self-portrait of Colt run with all the news stories was terrible, but said she liked the one from the Island Market security camera on Orcas that was now featured on wanted posters. "Colt said that's not him, but it looks like him to me . . . and I think that's a good picture of him . . . if it's him."

Pam said she and Colt kept up on everything by telephone, that he called her frequently on an untraceable phone "like the president has." Whenever they heard clicks or static on the line, Colt said it was the FBI listening in and he "says derogatory things to them." She said they talked for hours each time he called.

"We always laugh on the phone. I mean laugh hard, really hard. And some people may not see the humor in things that him and I see. Some of it is probably not very . . . definitely not politically correct. I am pretty prejudiced because of Vietnam, never really got over it, and Colt knows that. He always brings up something that makes me laugh about Orientals."

Colt was following the press about himself and Pam said he'd been getting angry at her lately for talking to the media. "I told him it's the only way to get his side of the story out there."

What her calls to radio shows, interviews in the local papers, and even call-ins to cable TV shows seemed to be doing, mostly, was to inadvertently deflect heat off Colt and onto her. She'd made herself an easy target, the one clear villain in the story, and had become a two-dimensional quote machine. Her gruff phone manner and gravelly "hisselfs" evoked Granny Clampett or, as some of the local cops referred to her around the station, Momma from the movie *Throw Momma from the Train*. When she told the hosts of Seattle's *Ron and Don Show* that Colt said his IQ tested three points below that of Einstein, one of them quipped that it sounded like hers was three points below room temperature.

Though her interviews didn't get beyond the "I'm proud he can fly planes" soundbites, the narrative Pam was trying to tell was that she could never control Colt, and "no one in the school system ever tried to help him," the social service people were "well-meaning but useless," and the deputies never tried to help the local kids. According to her, Colt was a good-hearted kid who loved the outdoors and airplanes, and who didn't steal because he needed to, "but because he can."

I asked Pam if she had any regrets about her part in Colt's upbringing. She said her biggest mistake was not moving Colton out of Island County once she realized everyone had it in for him.

I ASKED IF COLTON had a plan. "Kids always have plans . . . whether they're good or bad." At one point, she said, Colt had given her the tail number of an airplane and said she should be ready to meet him. "He wants to come get me and me be with him. Go live the good life."

Colt's idea of the good life, she said, was "having a yacht and living on a tropical island." The only way he'd ever talked of earning that good life was being a pilot. "I told him, 'You graduate and we'll send you to flight school.' Evidently he don't need flight school."

He did, however, recently tell Pam: "Don't be surprised if you get a strange phone call one day from either the government or a private company that wants to hire me to do secret work." She said Colt assured her that he wouldn't do anything for the federal government unless he had a twenty-year contract.

She stressed a number of times that she was proud of Colt for his abilities, including being able to evade helicopters and SWAT teams. "He's doing it because he likes to see if he can. He thinks it's easy—he's said that. And he's sure making them look like fools."

When a radio interviewer once prodded Pam, saying it sounded like she was rooting for him, she said, "Of course! I'm his mother!"

I ASKED IF PAM thought Colt might be doing some of these things for the press attention. "No, he's his own person, very much. He's not going to do anything because of what's in the media."

She said he was, however, following the news and his fan club online. "He laughs, reads me a few things over the phone, and we crack up. I told him the other day that when this is over, you have your pick of any woman, they're in love with you." I asked about his reaction to that. "He don't care, he's not into a girlfriend. He's got other things on his mind."

It didn't seem contradictory to Pam that Colt thought the media coverage was absurd and yet he'd told her to be ready to drag the old gate across the driveway because he was planning "something big" that would have "the paparazzi" crawling all over the place.

With that warning and the recent story from Granite Falls, Pam seemed fatalistic about Colt's chances, saying she didn't think he'd make it out alive, "not if he took a shot at those cops." She said that "everyone makes their life plan before they come to this earth," so "whatever Colt's going to go through, whatever's gonna happen is gonna happen, he planned it that way . . . It's predetermined."

Pam said she was trying to get Colt a bulletproof vest. I asked if he told her he wanted one. "I don't care if he does or not. I'm getting him one and he's going to wear it. Sometimes a mother has to put her foot down."

WHEN I STOPPED BY the next day to take photos of Melanie, it appeared that it soon wouldn't be safe for anyone to put his foot down around Pam's property. Her friend had arrived the previous evening. There was a big contractor bag filled with empty Busch Ice cans on the deck. Inside, Pam was doing her version of coquettish. She'd apparently been able to leave behind the weirdness for at least a few hours. For me, it was a whole new level. While Pam happily chatted on the phone, I sat at the kitchen table with Tim. Both physically and in his calmly menacing manner, he reminded me of David Carradine in *Kung Fu*. I wasn't surprised when he told me of his martial arts prowess. He said he didin't want to be identified because he had enemies from his time in prison. He was in there, he said, because he "broke a cop." He added, kind of unnecessarily, that he had a real problem with authority.

Tim also told me that if he wanted to, he could find anyone—anyone—in two days. I wanted to tell him that things have changed a little in the last thirty-seven years, and now a ten-year-old with a Web connection can find anyone in two minutes . . . but I didn't. It didn't seem like the time for jokes. Instead, it was booby-trap time.

Tim picked up a shotgun shell and hunting knife, and patiently showed me how he was carving away the ends of the shell casings to empty the pellets while leaving the wad and gunpowder in place. Then, he explained, you simply add a cap that impacts the primer when stepped on, and bury it out in the yard. Voilà, a homemade "toe-popper." It wouldn't kill anybody, he said . . . unless of course he went into shock. It was just designed to blow off part of a foot. To complement the poppers, he planned on adding camouflaged nail boards, poor-man pungi sticks, most effective when dipped in shit.

Pam said these would keep the media and the police away. I questioned the wisdom of setting booby traps for the police. "If I put a sign down at the end of my driveway saying 'Property Is Booby Trapped, Enter at Your Own Risk,' I think that covers me . . . And I don't care if it does or not. I'm not gonna have cops running around my property at all hours of the day and night . . . It's just unnerving."

They never made the "Booby Trapped" notice, but Tim did paint IF YOU GO PAST THIS SIGN YOU WILL BE SHOT on a big piece of plywood and posted it at the front of the drive.

23

My *Outside* magazine story about Colt hit the newsstands in mid-January 2010. I heard from a number of locals how unhappy they were that I was giving this kid, who was "a media creation," national attention. Better, one said, that we should keep silent so it would all just go away.

Friends joked with Sandi that because of the story, Colt was sure to come back to the island now and pay me a visit.

According to Pam, though, Colton already knew who I was. "He checks out everyone I talk to," she said. "And he's been reading your Web thing." Since there was no conclusion to the story by my deadline, I'd begun posting updates on a blog called Outlaws & Outcasts. Colt followed the posts as well as the Web sites that carried my travel-adventure stories.

Three weeks later, on February 10 at around 11 p.m., aviation authorities keeping guard over the antiterrorist no-fly zone wrapped around the Vancouver Olympics noted a small plane taking off from Anacortes Airport. The exclusion zone dipped to just north of Orcas Island, and any aircraft entering it had to utilize a special transponder code. This one wasn't transmitting the correct signal. ATC tracked the plane as it flew an erratic course, teasing along the no-go line, but they kept from pulling the trigger on any of their contingency plans, such as launching fighters armed with Sidewinder suppositories. They monitored the plane until it disappeared from radar over Orcas, and then forgot all about it.

The plane, a $650,000 Cirrus SR22—the same model Colt had stolen for his first night flight—touched down at the north end of the Orcas runway and was found bogged down in the muddy grass alongside the airstrip. It was a decent landing in that at least the plane was still flyable, with only minor damage to a gear cowling.

At 8:15 the following morning, Kyle Ater opened the door to his Homegrown Grocery and saw cartoonish bare feet drawn on the floor. He figured it was an employee prank. "I thought, Oh, these won't be hard to clean up because it's just chalk. Then I took a couple more steps into the store and saw the tills laid out on the floor and water pouring out of the sink."

The footprints trailed all around the store, up and down the aisles, ending at the side door with a "C-Ya!" The cash drawer was smashed open. "I went over to the sink to turn it off, and the security system was in there, underwater, along with my pliers, knife sharpeners, and a screwdriver." He called the police. "I'd been getting a whole new level of service from them since all the Colt stuff started because of the media attention." Kyle put on rubber gloves to keep from contaminating the scene and the officers arrived quickly. "But Steve Vierthaler told me, 'Don't worry, we won't be sending anything to the crime lab because they won't be able to look at it for a year.'"

Kyle says he and the deputies were thinking the break-in was a copycat because Colt had never done anything like draw footprints. "While they're shooting pictures, though, a radio call comes in saying, 'We've got a plane in the grass at the airport.' We all hear this and instantly everyone says, 'It is him!'"

The cops ran out of Homegrown and rushed to the plane, which had been sitting on the field for eight hours before airport manager Bea Von Tobel arrived, saw it, and thought, Oh no, not him again. The red-and-white Cirrus was pulled out of the mud and towed into a hangar belonging to Chuck Stewart (not his real name), the wealthy former CEO of a sportswear company.

Kyle wasn't really surprised to hear about the plane. It meant that Colt had finally got him. "He was mad that I'd beat him the previous year, that I'd kept him from breaking in by staying here every night for two months while he hit all those other businesses in town."

Sleeping on the floor with a .44 Magnum strapped to his leg hadn't played well with the mild-mannered organic grocer. "The stress caused a huge spike in my blood pressure, so I had to start taking my Chinese herbs. I couldn't keep staying here forever, though. It was exhausting. I needed to be at home in my own bed. So I basically spent all my year's profits on this security system." Kyle upgraded to a top-shelf sixteen-channel, high-resolution night-vision "really bad-ass system" that he could monitor from home on the Internet and communicate with via his iPhone. "It gave me a false sense of security . . . I mean this is a health food store; how many levels of surveillance do I need?"

A total of $1,200 was gone from the tills. The key to the upstairs office had been in the cash drawer, but it wasn't used. Instead, the office door had been busted open. The business's main computer was destroyed. "He thought the central server was the security backup, so he broke it open and jumped up and down on it, shattering the cards." The actual surveillance system was in a self-contained unit. Colt had tilted all the cameras down and unhooked them from the system, then realized the monitor also housed the memory. "He cracked it open to reach in and see if there was a hard drive. He would have gotten it if he took out the twenty-four screws, but there wasn't a Phillips-head around. So instead, he put it in the sink and turned on the water."

Downstairs in the store, working by the light from the beer and wine displays fronting the walk-in cooler, Colt raised all the covers over the vegetables bins and slid open all the deli cases. "He left them open and we had to throw out all the food," says Kyle. He didn't touch any of the beer or wine, but Kyle was sure he took some organic produce. He also went into the walk-in and took an entire two-by-three-foot baker's tray loaded with raw meat-and-cheese croissants that were proofing. "No way you could think they were ready to eat," says Kyle.

Colt also lifted a big hunk of dessert, an entire organic cheesecake. This one was blueberry, not strawberry like on his shopping list collage, but close enough.

As soon as I turned on my phone that morning, it rang with news of the stolen plane. Already, though, the Homegrown story had twisted into "the police dusted the floor and found footprints." I got to Kyle's expecting evidence of human footprints and instead had to laugh when I saw all the big "goofy foots" drawn on the floor. They even kind of fit in with the hippie vibe.

The first thing that struck me about the footprints was that there were a lot of them—thirty-nine, so many that they almost created a paisley pattern on the floor. Nothing about Colt said "Hitchcock fan," so I assumed it wasn't an homage to *The 39 Steps*. The drawings weren't terribly intricate, but each had an arched shape and five toes, so it must have taken fifteen minutes or so to move around the store and chalk them all. Why take the risk of pausing in the middle of committing a felony to do all that? If you wanted to send a message, wouldn't two feet have done it just as well as thirty-nine? While it could have been manic overkill, it looked to me more like Colt telling us how confident he was in his skills versus the police. He wasn't afraid of dawdling at a crime scene. The smashed and drowned security system, though, seemed twisted. Why go to all that trouble to make sure no images of you survived at the same time you signed your autograph thirty-nine times? Of course other than his own self-portraits, Colt was severely camera shy.

The "C-Ya!" he tagged onto the end was in jaunty bold letters. Knowing the extent Kyle had gone to keep Colt out of his store, it was easily seen as a "Na na, you can't stop me, I'm smarter than you!"—the same kind of tweak as restealing a bike out of a police station, or breaking a dog out of a pound, or returning again and again to take food from a home that kept upping its security measures. For a gamer, it was a great challenge.

When I went to the airport and saw the spot where the Cirrus ended up in the grass, something else occurred to me. The plane apparently landed at the north end of the runway and stopped quickly. That's the quiet end of the airport bordered by the Ditch, a field and woods, so it made sense to land there just to make sure no one saw you run off. But it also made perfect sense if your real plan was to land, run to town for a quick snack and to leave your mark à la Zorro, and then take off again. That would be an all-time "You can't catch me!" Secret-Agent Double-0 Smart-Ass, level 30 game move. It would take two daring night flights and two landings, the ultimate in-your-face to all those who'd been joking online that Colt must not have read the second half of the flight manual.

He'd told Pam to get ready for the paparazzi . . .

Two guests at Smuggler's Villa reported hearing a plane revving its engine again and again at 4 a.m. that morning—as if the pilot was trying to get it unstuck. The timing fit.

One last detail that struck me about Homegrown is that the footprints were drawn with chalk from the menu board. Was the tag a spur-of-the-moment decision—he saw the chalk and a bell went off? Or did he already know Homegrown so well that he knew the chalk would be there?

A local Eastsound woman later told me she'd seen someone suspicious in Homegrown the previous fall. "He caught my eye because he was extremely tall, barefoot at a time of year when even the barefoot folks around here are wearing shoes, and because he had this shit-eating grin on his face." When Colt's photo ran in the paper, she recognized his face even though there'd been something slightly different in his appearance. "When I saw him, he had on a dreadlock wig."

Pam told me that Colt said he'd been going out in public in disguises, telling her, "You wouldn't even know me, Mom." He never said, though, whether one of his characters was Rasta Harris-Moore.

THE ONE UNASSAILABLY DISTURBING fact was that Colt was now embracing the Barefoot Bandit persona. He was actively courting the media. No, he wasn't its creation, but he was digging the attention. Later, we learned that Colt had already been on the island in January, hiding inside Chuck Stewart's hangar. To take the chill off a cold winter's night, Colt squeezed his six-foot-five frame inside a Mini Cooper stored in the hangar and turned on the seat warmers. He stole a notebook and flashlight out of the glove compartment, and in a detail the cops—all amateur psychologists—love, he broke off one of the side mirrors to look at himself and feed what they believed was his narcissistic personality disorder.

What the visit to Stewart's hangar meant was that Colt had been able to move on and off Orcas without being noticed, without having to steal a boat or a plane. The Anacortes plane was a prank done solely for the thrill and the headlines. That kind of behavior tacked on to the guns and the cop teasing meant that the danger to both Colt and everyone else had cranked up immeasurably.

. . . .

THE FEBRUARY SUN SANK behind the islands at 5:30 p.m. Back home, after an uncomfortable talk with Sandi about being more vigilant, taking the keys out of her car, locking down the house, and using the new safe, the woods around our cabin once again seemed darker.

Where was he? If he had planned a hit and run, he was probably still looking for a quick way off the island. Flying was out, as the wind picked up wildly after dark. And surely the police now had eyes on the marinas. Or not.

At eight, I drove to Deer Harbor Marina to look for Colt or for people looking for Colt, and didn't see either. By nine, I was in Eastsound and went to the airport and the Ditch and drove up and down the streets. Everything looked deserted. I drove down Orcas's own Haven Road and parked by the Odd Fellows Hall, about 150 yards away from the huge NO TRESPASSING sign that marked the ancient Indian burial ground at Madrona Point.

Walking down the road, I expected a cop or FBI agent to jump out at any moment. This spot seemed a no-brainer for a stakeout, so I hunched my six-foot frame even shorter so no one could mistake me for the Bandit. Once I passed the warning sign and lost the glow of Eastsound, though, size didn't matter. It was a black, moonless night and no one could see a thing. I kept to the path only by altering course whenever I tripped over a rock or bush. Slowly my eyes adjusted to the point where I could see a faint radiance of water and sky through the crowd of black, skeletal silhouettes of madrona trees to the west. About fifteen minutes in, I stopped and sat on a log. I couldn't see or smell any campfires. The only option seemed to be to sit and listen. However, by this point the wind was gusting over 30 mph, hissing loudly through the trees. A regiment of infantry could have marched by without my hearing them. If Colt was heading in or out, though, he'd have to use this trail. Then I wondered what the hell I'd do if he did.

The cold wind cleared the skies, and stars came out above the trees, which were being whipped into a frenzy. Every big gust broke more widow makers out of the tall firs, the branches cracking like gunshots and then crashing to the ground. It was not a good night to be camping or hiding in the woods.

It also wasn't a good night to be sitting there. I got up and started to trip my way back down the path. Just as I reached the huge gnarly Doug fir that guards the entrance, a long, agonized screech came out of the black woods. A raccoon was decapitating a squirrel or something . . . I didn't stop to find out. I drove home thinking that along with dealing with some crappy weather, if Colt was spending a lot of time in the woods he must be having some wild, spooky nights.

Back at the cabin, I settled in to transcribe notes. Then at midnight, the dog went off. Murphy rushed from door to door inside the tiny cabin. As soon as I opened the front door, he growled and lunged outside. I grabbed him by the scruff but he dragged me off the porch, determined to get at whatever was under the house. I wrestled him back inside. Sandi, who'd been pretty cavalier about things up to this point, was wide-eyed. Murphy had never done anything like that in his three years on Orcas.

While I was in town earlier that day after hearing Colt had returned, I'd gone by our storage unit. It took me over an hour of digging through boxes but I finally found something I hadn't seen since packing it away in Orlando. Now I pushed a handful of shells into the twelve-gauge pistol-grip "street sweeper" shotgun. "Probably nothing," I said, shrugging, then went outside, telling Sandi to lock the door behind me.

There was nothing under the house. I walked up to the parking pad and no one was there either. I checked the cars, I snuck up on the outhouse and peeked inside. Then I hiked up the long driveway that cuts through the woods. I felt like an idiot, but I called out to Colt several times.

THERE WAS NO SIGN of Colt that night or the next. Any hope that he might've hightailed it off the island again was dashed the following day, though, when word spread that Chuck Stewart's hangar had been broken into again.

The Olympics happening just fifty miles north meant an already increased security presence in the region, and Orcas suddenly got the attention of a host of federal agencies along with additional state and local law enforcement. At the same time, a number of islanders decided that they'd had enough and suited up for some Colt wrangling. It was an entertaining mix. One father-and-son team patrolling the Eastsound streets dressed in full camo gear spotted movement in the bushes and rushed in to grab what turned out to be two FBI agents. A baker heading to work at 5 a.m. rounded a corner and saw two guys peering into his restaurant with night-vision goggles—more FBI agents. Anyone male near town in a car or on foot between dusk and dawn was a target. One acquaintance who drove to the gym early each morning in his rattling pickup got stopped again and again.

The FBI also set up a camera in Bea Von Tobel's airport office and fed video to their Seattle field office of every plane arriving or departing Orcas. Officially, though, the FBI continued to say they were not interested in the case of what was merely a local miscreant.

At the north end of the island, U.S. Coast Guard cutters cruised back and forth just offshore with their chase boats lowered, ready to snatch up anything trying to bolt out of the Ditch. Along with the coasties, DHS Customs and Border Protection 900- and 1,200-horsepower Interceptor Class patrol boats circled Orcas, sweeping the island and surrounding waters with their FLIR (forward-looking infrared, aka thermal imaging) and radar. U.S. Navy warships stood by along the border focusing their surveillance equipment on anything that moved. There were so many electromagnetic waves sweeping the area that we figured everyone on the island was now sterile.

SMUGGLER'S RESORT, SITUATED RIGHT on the Ditch and adjacent to the airport, served as a convenient base for all kinds of agents now sent on stealthy missions to capture Colt. They all came to Orcas undercover and, this being a small island, kept their secrets sometimes as long as fifteen minutes.

"They had multiple layers of undercover people here," says Smuggler's Mike Stolmeier. "I got different groups of from one to four guys staying in the condos and being real vague about their visits. But they'd always request the unit closest to the airport and then they'd casually try to pay with government credit cards. 'Oh, we're on leave from Iraq for a month.' Yeah, right you guys . . . this is what you would do if you're on a one-month leave, come to Orcas off-season when there's nobody here and nothing to do. My favorite was a couple of guys, outdoorsy types, who'd been looking around and then came in acting real nonchalant and started asking questions about the marina and the airport and 'Gee, does anything unusual ever happen around here?' So I said, 'Yeah, occasionally we get guys acting kind of suspicious.' They didn't get it, and one asked, 'So you've actually seen people acting suspicious?' I handed him a slip of paper with their license plate written on it, and said, 'Yes, the two guys in this car.'

"The biggest batch were four guys who stayed a full week. Definitely tactical types, go-get-'em thirty-somethings, in and out of the condo all day and all night. They were dressed Eddie Bauer–style—trying to fit in on the island. Only thing was that they weren't fishing."

Some of the sightings were FBI tactical units, but there were other acronyms involved as well. The Department of Defense won't confirm anything other than to say they "kept in touch with other agencies" about Colton Harris-Moore's adventures on Orcas, but a couple of sources claim the DOD had their guys out here at least checking out the situation if not actively searching. One thing Colt probably didn't know was that Secretary of Defense Robert Gates has a vacation home on the island. Secretary Gates declined to comment on whether he pulled a few strings to be neighborly and try to end the crime spree, but when things started escalating, some residents were pulling for him to send in Delta Force.

It was also an election year, and sixty-two-year-old Bill Cumming was widely expected to run for sheriff again. The longer the hunt dragged on, though, the more disgruntled his electorate. With federal help, San Juan County deputies baited a trap for Colt, leaving the keys in a white Chevy pickup rigged with tracking devices and hidden cameras. They even parked it outside a hangar. The day after they secretly set it up, an islander driving members of the high school golf team passed the airport. The kids all pointed to the pickup: "There's the decoy the cops put out!"

Five days after the Homegrown break-in, Sheriff Cumming put out a notice telling all San Juan County residents to consider getting alarm systems, and asking us to "wipe down all your surfaces," like windows and doorknobs to make it easier for the cops to get fingerprints, and smooth our gravel driveways so they'd be able to find footprints and tire tracks when we got hit.

For the few island residents not already feeling paranoid, that did it. Good night and good luck.

. . . .

THE FEDERAL FRENZY ON Orcas died down after about two weeks of the "undercover" agents coming up empty. FBI and DHS assets remained on call, though. Orcas went back to not even having twenty-four-hour police coverage. From 5 to 6 a.m. every morning, the island had no deputies on duty, a fact obvious to anyone who kept watch on the cop shop.

On Sunday morning, February 28, the sole young deputy manning the graveyard shift left the station and drove his police cruiser home to Deer Harbor. It's a twenty-five-minute drive, one way; forty minutes during the summer when chances are you'll be behind an "I brake for trees" tourist; or twenty minutes if you ignore the speed limits and risk offing yourself via a deer through the windshield or a skid off the cliff into Massacre Bay.

As soon as Colt knew the town was left unguarded, he came out of the shadows and approached Orcas Island Hardware. After the previous summer's burglary, owner Scott Lancaster had called Colt a "cockroach" during a TV interview. That gave the Barefoot Bandit three possible reasons for coming back: replenishing his tool collection, collecting more cash, and revenge. Or maybe he was just stopping by to do a return: he brought along the bolt cutters he'd stolen in the first burglary.

Scott had moved the piles of bagged mulch that Colt climbed the last time. He'd pulled the pallets far enough away from the sloping roof that he didn't think even Spider-Man could jump across to the building.

Colt once again scaled the tower of bags and then leaped, barefoot, across the void and onto the dew-slicked metal roof. His footprints led to each corner of the building, where they show he squatted like a gargoyle gazing out over the sleeping town. Satisfied the coast was clear, he went to the same warehouse window he'd found open last time. Scott, though, had jammed 2×4s into every frame, making them impossible to lift. Colt padded around the roof looking for another way in. He pried up a piece of metal siding, but realized it would take too long to make an opening large enough for him to squeeze through. He went back to the window, busted a small hole in the corner, then used a screwdriver to poke away the 2×4. The window slid open and he ducked through.

When the Cirrus showed up and Homegrown got hit, Scott had told his wife that he was going to start sleeping in the hardware store. "You

idiot," she said. "We spent four thousand dollars on that fancy new security system just so you wouldn't have to do anything like that."

As Colt started to climb down out of the loft, his body heat lit up an
infrared sensor, tripping a silent alarm at 5:28 a.m. (In a stroke of luck for
Colt, it was only *almost* silent.) Unaware that the security system was already calling the sheriff's office, he continued down to the ground floor
and went to the door leading to the shop. It had always been left open before the first break-in, but it was now locked. Colt went to work with pry
tools.

Meanwhile at his home outside of town, Scott received a 5:30 wake-up
call from the alarm company and jumped out of bed. When the alert went
to the police dispatcher in Friday Harbor, they contacted the on-call deputy. Even though officers lived just a few minutes away from the hardware
store, dispatch called the deputy who'd just gotten off shift and was
aboard his boat all the way out in Deer Harbor. It took him forty minutes
to get back to town.

Inside the warehouse, Colt wasn't getting anywhere with the metal-
framed commercial door, so finally he busted its window, reached through,
and unlocked it. When he pushed it open, though, something was wrong.
He could hear a little buzzer going off up at the front counter.

Scott arrived at the store ten minutes after he got the call. He went
directly to the back and looked up at the window Colt had used before. "It
was still dark so I couldn't see too well, but it looked wrong." Then he
waited. "I didn't want to go in until the deputy got there. I had this gut
feeling that Colton was in there or else still close by, watching."

The deputy arrived a half hour later and waited until a second showed
up before entering the store. They walked down the display aisles to the
back and found the bolt cutters. But Colt was gone.

Just down the street at Homegrown, Kyle had been back manning his
tower ever since the break-in. He'd had many more hours to, in his words,
"obsess" about Colt, and says he was starting to believe the kid might be a
werewolf. That night, Kyle had been very uneasy. "It was the full moon,
and I knew he'd be active, running through the woods growling and howling." Kyle and Cedra had seen what they describe as a white wolf lying in
a doorway across the street at 11 p.m. "Our dogs would usually be like
'Let me at 'em,' but they were really spooked by this thing."

Later, the sound of footsteps in the courtyard between Homegrown and the yoga studio woke Kyle. He went down and found a deputy passing through. "He said nothing was going on, but yeah, right . . . the town was starting to get all ruffled up."

The ruffling was unlike anything ever seen before on Orcas Island. Within a couple of hours, Whatcom County SWAT, Washington State Patrol, K9 teams with German shepherds, and all available San Juan County deputies were fanning out across Eastsound. Townsfolk hoping for a sleep-in Sunday were rudely awakened by the incessant brain-rattling thwops and sharp turbine whine of an ebony Homeland Security UH 60-A Black Hawk helicopter that showed up to tightly circle the town again and again and again for hours.

Idyllic Orcas Island looked like a war zone. Residents gathered at windows and on the street, craning their necks to watch the helicopter, and then shaking their heads as men in body armor with automatic weapons strode up and down the roads.

From the limited search perimeter both the helicopter and the ground forces were using, it was apparent they felt Colt had gone to ground within a very small area around town. However, he'd had at least a ninety-minute head start before any meaningful search began and was known to just run full out whenever threatened. I'm no manhunter, but a full five hours after Colt slipped out of the hardware store it looked like they were working a perimeter that Stephen Hawking could have run past in less than an hour and a half.

All day long, Scott Lancaster says local guys were driving up, guns in their cars, saying they were going to put a stop to this. "I thought, This is not good."

24

With all the obvious law enforcement activity around the airport, including the Black Hawk using it as an Orcas base, you'd think Colt would head to one of the far corners of the island and hunker down. Instead, he did the exact opposite. The kid who loved planes couldn't stay away from them.

At former astronaut Bill Anders's hangar, his assistant noticed powder on the floor. "Later we realized it was from someone lifting and moving the ceiling tiles, as if they were looking for a security system or a place to hide up there," says Bill. At the time, though, they didn't think too much of it since nothing was missing and they hadn't noticed any forced entry. Bill put his Cessna 400 to bed in the hangar as usual, with the keys left hanging from the plane's baggage compartment door. "I always did that because then I know for sure the mags aren't left hot," he says. He left the island for two weeks, and when he came back, he found the plane's POH sitting out, open, on a small table next to the airplane.

"That never leaves the plane," says Anders.

The ceiling dust and the POH mysteries were explained when a San Juan County detective found pry marks on Anders's doors. When they pulled up the records for the hangar's phone line, they revealed a number of calls to Pam Kohler.

The remaining mystery was why the plane, a sitting duck for two weeks, hadn't been stolen. Anders always gassed up at his museum, and hadn't bothered to stop before his last trip, knowing he needed only a small amount of fuel to make the hop back to Bellingham. Colt would

have figured out there wasn't enough fuel to take him far simply by turning on the gauges. Still, Colt studied up on the Cessna 400, aka Columbia—a model he had never flown before. Maybe next time he came back to
Anders's hangar he'd find it with filled tanks . . . or maybe he'd find another
400 somewhere else when the time was right.

Possible Colt sightings now poured in to the police. Bill Cumming
laughed when he told me, "Any kid on Orcas who's at least six feet tall is
getting a lot of attention." A friend who lives on low-bank waterfront just
down the road saw a shadowy character she's sure was Colton kayaking
past her home very late on a February night, navigating by headlamp. The
San Juans are one of the world's best places for sea kayaking. There's endless interest along the miles of serrated coastline, with views through clear
water down into kelp forests and rocky reefs covered in purple starfish.
Paddlers off the west coast of San Juan Island often get the privilege of
seeing killer whales at eye level. However, kayaking in the San Juans is a
daylight sport. Boat and ferry traffic, treacherous currents, and unforgiv-
ing cold water make midnight paddling in a major channel in the middle
of winter almost as foolhardy as flying a plane without taking a class. The
headlamp fit Colt's MO, as did bucking conventional wisdom. Later that
night, she heard someone trip over her garden wall.

Still, though, the most reliable sightings came from around the airport
area. When sheriff's deputies took a close look at the hangars, they found
four more besides Bill Anders's and Chuck Stewart's that had evidence
someone had gotten inside to snoop around. And they suspected Colt
had broken into even more. Just north of the hangars, a local guy who'd
been hired to keep watch over the Ditch twice saw someone lurking
among cars in the lot. He says that both times when he went to check it
out, a big guy he identified as Colt stood up, got right in his face, and
"intimidated the hell" out of him before turning and running off into the
woods.

Colt's Winter Olympics stunt had, as expected, brought a flood of press
attention and thousands of new members to his fan clubs who all rooted
for him to "Fly, Colton, Fly" and never give up. Around this time I tracked
down Colt's prison buddy Josh, who told me about the guns and Colt's

"They'll never take me alive" boast. Then Pam told me Colt was sure he'd get twenty years if he got caught. She also said he recently told her he's "done with people." Together with Colt's history of depression, all of this convinced me that the danger had ratcheted up to the point where somebody was going to die: Colt, a cop, or an innocent bystander. I could easily envision one of the many elderly folks on Orcas or Camano finding him in their home and keeling over from a heart attack.

Since Colt was reading my blog, I decided to cross the line and address him directly. On March 9, I wrote a post titled "What Should Colton Do?" I told him that no way was he going to get twenty years if he gave himself up, but he would if somebody got hurt, even by accident. I told him it was easy for those sitting at home to type "Keep running!" because he was providing entertainment and vicarious thrills. When he died, though, or was sitting in a cell, they'd just go back to playing video games. I wrote that the only smart choice if he wanted to eventually go for his dream of being a real pilot was to turn himself in.

CHUCK STEWART'S BIG HANGAR is the closest one to Smuggler's and the Ditch. Colt had taken an interest in that building from the beginning: blankets stolen from it in 2008 were found at one of Colt's campsites. He'd been back inside several times since then to study the POHs for Stewart's two planes. Deputies responded to each call, but couldn't figure out how anyone had gotten in. Colt's first peek into Stewart's hangar had to be a hallelujah moment. Stewart's aircraft were dream machines for anyone interested in flying. One, a $4 million Swiss-made Pilatus, is the hottest single-engine turboprop on the planet. Used by everyone from Immigration and Customs Enforcement (ICE) to air force special forces, the Pilatus carries up to ten people and cruises at more than 300 mph with a range over two thousand miles. It's also built to use short runways and land on rough dirt or grass strips. At nearly fifty feet long with a fifty-three-foot wingspan, the three-ton Pilatus was a magnitude more plane than Colt had ever attempted. However, a look at the POH revealed something very tempting. Its stall speed was only 5 mph higher than that of the Cirrus, which Colt had successfully landed twice.

Stewart's other aircraft was an amphibious DeHavilland Beaver, the ultimate bush plane. With its floats bolted on, the Beaver offered a pilot leaving Orcas Island access to the entire Inside Passage, with countless isolated inlets and bays in British Columbia. It would mean another huge leap in skill and luck to safely land on the water, but if the plan was ever to kiss society good-bye and get lost in the wilderness, here was the ideal vehicle.

The sweetener, especially for a teenage boy, was that both of Stewart's planes had very cool custom paint jobs, with vibrant black-and-blue smoke and waves streaming along the sides of their bright white fuselages. Actually, forget the teenagers: boys of every age on Orcas coveted those planes, as well as Stewart's hangar, which also had a two-story pilots' lounge built inside. As a model for a dream life, Stewart's would be irresistible to Colt. Beyond the hangar filled with fantasy planes and the clubhouse, Stewart lived in a large waterfront compound on the west side of Orcas with a dock and water toys. He was fabulously wealthy, had a jet plane by the time he was forty, and hobnobbed with famous sports stars. The part of Stewart's life that would have been alien to Colt, considering the take-it philosophy he'd espoused to Harley and Josh, is that Chuck had worked for it all.

Leading citizens in the Orcas community, Chuck Stewart and his wife raised their boys here, worked with local sports teams, provided support for numerous charities, and even built a school on the island. "He was one of the guys that was always there when I needed him," says Ray Clever, a former Orcas deputy who had a short list of wealthy residents—"my sugar daddies"—who he counted on to support various programs he started to help local youth, especially at-risk kids.

Clever spent twenty-six years as a San Juan County cop after starting his law enforcement career in California. He went through the Los Angeles Police Academy and reminisces fondly about the days when it was permissible to choke people out. "My favorite was the time I choked out two lawyers at the same time. They'd dined and dashed on a $300 tab, and when I stopped them they told me to 'fuck off' and started to walk away. I got one in each arm and choked them unconscious. The fact that they were lawyers was just a bonus."

Clever acknowledges that he was "a little jerk at times" with his new-found police power. "Every cop has to go through that. If they tell you that they haven't they're a lying son of a bitch." One day a veteran who'd seen it all pulled him aside. "He reminded me that I wore a police uniform, not a judge's robe, and that my badge wasn't big enough to hide behind but it was big enough that it was going to hurt when someone shoved it up my ass."

On his very first day on the job in the San Juans, Clever became one of the investigating officers for a five-year-long case, the famous Lopez Island bang-bang, chop-chop, burn-barrel murder featured in the Ann Rule book *No Regrets*. During his years working on Orcas, Clever was regarded by some as "the only real cop the island ever had." Others remember him for once shooting and wounding a suspect who attacked him, leading to a lawsuit that the county's insurance company settled.

Clever remained aggressive—"In my younger days, no one I chased ever got away"—but he was able to adjust to small-island community policing so well that parents of kids flirting with trouble would have him come over to put the fear of God and jail into them, after which, to those who chose the right path, he became Uncle Ray.

At sixty-five, the former all-American swimmer has added some girth around the middle, but it's like the meat on a summer bear—solid. Clever retired from the force before Colt became an issue, but was pissed that someone was running rampant on Orcas and picking on his friends. And he wasn't impressed with how well the sheriff's office had done against Colt so far.

The sheriff, though, was taking the Stewart break-ins seriously. According to Clever, one of the island's young deputies was detailed to set up a one-man stakeout inside Chuck's hangar. He spent an entire night there, and later told other officers that he'd been very uneasy inside the dark, echoing hangar. He said he had a creepy feeling that someone was watching him. He kept hearing noises that didn't make sense and said he was very happy once daybreak came.

Meanwhile, the FBI (still officially not interested in the case) was running a trap and trace on Pam Kohler's phone line. They saw that calls had been made from a number belonging to Chuck Stewart. According to Clever, when they contacted Stewart and told him about the trace, there was a chilling *When a Stranger Calls* moment because the phone calling Pam's number wasn't the one in the hangar. On March 11 and 15, calls had been made from inside Stewart's house.

Even more disturbing, says Clever, was that the family had been home on the dates the late-night calls were made. Chuck Stewart was incensed that someone was messing with his family. "If [Chuck] himself could have laid hands on this kid there would have been bloodshed. He would have torn him apart; he was that angry." Chuck wanted action and his connections went well beyond local government. He had friends in very high places and, according to Clever, an FBI official flew in from Washington, D.C., to kick some asses into gear.

Together, Sheriff Cumming and the FBI came up with an elaborate plan to finally put an end to the Barefoot Bandit's run. Since Colt had taken such an interest in and was apparently tracking Chuck Stewart, they'd set a trap at his home. Tactically, the place seemed ideal. Stewart's property lies on two scalloped beaches in an area called Lover's Cove at the base of Turtleback Mountain, just north of the turtle's head. The mountain here rises precipitously to over one thousand feet in less than half a mile—so ridiculously rugged and steep that when trying to go uphill you're forced to scramble on all fours. Two narrow gorges that feed down to the cove would funnel anyone trying to escape into narrow choke points. There are only five homes on that section of coast, with just two private roads leading in and out. To the west lay the 45-degree water and deadly currents of President Channel.

Even though the terrain negated Colt's sheer speed, the authorities still had to be prepared to chase him on foot, something the Orcas deputies were not up to. The plan called for an elite FBI tactical team—gung ho, highly trained, and in excellent shape—to form a heavily armed ring around the outside of the house. The other part of the trap would be laid inside the home, where two FBI supervising agents and the San Juan County detective who'd been in charge of the Colton case from the beginning would be waiting to grab him. Local deputies would seal the roads and form the outer perimeter. Cumming also had the nuclear option, with a Homeland Security Black Hawk, a Whatcom County Sheriff's helicopter, dog teams from Whatcom and Snohomish Counties, tactically trained Homeland Security agents, and two five-man teams of Marysville manhunters all standing by to launch into the operation if needed. In all, there were thirty-five local and federal law enforcement officers and all their high-tech assets arrayed against one barefoot teenager. On paper, it seemed a lock.

The operation was planned for St. Paddy's Day, March 17. The Stewarts went off island, leaving their home and hangar irresistibly empty. It was cold, a damp 40 degrees at sunset, when a large group of us began to gather east of town. We kept warm with fiddles, bodhrans, brown bread, and Jameson, and for once it seemed like operational security held because there wasn't a word around the bonfire about the Lover's Cove stakeout. While we ramped up the *craic*, a delivery truck made its way down the winding road etched into the steep hillside leading to the Stewarts' place. No one knew where Colt was and whether he had the area under surveillance, so the commercial van was used to secretly infiltrate the cop and two agents into the house. The inner trap was set.

Meanwhile, the FBI tactical team was still on the mainland, racing down I-5. That's when the best-laid plans started to go awry.

Living in the San Juans means dealing with the ferries. Each island gets a quota of cars on every boat. In the winter, you can arrive at the terminal a half hour before a sailing and still get on. At the other extreme is the Fourth of July weekend, when a line of cars can back up into downtown Anacortes and you may have to wait eight hours to get on a ferry. Residents know to plan their summer lives so they never have to leave on a Sunday or come back on a Friday unless it's a dire emergency. The rest of the year, you know to adjust your schedule to allow enough time to get to the ferry landing. The FBI declined a Freedom of Information Act request for the details of their St. Paddy's Day ferry travel, but, simply put, the highly trained tactical team missed the boat.

If an Orcas resident misses the ferry and it's just a matter of making him late for dinner, he curses and then heads back into Anacortes to load up on relatively cheap groceries and gas, and maybe gets a fast-food fix at the McDonald's. If, however, it's very important that he get out to the island and can't wait for the next boat, there are a number of options. Two different small airlines fly from Anacortes to Orcas for $69 a person. For $350, a fast charter boat will run small groups and their gear to Orcas in less than a third of the time it takes on the ferry. So, if you positively, absolutely have to get there, no problem. Now, if you're an FBI tactical team that's going to be late for the big stakeout, you have those options plus even more. Your federal brethren in Homeland Security have super-speedy 1,200-horsepower interceptor boats, in both Coast Guard and Customs and Border Patrol flavors, based just up the shoreline in Bellingham. Plus you have San Juan County's own Sheriff's Office boat available. There's no reasonable excuse why the FBI team wasn't able to get to Orcas on time. But they didn't.

This left the two FBI special agents and the San Juan detective inside the Stewarts' house with a choice: stay inside or move outside. Colt had already proven he could escape stakeouts set up inside homes just by turning and running. The only time he'd ever been caught was when he was found inside a home and then bottled up from the outside. The story from a San Juan deputy who worked the case is that the three did move outside the home for a while, but then went back inside because they got cold. (When that detail leaked out, Orcas residents began to call it the Cabela's moment because if the cops had worn their longjohns, they would've been comfy enough to wait outside and probably could have caught Colt.)

When the FBI SWAT team finally made it to the island, they were met by an Orcas deputy and led out past Jack Cadden's Bonny Brook Farm to the private switchback road that heads toward Lover's Cove. It was decision time again: go all the way to Stewart's and risk scaring Colt off if he was already lurking nearby, or hold back and wait. They decided to wait and parked on a small patch of ground where several driveways converged about a mile from the target house.

After midnight, a truck approached the crossroads. According to Ray Clever, the FBI agents and Orcas deputy let it pass unchallenged. Any local islander seeing a cop car or a mysterious black SUV parked on the side of his residential road would have stopped to ask what was happening. The person driving this truck, though, kept going. Another suspicious fact about the truck was that it belonged to the Stewarts; it was the one they'd left at their hangar.

And, of course, Colt was driving it.

COLT DROVE TOWARD THE Stewarts' home, but stopped short and parked the truck sideways across the road, blocking anyone from driving in or out. It appeared he smelled a trap, probably from sighting the vehicle parked at the crossroads. The odd thing is that instead of taking off into the woods, Colt continued on foot up to Chuck Stewart's house. Game on.

There are two stories told by different San Juan County police officers at this point. One says that as Colt was about to open the front door, he heard motion in the house and turned and ran. The other says that Colt actually opened the front door, walked in, and flipped on all the lights.

Conventional wisdom would be that hitting the lights was a stupid move on Colt's part. Actually, by Clever's thinking, it was brilliant.

"If he'd come in and left the lights off, and there were people in there that knew how to play this game, they'd have come out of the dark and taken him down. So instead, he surprises *them* by turning on the lights. The FBI agents hesitate just for a moment, thinking, Well, maybe this is somebody that belongs here. The kid's got it preplanned . . . He doesn't hesitate. He one-eighties and he's gone."

When he heard the agents react, Colt turned and ran off into the darkness. Sheriff Cumming later reported that Colt was positively identified, and from what one of the officers told a local resident, they were close enough to see that he had night-vision equipment.

At 1:15 a.m., Bill Cumming lit the bat signal. Colt was trapped down in Lover's Cove, but the sheriff didn't want to take any chances. He called in all the backup and reinforcements at his disposal. Even if Colt was only a property criminal, this kid had embarrassed his department, cost it the confidence of residents, and pissed off VIPs. He'd now get the full shock-and-awe treatment. Deputies sealed off the roads. The FAA even set up a temporary flight restriction (TFR) around the entire west side of Orcas in order to clear the airspace.

The sheriff's office put out word that a capture was imminent. Mission accomplished.

BACK NEAR THE TOP of the road leading to Lover's Cove, Henry and Donna McNeil had been asleep for hours. Donna works as postmistress at the Orcas Landing office, and her family has been on the island since pioneer days. Donna grew up with her grandparents' stories of how during the Depression folks on Orcas who knew how to hunt and fish helped feed their neighbors who didn't. She was raised as a throwback island gal, crabbing, fishing, and hunting, even earning her high school spending money by selling raccoon pelts. As a young girl, she rode her horse all over Turtleback, and knows every one of its deer trails and skidder roads. She'd seen a lot of things on the mountain, but never expected anything like this.

The dogs went on alert first, which woke Donna up at 1:30 a.m. "Then there was this grumbling that got louder and louder, and suddenly the whole house is filled with light shooting in all the windows and skylights." Waking up into what looked like a scene from an alien invasion movie, Donna jumped out of bed and ran to the door. Down on Jack Cadden's field, a Black Hawk was dropping off the manhunters. "We had no idea what was going on. We never expected Colt to come out here; he was an Eastsound problem, so we had no clue." The helicopter took off and came right at them, stopping only one hundred feet away and hovering at eye level over the road that ran next to their hilltop house. "The pilot turned on a red light in the cockpit so we could see him," says Donna. "And then he waved."

The chopper would move down toward the cove and sweep the area, then come back to hover near their house, over and over. Donna turned on her police scanner and could tell they were chasing someone. At 3:30 a.m., they saw a light out in the trees and Donna called the sheriff's office. "They told me, 'Just stay in your house,' but wouldn't give me any more information." That didn't sit well with Henry. "Horseshit, this is my property," so he strapped on a .45 under his bathrobe and went out in his moccasins to check around. As he walked to the edge of the woods, he saw flashlights swinging, heard voices hollering back and forth and radios going off, and saw dark figures moving through his private skeet-shooting range. One of the lights caught Henry in its beam and immediately men started shouting, "Halt! FBI! FBI! FBI!" Henry held up his hands and shouted back, "Homeowner! Homeowner!"

The FBI tactical guys asked Henry to go back inside, but he told them he was going to look around his property. He went over to an old blue pickup parked on a patch of clay that'd turned mucky from the recent rains. Henry shined his light on the ground to make sure he didn't step in the mud, and checked inside the truck.

Donna called the county again, demanding some information. Finally, a deputy pulled into their driveway and said that they were after Colton Harris-Moore. Donna told him about the abandoned farmhouse back in the woods on her parents' property. "He sluffed it off, saying, 'We don't think he's gotten this far. He was spotted down at the crossroads.'"

HOMELAND SECURITY CALLS THEIR UH-60 Black Hawks "tactical apprehension aircraft," and outfits them with cutting-edge catch-'em gear. The copters' Star Safire FLIR is so sensitive that it can zoom in not only on a warm body, but just on the residual heat where someone has touched an object. It makes tracking someone who's barefoot even easier than if he were wearing shoes because he leaves a trail of warm footprints that show up white against the cold ground. Conditions were ideal, as it'd dropped into the mid-30s, making warm bodies stand out even brighter. One thing Colt had going for him was the tree cover, since Orcas is primarily forested in evergreens. The thick layers of fir and cedar acted as insulation to hide his thermal signature. Unlike the Ace Hardware chase, though, the searchers knew basically where Colt was. He might be able to hide from the Black Hawk by finding a big fleshy cedar and hunkering down underneath, but as soon as he stopped moving, the dogs should have caught up to him.

Since they had information that Colt used police scanners, the searchers even used a special tactical frequency he couldn't eavesdrop on. That, though, caused communications trouble since not all the cops had the same radios. Turtleback also blocked signals, and an Orcas deputy had to station his vehicle on the road just beside the McNeils' so he could relay messages among the teams.

Early in the morning of what was now the eighteenth, a request went out to the Orcas Island Fire Department Auxiliaries to set up a big pancake breakfast for the search teams. Everyone assumed it was going to be a celebration.

The Orcas rumor mill also had to put on extra workers once the sun came up. Reliable word varied from "They've got him trapped against a cliff" to "cornered in a shed" to "He went in the water." TV reporters were tipped off and Seattle crews started toward the island. As the hours passed, though, it became apparent—at least to locals—that things weren't wired as tight as they appeared.

Tactical hunter teams started going from house to house, waking residents for permission to search their properties. One resident asked if there was any danger. "Don't worry," he was told. "We have Turtleback Mountain surrounded."

It's not wise to laugh at someone holding an automatic weapon, but anyone who knew Orcas could tell you that unless the U.S. Army's Tenth Mountain Division was also deployed out in the bushes, there was no way Turtleback was surrounded.

AFTER DONNA MCNEIL LEFT for work, Henry went back out to walk the property. He stopped at the chicken coop to make sure the birds were okay and found a surprise—no eggs. They'd been off the island on the seventeenth, and the hens had been laying five a day all month. There should have been ten eggs. It's hard to imagine someone running from a helicopter stopping to pick up eggs, but they never found an explanation. It also lends some credibility to the idea of searching every "farmhouse, henhouse, outhouse, and dog house."

Whether or not there was a fly-by egg heist, the next thing Henry found was less equivocal. In what had been a smooth patch of clay mud near his pickup three hours before, he now found a big bare footprint. He called the police and Donna, who came back home to find a yard filled with black cars with no license plates. Seven guys—FBI, Marysville troopers in full camo, Homeland Security agents in all-black tactical gear, and deputies from Snohomish and San Juan Counties—were all puzzling over the print like they were Bigfoot fanatics. They also spotted a number of partials and a second full footprint near the chicken coop. "The head FBI agent said, 'No, that's not his print,'" says Henry. "He said it was too small, like a size nine." (A professional tracker hired by CBS News later estimated that the prints were made by someone who wore a size thirteen shoe.) "Then he asked us if we'd been running around barefoot that night. Yeah, right."

Whoever made the tracks appeared to have been making a detour around the deputy sitting in his truck relaying radio calls. Henry asked why they weren't bringing a dog up since the prints were certainly fresh enough to track. "They told us that the dog team had gone back to the mainland at five-thirty a.m."

Donna asked the searchers if they'd found anything at the old farm-

house. "They all looked at each other. The Orcas deputy hadn't told anyone about it. They got all excited, so I asked them if they wanted me to
take them to it. They said, 'No, ma'am, these are professional trackers.'"
It was full light out, and Donna says she described exactly how to get there.
More than thirty minutes later, she says, a call came in from the professional trackers reporting that they'd gotten lost heading to the two-story
farmhouse a quarter mile away.

THE SEARCH CONTINUED THROUGHOUT the day. Local squad cars crawled
down Crow Valley Road with their trunks open and filled with piles of
Marysville manhunters, legs and rifle barrels sticking out. The FBI agents
charged past in black vehicles, driving back and forth from one fruitless
hot tip to another. Roadblocks were set up, taken down, and then set up
again on the same roads. The Black Hawk and sheriff's copter continued
to sweep the terrain with their surveillance pods while patrol boats scanned
the shoreline.

At 3 p.m., Sheriff Cumming told the troops to start winding down. At
4:11, he put out a press release: "The extensive, intense search for Colton
Harris-Moore on Orcas Island has now been scaled back to an ongoing
investigation . . . This is an ongoing, multi-agency investigation involving
both county and mainland-based law enforcement agencies. Therefore, no
interviews and no additional, specific details of the search activity or the
investigation will be available."

THERE WAS A STRANGE reaction on the island. On the one hand, many
people thought the big paramilitary overkill was ridiculous. However, there
were now also a lot more folks officially scared. The story that this was just
a nonconfrontational property thief and squatter didn't jive with black
helicopters roaring around all night and day, and heavily armed men going
door to door. Local authorities on tourist- and retiree-sensitive Orcas had
long given the sense that this kid was just a nuisance. If he'd been a serious
threat, like a murderer or a rapist, then they'd have really gone after him
and, boom, it'd all be over. But now everyone wondered: If this *was* someone
who'd been leaving behind a trail of bodies instead of just bare footprints,

what would they be doing? Sending in helicopters, manhunters, dog teams, and the FBI? Done, done, done, and done. With no results.

Evidence that a lot of residents were thinking about their personal security was the sudden rush of orders with our local gun dealer for "less-lethal" rubber bullets. Designed to stop someone without killing him, these shotgun rounds used to be called nonlethal, but depending on where they hit the target, they weren't.

One of the last tips on the eighteenth came from Carolyn Ashby, who'd been sitting at her kitchen table in Crow Valley, three-quarters of a mile from Turtleback, watching the helicopters. At 3:30 p.m., she and her daughter spotted a "great big" man dressed in a black hoodie acting very strange in one of their cow pastures. While Carolyn was on the phone with the police dispatcher, she lost sight of the guy. "I carried the phone out onto the porch, and suddenly he walked out from behind a shed. I said, 'There he is!' and he took off running. He ran through the tall grass uphill . . . I've chased cows through that field and it's not easy." Ashby's Holsteins and horses lifted their heads and watched the stranger run by. "They must have been thinking, Oh boy, he's in trouble, because the cows know they get in trouble whenever they break into that field."

A deputy responded and a helicopter hovered over their property for about an hour, but to no avail. "My son-in-law is six-four and they swooped down on him, but they could never find the guy in the field."

Carolyn and her husband Eb's grandsons are the fifth generation of their family on Orcas. In all their time here, she says nothing like this had ever happened. "Things just aren't the same anymore. My daughter takes a baseball bat when she goes out at night to get wood. When you let the dogs out after dark and they take off after something, you're scared to open the door and let them back in because you don't know what's out there. You feel trapped inside your own house."

A number of older folks took the threat so seriously that they started planning to move off the island. They could take the added expense, the long trips to get mainland medical treatment, the extra day it took to get anywhere else in the country to see grandchildren, and all the other inconveniences of living in the San Juans because it was such a peaceful and safe setting. But they hadn't signed up for Black Hawks chasing fugitives through their backyards.

25

———

own on his 120-acre spread at the base of Turtleback where he raises cattle, eighty-five-year-old Jack Cadden had been rooting for Colt to wise up, quit his shenanigans, and go off and get a life somewhere. "He was a smart bastard, kept the deputies busy. If he'd a put all that smarts to a good use he woulda made something out of himself. To tell you the truth, I kinda hoped they never would catch him."

When Jack found out that it was because of Colt that the "son-of-a-bitch helicopter" kept waking him up, he did something that he'd never done in his seventy-eight years on Orcas: "First time I've ever locked a goddamn door on this island!"

That a guy like Jack was locking his doors says something. As a seventeen-year-old marine, Jack took part in the invasions of Guam and Okinawa, got shot twice, and came home with two Purple Hearts, a Silver Star, and a Japanese sword that, Jack says, "one of their officers didn't need anymore."

Jack Cadden ain't scared of the dark or anything else. Now, though, because of Colt he had to leave lights burning all night.

If Colt came into his house, Jack said, he'd just handle it. "If he made me, I woulda shot him in the leg or foot or something."

Unlike other guys who'd been puffing up and talking about shooting people during all this, you had to take Jack seriously. And though I know he would've given Colt every opportunity to back away before putting an extra hole in him, Jack actually had previous experience shooting at barefoot guys. And that's worth a quick Farmer Jack story:

"This is back in the days when there was quite a batch of hippies around the island—crazy bastards. Nancy and I were sitting eating break-fast, and here comes this strange-looking guy across the field. I picked up the old twelve-gauge that I kept loaded in the corner and went out on the porch. Well, sure enough he comes up toward the house. I said, 'I don't know what the hell you want around here, but you better get gone.' He picked up a stick and started waving it around, so I let one fly right over his head. Man, he took off down the road, right across that sharp crushed rock, barefooted! I came back in and Nancy'd called the law. About a half hour later, this sheriff's car comes up the driveway and they had the guy in the backseat. They says, 'Is this the guy?' And I said, 'Sure looks like him. What did you bring him back here for . . . you want me to shoot him now?' They said, 'Oh no no no no!' "

SPECULATION BY THE EVENING of the eighteenth was that Colt lay crum-pled on the rocks below the west coast cliffs. Other stories circulated that Turtleback was riddled with caves and that's where he was hiding. A de-tective called Donna McNeil to ask where the caves were, and she ex-plained that though there was a mine shaft from an old gold mine, it was now in a homeowner's front yard and had been filled in. She did tell them about a couple of quarries on the mountain, and says that a search near one of them turned up a campsite tied to Colt.

FBI agents and Marysville manhunters stayed on the island after the big chase and canvassed homes around Turtleback, asking the residents if they knew "any good hiding places," but turned up nothing. Months later, hikers stumbled upon a campsite on the mountain where it rises to a com-manding view above Crow Valley. It was a spot less than a mile and a half from Stewart's and only a half mile from the Brodys' home. The camp was littered with water bottles, food wrappers, and three Pilot's Operating Handbooks taken from airplanes.

There were a couple strange incidents in the days after the big chase, both in an area between Turtleback and Eastsound. In one, a man came home to find his shower running.

Then, remarkably, on March 22, Colt went back to Chuck Stewart's home. He broke in and stole Mrs. Stewart's set of keys, bottles of Pel-legrino water, and one of her son's sweatshirts. The Black Hawk launched, but again found nothing. On the twenty-sixth, Chuck climbed into his Pilatus and saw that the plane's POH had been pulled out and opened up to the "start" checklist. Then on April 1, his caretaker discovered that the hangar's alarm system had been tampered with.

One night during all this activity—he's not sure exactly which—Josh got a phone call. "Colt was inside a hangar he'd broken into. He called late and said he could hear the helicopters flying around. We didn't talk long, though. He said he had to run." Josh says Colt's manner was just like always: "Totally relaxed."

After that, Colt lay very low. There were no credible sightings for several weeks. The police believed—or at least wanted to believe—that their massive show of force had chased him off the island. Residents, though, seemed tuned to something, some energy that Colt brought to the island. It was the same feeling you get when you're walking through grizzly bear or cougar country—that little background buzz, a tickle on the neck. And that was still around.

In our cabin it'd become an uncomfortable running joke. Every time we heard a strange noise in the night, either Sandi or I would yell out, "Knock it off, Colt, we're trying to sleep!" Then we'd laugh. And then we'd listen harder.

Murphy felt it, or maybe he was just feeding off everyone around him. He definitely acted more alert as we did our daily two-mile hike through the Deer Harbor woods. There was one spot not far from the cabin where several days in a row he stopped and stared into the trees, refusing to budge until I put all my weight on the leash. Since early March, there'd been a persistent rumor on Orcas that there was a $500,000 reward for capturing Colt. Where before there'd been just a few vigilante types roaming Eastsound, now there were guys all over the island arming themselves and taking to the trees. I emailed Sheriff Cumming, asking him to make some kind of statement saying there was no such huge reward (at this time there was a total of $3,000 offered among rewards posted by Orcas, Camano, and Crime Stoppers). But he never put the rumor to rest. It occurred to me that the cops had no reason to quash it since the supposed big reward put a whole lot of camo-wearing, off-season deer-hunting, shit-kicking mossnecks out in the field shaking the bushes. Plus, with only a $3,000 reward, it was just as likely that one of these guys would shoot Colt and mount him over his fireplace instead of turning him in.

With the rumored bounty on top of all the anger, it wasn't the safest time to go traipsing through people's woods. After Murphy stopped at the same spot the third time, I called the neighbor and asked if I could hike in to check it out. I found what looked like the perfect campsite, but no one was around and there was no evidence except for a large pile of scat. I ran down the possible suspects: too big for a raccoon, too far from the water and not fishy enough for an otter, no stray dogs around . . . The only wild animal in the area big enough would be a deer, but their droppings are usually in Milk Dud form . . . What the hell was I doing? This kid actually had me kneeling in the woods examining excrement like Kolchak the Crap Stalker.

IF I WAS GOING goofy, at least I wasn't alone. Most of the people I spoke to admitted they'd been calling out to shadows and noises in the dark woods. Five days after the big Lover's Cove debacle, I spent an evening manning the Eastsound lookout atop Homegrown with Kyle and his .44 Magnum. He hadn't been getting much sleep since the break-in.

"This store makes a million noises," said Kyle. "Refrigerators clicking on and off, the wind flapping the vents, birds landing on the skylight . . . One night I heard this banging downstairs, grabbed the gun, and ran down, but there's nothing there. We figured out later it was Pumpkin's tail wagging. Another time we scared the shit out of one of the deputies who'd climbed up the outside stairs because he thought he saw something up here. The dogs heard him and I come running out of the office in my underwear with the gun, and we're yelling, 'Hold it right there!' at each other. So yeah, we're nervous, but you're only paranoid if he's *not* out there . . . and we know he is."

It was a quiet night in town, but every ten minutes or so, someone would walk by and Kyle would jump up. "See!" It seemed like suddenly every kid on Orcas was at least six-three and wore a hoodie that made him look taller. Kyle had bumped into some of the young guys wandering around. "They were out there packing Tasers, looking for Colt." Kyle's theory was that some of the other kids out wandering at night were actually helping Colt: "Maybe they're acting like decoys."

The speculation about whether Colt had help on Orcas seemed to end when investigators reportedly found a note written in what looked like a female's handwriting that he'd left behind in Stewart's truck. According to a detective familiar with the case, the note was addressed to Colt and warned him about a deputy who lived in a marina, presumably Deer Harbor. It also gave directions to a home and it included tips such as which car to look for in order to tell if the owners were around. The note discussed a plan for stealing a boat and heading for Alaska. "It talked about finding a long-range cruising boat," says the detective. "And appeared to involve at least two people other than Colt, although we wondered whether Colt had invented all this and planted it as a diversion to throw us off his trail."

There were about a dozen boats moored at Deer Harbor Marina that could make the six-hundred-mile journey to Alaska without having to risk stopping for fuel. Cruising-style boats trade speed for long range, though, so there'd certainly be a lot of opportunities for the authorities to spot a boat during the approximately seventy-five-hour trip. But it had to be an attractive thought. If you ran only at night and laid up in one of the myriad secluded coves during daylight, chances of discovery were much less. And when you got wherever you were going, you'd have a comfortable floating home. Paint over the boat's name, and it's not inconceivable that you could anchor someplace almost indefinitely. The issue then would be, as usual, feeding yourself. The other problem was timing. Usually only commercial fishermen make that trip outside the calmer summer season. Winter winds and waves make the exposed stretch between the north end of Vancouver Island and the start of the Inside Passage a rough place for even large ships.

WHEN KYLE PULLED OUT his insurance file the day he got hit, he discovered something disturbing beyond how much the cash loss and $5,000 in damage was going to cost him out-of-pocket. "Not long after I bought Homegrown in 2006, I had a break-in. When I looked at those records, I realized that other than the chalk footprints, it was the exact same burglary. Same method and place of entry, same way of laying out the tills. It was total déjà vu." In the previous break-in Kyle lost high-tech goodies, a cutting-edge laptop, and an external hard drive loaded with all of his music. The crime was never solved or even really investigated. Kyle, though, was now sure it had been Colt.

"He waits until you think he's gone and you let your guard down and then he strikes again." Kyle was convinced Colt was feeding off the island's energy. "It feels like I'm going to wake up and he'll be leaning over about to bite my neck."

COLT'S FASCINATION WITH RETURNING to hit the same places was very unnerving. In April, two events happened that involved previous victims. One seems like just another opportunistic break-in, while the other was much more unsettling.

At 11:15 p.m. on the eleventh, the telltale turbine scream of a Black Hawk tore the air just above our cabin. My first thought was that it was heading to Lover's Cove again, and I wasn't looking forward to spending the night making small talk with a deputy manning the roadblock. As I walked outside, though, I could still hear the helicopter. Up the hill where our knoll falls into what we call the Dark Forest, the Black Hawk's blinking red light showed through the trees. It was close. I jumped in my truck and drove to where Deer Harbor narrows to a fifty-foot bottleneck between the bay and a shallow wetland. The Channel Road Bridge crosses at that spot; it's the only way those of us living on the west side of Deer Harbor can get to anywhere else on the island. I stopped in the middle of the bridge and watched the helicopter as it hovered almost directly above, its brilliant NightSun spotlight hunting the woods and fields of Cayou Caye.

Earlier in the day, Ryan Carpenter, owner of the Deer Harbor Inn Restaurant whose credit cards were used to order spy cameras and a flight helmet in 2008, had gone to do some work on a house he rents out. The three-bedroom home sits high atop a hill, its windows offering a gorgeous view of the entire harbor. Ryan walked into the living room and noticed that the wooden blinds had been lowered. "They were old and didn't work too well, and whoever lowered them broke bits and pieces off trying to get them down." Ryan switched on a light and saw that someone had been playing house.

He had cooked popcorn and eaten it by candlelight—leaving a pool of wax on the floor. Next to the wax sat a water bottle and a couple recent newspapers. One of them, a copy of the *Islands' Sounder*, was marked "Lobby" and had been taken from the Inn at Orcas Island, just down the road.

Conveniently for whoever had been inside snacking and reading, Ryan himself had moved a king-size mattress into the living room from a bedroom where he'd been working on the oak floors.

Ryan didn't call the police. Instead he called his brother. "I told him that the Barefoot Bandit had been there and maybe we could catch him for the reward."

Ryan worked his shift at the restaurant, and was walking home at nightfall when he noticed a light burning in the rental. He figured he must have left it on. "I stopped home to tell my wife I was going over to turn it off. Then I stepped back outside, looked over, and it was already off. That's when I got a little scared." He called 911 and the sheriff's office told him someone would be right there. He then called his brother, Matt, who grabbed a baseball bat and came over. "The adrenaline was pumping," says Ryan. "And we're waiting and waiting."

After forty minutes, they couldn't take it anymore and, together with their innkeeper and his dog, they went across the road to the house. The innkeeper went in the front door while Ryan went in the back. No one was in the house, but the *Sounder* and *Seattle Times* were gone. "It's like he just came back for the newspapers." When they went back outside, they heard something or someone crashing through the woods. "It could have been a deer, but didn't sound like it."

Ryan says that fifteen minutes after they went into the house, he saw the first deputy. "They reprimanded us for going in before they got there because it could have been dangerous, but it seemed like it took them a long time to get there."

The Black Hawk arrived two hours after Ryan called and stayed on station until after midnight, delighting local residents who got to stay up late and make shadow puppets when its spotlight shined in their windows.

With the action so close, neighbors now said they planned on putting a sign at the bottom of our road directing Colt to my cabin.

THE NEXT COLTONESQUE EVENT that month was more serious. Chuck Stewart and his wife were in their bedroom overlooking President Channel. A light suddenly appeared out on the black water. Tug boats pulling log booms and the occasional commercial fisherman traverse the passage between Orcas and Waldron Island at night in April, but few other boats. The light swung back and forth, but it looked too small for a boat's spotlight. As it came closer, they realized it was a headlamp worn by someone in a kayak paddling toward their property. They knew no sane kayaker—or even a tourist—would be out there at night.

They immediately called 911 and Sheriff Bill Cumming himself jumped into the police boat over on San Juan Island along with two deputies. The sheriff put the lash to *Guardian*'s turbo diesels and the thirty-five-foot aluminum catamaran (bought with money from a drug seizure) made it on scene even before an Orcas deputy could get there by car from Eastsound. Pulling up off Stewart's beach, they fired up an infrared scope and spotted a figure approaching the house from the water. The Stewarts have a dock, but like everyone else, they remove the lower, floating portion for the winter. This meant the *Guardian* was unable to let the deputies off. The Orcas officer in his patrol vehicle then came down the hill with his lights flashing, and the suspect fled into the night. It seemed almost inconceivable that the same guy who'd walked into an ambush that put thirty-five cops on his ass would come back to the same place and try it again.

"After that," says Ray Clever, "I said enough of this bullshit. Here's [Chuck's] wife, petite blonde, just the soul of an angel, generous and kind, and she's terrified in her own home. She was ready to close down the school, take everything they own, and get the hell off Orcas. She was in tears, asking me to get her a gun and teach her how to shoot. That really got to me. I called [Chuck] and said, 'I'm yours, won't cost you a dime, how can I help?'"

Clever went out to their home to check out its security and came up with some self-defense responses in case they had any more unwanted visitors.

Next he and Chuck went to the hangar. By now there was evidence that Colt had been in there at least four times, but the police still had no idea how he was entering. There were no pry marks on the man door or the large hangar door, so the supposition was that he'd been using a key, though no keys had been missing until the seventeenth.

They stepped inside the man door at the southwest corner and Ray began a methodical scan. "We started at the floor level—anything out of place? Any panels loose? No." They surveyed 360 degrees and then looked higher. As they were checking out the north end of the hangar, where the two-story pilots' lounge with its kitchen and sleeping area stood as a building inside a building, Chuck noticed something. The hangar has translucent fiberglass panels that act as vertical skylights, and there was one small section, a six-inch strip, that looked brighter than normal near the top of the lounge. Chuck said, "That's not right." The pilots' lounge doesn't reach the top of the hangar, so there's a gap between its plywood roof and the ceiling. "We walked up and tried to open the attic door," says Clever. "We can't budge it. That ain't right either."

They went outside. Attached to the north end of the huge hangar is a shed-roofed storage building. There were crush marks on the downspouts coming off the roof. They pulled out a ladder and climbed up onto the roof that starts about ten feet off the ground. "We walk up to where it's attached to the side of the hangar and there are two piles of human shit up against the wall."

The light strip they'd noticed was a gap where Colt had cut out the fiberglass panel and then replaced it, creating a hatch. "We pulled that off, lean in, and here's a mattress, food, gallon jugs of water, clothing, stuff like [Chuck's] son's BlackBerry that'd been taken out of their house, an iPhone, a whole box of junk." Colt had taken stamps, scissors, bed linens, an insulated mug, a DVD, a mirror, even Glass Plus from the Stewart home to outfit his hideaway in their hangar. He also had a sleeping bag and piss jars. "Then we find the .22 handgun that'd been stolen over in Granite Falls after that plane crash. Then, finally, we find the flight manual from the plane he took from Anacortes in February."

They left everything where it was and replaced the hatch. Clever's cop juices were flowing and he told Stewart that this would be the place to catch Colt. Chuck Stewart agreed to fund a private stakeout.

. . . .

CLEVER DIDN'T THINK APPREHENDING Colt would be easy. "He's not some scared kid, he's out there planning, and it has worked well for him for a long time."

It would take some time to put together his Orcas A-team and gather some special equipment, but Ray didn't want to risk missing Colt. He decided to start running the stakeout with just his thirty-five-year-old protégé, Vitaly. They set up in a storage unit near Stewart's hangar, but ran into a snag the very first night. The storage unit had an alarm system, which had been turned off. However, unbeknownst to them, it was programmed to automatically reset. When Ray opened the door, the alarm went off and an Orcas deputy responded. "If Colt had been watching, he might have seen us," says Ray. "But it's next door, so we didn't worry too much that we were blown."

Over the next week, the stakeout evolved into an elaborate trap. Ray met with John Gorton, Orcas Island's English-born octogenarian electronics wiz who, after twelve years as a radar engineer with the RAF, spent the rest of his career working on top-secret defense systems for Hughes Aircraft. Gorton moved to Orcas twenty-one years ago at the same time as the Stewarts, and has known the family since then. He runs a video production company on the island, and has been asked to set up a few surveillance systems over the years. Before Colt, though, the jobs tended to be Orcas in nature, such as setting up night-vision cameras for someone who wanted to know who was knicking the fruit off his apple trees.

For Stewart's hangar, Gorton designed a system using a series of audio and infrared video sensors that fed monitors in the storage unit. They knew they had a challenge because of Colt's obsession with surveillance equipment. "The problem with infrared cameras," says Gorton, "is that in a pitch-dark room, you can see the illumination diodes if you know what to look for." Gorton, though, had a connection in the tech business who sent him a prototype of a new kind of IR camera, one with a totally invisible light source.

The cameras and microphones would let the stakeout team know when Colt was inside the hangar. Clever and Stewart felt sure that Colt was planning on coming back for the Pilatus. "Once he climbed down from his nest to the hangar floor, we had him," says Clever. The first thing they'd done was replace the hangar's locks. There'd been deadbolts with knobs on the inside—one twist and you're out the door. Now, you needed a key to get in and to get out. All the locks had also been rekeyed so there was no chance Colt had a copy.

Once Colt entered the hangar, three of the four-member team would rush out of the storage unit and cover the exits while the other kept watch at the monitors. Vitaly, says Clever, is the fastest guy he's ever seen. "He could run that boy down, no doubt." Ray also recruited two men he does martial arts training with, Chuck Silva and a local high school teacher, Corey Wiscomb.

Corey had been at the center of a recent Colt-related controversy. He'd given students in his Math with Business Applications class a challenge: come up with a business and launch it online within four hours. These were all Orcas kids living through the biggest news event to ever hit the island. They understandably thought of Colt, and designed a T-shirt that showed a silhouette of someone running from other figures and a cop car, with text that read: "You Betta' Run, Colt, Run."

There'd been some local students on Colt's Facebook pages urging him on, but those were underclassmen. These guys and gals doing the T-shirt were seniors, and they said they understood the problems that the Barefoot Bandit was causing in their community. Groups of Orcas High boys were even heading out into the woods on weekends to search for Colt. The words on the T-shirt, they said, meant "We're coming to get you!" Their plan was to donate all proceeds from sales to Colt's local victims, and they stated such on the Web page. It seemed like a no-brainer to the kids. With the atmosphere of fear and hate growing on the island, their project even had a sweet touch of doe-eyed idealism to it. "We thought it might help start the community's healing process," says student Alison O'Toole.

The project became a twofer. Along with the practical experience of starting a business, the kids also got a civics lesson. A number of islanders went apeshit on them. One business owner said that if they didn't immediately pull it all down, he'd refuse to ever let any Orcas High School student into his store again. There was also a referendum coming up on a bond for repairs on school buildings, and some folks threatened that they'd fight against it if the kids didn't cease and desist. "We were totally shocked by the reaction," says student Sam Prado.

The final decision was supposedly left up to the students, but there was a flurry of phone calls that went much higher than the twelfth grade. Ultimately the kids backed down, getting a cold-water baptism in small-town politics.

One of the reasons Ray Clever says he asked Corey to help with the stakeout was because he knew he'd "taken crap for the T-shirt thing." The main reason, though, was because he and Chuck Silva are what Clever calls "bloody proficient" fighters. "If Colt put up a struggle, it would not have gone well for the young man."

Not that the plan was to let it get to hand-to-hand combat. Chuck Stewart outfitted Clever's team with bulletproof vests, shotguns loaded with less-lethal baton rounds "to knock him down," and Tasers "to sizzle him like bacon." They also carried high-powered strobes designed to disorient him. Clever would be the only one armed with lethal ammo. "I had no intention of shooting him . . . unless he presented, then all bets were off."

Ray asked the sheriff for a police radio so if it all went down, his posse could keep in touch with the deputies to make sure everyone knew where everyone else was and make sure nobody got shot accidentally. Instead of a radio, they sent a police scanner, which Ray took as a slap in the face. Just in case, he outfitted his team in bright red T-shirts and got word to all the Orcas deputies to not shoot the guys in red.

After Ray told the sheriff about finding the gun in Colt's nest, Bill Cumming wrote an email to all the Orcas deputies, saying, "This information raises the threat level . . . You are to use this information as though he is armed and take all appropriate precautions with him. Also, under no circumstances are any of you (us) to discuss this information with anyone other than those who NEED to know."

Ray and his team continued to work their day jobs, then every evening at dusk they sneaked into the storage unit, where they took turns watching the monitors and sleeping on a mattress laid on the cement floor.

While the Clever team lay in wait for Colt, others were actively tracking him through the Orcas woods. Colt not only had manhunters on his trail, but now, most fittingly, a Sasquatch hunter. Seventy-year-old Richard Grover brought his four decades of experience in tracking Bigfoot to the search for the elusive Barefoot. A real hope would be that he'd bag both: find Colt *and* Bigfoot so Orcas could score some more tourist traffic. Grover hunted around Orcas using a dowsing rod tuned to certain energies. Deputies say he actually scared up a teenager wandering through the woods, but unfortunately it turned out to be neither Colt nor a postpubescent Sasquatch.

ON MAY 10, I got a call from Pam. The FBI agents had been by again. "They told me a boat was stolen off Orcas about a week ago and they think Colt mighta done it." They asked Pam if she knew where Colt was headed. She told them no. Then she says they told her it might not matter anyway, because the boat hadn't turned up anywhere and that could mean it sank.

"They always try to affect me, get me to cry, but it takes a lot to get me to cry. I told them Colt's a good swimmer. They said, 'Yeah, but the water's so cold now that he'd get hypothermia and drown . . .' So I asked them how long it takes for a body to float up. They said a couple of weeks."

I'd never heard Pam shaken up like this. She'd been philosophically fatalistic, but the FBI saying Colt could already be lost beneath the frigid waters seemed to hit her with a cold splash of reality.

She hadn't heard from Colt in months, and asked me if I'd write a post on my blog telling Colt to give her a sign that he was alive. One thing her manner told me—and I presume told the agents—is that she really had no clue where Colt was. I figured the FBI was just trying a particularly heartless tactic to try to shake some information out of her. But . . . maybe they were telling the truth.

It made sense. Things had been very quiet on the island; no Colt sightings for a month. With the Orcas ferries and airport under surveillance, if he didn't have someone to hide him in his or her trunk, then stealing a boat would be the easiest way off. I checked the marinas for reports of stolen boats, and there were none. But the island also has many private docks, and there are plenty of dinghies and kayaks beached in waterfront yards. A very strong kayaker who knew how to read a current chart could island hop to the mainland. He'd have to cross a shipping lane, though, presumably at night when ships don't see or stop for kayaks because the radar reflections off the low-riding craft are about the same as a floating tree branch.

Setting sail on these waters at night whether in a kayak or small boat always entails some risk. The Salish Sea's cold currents claim paddlers and boaters even when they're not skulking around in the dark. The more I thought about it, the more likely it seemed that Colt could indeed be dead, a blanched body wrapped in kelp on some lonely pebbled shoreline. It was a disturbing image that had a stronger effect on me than I expected. So late that afternoon, I wrote a short blog post telling Colt that his mom was worried and asking that he give her a sign to let her know he was okay.

The next morning, May 11, as I rounded the curve to drive onto Channel Road Bridge, I suddenly slammed on the brakes. There was a thirteen-foot-long bare foot taking up the entire right-hand lane. I guess you could consider that a sign.

If Colt did it, I was glad he wasn't dead. At the same time, though, it was a little chilling. I felt like the planchette just moved itself across the Ouija board. I scanned the woods surrounding the slough, sensing that I was being watched.

The footprint didn't look like the thirty-nine left on Homegrown's floor. Of course the difficulty factor between drawing eighteen-inch-long feet with fat chalk and running up and down a bridge in the middle of the night with a can of black spray paint outlining a foot the size of a Volkswagen Beetle is immense, so artistic allowances must be made. I stood on top of my truck and took a photo, which I emailed to Bev Davis to show Pam. Word came back right away that Pam was positive Colt had painted it for her.

Pam told me she called up the FBI agents and verbally thumbed her nose at them, saying that Colt was definitely alive and now she *did* know where he was, so there.

LATE THAT NIGHT, a rock or something else hard hit the metal roof of our cabin. Once again I found myself standing outside in my boxers staring into the blackness. This time, though, I didn't bring a gun. The footprint on the bridge was about communicating, not threatening. No one showed himself or answered my calls except for a lonely screech owl. If the big foot on the bridge was an "I'm okay," it was also a "good-bye," because that was the last sign of the Barefoot Bandit on Orcas Island.

It was also the stepping off point for the most famous outlaw road trip since Dillinger's last run.

PART 4

OVER THE LINE

WANTED
BY THE FBI

INTERSTATE TRANSPORTATION OF A STOLEN AIRCRAFT

COLTON A. HARRIS-MOORE

Captured   Captured   Captured

Aliases: Colton A. Harris, Colton Harris, Colton Moore, Colton A. Moore, Colton Harris-Moore, Colton Koehler

DESCRIPTION

Date of Birth Used:	March 22, 1991	**Hair:**	Brown
Place of Birth:	Washington State	**Eyes:**	Green
Height:	6'5"	**Sex:**	Male
Weight:	205 pounds	**Race:**	White
NCIC:	W277849912	**Nationality:**	American
Occupation:	Unknown		
Scars and Marks:	Harris-Moore has a scar on his left arm from a knife wound.		
Remarks:	Harris-Moore may be in possession of stolen firearms.		

CAUTION

Colton A. Harris-Moore has been charged with interstate transportation of a stolen aircraft, and a federal warrant was issued for his arrest on December 11, 2009, in the United States District Court, Western District of Washington, Seattle, Washington. This stemmed from the theft of an airplane from Bonners Ferry, Idaho, on September 29, 2009. The plane crash-landed after running out of fuel 260 miles away near Snohomish, Washington.

Additionally, Harris-Moore is wanted locally for escaping from a Renton, Washington, group home in April of 2008. He had been ordered to stay there after pleading guilty to

26

—————

I t's about a four-mile kayak paddle from inside Deer Harbor to the closest spot on San Juan Island. However, that doesn't count tides, winds, or currents, which, if they're against you, can make that distance the equivalent of a moon shot. From Orcas to Friday Harbor is a forty-minute ferry ride, available to walk-ons and car passengers five or six times a day depending on the season. You can also run between islands via small motor boat in twenty minutes. If you managed to Doctor Doolittle yourself onto the back of a Steller sea lion, it could carry you there in about an hour. The point is, we had no clue how Colt got from Orcas to San Juan Island. No reports came in of stolen boats, cars, or planes. It was possible someone smuggled Colt onto the ferry in his or her car. But if so, why? Why not simply get on one going the other way, toward the mainland, and drive him wherever he wanted to go? Unless, like before, this was just a way to keep playing the game, making things intentionally more difficult, all ego and craftiness, complicating things just to keep the adrenaline flowing.

Two days after the footprint on the bridge, Colt broke into a home at the southern tip of San Juan Island where it tails toward Lopez. He snagged the owner's mountain bike and the keys to his twenty-four-foot SeaSport, a Northwest-built sportfishing boat. Late Thursday night/ Friday morning, he drove the boat out into Griffin Bay and then curled around Cape San Juan heading east. He cruised by Goose Island, where the honking comes from seals and sea lions, not geese, and then crossed the fast-moving waters of Cattle Pass—named for a load of cows shipwrecked by the Hudson's Bay Company. On the Lopez side of the channel,

Colt skirted Deadman Island and then grounded on Shark Reef. In an attempt to get as close to shore as possible—and maybe in order to cause the least amount of damage to the boat—he raised the engine's outdrive. He also switched off the batteries before hopping ashore with his gear and the bike.

Lopez is the third largest of the San Juans. Folks from Orcas and San Juan Island good-naturedly refer to it as "Slowpez" for its countrified atmosphere. The one-finger wave (index finger, thank you very much) is a universal, year-round ritual on Lopez—not just an off-season nicety among locals as it is on Orcas. Lopez's most notable resident when he's not in Seattle or cruising the world aboard his 416-foot super-mega-yacht, *Octopus*, is Microsoft cofounder Paul Allen, who owns a 387-acre peninsular chunk of the island.

Much of Lopez is farm-flat and great for biking. By Friday evening, Colt had ridden the 8.5 miles up to the northeast corner of the island. Cameras at Spencer's Landing Marina caught him coming down the ramp to the dock at 11 p.m. wearing a big backpack. He looked around carefully at first, spotted a camera tucked up under an eave, and bolted out of its range. He didn't leave the marina, though, and was tracked on other cameras as he moseyed up and down the four long docks, stopping here and there among the 110 slips like he was at a boat show. He calmly shopped all night, boarding at least six boats. "He was very relaxed, not gun shy about anything," says Kim Smith, who, along with his wife, Michelle, manages the marina. "It was like he knew the place."

The slips at Spencer's Landing are all taken by full-timers, not strangers—"transient boats" in marina parlance—so there aren't many security concerns. Plus this is Lopez Island: five of the boats Colt went aboard had been left unlocked. Inside one, he pulled out a chart to study the waters south of the San Juans that included Camano Island. In others he turned on lights and electronics, kicking the tires, checking fuel levels. Each boat was filled with gear, but he didn't take anything except, apparently, a nap in one of them. Every boat Colt surveyed was capable of making the trip he had planned, but he kept looking for just the right boat. Shortly after 5 a.m., he found her.

She was a Coastal Craft 300, a thirty-foot-long, aluminum-hulled flybridge cabin cruiser christened *Stella Maris*—a $400,000 pocket yacht. "It's a real looker and had all the electronics you could want on it," says

Kim. With a top speed of thirty-two knots and a range you could stretch out to eight hundred nautical miles, she was definitely an Alaska-capable boat. Colt stepped aboard, but found the cabin locked. He spent half an hour unsuccessfully trying to get inside. At 5:45 Saturday morning, with the sun coming up, he walked back up the dock and left the marina.

Later Saturday morning, a deputy came by and told Kim about the boat stolen on San Juan Island and found on Lopez. He said they figured it was Colton Harris-Moore and that he might be looking to steal another boat. Kim had a couple of large yachts in the marina he'd been doing engine work on, so he secured those as best he could. Since it was a weekend, people who used their boats as second homes would be living aboard at the dock. Kim figured that activity plus the security cameras would dissuade anyone from nosing around. The owners of the Coastal Craft, two Seattle women who also have a weekend home on Lopez, took their boat out that day to jig for cod. When they returned from fishing that afternoon, *Stella Maris* had about 150 gallons of fuel left in her tanks.

Just before 9 p.m. that evening, May 15, Colt came barreling back to the marina on the mountain bike. He parked it at the head of the main dock and went directly to the *Stella Maris*. A couple from Seattle were on the deck of their sailboat just one slip away, reading books in the twilight. Colt ignored them, though, and went aboard. Fully exposed to anyone who might look up or walk by, he worked on the Coastal Craft's front hatch for nearly half an hour. The hatches are designed to stay watertight even if a large wave crashes over the bow and are very difficult to break into without causing extensive damage. But Colt finally got it open and climbed inside.

He turned on the interior lights and methodically searched for what he knew he'd find: ignition keys. They were in a drawer, hidden beneath silverware. Once he knew he could start the boat, he jumped off and went back to grab the bike. He lifted it aboard, unplugged the shore power cord, cranked the diesel engine, and cast off the lines.

At 9:30 p.m.—with the Seattle couple still contentedly reading—Colt flicked on *Stella Maris*'s spotlight and motored out of the marina with the fenders still dangling off the sides of the boat. He cruised up around the tip of Lopez, and then set a course not north to Alaska, but south for home.

When Kim got to work the next morning, he noticed that *Stella Maris* was missing. No big deal, he first thought, because the women could have come by early and headed out fishing again. Then he saw that the dock lines and power cord were just thrown onto the dock, not neatly coiled like the owners always left them. "I went to the office and looked at our security footage from Saturday night," says Kim. "Sure enough, here's the kid taking the boat." He called the sheriff. His wife, Michelle, suggested they check the footage for Friday night. There, live on tape for more than six hours, was Colt boat shopping.

On Sunday morning, a Coast Guard Safe Boat found *Stella Maris* adrift off Hat Island, aka Gedney, which lies about three miles below the southern end of Camano. With no one aboard, they figured the operator had fallen into the water and launched a search-and-rescue (SAR) mission.

Kim got in contact with the owners, then told the coast guard they were okay. He asked one of the Guardies whether the *Stella Maris*'s dinghy was still aboard. When they said yes, he asked if there was a bicycle. "They said no, and I said, 'He's gone.' "

There was no damage to the *Stella Maris*; the owners say Colt took good care of their boat. The only visible evidence that someone had been aboard were a couple of used towels and a wrapper from a Snickers bar.

Kim says he then found himself in the middle of a turf war. The San Juan County sheriff didn't want him to share his surveillance footage with the Island County Sheriff's Office, and Island County didn't want to share any information with the coast guard. Kim finally threw up his hands and turned over the recordings to San Juan County, which later released a couple of still frames to the media. According to Kim, they weren't even the best shots from the video, which had enough resolution to tell Colt had neatly trimmed his hair since his famous photo, plus had let his sideburns grow.

The authorities never recovered a GPS track from the boat and didn't know which route Colt took from Lopez south—but it's easy to guess. The long way is seventy-five miles; the short route is fifty. The shorter path would take him through Deception Pass at night. When the tide is ripping at Deception, two million cubic feet of water per second flow through the narrow pass, with the current reaching nearly ten knots—faster than the cruising speed of many boats. It's such a choke point that water levels inside and outside the pass can differ more than three feet, making a trip through at full flow seem like running a swirling, whirlpooling rapid. With any kind of storm surge or wind opposing the rushing water, waves can stack up ten feet high. Boats without enough power to muscle through can be spun around and spit into the rocks. It's one of the most spectacular and dangerous spots in all the Salish Sea.

What would Colt do? He wouldn't hesitate to take Deception. It would explain stealing the boat earlier than his usual post-midnight hours of operation. He would have checked the tide tables and known to get through Deception somewhere close to slack water. Leaving the dock at 9:30 and running at eight knots—a smart nighttime cruising speed—put him on schedule to be through and into protected water behind Whidbey Island by the forecasted midnight slack tide.

THAT SUNDAY AFTERNOON, PAM was hanging around the trailer as usual. "I heard a whistle from the woods . . . didn't sound like any bird I knew." She didn't pay much attention, though. "Then I heard what I thought was my idiot friend coming up the drive, babytalking to Mel. I waited for him to come up to the house, but nobody came. Then later, Mel went off into the woods at the back of the property and came back with a fresh rib bone."

Pam says Colt never actually came to the house, and doesn't know if that was him stopping by to see Melanie and give her a treat. When I told her the boat he'd taken was a yacht, she said, "Well, that's Colt's style."

At 11:30 that night, Pam was in bed watching a Western with the sound cranked up. "I hear a voice calling to me, asking which window or door I was going to meet them at. I yelled, 'Let me get my bathrobe and slippers on!' I heard them calling again in a voice like trying to sound like a young person, like they were trying to make me think it was Colt. I yelled out that I was getting my shotgun. I cocked it, had it ready to go, and went to the front door. I had my hand on the handle, then stopped and thought no . . . Instead, I went to the kitchen window and moved the curtain to look out, and suddenly a bright light was in my eyes. I yelled, 'Get that goddamn light out of my eyes!' Gawd that just pissed me off . . . I hate that."

It was the FBI. "They said they knew Colt was here today and started threatening me right and left. 'We know you've been helping him and you're going away for years!' I said I haven't seen him and I don't know where he is and if you don't believe me then give me a lie detector test. They said, 'Oh, we don't do that.' I said well then arrest me or I'm going back to bed. They didn't say anything, so I closed the door and locked it and waited until I thought they were gone. Couldn't relax, though, so I turned off all the outside lights and went out and sat on the deck, listening and looking for those little flashlights they all carry."

BY THE EIGHTEENTH, ISLAND County deputies discovered that the Wagners' house and beach cabin had been broken into again.

"We'd secured everything after the last time," says Bill Wagner. "So he had to break the lock on the main house to get in. And he also broke the door on the cabin. That's the first time he'd ever done any damage at our place."

Inside the beach cabin, the Wagners' hookah rig—a floating compressor that feeds scuba regulators—had been inflated but not used. An outboard motor and gas can had been carried out to the beach. Both were left on the sand, the outboard with its engine cowling off, as if someone had trouble getting it started. Missing, though, was the Wagners' eight-foot Livingston dinghy.

When Colt faced charges the last time, the Wagners told the court they'd pay for school books, "or anything that might help his education while he was in juvie or after he got out," says Bill. Now, he said, while he wasn't angry about the boat or the damage to the doors, he was worried that Colt was "way beyond" needing just a nudge onto the right path. "He's an extremely bright kid who could have done anything. Now, with the planes and the boats and the fame, it's evolved to the point where he's become something he never thought he could be . . . He thinks this is his one chance to really live life."

Bill wasn't under the illusion that it was going to end well for Colt in the short run, but said of the "kind, helpful" kid he came to know during those Camano summers, "He deserves a happy ending."

BACK ON ORCAS, THERE was a definite exhale after the *Stella Maris* was found off Camano. Ray Clever and his team pulled up their stakeout at Chuck Stewart's hangar and slept at home for the first time in thirty nights. Kyle Ater, the holistic Dirty Harry, did the same, leaving Eastsound in the care of our handful of deputies and a host of new security systems.

Something about Colt's exit from the island this time made it feel permanent. The extra energy, the id in the air, was gone. So Sandi, Murphy, and I were especially surprised at dusk on the twenty-first to once again hear a banging under the cabin. We looked at one another for a moment. Then it happened again.

I dragged Murphy away from the door and went outside into the dim light. I started to bend over and look under the cabin when movement in the salal behind me caught my eye. I spun, and would have been less surprised to see Colton Harris-Moore sitting there eating a pizza. Instead, it was a peacock, a full-blown, shimmering electric-blue-and-green peacock with a five-foot-long, hundred-eyed tail, staring at me. The big bird wasn't afraid at all. Sandi brought me a piece of seed bread and he ate it out of my hand, then calmly posed for pictures.

Some folks in Crow Valley were the only ones who kept a small flock of peafowl, but we called and they weren't missing any. It was a bizarre visitation. Depending on which mythology you follow, the peacock symbolizes compassion, the heavens, or immortality, as in rebirth—like a phoenix.

The peacock's cries haunted our woods that night, then he moved about a mile away and adopted friends of ours. A year later, he's still roosting on their pickup.

PUSHING OFF FROM THE Wagners' beach on the west side of Camano during the right tide and sea conditions, it's not a bad paddle across to Whidbey Island. The currents can even help carry you south to a sandy point near the little town of Langley. From there, it's about eight miles down to the bottom of Whidbey and the next dot that the police connected to Colt's run.

On the night/morning of the twenty-third/twenty-fourth, a boat went missing from Sandy Hook, a dense development with sixty-some private docks biting into a skinny strip of water so it looks, from the air, like an alligator's snout. Residents believe someone had been lurking around the neighborhood for at least a night or two, carrying out several break-ins and sleeping aboard a boat. One dock held a twenty-seven-foot Maxum powerboat. During the night, a thief rowed across the hook and exchanged his small dinghy for the sleek Maxum, ripping out the ignition to hotwire it.

After a short six-mile trip southwest across the passage to Eglon, near the top of the Kitsap Peninsula, the boat was beached. Bare footprints led away down the sand.

The boat theft made the news, noting the possible connection to Colt—including the fact that the forensic evidence was turned over to the FBI. The FBI doesn't waste its time on run-of-the-mill boat thefts, so this was a strong indication that they believed it was Colt and that he was on the move heading south. Despite that, there was already a full head of steam ramping up the Barefoot Bandit chase back on Camano, which was now likely six days and two steps behind Colt.

The media focus turned back to the South End. Pam called the cops on a TV crew that sauntered up past the YOU WILL BE SHOT sign in order to get the "I'm getting my shotgun" footage—which it did. The responding deputy noticed the nice new wooden stairs that had replaced the cinder block pile leading to the deck. "He asked me if they were booby trapped," says Pam. "I told him no, but said there were others all around my property."

Pam got continuous media offers, but refused to go on camera. One major network sent her a box of fruit, which had no effect, as she said she "wanted the green stuff" and wasn't talking veggies. She told me I was lucky that I got in early, before she started charging people for interviews.

THE EVERETT HERALD REPORTED that Bigfoot hunter Richard Grover now pointed his dowsing rod toward Camano. South Enders hoped he would at least help locate a few of their old moonshine stills lost amid the nettles. As the story got bigger, more new characters entered the fray. In early May, an Orcas native attending school on the East Coast started a blog and Web site called Catch the Barefoot Bandit. Using the nom de plume David Peters, he cast his efforts as a direct counter to the fan clubs and T-shirt sellers. On his site, community members could fight back against Colt by donating to a reward fund—with the thought that eventually it would get high enough to tempt someone to turn him in—and by buying T-shirts, mugs, kitchen aprons, and so on with Colt's picture and mocking messages such as "Turn yourself in and we'll give you the second part of the flight manual—you know, the part about landing."

Peters contacted Mike Rocha, a fugitive recovery specialist, aka bounty hunter, to ask what it would take to get someone like him interested in hunting Colt down. Beyond bounty hunting, Rocha's various companies offer surveillance, execution of high-risk warrants, "anti/counter terror services," and Spetnaz-trained teams that can teach you to defend your "important bridges and transportation routes . . . from enemy combatant attacks." They basically do anything that involves wearing black tactical gear, kicking down doors, taking lots of target practice, and other things that go well with the soundtrack of "Let the Bodies Hit the Floor" that plays on his Web site.

The swaggering Rocha, a Vin Diesel double including the shaved head, saw an opportunity to promote his companies and maybe change the public image of bounty hunters from Dog "the" to something at least less hairy. A bail bond company he's connected to donated $2,500 toward the reward, and Rocha volunteered his team of door kickers. A sticky issue, though, was that Colt wasn't a bail jumper. When an arrestee bails out, he signs a contract that explicitly gives the bond agency the right, should he skip, to break into his home, kick his ass, cuff him, and drag him to prison. In Colt's case, however, the bounty hunters had no legal authority beyond any regular citizen to chase or arrest him. And they couldn't go onto private property without permission.

Rocha came out to Camano and left Pam a note explaining how he could arrange a "win-win" situation. According to Pam, Rocha wrote that she or Colt's friends could turn him in and collect the $5,000 reward, then All City Bail Bonds would post Colt's bail for free and have a lawyer standing by to work the case pro bono.

Colt was an escapee, though, and he still owed Washington State jail time on his previous sentence. If he was caught or turned himself in, Colt could automatically be sent to prison to start serving out the remainder of his three-year stretch even before new charges were filed. So bail was moot.

Rocha eventually met in person with Pam. She liked his look, but didn't like what he had to say. Things got testy to the point where she wound up telling him that if any of his guys shot Colt they'd have to watch their backs for the rest of their lives.

ON THE TWENTY-SEVENTH, THERE was a sudden burst of activity on police radios. "Usually cops are very laid back on the radio," says Shauna

Snyder, who heard them on her scanner. "But they sounded gleeful." The excitement was over a teenager captured on an Island County beach. "Residential burglary . . . one in custody" was the call that caused all the titter. Word spread very, very fast. At the trailer, the phone rang. A reporter called Pam to get her reaction to Colt's being caught.

Problem was, it wasn't Colt.

"They should double-check this crap before they call a mother and say that her kid is arrested!"

By the thirtieth of May, Colt had made it 127 miles from Eglon down to Raymond, Washington, a little village on the Willapa River. Driving along Highway 101, Ocean Avenue, toward the town of South Bend, Colt stopped at a Vetters Animal Hospital. He took a ragged piece of paper and wrote a note:

> *Drove by, had some extra cash.*
> *Please use this money for the care of animals*
> *—Colton Harris-Moore*
> *(aka "The Barefoot Bandit")*

He attached a $100 bill and put it in the front door of the clinic, which does considerable work with abandoned pets. The receptionist found it and, according to the vet, didn't recognize the name. She thought it might be from one of their regular clients. The vet herself, though, had heard of Colt. She didn't know if the note was real or not, but called the local sheriff, who ultimately got in touch with the Island County Sheriff's Office. They told him it sounded like Colt, but that they'd like to keep it quiet until they could check forensics.

The vet wrote about her brush with the Barefoot Bandit to a friend, the libertarian author Claire Wolfe, who mentioned it on June 1 in her Living Freedom blog online at *Backwoods Home* magazine. Wolfe writes often of "outlaws," though makes a distinction between common thieves and those who run afoul of rules set up by what she considers an intrusive government. "Colton Harris-Moore may not be a true Freedom Outlaw. He may not even be a particularly good guy. But you gotta admit, the boy does what he does with panache. And in this day of omni-surveillance, it's encouraging to know that some untrained kid can spend years outfoxing 'authoritah' and surviving in the cold northwestern forests."

Once Wolfe published her blog online, the news that Colt was likely at least as far as Raymond and only thirty miles from the Columbia River— Washington State's southwestern border with Oregon—was out there. It popped up on my "Colton Harris-Moore" Google alert on June 1, but the story didn't hit the papers for seventeen days (by which time Colt was already halfway across the country).

The delay must have been surprising if not disappointing for Colt, because here was another action specifically tailored to get press attention. He did, by all accounts, love animals. The only civic statement anyone I spoke to could remember Colt making was when he told his mom that the penalties for animal abuse should be harsher. Pam took this and tagged it on to any mention of making money off of Colt's notoriety. After his legal expenses (though she expected a lawyer to take his case pro bono just for the press), and after building a house on her property that she'd eventually leave to Colt, she said any leftover money would go to starting an animal shelter, because that's what he would want.

The vet note showed that Colt was further embracing his media construct: he signed this note with his full name, Harris-Moore, the name used by the press, not his usual Colton Harris. Outlaw legend–burnishing and Facebook fan–wise, it was a smooth PR move. Who could hate a poor kid from a rough home who loved animals? Rob from the rich and give to the pups.

The $100 gift itself, though, was confiscated by the police. To them, the money was evidence. The note was also evidence: another sign that Colt was cocky enough to not worry about covering his tracks . . . "You can't catch me."

THAT MONDAY, MAY 31, was Memorial Day. Colt continued down 101 until it hit the Columbia River. Then another puzzler. Turn left and he could have simply driven south and crossed the Astoria-Megler Bridge. Drive a little over twelve miles, and he'd have been in Oregon. A few minutes more and he'd be at his next intended stop. No muss, no fuss . . . no fun. Instead, he went right and headed for Cape Disappointment.

In 1775, a Spanish explorer sailing up the Pacific Coast figured that the huge volume of brown water flowing into the ocean at 46 degrees 15 minutes north meant there was a river mouth *aquí*. The waters looked so treacherous, though, he didn't risk trying to confirm it. Later on, a Brit poked his bowsprit between the two points of land but didn't believe it was a river, so he renamed the northern headland Cape Disappointment. It was an American merchantman, Captain Robert Gray aboard the *Columbia Rediviva*, who finally braved the current and waves at the mouth to claim North America's fourth-largest river for the adolescent United States in 1792, naming it after his ship. As with most New World "discoveries," Gray was greeted by the Indians who'd been living there forever. These were the Chinook, who lent their name to the king salmon.

Tucked in behind Cape Disappointment lies the Port of Ilwaco, the closest marina to the infamous Columbia River sandbar or, as it's known to mariners the world over, simply "the Bar"—often said with a shudder. More than two thousand vessels have sunk around the Bar, which is the most crowded crypt in a stretch of Northwest coast called the Graveyard of the Pacific. What makes the area so perilous is the battle between the outflow of the mighty river and the Pacific's winds and waves that takes place atop the huge sandbar. In the right (wrong) conditions, the mouth of the Columbia can transform from a tremulous smooth swell to twenty-foot-tall breakers in the time it takes to ask, "Where'd we put the life jackets?"

The seas here are so consistently hellish that the U.S. Coast Guard bases its National Motor Lifeboat School at Ilwaco in order to train Guardies to handle anything the ocean can throw at them. The guard also mans a busy search-and-rescue base at Cape Disappointment that includes three lifeboats specially designed to operate in Bar conditions, which means being able to roll over and then right themselves and keep going with only minor soiling of the crew's survival suits.

That said . . . there's excellent salmon fishing just outside the mouth of the Columbia, which makes Ilwaco a great place to keep a boat as long as you know what you're doing and always respect the Bar. Larry Johnson of Tumwater, Washington, keeps his *Fat Cat* there during the summer. *Fat Cat* is a thirty-four-foot Ocean Sport Roamer, a muscular twin-diesel $400,000-plus fishing machine built, coincidentally, at a small factory on Camano Island. Larry had used his boat Memorial Day, then put her safely to bed in her slip that evening. Boaters are second only to plane owners in their obsessive relationships with their craft, and Larry even has a sort of baby monitor for his. "There's a webcam at the port that you can control by computer, so I sign on and check the boat every day."

Not that he thought there was much to worry about. Boat theft didn't happen at Ilwaco. The marina had security cameras and, as a bonus, a woman lived full-time aboard her boat moored next to *Fat Cat.* Larry kept his boat locked, but like many folks who have to travel long distances to their marinas, he kept a key squirreled away, hidden under gear, just in case he ever forgot his.

The surveillance camera sweeping the port showed *Fat Cat* right where she should be at midnight on the thirty-first. At 12:45 a.m., though, it showed an empty slip. In the meantime, Colt had crept aboard, rooted around the cockpit (on a boat, the cockpit is the open deck area behind the cabin, not, as on a plane, the place where the driver sits), and found the key. Once inside, Colt unsnapped all the window curtains, carefully rolled them up, and stowed them neatly on a shelf. He started the engines, cast off, and motored out of the marina.

To get where he wanted—across the Columbia to the town of Warrenton—Colt had to thread his way down a snaky channel that winds around several small islands and past constantly shifting sandbars just to reach the river. Charts of the area are cluttered with icons for sunken ships along with notations that even some navigational buoys aren't marked because their positions have to be changed so often due to the deceptive sands. The channel took him right past the Cape Disappointment Coast Guard station, where he would have had to slow to "No Wake" speed alongside their dock.

Just past the station there's a beach jutting into the channel that would have been invisible on this dark night with just a sliver of moon hidden behind an overcast sky. Around that and past Sand Island, the *Fat Cat* would finally be in the river.

Once on the river, Colt could open up the throttles, but the danger wasn't over. The most perilous part of the Columbia is actually crossing the Bar, and Colt didn't have to do that, though, as Larry says, "he was close enough to spit on it." Even behind the Bar the crossing can be hairy, with sloppy seas to contend with, and on the other side Colt had to snug into

the Oregon shoreline to avoid grounding on the Desdemona Sands. Then
he needed to pick out the flashing beacons marking the Skipanon Waterway against the lights of Warrenton, Oregon, a town of five thousand built
on tidal flats across Youngs Bay from Astoria. Colt made it and motored
down the Skipanon to a commercial pier north of town. He docked the
boat, tied her up, shut her down, locked the door, and put the key back in
its hiding place.

Tuesday morning, Larry logged on and pulled up the Port of Ilwaco
camera. "I couldn't believe it," he says. "I downloaded the image three or
four times and then called the port." The marina sent someone down to the
slip and called him back, confirming his boat was gone. Larry phoned the
coast guard while Ilwaco called all the marinas around Washington and
Oregon. They soon got a call from Warrenton that they'd found *Fat Cat* at
their dock, tied up among much larger commercial fishing boats. When
Larry heard where it was, he assumed that it had been taken by someone
very experienced with boats and with navigating the local waters.

More evidence of that came when he arrived at the boat. "There wasn't
even any cosmetic damage." The boat has a full electronics package, with
integrated radar and chartplotter, but it didn't look like that had been
used. "The covers were on the electronics, switches off, and there were no
new tracks saved on the plotter." That really puzzled Larry. "With the
channels poorly marked and the Bar out there, to have done that at night
without navigation equipment . . . I don't know how you'd do it. He got
real lucky."

One explanation is that Colt carried his own portable GPS unit—he'd
stolen plenty of them by this time. With lots of time to plan, he could pull
up charts on his laptop, plot his routes, then transfer them to a GPS. That
doesn't make what he did easy. He still had to contend with everything
Mother Nature could dish up, and he had to drive the boat across a big
black expanse of moving water while navigating from a tiny screen.

"Why you would steal a boat to get to Warrenton I have no idea," says
Larry. "It takes a long time and you have all the risks out on the river. In-
stead, you can drive a car across the bridge and be there in a few minutes."
And conditions weren't ideal: Larry couldn't bring his *Fat Cat* back to
Ilwaco for several days because the river was raging with eight-foot swells.

The Warrenton chief of police, Mathew Workman, says that as soon as they recovered the stolen boat, Colt was the prime suspect. "Mr. Moore had been put on our radar . . . and we fully expected to have something else happen in the area because that seemed to be his MO. When we didn't have anything reported stolen that day, we were concerned he could be staying in one of the vacation homes that we have around here."

Workman, forty-two, was a twenty-year police veteran who'd been chief in Warrenton since October 2008. He says that he got the word out to all Clatsop County police to be on the lookout. "Then I contacted the TITAN Fusion Center down here and asked if they could put something out to all law enforcement in the area."

TITAN Fusion Centers are a post-9/11 Homeland Security big fix that allows local, state, and federal law enforcement to share intelligence and connect the dots on a broad range of subjects, including gangs, organized crime, and serial criminals working a local area, as well as activities that might be terrorism related. Workman says he was told that the information he presented to the Fusion Center didn't "meet their criteria" for forwarding it among other agencies.

Despite TITAN's turndown, law enforcement in Clatsop County, Oregon, as well as Pacific County and Island County, Washington, and the FBI, all knew that Colton Harris-Moore was in Warrenton. And anyone with a twitching EEG knew about his predilections for airplanes. For some reason, though, no law enforcement agency made the obvious move to get in touch with the first place that would come to mind when wondering what Colt would do next. Less than two miles from where he docked the *Fat Cat* lay the Warrenton-Astoria Regional Airport, offering two scenic runways on the shores of the Columbia. John Overholser, the airport manager, says that he received no word, no warning, and had no idea that the Barefoot Bandit was even in Oregon.

At some point on the first, Colt made his way from the Warrenton commercial dock to the airport. Inside the fence that evening, a Cessna 185 sat unattended out on the ramp. It was a proverbially dark and stormy night, one when pilots with hundreds of hours in the left seats of airplanes they know by heart would beg off taking them up. But someone walked through the rain and gusty winds out to the Cessna. Regardless of the weather, the 185 had some things going against it as sensible transportation for Colt. This model sits on two big front wheels with just a tiny turnable gear under the vertical stabilizer to keep its butt off the ground. The configuration gives the aircraft a distinct nose-up attitude—thus the nickname for this style: tail-dragger. The vast majority of early planes had this setup, though nowadays almost all designs incorporate the tricycle-style wheels like the 182s and the Cirrus.

Cessna stopped building 185s back in 1985. Colt always said he preferred newer models, and landing tail-draggers takes much more practice as they have the tendency to tip over on their noses or ground loop (spin in a circle). But out came a flathead screwdriver to try to pry open the plane's doors. Nothing gave easily, though, and he may not have been trying too hard. If he had gotten inside, he would have found the fuel tanks empty.

Colt, police say, then headed for the small terminal. An outside light illuminated a window that looked like the easiest entry point, so he unscrewed the light fixture and laid it on the ground. He untwisted the bulb until it went out, throwing that side of the building into darkness. His trusty screwdriver made short work of the window latch and he climbed inside. It turned out to be a kitchen, and as Colt stepped down, his foot landed on the stove, bending one of the burners. The only stuff in the kitchen was, according to Rich Rasmussen who works at the airport for Hertz, "some pretty nasty food . . . been expired a long time," so Colt moved on to the rental car office.

The door to the Hertz office had some play in it, so first Colt tried to jimmy the lock. That didn't work, so he simply put a shoulder to it and busted it open. It appears he didn't dawdle in the office—two hundred dollars were left behind in the desk—and instead just picked two sets of keys out of a glass bowl, one labeled for a Dodge Journey, the other for a Ford Fusion. The Dodge was right out front.

WHILE COLT WAS BOATING across state lines and shopping planes in Oregon, residents back on Camano Island were gathering for a meeting at the Elger Bay Elementary School. It had been set up by Josh Flickner and David Peters to introduce the community to Mike Rocha and his team. Some locals, though, weren't too receptive to the idea of armed bounty hunters skulking around the island. One woman said she wasn't comfortable having them walking through their backyards with automatic weapons. Rocha reassured her, saying they wouldn't do that. "We carry *semi*automatics," he said. That got a laugh. What didn't was when one older guy stood up and said of Colt, "Most of us want him dead!" The crowd of more than two hundred responded with groans. Flickner got up and said the man wasn't speaking for anyone but himself. The "dead!" quote, though, made the evening news.

Rocha told the crowd his men were already out working the island. Sheriff Brown wasn't at the meeting but announced that he wouldn't be sharing any information with any private group, including bounty hunters. That certainly seemed accurate, because while the bounty hunters began shaking the bushes on Camano, the police and anyone paying attention knew Colt was already south of the state border.

AT 7:30 A.M. ON the second, Rich Rasmussen noticed that the Dodge Journey was missing. Last thing he expected, though, was that it had been stolen. He figured another Hertz employee had borrowed it. What made more of an impact on him was that the key to his office door was working much better. "It'd usually catch a little and you'd have to wiggle it . . . That morning it just turned," he says. "I thought maybe it was a miracle." When word came back that the Dodge wasn't with Hertz staff, Rich called the cops. "They said, 'We've been waiting for your call.'" The police told the airport manager, John Overholser, that once the stolen boat showed up, they figured it was just a matter of sitting by the phone and sooner or later they'd get a call about something else getting ripped off.

COLT DROVE THE DODGE Journey south on Highway 101—the Bandit with no driver's license cruising one of the world's great road trip routes. From the time he dropped the C-note at the vet's in Raymond, he'd had the Pacific Ocean beside him nearly the entire time. The only downside to 101 in Washington and Oregon is trying to ignore the patchwork of clearcuts that make the region look like a green dog with mange. Of course since Colt traveled nocturnally, he missed most of the sights. South of Seaside, Oregon, he veered southeast into Yamhill County, Oregon's wine country.

He ditched the wagon in Dayton and made his way three miles to McMinnville at the north end of the Willamette Valley, thirty-eight miles south of Portland. If Colt hadn't been on the lam, this would be a natural stop. The town hosts the country's second-largest annual UFO Festival—only the one in Roswell, New Mexico, is bigger—which seems like it might attract a kid who specialized in unidentified flying. The serious draw, though, is the Evergreen Aviation & Space Museum, retirement home for Howard Hughes's famous flying cargo ship, the *Spruce Goose*, the largest airplane ever built. The *Goose* (actually made of birch) is housed in a gigantic glass-walled hangar that's lit up beautifully at night.

Just across Salmon River Highway from the museum lies McMinnville Municipal Airport, a busy little hub that serves as a base for more than 130 prop planes, jets, helicopters, and gliders. The cluster of businesses and offices on the field include the FBO/flying school Cirrus Aviation along with Northwest Air Repair, and the ten-thousand-square-foot area command of the Oregon State Police—a big-ass cop shop. There's also a National Guard armory on the property, and just south of that lies Airport Park, a heavily wooded campground that's open to the public. Fliers who come to McMinnville to check out the museum often camp at the park, which runs practically right onto the taxiway.

Northwest Air Repair is owned by U.K.-born Graham Goad, who also serves as the airport's manager. His younger brother Adam worked at McMinnville as a flight instructor for a helicopter company.

According to Graham, the first weirdness happened on Thursday, June 3, "when Connie, who works at the FBO, went to get her lunch out of the fridge and noticed it was gone." Lunch-bag larceny wasn't a common occurrence at McMinnville. No one made a big deal out of it, though—some folks just aren't that fanatical about their food. And some folks are. When Graham walked into his hangar office on Monday the seventh, he immediately noticed that something was horribly, horribly wrong: three of his Johnsonville Beddar with Cheddar brats were missing.

Graham loves those fat tubes of beefy cheesy goodness. Often he'll just nuke a couple in the microwave and gobble them down without even bothering to bun 'em or add fixings. He doesn't take brat banditry lightly, and with a notorious forager known to be in the area, he quickly came up with a suspect. "My brother Adam has a key to my shop and he sticks his head in my fridge all the time."

Adam, though, swore up and down that he didn't do it. Graham scratched his bald head and almost had himself convinced that he just might have been eating so many himself that he'd lost count. But then he noticed a couple more odd things around the office. His computer had been reset, and his WiFi signal booster had been unplugged, disabling the camera that sent images of his shop to his desktop throughout the day. Minor, compared to the missing hot dogs, but still evidence that something fishy was going on.

BACK IN WASHINGTON ON June 3, another bizarre twist. An anonymous donor made a public offer to Colt: turn yourself in and I'll give you $50,000. The offer was made through Jim Johanson, an Edmunds-based attorney and former state rep whom fugitive-recoverer Mike Rocha described as "a friend of our company." Johanson says the donors were "just some people that didn't want to see anything bad happen to Colt or anyone else, like law enforcement." Part of the deal was that Johanson would also represent Colt pro bono, "no strings attached." The free lawyer and $50 grand in "no longer walking around" money had a deadline, though, set to expire June 8 at 3 p.m.

I couldn't find a law enforcement officer anywhere who'd ever heard of such a thing as allowing a fugitive to basically collect a bounty on himself. If it worked, it could start a whole new trend. Go directly to jail and *do* collect your $200.

"He's not gonna turn himself in," said Pam. "Give up your freedom for a lousy fifty thousand dollars! What the hell can you do with that small amount of money? Maybe get a really nice car."

The deadline came and went without a peep from Colt. The prospective donors have remained anonymous.

ON WEDNESDAY MORNING, JUNE 9, Graham Goad arrived at his McMinnville shop and noticed that the back door was unlocked. Inside his office, Graham's computer screen wasn't how he'd left it and his wireless booster was again unplugged. He called Adam in and demanded to know if he'd been messing with his stuff. Again, Adam pleaded innocent. Then it was his turn. He pulled his head out of his brother's fridge and asked, "Graham, how many hot dogs did you eat yesterday?"

Oh no, Graham thought, not now, not when he'd just stocked up on the special smoked sausage dogs. Graham did some quick hot dog calculus that put Captain Queeg's geometric strawberry logic to shame. He ran the figures again and double-checked the net number of wieners left in the wrapper. The result was inescapable: six dogs had fled the pack.

"That's when I realized, 'Hey, somebody's been in here!'"

Graham walked over to the FBO for a cup of joe and mentioned the theft. "One of the people there said, 'Ho ho ho, maybe it's the Barefoot Bandit!'"

Graham and other local pilots had heard of Colton Harris-Moore and his affinity for airports and aviation. "We knew he was doing this kind of thing," he says. "But naw, we figured he was still stuck up there in the San Juans. We didn't think he'd venture this far."

Of course the information that he was most likely in Oregon and shopping the state's small airports was already there for the disseminating. Here again Colt was serving as a war gamer for law enforcement and Homeland Security. He wasn't a serial killer or an Al Qaeda sleeper, but he was someone already accused of stealing four planes, more than a million dollars in property, and committing dozens of other felonies. He was very high profile and certainly would be a feather in the cap of whoever caught him. The FBI was actively hunting him and you'd hope they have big ears.

The Dodge Journey stolen from Warrenton-Astoria was recovered by the Yamhill County Sheriff's Office in Dayton at 7 p.m. on June 3. That's less than two miles from McMinnville Airport, which has that State Police Command Center right on the property. Yamhill contacted Warrenton that day and Chief Workman called state authorities and the TITAN Fusion Center. The Fusion Center declined Workman's request to get the report out, and though a window-licking squirrel could have looked at the info and Colt's well-known MO and come up with McMinnville Airport as his target, no one in law enforcement even called the airport to give them a heads-up.

Instead, on June 3, just after Pam says she'd poured herself a beer, the FBI drove up to Haven Place on Camano Island. They were there to ask once again that Pam let them know where Colt was. One of Pam's standard lines had become "If you don't believe me, give me a lie detector test!" The

FBI agents always declined. This visit, though, the FBI agents told her they were going to set one up for her, but that it would take a couple of weeks. Suddenly Pam wasn't so sure. "I'm going to have to think about it . . . I don't trust these polygraphs."

Pam had bought herself a small tape recorder and now recorded the police and FBI whenever they questioned her. During this visit, the tape ran out. The FBI agents stopped the interview and one of them inserted a new tape for her. They all saw the humor in that, and telling the story, Pam went into a fit of throaty laughter that ended in a hacking cough.

"They were real nice like they used to be," she said. "And I gave them a big damn lecture about shining that damn flashlight into my face the last time. I said, 'Don't you ever do that again!'" The agents, Pam says, told her they didn't have too much time to look for Colt "because they were after bin Laden and stuff like that. I told them that Colt and his dog could find bin Laden, and one of them laughed and said, 'Yeah, he probably could.'"

Friendly as they were, they did, however, leave Pam with a copy of U.S. Code, title 18, chapter 1, section 3, the law regarding actions such as harboring or hindering the apprehension of a criminal that would make someone an accessory after the fact.

She sighed and said that her life revolved around Colt's problems. "I get so tired of thinking about it . . . I go to sleep thinking about it and I wake up thinking about it." Other than her movies, she said, she has only one escape. "It's called beer," she laughed, then added, "I'm serious."

As Pam was reading the paper the FBI agents left her, a spider crawled across it and she suddenly yelled, "They bugged me!"

LATE IN THE EVENING on the eighth, the telephone rang in the trailer. Pam picked it up and recognized a voice she says she hadn't heard for months. "It was Colt . . . I was shocked, but it was great to hear from him. He sounded good, relaxed, says he's fine." Pam says she asked Colt where he was and got silence for an answer. "He says he got rid of the cell phone he used to use and now he's on a throwaway." Pam warned Colt that the heat was on. "I told him to lay low, real low, because of the stupid bounty hunter . . . but he already knew about him." As usual, Colt had been following all the news about him. He told Pam, "I read where you said that I wouldn't be interested in no lousy fifty thousand."

"I said, 'I was right wasn't I?' And he said, 'Yeah.'"

Pam had just gotten in touch with John Henry Browne, who, depending on who you ask, is either Washington State's most effective criminal defense attorney or its most hated. Or both. Over a long career, the sixty-four-year-old Browne has been attracted to numerous high-profile cases. Early on, as head trial lawyer for the King County public defender's office, he represented serial killer Ted Bundy. Since going into private practice, he's specialized in clients who've been similarly popular in the public's eye, such as a man who set a warehouse fire in which four Seattle firefighters died. Browne, brash, theatrical, and six feet six inches tall, sees himself as a great equalizer for the individual against a too-powerful government. He has a reputation for aggressively attacking the prosecution's witnesses, which he's paid to do, and taunting and threatening prosecutors, which just seems to be his favorite hobby.

Browne confirmed he was interested in Colt's case. Maybe having a headline-making lawyer to defend him would convince Colt to turn himself in before somebody got killed. I figured it was worth one more shot, and on June 7 wrote a blog post to Colt that included John Henry Browne's cell phone number.

WHEN I NEXT SPOKE with Pam, she said she'd told Colt about the lawyer, "but he didn't act interested."

Pam, though, was almost bubbly in this conversation. Colt had finally reached out to her again, and she was feeling like she'd taken control of some things. She had John Henry Browne, and she was setting up a defense fund for Colt.

"I have people saying hi to me that haven't said hi in friggin' years," she said. "Yesterday down at Elger Bay store, two of the cashiers that have always had their noses in the air to me were suddenly saying, 'Hi, Pam, how ya doin'?' What the hell is that? Oh, we better hurry up and make friends with her because she's gonna be famous. What the hell?"

Pam said that Colt was studying a foreign language but wouldn't say which one. In one of their conversations, she said, he also mentioned a girlfriend. "So I told him about birth control 'cause I guess she stayed with him for a while . . . I said, 'Now, Colt, you're not supposed to have any kids until you're quite a bit older. And he said, 'Oh, don't worry, Mom.'"

Colt had asked her for some other advice, too. "He wants me to write down my words of wisdom for him. And I said, number one: don't get involved with Orientals or black girls. But then the next time he called me I said I take all that back. I said, 'Colt, if you love them, then I don't care what their color is, because real love is not easy to find.' He said, 'Well, she's gotta be able to build a campfire.' I said, 'Okay, what else?' He said, 'She has to know how to cook and she has to know how to set up a campsite and fish.' Anyway, he went down his list and what he was describing was me! I felt good about that."

BACK IN OREGON . . . SIX days and nine hot dogs after law enforcement knew the Dodge had been dumped within walking distance of McMinnville Airport, the owner of the FBO called Graham Goad and told him a rental car was missing. One of the services offered by the FBO is to line up cars for incoming pilots. A silver GMC Acadia was stolen while waiting for Enterprise to come pick it up. That same day, the ninth, they noticed that the stock of AA batteries in the supply closet had been raided. Then the owner of a private hangar went to turn on his handheld GPS and it wouldn't work. When he opened the back to check the batteries, they were gone.

Graham and the owner of the FBO called the Oregon State Police station seventy-five yards away, but the Staties shrugged and told them to call the city police—they had no interest in a stolen rental car and disappearing hot dogs. The McMinnville PD showed up and took a report, but didn't do any forensic work. It was Graham who found where the back window to his hangar had been pried open with a screwdriver.

A week later, Graham's youngest brother, Matthew, who lives up in Everett, Washington, sent him an email link to a newspaper story about Colton Harris-Moore being tracked to Oregon. "He says, 'Hey, this guy is in your area!' I said, 'Yeah, we figured that out, thanks for the timely heads-up.'"

. . . .

"No, I never heard anything," says Alan Daniels, manager of Oregon's Ontario Municipal Airport. He'd received no warning about any airport-surfing plane and/or car thief at loose in the region, certainly not near his airport, which offers a single five-thousand-foot runway right alongside a golf course. Hook your approach to runway 32 at Ontario, and you could land your Cessna in a water hazard.

Ontario has a population of eleven thousand or so, making it the biggest town in Malheur County. "We're just a quiet little community out here in the desert," says Daniels. "It's not the edge of the world, but if you stand on your tiptoes you might be able to see it." Ontario grew up on the Union Pacific Railroad and lies on the Snake River where it begins to serve as the squiggly divide between Oregon and Idaho. The area farms out potatoes, onions, and beets, but the town's main claim to fame is that it's the home of Oregon's largest state prison.

The Ontario airport is close to a major highway, and several other arteries intersect in and around the town. Ne'er-do-wells like the easy on-and-off access. "Our crime rates," says Captain Mark Alexander of the City of Ontario Police Department, "are up there with bigger cities just because we have such a transient population." Captain Alexander says they get a lot of people coming through town because they've got themselves a Walmart and no sales tax. Plop that combination close to the border of a state with 6 percent sales tax, and sooey, it's feeding time. "Any given day at Walmart, 75 percent of your license plates are Idaho."

Alexander says he hadn't heard of the Barefoot Bandit. "You gotta understand, we're just flooded with 'Be on the lookout of all kinds of people,' and that's just from around here." That doesn't mean their airport was totally off police radar. "We've had some hangars broke into before," says Alexander. For that reason, officers do drive-bys around the airport every once in a while. One of them cruised through at 10:30 p.m. on June 9, and saw nothing amiss—because you can't see what's already missing.

Local pilot Gary Taylor, fifty-two, flies corporate, a Learjet, out of Ontario Muni. He'd pulled up to the airport that day at 3 p.m. in his white 2008 F250 diesel pickup. He parked the big rig next to the hangar and his copilot cruised up alongside in her Prius.

Gary, who's been flying since he was sixteen, went inside to wipe down the jet with an ugly blue bath towel he'd bought just for the plane's exterior. Once he had the Lear sparkling, he tossed the towel and his keys into the pickup. "I don't like to fly with car keys and take the chance of losing them on a layover." The Ford had a keyless entry, so he always stuck his keys up under the driver's seat and locked the doors. On the front seat, he left a $1,000 Bose noise-canceling pilot headset and a brand-new jacket. Normally, Gary would have tucked his truck into the hangar, but this was scheduled to be a short flight, just a hop to Salt Lake City and back, so he left it outside. They fired up the jet and took off at 4 p.m., expecting to be back by 9 p.m. that evening.

Instead, it wasn't until midnight when they taxied back to the hangar. The big truck was gone. "At first," Gary says, "I thought it was some of my sick friends playing a joke on me." He didn't find it funny. "It was late and I just wanted to get home." He made a couple of calls and realized this was no joke, then called the police.

The cops told him not to worry—too much. They said that it would probably show up later that night. "They said it was pretty common for . . . you know, Hispanic people to go out and joyride for a little while. They told me the cars usually show up in town."

As they poked around, it became apparent that the pickup might not have been the thief's first choice. He'd used a screwdriver to try to get in the Prius. Then they discovered that he'd also tried to force open the hangar's man door. Typically, those are flimsy, but Gary had reinforced it with a steel plate. It turned out to be a lucky break for the burglar: if he'd opened the door, he would have tripped the silent alarm.

The next day, Gary was driving toward the hangar when he noticed something that caused him to hit the brakes. A jerrican of fuel and a hand truck that had been in the bed of his missing pickup were sitting alongside a silver GMC Acadia parked not far from the Lear's hangar.

"I thought that is really way too weird."

It got weirder. When Gary walked up to the Acadia and looked inside, he saw his ugly blue towel.

He called the police out again. The towel, they theorized, had been used to wipe down the prints on the stolen SUV.

Gary's truck wasn't found in town. Two nights later, though, at 2:15 a.m., he got a call from a deputy from over in Ada County, Idaho, who told him they'd found his F250 on a farm road grandly named the Emmet Highway in a little town of less than two thousand called Star. The truck had gone about thirty miles down 84 and then east about ten miles, ending up in the middle of a field where the corn crop was just starting to sprout with stalks about six inches high. "I asked if my headset was in there and the sheriff said yes. The keys were gone, though. They didn't bother with prints or anything, he just said, 'Come get it *now*,' because the ignition key was missing and they were afraid whoever took it was going to come back."

Gary was able to get ahold of a tow company to go put the truck up on a flatbed, but they refused to bring it all the way to his place and he had to go meet them halfway. When he got to the pickup, Gary says he noticed a couple of things right off. First was olfactory, and it wasn't a new-car smell. "Horrendous body odor. That freaked me out . . . I wasn't sure I could take it." The second thing was that the seat was pulled way up, as if whoever was driving it was real short, or he'd moved the seat up so he could stretch out and sleep in the back. Then, when he turned on the engine, the radio started talking Spanish—not the station he'd left it on.

Because Ada County didn't bother to do forensics, there's no clue who took Gary's truck—other than the person who did might not have bathed in a few days, and he either spoke Spanish or . . . was possibly learning the language and wanted to practice. Or the truck may even have been stolen twice, both thieves realizing they weren't going to get far without having to stop for fuel, which isn't a smart thing to do considering that almost every gas station in the country has surveillance cameras.

What is known, though, is that Colton Harris-Moore was in Ada County at that time, where he stole a 2006 Ford F150 and continued his road trip. He did a big 372-mile swing below the Sawtooth National Forest amid the western foothills of the Rocky Mountains and then drove down into the Teton Valley to a town called Driggs, Idaho. There at Driggs Teton Peaks Municipal Airport on June 12, he traded the pickup for a gray Cadillac Escalade, which he stole from a private hangar. The airport had a number of cars around, all with keys in them, but Colt picked the top of the line, the favorite SUV of rap stars.

He dumped the Escalade in Cody, Wyoming, the following day. Moving between those two points, the most likely route is through Wind River Canyon, past Kirwin, a spot that Amelia Earhart liked so much that she was having a cabin built there while she attempted her ill-fated around-the-world flight. The other choice would be up through Yellowstone National Park and across the Wapiti Valley, a drive that Teddy Roosevelt called "the most scenic 50 miles in America." It's the perfect path for a summer road trip, but risky due to having to stop to pay a park entrance fee to a ranger. Regardless of the route, both drives run through such breathtaking vistas that it should be a felony to do either one of them at night.

Colt was now getting into real bandit country. In 1832, Driggs was the site of a huge fur trapper rendezvous that, beyond the usual alcohol-fueled shenanigans that made those gatherings famous, ended with the deadly two-day battle of Pierre's Hole, where mountain men along with their Nez Perce and Flathead friends fought a band of Gros Ventre Indians. And Colt certainly wasn't the first rustler to make a run through Teton Valley, though historically it served as a hideout for those who filched cattle and horses instead of boats and planes. Crossing into Wyoming, the red hills and frontier towns still faintly ring with the ricochets of Robert LeRoy Parker and Harry Longabaugh, aka Butch Cassidy and the Sundance Kid, along with Wild Bill Hickok, Doc Holliday, Calamity Jane, and Frank and Jesse James.

The local legend most akin to Colt was probably Ed Harrington, a gentleman bandit whose lasting celebrity came from a July day in 1914 when he held up fifteen stagecoaches. They were sightseeing coaches, each filled with tourists visiting Yellowstone Park, so it was like robbing the faux boats as they make their way through the Pirates of the Caribbean ride. Harrington was very polite, used the magic word "please" when asking folks to deposit their cash in his sack, and didn't hurt anyone. He got so cocky with how well his plan was working, though, that he allowed his victims to take snapshots of him as souvenirs. Harrington collected more than $1,000 in cash and jewelry, but was later identified and spent five years in Leavenworth.

The Wild West was once policed by characters like Wyatt Earp and Bat Masterson, who were just as wild as the famous outlaws they corralled and sometimes caroused with. Today, it's men like Detective Ron Parduba and George Menig of the Cody Police Department. Both are former NYPD.

New York cops all think they've seen everything, but when Parduba and a fellow officer, John Harris, went out to investigate a break-in and stolen truck at High Country Roofing on June 13, they found a distinctive piece of evidence: a giant bare footprint. Harris saw the print in the mud and said it looked "like Bigfoot." Cody police suspect Colt first went for an Escalade parked at a body shop—'cause that's how he rolls—then realized it was too damaged and took the roofing truck instead. At some point during his time in Cody, the Barefoot Bandit cut his foot. As he drove the truck east, he bled DNA onto the floorboard.

The truck made it only two counties before it ran out of gas. Colt ditched it along the highway, leaving the keys in the ignition. A quarter mile away, he sneaked into an unlocked garage and made off with a Lincoln Mark LT, a $40,000 luxury pickup that's very popular in the carports of the Mexican cartels. The Lincoln was found later at a small airport, a giant footprint on its bed cover.

Detective Parduba reported the Bigfoot sighting to Assistant Chief Menig, who saw a media report on the Barefoot Bandit. Together they concluded that all the evidence fit Colt's MO and made a call back to the trailhead. Island County's Ed Wallace says Menig's call was the first hint of Colt's location he'd received since Oregon.

THE LINCOLN PICKUP MADE its way to Buffalo in Johnson County, Wyoming, in the foothills of the Big Horn Mountains just north of Crazy Woman Canyon and the legendary outlaw sanctuary Hole-in-the-Wall. The most famous denizen of Hole-in-the-Wall was Butch Cassidy who, historians say, first soured on authority figures at the age of thirteen when he rode to town on his day off to buy some jeans, but found the store closed. He broke in, got his pants and a piece of pie, and left an IOU. The store owner pressed charges, however, and an outlaw was born.

Butch and Sundance stayed in Buffalo at the Occidental Hotel, as did Calamity Jane and Buffalo Bill. Today, folks drifting into town are more likely to be about coal and methane production than gunslinging, but the area's still primarily big skies and open spaces. Only 8,500 people live in all of four-thousand-square-mile Johnson County.

Jim McLaughlin, who's the manager and fixed base operator for the

Johnson County Airport two miles north of the town center, fits the rugged landscape he's occupied since 1978. That, though, still doesn't make him a local. "Not in this town," laughs the easygoing seventy-two-year-old great-grandfather. Jim raises a small herd of cattle and there's a bit of John Wayne in his voice, but he says he doesn't get along so good with horses. "I'll stick to planes—they're a heck of a lot safer." He flies and maintains Cessnas and Supercubs, and other than most weekend evenings when he's out dancing, Jim says he seems to spend all his time at the airport. He hadn't, though, gotten any calls about Colt even though his was the closest airport to the Barefoot Bandit's last known whereabouts.

"I'd heard a little bit about him a long time ago, but I didn't think anybody like that would try something here because, you know, it's kinda dangerous around these parts—a lot of guys pack weapons."

Jim's first hint of something odd was on Saturday, June 12, when he slammed his hangar door shut and the padlock fell out, broken. "At first I thought maybe it was just old and rotted." Then, when Jim came in on Monday, he realized that more than entropy had been afoot. Eight Snickers bars had been swiped from the FBO counter, and when he went to his hangar he noticed a bunch of tools—big screwdrivers, pry bars, and channel locks—was missing. Jim walked the rest of the private hangars and saw that six of them had been broken into. In one, there'd been both a Suburban and a $65,000 sporty-luxe Cadillac CTS-V—"One of them go-fast ones," says Jim. Both vehicles had full fuel tanks and the keys inside. "He wanted a Cadillac." Sometime Saturday night, Colt had closed the hangar door behind him and drove off in the supercharged sedan.

Jim called the law but didn't expect much. "They don't go out to a shooting here until they're sure the bad guys are out of ammunition." The police took a report but didn't do any forensics at the airport. "They might know where the fingerprint kit is, but I've never seen them use it." Jim says the police didn't mention anything about the Barefoot Bandit and didn't have any suspects in mind. "They were . . . disinterested." The police did collect some of the tools that had been taken out of Jim's hangar, but he says he's not sure if that was for evidentiary purposes. "Probably a cop needed a big screwdriver."

Later, the fancy Lincoln pickup stolen just a ways out of town was found—sitting in the Johnson County Airport's lot.

. . . .

THE CADDY WAS RECOVERED a few days later, undamaged, 163 miles away in Spearfish, South Dakota. To get there, Colt drove through Crook County, Wyoming, and its most famous town, Sundance, which lent its name to Harry Longabaugh, the Sundance Kid, after he did a stretch in its jail for horse thieving at the age of eighteen.

Spearfish takes its name from the Sioux Indian practice of spear fishing in the local creek. It's a Black Hills town of 8,600 just ten minutes north of Deadwood, the notoriously lawless gold rush town where Wild Bill Hickok was gunned down.

The Cadillac was ditched just a mile from Spearfish's Black Hills Airport. By now, anyone could guess where strange things started happening next. The FBO at Black Hills is Eagle Aviation, run by Ray Jilek. Did Ray get any warnings that something wicked his way comes? "None."

Ray runs a tight ship. "We balance the till every night and again in the morning," he says. When they did the count Monday morning, the fourteenth, it was off. "We were four dollars short." The missing four bucks wasn't near as strange as the fact that several hundred dollars was left behind in the cash drawer. "It was really puzzling . . . It just didn't seem rational," he says. Someone less precise might even think they'd simply miscounted, but not Ray. He started looking around and found that a number of locks had been subtly jimmied.

"Everything was put back as close as possible to the way it was left, but you could tell." One of the doors that'd been opened led to a hangar with two unlocked planes. "We had portable GPS units and headsets and all that kind of stuff inside . . . but nothing was taken." He began to think it was probably just kids—until he got to work the following morning.

This time the till was empty. "It'd been pried open with a screwdriver." Ray says the burglar took his big orange-handled Snap-on screwdriver and sledgehammer and went to work on a four-drawer fireproof filing cabinet. "He beat on that thing, must have been for an hour to gain access to it only to find out there was nothing inside, absolutely nothing." The planes were all accounted for, but one other count was off. "There were 15.8 gallons of high-grade aviation fuel missing."

Inside the FBO is a lockbox where folks who keep cars at the airport store their keys. When a sheriff's deputy found the stolen Caddy the next day, "that's when they started putting two and two together," says Ray. They figured there'd likely be a vehicle missing from the Black Hills Airport, and sure enough, when they went out and counted, a Ford pickup was gone. "He'd pumped the aviation fuel into the truck and took off sometime late Monday night or early Tuesday morning."

The mystery that remained was the first night's $4. "We were thinking about that and suddenly looked over at the vending machines." Ray speculates that Colt got hungry and needed some singles to get a Coke and a candy bar, maybe a Snickers.

THE BLACK HILLS FORD drove through the spectacular desolation of the Badlands and pulled up to the Pierre Regional Airport in the capital city of South Dakota. This was the largest airport Colt hit during the summer of 2010. Pierre's two runways stretched across its 1,700 acres and handled commuter airlines, including Delta Connection. Lindbergh once landed here in the *Spirit of St. Louis* during a goodwill tour.

A ten-foot-high fence surrounded the secure side of the airport. According to what airport manager Mike Isaacs and the local police figured out from the evidence, Colt found a natural entry past security and into the terminal building. A lone tree, a crabapple, stood in the parking lot and branched out toward the terminal. It was an easy climb, then out on a limb and onto the roof. Footprints—sneakers—led from the tree across the flat roof to a second-story door. "No one would even think to lock that door," says Mike. "There's no outside access to it—unless you climb the tree—and it's only there to take weather observations for the FAA." Once inside, Colt had access to the entire airport. "He could have messed with all the TSA's equipment, but he didn't."

What he did do, though, was stealthily attempt to jimmy nearly every lock in the terminal using a screwdriver. "The more we looked, the more we found these little pry marks here, there, and everywhere. He could have easily broke a window and gotten into my office and taken laptops and all kinds of stuff, but he didn't."

Colt tried the cash box at the Delta counter but couldn't crack it. He did get into the lockboxes at Avis and Budget, and took the key to a rental car. He then went outside on the runway side of the airport and found an open door at the firehouse. Upstairs in the chief's office around 4 a.m., Colt got on the computer and pulled up Google Earth, zooming in on the satellite view of the airport and surrounding area. He grabbed the chief's iPod touch on the way out and stopped by the firefighters' break room where he microwaved himself a Hungry-Man frozen dinner and took a Diet Coke.

When he got back outside the fence, Colt had some good news and bad news. The Avis key he'd taken fit a car in the lot, but the car had been totaled. So he jumped back into the pickup he'd taken in Buffalo and continued east.

"I was surprised," says Isaacs. "After I found out that he had a history of this, I was a little shocked that nobody had sent out anything to the airports." Isaacs says he tried to make up for that by calling 866-GA-SECURE, a hotline for reporting suspicious activity around general aviation airports that's a partnership between AOPA and the TSA. Calls ring at the TSA's Transportation Security Operations Center. "I also called our state aeronautics office and the other local airports and let them know to watch out."

COLT HAD NOW MADE it to the exact center of the country, 1,200 miles away from the comfort of his misty Northwest woods. He was adamant about sticking to the conspicuously predictable MO of hopping from airport to airport. The FBI, TSA, and police departments stretching back to the Pacific coast all had more than enough information to guess his next moves. It appeared the game was coming to an end.

Meanwhile, on June 16, local Seattle television aired footage of a team of masked bounty hunters gearing up and going out to hunt Colt. They patrolled dark roads and woods and hid in the weeds around an airport . . . on Camano Island.

On Orcas Island, high school yearbooks came out. The junior class photos included a kid who'd spent so much time on the island he might as well have enrolled and joined the Vikings basketball team. Colt's was the only self-portrait.

. . . .

Jack McCall, the guy who shot Wild Bill Hickok in Deadwood while he held aces and eights, was originally set loose because Hickok had maybe killed his brother. McCall was rearrested, though, and taken to a place where the law existed more formally than it did in Deadwood. That place was Yankton, Dakota Territory.

Yankton, South Dakota's River City, lies on the north bank of the Missouri. It's nearby airport is Chan Gurney, where Gary Carlson runs the FBO.

I'll get this out of the way quickly: Gary, did you get any advance warning that there was someone in the area, state, or region who was targeting airports?

"None, no, not a one."

Carlson's first inkling came when he rushed into his office at 7 a.m. on a hectic June 17. He had a jet coming in early and was hurrying to have everything ready. He slammed his door behind him and noticed that it sounded funny. Then he went to his desk and saw that someone had turned his monitor off. That wasn't right. When he'd left at 9 p.m. the night before, he'd put it into sleep mode, just like always. He went back over to the door and saw that the lock had been jimmied, then immediately ran out to make sure all the planes were okay.

They were, but his big Craftsman screwdriver was missing out of the toolbox, and that matched the damage on the security door. He also noticed that blankets were gone from the little spot the FBO has for pilots in need of a nap between flights. A brand-new Chevy pickup had been delivered to the airport by a local rental company for the people jetting in that morning. Its key was gone, but the pickup was still parked outside. This was interesting. The Chevy had OnStar, which has a stolen vehicle tracking function that can alert police to its exact location, speed, and direction via GPS. Beginning in 2009, OnStar even added the ability for operators to remotely slow a vehicle once the police confirmed it'd been stolen. A smart thief would know this and pick another car. But OnStar is also standard on all Cadillacs, like the recently boosted Escalade and CTS-V. It made sense to take those cars only if the thief was cunning enough to know that they wouldn't be noticed missing until he'd already gotten to his next stop.

But what if the traveling thief had decided for some reason to stay put for a while?

Gary called the police, who immediately suspected Colt and knew what to look for. They quickly located the Black Hills pickup in the airport parking lot. Detectives jumped on Carlson's computer and saw that someone had been online at 1 a.m., surfing AirNav.com, "the pilot's window into a world of aviation information." AirNav tells you everything you'd want to know about every airport: number and type of planes based there, how busy it is, hours of operation, FBO services, and whether there's a manned tower. The site also links to satellite photos of the airport and surrounding area, which the computer history showed had been pulled up.

The fact that not much was missing from the airport led local detectives to believe Colt might be coming back for a second bite like he did in Spearfish and at least four other airports. So they came up with a plan to stake out the building that night. The police also began a search of the area, paying special attention to a copse of woods just south of the airport.

Those woods, a mix of elm and cottonwood, fully leafed in mid-June, form the northeast corner of a residential neighborhood adjacent to the airport. Inside the trees, you have an excellent spot to watch the area homes and see which ones remain dark after sundown. It's less than a third of a mile from the airport to the street entrance of the development, or you can walk across a soybean field that takes you right to the backs of the houses.

Colt walked over and began snooping around. Police say that he visited numerous houses in the neighborhood, but didn't find just the right one until he broke into the home of Kelly and Lisa Kneifl.

The Kneifls and the four youngest—ages fourteen, twelve, eight, and five—of their seven kids had just moved into the rancher a month before. Kelly and Lisa travel often for their jobs and it had been a very busy year. They'd barely even begun to unpack the house, but managed to block out a week for a vacation. That's where they were, up in the mountains of Pennsylvania, when Colt came calling.

Several things made the Kneifl house ideal, even beyond the fact that the family was out of town. There was plenty of food, the kind of stuff teenagers love, like frozen pizza and chicken nuggets, packaged deli ham and chicken, and a whole vat's worth of sugar-free Jell-O pudding cups. The home also backed up to open fields and ongoing residential construction. If someone inside was careful about turning on the lights up on the main floor, and spent most of his time in the large finished basement where the only light visible from the outside would be through the egress window facing the fields, it'd be possible to remain unseen indefinitely, even by the neighbors. Plus, the Kniefl boys had a kick-ass video game collection and three platforms—Xbox, Wii, and GameCube.

Colt chose one of the boys' beds downstairs for sleeping. He spent the rest of his time on the couch in front of the TV in the basement family room. That's where he ate, neatly piling his food wrappers and building what would become a leaning tower of Jell-O pudding empties.

In the middle of the night, officially early morning on June 18, Colt was wide awake and busy. He nuked himself some chicken nuggets and arrayed them in three precise rows of three on one of the Kniefls' square plates. He set the clothes washer going, and with his nuggets cooling by the couch, jumped into the shower. When he got out, he turned on one of Kelly's beard trimmers and started giving himself a buzz, cutting about an inch off his hair. Then he heard an unwelcome rumble . . .

Kelly and family had a long, long day getting home from Pennsylvania. They drove to Pittsburgh, flew into Omaha, and then had a two-and-a-half-hour run home. It was 3 a.m. when a blurry-eyed Kelly finally pulled into the driveway, hit the garage door opener, and roused the troops.

Lisa gathered up her five-year-old daughter and carried her to the door leading into the house. She noticed that the door was slightly ajar. "I don't remember leaving this open," she said to Kelly. Lisa stepped into the mudroom and flicked on the light. That's when she saw that the door at the end of the hall leading to the interior of the home was also open. She was looking at it, just about to mention it to Kelly, when suddenly a hand reached out and slammed the door shut. Lisa screamed.

Kelly charged in and flung the door open like an angry grizzly. He was ready for almost anything . . . though he was still momentarily shocked to find a naked man. Colt ran away at full speed, and Kelly, a six-foot-three 340-pound former football player, took off after him, roaring, "Get out of my house!"

With Kelly right behind him, Colt fled deeper into the home, then suddenly made an acrobatic leap over a banister, landing three-quarters of the way down the basement stairs. Kelly had to backtrack to the top of the stairway and then rushed down, still screaming at the top of his lungs, "Get the hell out of my house!"

As Kelly neared the bottom of the stairs, the only light was a dim glow from the egress window off to the left; the rest of the basement was in total darkness. He was a clear target, though, silhouetted by the light coming from upstairs. Kelly's roars were suddenly matched by a young voice shouting back at him from about fifteen feet away: "Stop! I've got a gun! I'll shoot! I'll shoot!" A red laser beam shot out of the darkness and hit Kelly. He stopped dead.

Lisa was watching everything from the top of the stairs. She turned and screamed to the kids, "Run!"

After freezing for a second, Kelly ran back upstairs. Out on the driveway, their twelve-year-old daughter had already dialed 911 on her cell. Lisa grabbed the phone and breathlessly told the operator that there were people in her house threatening to shoot her family. Kelly yelled for everyone to get back into the car. He slammed it into reverse and backed out and down the street, stopping two houses away. He pulled into a neighbor's driveway, where he could still see the front of his home. He momentarily considered driving to the other side so he could shine his headlights on the basement window, "and then I thought, He's got a gun, I've got the kids, that would make no sense at all."

Down in the basement, Colt ripped open the washing machine mid-cycle, breaking the latch. He grabbed for his sopping-wet clothes—missing a pair of gray-and-black Calvin Klein boxer briefs in the bottom of the drum—then scooped up the rest of his gear and slid open the basement window.

About six minutes after the Kneifls dialed 911, Kelly saw two officers cautiously approaching the house on foot. A few minutes after that, a third officer showed up, and finally one of them circled around to where he could see the basement window. Several minutes later, the 911 operator told Kelly that the officers wanted to talk to him. He drove to another neighbor's driveway, where a cop was waiting, wanting to know about the house's exits and what weapons were inside. He said they had a SWAT team on the way.

It was nearly an hour before the four-man SWAT team arrived in full gear, assault rifles strapped across their chests. In the meantime, Kelly had sent Lisa and the kids off to a hotel to try to get some sleep. He drew the police a rough blueprint of his home, and they then told him to pull back out of the line of fire. Kelly didn't have a house key to give them, so the tactical team hoisted their metal battering ram and approached the front door—they felt it was a safer entry point than going through the garage. Bang went the door and Kelly watched them pour inside "hoopin' and a hollerin'."

By the time they'd cleared the house, finding no one inside, it was 4 a.m. A canine team began working the area and the police asked Kelly to help them find his shotgun and rifles, which were all accounted for, along with Lisa's jewelry and the cash he'd had stuffed in a drawer. A detective led him through the house, room by room, taking photos and asking how things had been left, what was missing or out of place. "Even the boys' bedrooms, nothing was really messed up," says Kelly. "Or at least not more than usual. Even the food wrappers around the couch were somewhat organized."

Later Kelly realized that Colt had gotten into his locking file drawer, prying it open with a screwdriver. It'd been filled with birth certificates and other important papers. "The only things missing, though, were all my vehicle titles."

The real disorder was in the basement bathroom, where it was obvious that someone had been interrupted mid-primp. A razor sat on the floor along with shaved whiskers. Inch-long head hair was all over the place, "on the floor, in the sink, on the counter, and even chunks of it on the window he'd climbed out."

All through the police search, the washing machine had been angrily beeping about its premature evacuation. Kelly finally turned it off.

After a short break at the hotel to see his family, Kelly returned to his street at daybreak to find a scene out of the movies. Law was swarming the neighborhood. Investigators pulled Colt's fingerprints from inside the house, while other officers canvassed the nearby homes, finding evidence Colt attempted to break into as many as a dozen. Police searched local construction sites and woods near the airport.

At 4 p.m., a search group from Codington County, two hours north, arrived with a trio of bloodhounds. Kelly watched them walk the dogs one by one around his house. Each hound picked up a strong trail leading from the basement egress window. The hunters worked the neighborhood hard until 11 p.m., while all afternoon and into the evening helicopters from the South Dakota National Guard sliced through the sky, searching for Colt from above.

Kelly had screamed so hard at Colt that he lost his voice for five days and had to hoarsely whisper reassuring words to his children as they called out night after night, frightened, saying they heard strange noises and were worried someone was in their house again.

When he began learning about Colt's history, Kelly found it reassuring that he'd never physically hurt any of his burglary victims. One thought, though, kept him awake long after the incident. "Thinking about it from his side, with this big bearded guy chasing him down the stairs screaming bloody murder . . . I must have come very close to scaring him into shooting me."

THE WORD WENT OUT to all law enforcement: Colt not only collected and carried guns, and might have fired a shot at cops in the woods, but now he'd actually threatened to shoot a civilian in his home. This amped things up immeasurably. If that laser was attached to a pistol, Colt had been a twitch away from making this a completely different story.

Colt told Josh that he'd use a gun if he had to, and he told Pam that he wouldn't shoot first, but that he'd shoot back. He just made it a lot more likely that he'd have to.

EVEN THOUGH CAUGHT WITH his pants down in the Kneifls' home, Colt made efficient use of the 3 a.m. darkness and the nine or ten minutes he had before the police got into position to cut off his escape. While law enforcement converged on Kelly's house, Colt's speed and stealth took him several miles east, far outside the search area. He broke into another home, stole the keys to a Toyota Sequoia, and hit the road.

Colt crossed the Missouri and made a straight shot south through sixty miles of Nebraska farmland to Norfolk, a city of twenty-four thousand in Madison County. Sometime after midnight on the nineteenth, he parked the Sequoia at Ta-Ha-Zouka Park on the Elkhorn River. The area had just experienced record flooding. The Elkhorn jumped its banks, swamped farms, and even tore down a railroad bridge and a pedestrian trestle that served as part of the state's Cowboy Trail. Three days before Colt arrived, residents had been out in force, filling and piling sandbags to try to keep the river out of their homes and businesses.

Less than a mile down 81 from Ta-Ha-Zouka lies Karl Stefan Memorial Airport. At 2:56 a.m., Colt walked through an unlocked door and into the airport services building. He found and disabled the surveillance equipment, but a technician was later able to recover the data, which showed the Barefoot Bandit. There was cash and equipment in the airport office, but Colt didn't bother with any of it. He did, however, grab a souvenir, a $40 hoodie embroidered with an airplane and NORFOLK AIRPORT. Colt then began snooping around the hangars, unsuccessfully trying to get inside a plane.

The airport folks—who'd received no prior warning—reported the break-in at 11 a.m. the next day. Police came and took a report, but it wasn't until workers doing flood clean-up at Ta-Ha-Zouka found the Sequoia that Colt's name came up. Norfolk PD told the airport manager she better check inside all the hangars, that chances were something big was missing. Something was: another Cadillac Escalade.

27

"I'm pretty sure he's thinking Grand Theft Auto at this point," said one of the detectives closely following Colt's run from back in Washington State. He told me he believed Colt was just going to keep stealing vehicles until he got wherever he was going. The joke around the Island County Sheriff's Office was that Colt was heading for Chicago to turn himself in live on *Oprah*. More serious speculation was that he might be heading for Winnebago County, Wisconsin, for the annual Oshkosh air show, the biggest fly-in of plane freaks in the country and considered a rite of passage for private pilots. As many as ten thousand aircraft flock to the show each summer.

I didn't have a clue where Colt was heading. Based on his interest in South American islands, I guessed he was studying Spanish, so Mexico had seemed likely until he turned toward the Atlantic Ocean. But I totally disagreed about the cars.

Wherever Colt was going, I was certain he wanted an airplane. When crumb after crumb on his trail turned out to be yet another Caddy or pickup, I did start to doubt my own theory—but only until I checked the weather. It'd been awful across the Midwest, with massive thunderstorms capable of smacking small planes out of the sky. It now made sense to me that Colt would hole up in a house like Kelly's near an airport, waiting for the right flying weather.

The question that was still driving me crazy, though, was, How had the law not caught up with him yet?

I sat down on Sunday evening, June 20, to test two theories. One, that Colt was looking to steal a plane, and two, that his MO was so predictable that the cops and FBI should have easily been able to get out ahead of him. So far, Colt had stolen Cessna 182s and Cirrus SR22s. He flew the 182s at daybreak. He chose SR22s for his night flights when conditions and navigation are edgier and he could use the assistance of the glass cockpit instruments. With the bad weather across the Midwest, I assumed that he'd lean toward taking an SR22, day or night. Then I looked at his last known location and direction. Colt had recently taken a dip south, but I always figured he'd do that eventually in order to avoid Chicago since he needed to operate in rural areas where people were lax about security. I felt he'd get eaten alive in a big city. It still looked to me like he was determined to head east. Colt couldn't risk stopping for gas, so his hops were relatively short. East out of Norfolk, Nebraska, the Iowa border was only sixty miles away. And, again, Colt wanted an airplane—they live at airports.

I simply Googled three words: Cirrus, airport, Iowa.

The top result was Classic Aviation, a Cirrus flight training center at the Pella, Iowa, airport. I picked up the phone and started to dial their number, but then looked at the time. It was 6 p.m. on Orcas, which made it . . . some hours later Central Corn Time. No one was going to be sitting around an FBO on a Sunday evening. I hung up and instead spent some time on Classic's Web site, learning that Pella means "City of Refuge" in Dutch and was settled by immigrants from Holland who planted lots of tulips. It also said that along with flight training on Cirrus airplanes, Classic Aviation offered a free courtesy car for runs into town to check out the flowers and delicious Dutch pastries.

I wrote down their phone number and put it on my to-do list for Monday.

After breakfast the next morning, I called Shane Vande Voort, owner of Classic Aviation and manager at Pella Municipal Airport. The first thing I said was "This call is either going to sound real crazy . . . or not." Shane laughed and said, "That's okay, I get a lot of calls like that." I asked if he'd received any recent calls from the FBI, NTSB, FAA, local police, or anybody else warning him about anything. Shane was silent. Yep, he thought I was crazy.

"How did you know to call me?" he asked after a long pause. I told him it was just a cold call, that I'd picked his operation simply by looking at a map and the kinds of planes based at the field.

"Well, no," he said, "I hadn't gotten any calls from the police in the past couple of days, though I wish I had . . . because I wound up having to call them myself this morning.

"We had a break-in last night," he said, then asked me who I was. I explained that I was a writer following a teenage burglar and transportation rustler named Colt who had an affinity for airplanes.

"How did you already find out that we got hit?" he asked.

I told him, again, that this was just a cold call based on a couple minutes of research.

"You're kidding me . . ." Shane said that the police were there doing their initial forensic work as we spoke. Not a word of this had gotten out yet.

"Did Colt get a plane?" I asked. Shane said no, that he and the police had already checked the planes and all were accounted for and everything looked fine. Shane told me that he'd locked up and left Sunday night at 9:30 (he would have been there if I'd called). He remembered leaving a hangar door open as he fussed around in the office. The police, he said, hadn't found any sign of forced entry, so he thought the thief might have sneaked in while he was still there, walked through the hangar, and just hid inside until he left.

Shane said he knew right away that morning when he got to the brick building that houses Classic Aviation that he had trouble. "There was grass all over, in my office by my computer, and in the upstairs bathroom the whole bottom of the sink was filled with dead grass." All the cash he'd had on hand, some $450, was missing, and his courtesy car was gone.

"But he didn't try to get a plane?" I asked again, feeling my wild blue yonder theory fading away.

"Nope," said Shane.

As the police pieced things together, they found that Colt had dumped the Norfolk Escalade at a tire company 1.3 miles from Shane's airport. "The interesting thing about that," said Shane, "is that there's a four-lane highway in-between, so he must have run across." That would have taken him through a lot of wet grassy fields.

When Colt got inside, he turned off two monitors in the front office, then went to Shane's and sat at his computer. At some point, he deleted the browser history, then unplugged the network cable, which he could use to get his own laptop online. Rummaging around inside the office and FBO, Colt found the cash drawer and also took sweatshirts, two boxes of Tic Tacs that were in Shane's desk, and keys to both Classic Aviation's courtesy van as well as a customer's Mazda Tribute. He also grabbed a pair of sneakers, size twelve, that belonged to one of the mechanics. Before he left, Colt went upstairs to the sink and washed the grass off his feet.

Shane said the police were scanning his computer trying to get any info on what Colt might have been researching (they didn't find anything). I asked whether Colt had taken any flight training materials (no) and asked again (and again) about the planes. "He had access to an older Cirrus SR20, a Bonanza, and a Cherokee, and he could have easily gotten into the hangars with nicer, new planes including the SR22s, but *no*, he didn't try," he said.

I couldn't understand why Colt didn't at least attempt a plane, while Shane couldn't understand why Colt traded in his late-model Cadillac Escalade for Shane's crappy $1,500 silver Dodge Caravan emblazoned with the Classic Aviation logo and phone number. "I can't imagine where he thinks he's going in that, with our name written on the side."

A local pilot had come to the field and started his plane at 5 a.m., so Shane speculated that he'd scared Colt into just taking the first car he saw that he had keys to. Since the van hadn't been located yet, Shane's main worry was that Colt was planning on coming back. He said he was already arranging to have surveillance cameras set up all over the airport, and just the thought of that disheartened him. "This is Iowa," he said. "It's a leave-the-keys-in-it kinda place, and this guy is capitalizing on that trust. That's low."

A FEW HOURS LATER, my phone rang. It was Shane. He said that because I'd been such a pain in the ass (or something to that effect but in a friendlier Midwestern phrasing) about the dang airplanes, airplanes, airplanes, he'd gone back out and rechecked them. "You were right," he said. "He tried to get into one of the Cirrus SR22s by prying open the baggage door with something like a screwdriver." The lock was damaged, but he wasn't able to get inside. (Much later, Shane also realized that Colt had taken a Cirrus flight manual from his office bookshelf.)

"It's kind of frustrating for me," he said. "All this Homeland Security and GA Secure . . . It seems like the word could have been sent out by the authorities . . . I shouldn't have to hear it from you."

Shane took it upon himself to start making calls, hoping that other airports wouldn't be left in the same position. He phoned Steve Black, at Ottumwa Flying Service just forty-five minutes down the four-lane from Pella. He told Steve about the break-in and warned him he was in the Bandit's path. Steve in turn called the local police. "They said they'd be making additional patrols out here," he says.

Word also went to the Iowa DOT's Department of Aviation, which sent out the first organized bolo-type (Be On the LOokout) "Urgent Alert" to airports at noon on the twenty-first. It encouraged them to secure their facilities and "possibly even work with local law enforcement to step up patrols." It only went statewide, though, and Colt was obviously on the move.

With adequate warning, ignition keys could have been secured and plane owners could have at least considered spending $100 on a throttle lock or wheel locks that make it much harder to steal an aircraft. The lack of official warning to every small airport in the country wasn't a money issue or a manpower issue, just a lack of common sense.

Colt was always good at staying one step ahead, but even he had to be surprised at how easy it had been up to this point.

THE WEATHER, THOUGH, CONTINUED to work against him. In Ottumwa, Iowa, where they were getting ready for the big balloon races scheduled for the twenty-third, they had heavy rains and thunderstorms. A tornado tore through the area as Colt arrived.

Sometime Monday night or early Tuesday morning—after the Iowa DOT warning and after Steve Black says he called the local police to alert them—Colt got into the main building at Ottumwa Regional Airport and tried prying on every interior door with a screwdriver. He then moved on to the FBO and busted into the cash drawer, taking all the bills. The bathroom was also left a mess, as if someone had been bathing in the sink.

When Black discovered all this Tuesday morning, he spotted the Classic

Aviation courtesy van out in his parking lot. The silver minivan was neat and clean, still had an eighth of a tank of gas, and all the clothing missing from the Pella terminal was inside. Even the keys to the Mazda Tribute were left sitting on the passenger seat.

That night, west of downtown Ottumwa, Colt climbed a fence into the parking area where the Frito-Lay company parks its delivery vans. First he tried to wrench open one truck's door, but it wouldn't give. The thought of all that crunchy goodness just inches away was too much to pass up, though, and he resorted to breaking a window. Along with the broken glass and disheveled snack packs, the *Frito Bandito Descalzo* signed the crime by leaving behind fingerprints and the hoodie he'd taken from the airport in Norfolk, Nebraska.

Just a short stroll from where the Fritos lay, Colt took a white 2010 Chevy HHR—a retro, fifties-style wagon—from the Ottumwa Water Works. The Chevy didn't fit the Cadillac SUV and Lincoln pickup pattern. It wasn't luxe, it was relatively underpowered, and it didn't have four-wheel drive. According to the Ottumwa police, though, it was "easy pickings" since the water department driver had left the keys in the ignition.

TO THE EAST LAY the Mississippi. Steve Black says he heard police officers speculating that Colt would next take a boat and roll on down the river to New Orleans. It would have nicely closed the literary loop on any Huck Finnishness of the tale, but a little bit of research would have told Colt about all the locks along the way where he'd have to interact with lock masters. Instead, he crossed Ol' Man River in the Chevy and made his way into a heavily wooded area outside Dallas City, Illinois, that's called Happy Hollow.

"Happy Hollow is sort of our Cajun country," chuckles John Jefferson, sheriff of Hancock County, Illinois. "People up there are pretty reclusive, pretty protective of their property, and a lot of them are not real fond of law enforcement. It's a different kind of community . . ."

The road taken by the Chevy into Happy Hollow, directly opposite the riverbank village of Pontoosuc, follows a streambed. "If you're not from that area," says Sheriff Jefferson, "you'll get lost in there—all these little roads shoot off." Colt may have been looking for a secluded spot to pull

over and get some sleep or else knew that there were vacation cabins
scattered around the Hollow. He got into trouble, though, because of the
weather.

The road in crosses a creek. Normally, water flows beneath the road-
bed through a culvert, but there'd been record rains all June, and the creek
swelled until it overran the road, coating it with a thick layer of bottom
mud and sand. If Colt had had an Escalade or one of the big four-wheel-
drive pickups, no problem. However, once the front-wheel-drive HHR got
hub deep in the muck, it stuck. Colt was not happy. When he couldn't free
the vehicle, he grabbed a shovel from the back and smashed every one of
the windows. He threw the shovel into the water and then took off on foot
into Hancock County's backwoods.

Residents found the stranded Chevy at 7 a.m. Wednesday morning.
After Sheriff Jefferson traced it back to Ottumwa, he was contacted by the
Iowa Intelligence Fusion Center, which told him they were "100 percent
convinced" that it was Colton Harris-Moore. Jefferson hadn't gotten any
advance warning, but he quickly got up to speed on Colt's MO and put out
a mass release to all the local media asking them to warn folks that Colt
was likely armed and not to approach him, just call the police. In the meantime, he told everyone to lock up their homes and cars, and if they happened to have a plane, lock that up, too.

I spoke with Sheriff Jefferson several times over the days following the
recovery of the HHR. Illinois-farm raised, he was serving his fourth term
in office (he's since won his fifth). And he apparently knew a thing or two
about kids doing goofy things. He was raising a crop of them: six of his own,
plus, over the last eighteen years, he and his wife had taken in thirty-five foster kids. "What worries me is that Colt is eventually going to graduate into
something bigger."

Jefferson had his deputies aggressively patrolling, but like law enforcement who'd chased Colt in every other jurisdiction, they were hampered
by the fact that they couldn't just go barging onto private property to do
searches—especially not in a place like Happy Hollow, where folks don't
take kindly to anyone poking around their cabins, badge or not.

The sheriff felt like he was doing all he could, but it still seemed like a
needle in a haystack situation. Jefferson oversees Hancock's 816 square
miles with just eight deputies and himself, plus some assorted small-town

police forces spread through the county. Considering the notoriety of the case, he expected someone more useful than the media might call. "I'm surprised there's been no help from the Feds, or that some kind of task force hasn't called." The Iowa Intelligence Fusion Center had collected the intelligence from their side of the line, but they said they weren't going to actively investigate or pursue the case. Jefferson and his deputies went out and talked to everyone aviation related, which was no small task. "There's a private airstrip about a mile and a half straight south from where he got stuck, and five small airports within twelve miles."

MEANWHILE BACK IN WASHINGTON . . . Harley Davidson Ironwing was back out on the streets hoping to hook up with his old buddy Colt. While he was in prison, Harley says a Snohomish County sheriff and a corrections officer questioned him about Colt. "I told them to go fuck themselves." Now Harley put the word out that he was a free man and ready to help Colt stay that way, too. "I'm the one person that can keep him out of prison. I guarantee it. I'll just call in a couple of favors."

On June 21, with Colt more than a thousand miles away, Harley's hard-luck story took a tragic turn. His foster mother, Karen Ironwing, died of cancer. She was the one who, Harley said, he was counting on to help give him some much-needed structure outside of prison. Harley didn't make the funeral—he still hated his foster brothers. That Friday, the twenty-fifth, Harley walked the aisles of the Stanwood Haggen grocery store. He was hungry and says he hadn't eaten for three days. He stuffed five packages of string cheese into his pants and went for the exit. Store employees saw him and gave chase. As Harley got to the door, he spotted a Sno County deputy and turned to run the other way. The deputy caught up and tackled him, with both men tumbling into an elderly couple, knocking down an eighty-four-year-old man. The old man went to the hospital (bruised but okay) and Harley went to jail, eventually sentenced to eighteen months for third-degree assault.

ON THE SAME FRIDAY Harley got pinched for the string cheese chase, police back on the Iowa side of the Mississippi found a stolen pickup dumped at Casey's General Store in Burlington. Colt had recrossed the river. This time, he says, he did indeed do it in a boat, and in a rowboat, much closer to Huck's raft than the large yachts he'd stolen before. He didn't strike out for the Big Easy, though, just struck out for the other side. Colt claims he lost a paddle along the way and had a harrowing nighttime crossing. Once in Iowa, he went north.

Casey's lies directly across the street from Southeast Iowa Regional Airport, which was just twelve miles north of the stuck-in-the-mud Chevy HHR tied to Colt. The airport had received the Iowa DOT warning in time, but it didn't help. A pilot taxied up to his hangar on the twenty-seventh and raised the door to trade his plane for the 2010 Ford F150 pickup he'd left inside. His truck, though, had already been gone for at least three days. A cop had even seen it on the twenty-sixth, 228 miles east at Vermilion Regional Airport in Illinois, but didn't believe it was stolen because it hadn't been reported yet.

The police were now two steps behind Colt, though he was doggedly, brazenly, sticking to his airport-to-airport MO, all the way across the country.

OUT AT THE OLD FBO building at Vermilion Airport on Thursday, June 24, thirty-nine-year-old Homer Woolslayer barbecued himself a steak and sat at a picnic table enjoying the evening. The airport was so desolate and so quiet he could hear the beacon rotating across the runway. A flight instructor and cropduster out of Tulsa, Homer first flew at eight years old, handling the stick of a Piper under the supervision of his oldest brother, who was already flying cropdusters. Always a risk taker, Homer raced motorcycles professionally until he realized he'd never make it to the top in that dangerous racket. After an ill-fated stint in his family oil field equipment business, he fell back on flying. He became a freelance instructor, and flew air ambulance missions in a Citation II jet.

In March 2010, just a few months before heading up to Vermilion, Homer had his Captain Sully moment. He had a student up in a 1976 Cessna 210 Centurion when the plane lost power on approach. Only five hundred feet above the Arkansas River with no time to maneuver, Woolslayer grabbed the controls and just had time to get the wheels down before flaring the plane onto a sandbar. "It was a nonevent," he says with a barnstormer's nonchalance. "There wasn't a scratch on the plane and we didn't bend it at all." Unfortunately, water was being released from a dam upriver, and he could only stand there and watch as it rose and swamped his Cessna, ruining the interior and wrecking the electronics.

During the growing season, Woolslayer hires out as an itinerant crop-duster. He'd gotten an offer to come up to Illinois and spray for Aero Crop Service. He'd be flying an Air Tractor 301, a tail-dragging radial-engine beast of an airplane. "It's real hard work," says Homer, "but there's a lot of romance to cropdusting because it's so dangerous. When the airplane is fully loaded, it's barely able to fly. You have to be real careful. Lose focus for a moment and you'll crash and kill yourself . . . But it's a neat job."

The plan was to spray ten thousand acres of corn in two weeks. Since Homer would be there only a short time, the owner of the dusting outfit, George, told him he could bunk out in an office in the airport's defunct terminal building. Homer set up a "Kmart condo," with an inflatable mat-tress and a few basics inside, and his barbecue just outside the door. The coals were still glowing as he sacked out on the twenty-fourth.

Homer didn't get to sleep through the night, though. At 4:25 a.m., something woke him up. From his air mattress, he could see through the office window to an outside door. He heard the knob rattling and saw the silhouette of a very tall man apparently trying to get in. "What the hell? I looked at the time, it was just before the false dawn." Homer pulled on some pants and went outside. He didn't see anybody, but did notice some-thing odd. "There's a vehicle, a really nice late-model Ford pickup, that wasn't there before. It stood out because every other car around had con-densation on the windows and this one didn't—it had to have just drove up." Woolslayer noted that the mystery truck had Iowa plates and saw that someone had tossed a travel-size bottle of mouthwash underneath it. "I figured this guy was coming to meet an early plane and trying to get inside looking for someplace to take a leak. After a while, though, when I didn't hear any planes coming or going, that kind of spooked me. It was weird, but finally I thought, Ah, forget it, and went back to bed."

Homer told George about it the next morning. "He perked up, but there wasn't much to do. He just said, 'Gawd, Homer, nothing ever happens at this airport . . . Now you show up and people are sneaking around trying to get into my office.'" They laughed it off and went to work, but because the white pickup was still there at the end of the day and whoever drove it hadn't flown off, Woolslayer had a funny feeling that the tall visitor would be back.

That evening, down at another part of the airport, Mike Vadeboncoeur was working late. He owns Midwest Aero Restorations and there'd been a lot of overtime lately as he put the finishing touches on a WWII P51 Mustang that was scheduled to appear at the big air show in Oshkosh at the end of July. At 9:45, he'd just taken a break to watch a YouTube video that his mom had sent him. The clip had a loud soundtrack, and in the sudden silence when it ended, Mike heard something outside his office. "There's a loose tile out there and it makes a certain sound, a squeak, when someone steps on it." Then he heard a door close. He got up and walked out into his secretary's office, calling, "Who's there?"

Mike hadn't received any warnings about Colt. All he knew was that someone else was in the building. Out in the hallway, lights that are always left burning had been turned off. "It just didn't make any sense, and I was pretty nervous." He was also angry. Just that day at lunch he and the guys had been discussing Chicago's strict gun laws. "I'm in favor of having weapons to protect yourself, and here I was, with somebody right outside that door, maybe with a gun, and I had nothing to defend myself with. It was a very sick feeling."

Mike decided that staying in his office wasn't a good idea, so he bolted outside onto the tarmac. He looked around, but there was no one there. He walked around to the front of the building . . . nothing. He tried the front door and it was securely locked. When he came back inside, he turned on all the lights. "I was really getting kinda spooked, but like an idiot, I grabbed the only weapon I could find, a broomstick, and went around checking every room in the building." Everything seemed fine, and he tried to convince himself that he hadn't really heard anything.

Down at the old terminal, Homer Woolslayer was lying on his back on top of the picnic table, belly full of barbecue and eyes full of stars. "It was a nice clear, dark night, and I was watching the sky and listening to the crickets and coyotes." Still, he hadn't forgotten about the prowler. "I had a feeling he'd come back at the same time." Homer says he's one of those people who does not need an alarm clock. "I can tell myself to wake up at a certain time . . . It's the weirdest thing." He set his internal alarm for

4:15 a.m., and it went off on schedule. "Then I just lay in bed waiting." He didn't have to wait long.

"Sure enough, he comes back, right on time at 4:27 a.m. I can see his silhouette, but he can't see me." Homer says he heard one door rattle and then the tall dark figure moved to the next. "I sat up in bed, watching him walk around trying to get in. I was a little bit nervous, and I didn't just rush out. I mean, he was brazen. He had to know someone was inside—the air conditioner was going, and the coals were still hot out in the barbecue. I'm thinking, What happens if I go out and try to tackle this guy? If he's desperate, he'll kill me. If he's not, and he's just some harmless guy, then in a few minutes we'll be laughing and drinking coffee. Or, if he's somewhere in between, he'll kick my ass and run. So I hesitated."

Finally, Homer jumped up and went to the window. He got a good look at the guy as he was walking away. "He was very tall, had kind of an awkward gait, like the cheap white sneakers he had on didn't fit him. He didn't have socks on, and was wearing jean shorts and a T-shirt with a sprint car on it, like from some local, small-time speedway, and he had on a ball cap."

Woolslayer went back to his bedroom and threw on his jeans. By the time he got outside, though, the tall guy was out of sight. "I walked clear across the airport out to the runways, about half a mile, but couldn't find him. I think he knew exactly how to get away, he heard me scurrying around to come after him and he doubled back on me. If I'd a known he was a pro I woulda used some different tactics on him."

SATURDAY MORNING, MIKE VADEBONCOEUR arrived at work still not sure whether he'd been imagining things the night before. He rechecked all the switches and circuit breakers and didn't find any problems that would've caused the lights to go off. Then he went out to his hangar and looked around carefully. At the far corner, he noticed that there was more light than usual coming in around a door frame. "Sure enough, it'd been busted open."

Colt had pried open the deadbolt on a hangar that housed a TBM 850, a Daher-Socate turboprop sports car of a plane, similar to a Pilatus but smaller and a bit faster. He then made his way into Mike's hangar, which housed warbirds in various states of restoration. "I'm sure he looked at those and thought, Well, I don't think I can start any of them," says Mike. After that, Colt came through the doorway into the FBO, turning off the lights as he passed, then noticed Mike. "I'm sure he saw me sitting there and went, 'Oops.'"

Homer Woolslayer says he walked around the airport with the other guys that morning and they discovered that as many as five hangars had been broken into. "I think this kid just walked into each and said, 'Well, that's no good, I can't fly that plane, and I don't want to fly that one . . .' He knew what his limitations were. Most of those planes were too sophisticated." Homer says that even the airplanes that Colt could have flown weren't the kind he was looking for. "He went into one hangar with a little trainer in it, a Piper Tomahawk, easy to fly, but some people call that plane the Traumahawk because they say it spins too easily . . . I was cracking up, because he wouldn't even steal one of those."

Homer and his boss talked about involving the police, but nothing was missing, "not a lightbulb. We're saying, 'Do we want the police out here?' I'll say there's a healthy suspicion of authority around these parts."

Mike didn't share that feeling, though, and called the cops. They checked around, saw the mysterious Ford pickup with Iowa plates and the broken hangar door, and they very quickly came up with a suspect: Homer Woolslayer.

"The police were very suspicious just because I was the new guy and I was living out there," says Homer. "One of them, this freckled guy in his thirties, was real aggressive, acting like he had some kind of mental problem, saying, 'You're out of state and I'm running your 10-26!' or something like that. We're standing around the Ford and he was shaking me down, demanding my ID, acting like he was going to arrest me. I finally just started cracking up, saying, 'Man, you're running my license to pull up whether I've run a tollbooth back in Oklahoma and in the meantime you're leaning on a stolen vehicle!' The cop got all huffy, and I said, 'I'm telling you, whoever did this rolled up in this Ford pickup and right now he's somewhere within four hundred yards of where you're standing, but instead you're interrogating me! You've lost your mind. I mean, what education do you need to be a cop in Vermilion County?'"

The police did run the plates on the F150 from Burlington, but its pilot owner was still on vacation and hadn't reported it stolen yet.

Along with the local cops, some other folks at the airport weren't so sure about Homer Woolslayer either. "I was the only thing that had changed, so they figured it was me." Video from the surveillance cameras sure enough showed an image of someone walking around the hangars in the middle of the night, trying doors. However, the images weren't clear enough to be conclusive. Homer's boss believed him, though, and wanted to make sure he was properly equipped in case the tall stranger came around again.

"These farm people and cropduster types out here in Illinois are armed and ready for anything, man," says Woolslayer, laughing. "If some army ever tries a frontal assault on that airport, they'd lose." His boss cracked open a special safe, and when Homer lay down on his inflatable bed that night, he was packing extreme heat: two handguns and a sawed-off pan-fed Saiga shotgun (basically a twelve-gauge machine gun). Just in case the spotlight he'd been given wasn't bright enough, he also had parachute flares "from some Eastern Bloc country."

Woolslayer went to sleep laughing to himself. "I'm in bed dressed like Rambo, bullets strapped over my shoulder. It would be nothing to be lying there with a shotgun waiting for a burglar back in Oklahoma, but I'm in this different state and I don't know the rules of engagement. I already knew this one cop didn't like me . . . so I started thinking I don't know if this is such a good idea. I mean, I wasn't going to kill him, but I was planning on scaring him and finding out what he was doing. You know, hell, if he was hungry I probably would have bought him breakfast."

However, nothing happened at the airport that night. Rambo Woolslayer got up, stripped off his guns, and went to the local diner. As he was sitting there, he overheard a waitress talking about a friend whose car had been stolen early that morning. "I said, 'Hey, your friend doesn't happen to live by the airport, does she?' She said, 'Yes, just a couple blocks away.' I started laughing and said, 'I know who took her car.'" Homer went back to the airport and told his boss that it was over, the guy was gone.

THAT DAY, SUNDAY, THE owner of the Ford pickup came home and noticed it was missing. The Iowa police connected it with the stolen car query from Illinois and called the Vermilion County sheriff with the story of Colton Harris-Moore, telling him that he'd probably have another stolen car or airplane any minute now. Conveniently, Vermilion already had the report from the waitress's friend whose car had been taken at 2 a.m. When deputies went to reinvestigate the car theft, they found a handheld GPS and an iPod left behind at the site. According to the sheriff, the GPS memory showed tracks to all the locations where Colt had committed his cross-country crimes.

When Homer Woolslayer heard about Colt, he looked around the airport and speculated that he had probably camped out in the abandoned control tower. "It's decommissioned, but you can still get up in it." Homer read up on the case and couldn't understand how anyone could call Colt a bad pilot just because he'd crash-landed a couple planes. "That's really arrogant. He knew his limitations, knew he couldn't take a cropduster or a warbird because there's too much torque roll for a new pilot. And the landings? This kid can't land and walk up to an FBO, so he has to put them down in fields—and he's been able to walk away from those landings. I think he knows how to fly, and he's actually pretty good. I wonder if there are award banquets in prison."

COLT HAD FINALLY OUTRUN the bad weather. Across the Midwest, skies were clear and sunny, winds calm, temperatures reaching the 80s during the day, high 60s at night. It was great weather to watch planes at the big air show, but also fine weather to fly them. Oshkosh was northwest, but Colt drove southeast.

The stolen car from Vermilion turned up 120 miles away in a church parking lot in Bloomington, Indiana. Sunday churchgoers noticed its out-of-state plates, and when they peeked in the window, they saw a purse and keys. Police arrived and established that the vehicle had been stolen, but none of the owner's personal property left inside had been disturbed. The only thing missing was the car's ignition key. Whether taken as a souvenir or perhaps as a courtesy to prevent the car from being restolen, it all matched Colt's MO.

The biggest hint was that the church stood a half mile away from the Monroe County Airport.

THE MONROE COUNTY SHERIFF'S Office began receiving calls from FBI and Homeland Security agents, catching them up on the suspect and the chase. The stolen car connected to Colt made the news, and anyone who bothered to look knew that the world-famous airplane thief Colton Harris-Moore was in Bloomington, very close to a small airport.

The sheriff's office made a call to the airport, but the manager, Bruce Payton, was off for a couple of days and the warning wasn't spread around until they finally connected on Wednesday.

"A detective came out the morning of the thirtieth," says Payton. "He said that I should alert people on the field to be careful and watch for this guy known as the Barefoot Bandit." Bruce went to his office and immediately downloaded everything he could find about Colt and passed it out to all the businesses and professional pilots. He asked the two FBOs to post the info and pass the word to any pilots who flew in. One FBO, Cook Aviation, took the warning so seriously that they hired a night watchman to guard their hangars. Monroe County is a fairly large airport with about a hundred general aviation aircraft based in buildings spread out over a mile of ground. Cook's guard wouldn't be in any position to see what was going on at other far-flung hangars.

Payton personally called all of the corporate flight departments at the airport. "I told them there was reason to believe this person might be in the area and to take extra precautions with their aircraft." He even stopped by the daily coffee klatch. "A few guys come down every day and sit out on the deck on the public side of the fence to watch the planes and have a cup." Before he could tell them what was up, though, one guy had to leave. As he was riding his bike back home, he saw a "scruffy young man, very tall and slender" walking on the nearby railroad tracks.

The only people left to give the word to were the private pilots based at Monroe. Payton went to one of the boys-with-big-toys beery barbecues held regularly throughout the summer down among the seven private hangars that sit at the far southeast end of the airfield, near the start of runway 24, the shorter of Monroe's two strips. "There were nineteen guys there that night," says Payton. "And I briefed everyone."

The barbecue bunch that Wednesday evening did not include all the owners, though. One who was missing was sixty-year-old John "Spider" Miller. Miller and one of his older brothers, Don, owned a 2008 Cessna Corvalis 400 TT—a plane very similar to the Cirrus SR22—that Spider had just flown out to St. Simons Island, a beach and golf destination on the Georgia coast.

Spider Miller was the middle child in a family with eleven kids, and he got his nickname early on from his habit of crawling all over everything. "When I was a young guy I used to say it was because the girls all thought I had eight hands," he laughs. "Now that I'm an old-timer, I'll settle for four . . . Actually, I'll settle for just crawling around." Spider's fascination with planes began at an early age, but he didn't become a pilot until he was forty-nine. Since then, he's worked his way through multiple ratings and flown his Corvalis, "a great little airplane," for both business and pleasure.

Both Miller brothers have beer distributorships. Spider is the president of Best Beers, though he prefers the title "repackage manager." If he'd been in town that Wednesday night, he might've wandered down to the barbecue, as he does occasionally. "They're all great guys, and I go more for the drinking than the eating . . . I actually like my product." Instead, he was relaxing in the Georgia sunshine, getting "robbed" on the golf course.

So the Vermilion car was found on the twenty-seventh. The public warning went out to the airport on the thirtieth. Now, days had passed without news of local vehicles going missing or any strange happenings at any other airport in the region. Colt had to be in the area, and he wanted a plane.

On Thursday, July 1, AOPA finally came out with an alert about Colt through its weekly email newsletter, which goes to virtually every private pilot, flying student, and anyone else remotely connected to general aviation in the country.

That same afternoon, Bruce Payton slipped out of work and headed down to Nashville to see a songwriter friend of his who had a gig. The trip was a birthday present to himself. Everything back at the airport had seemed secure, and even though he hadn't noticed any additional police or FBI activity, Payton felt sure they must have had the place under surveillance. The entire facility is surrounded by a ten-foot-tall chain-link fence topped with three strands of barbed wire that are angled out, making it extremely hard to climb. "It looks a lot like a prison," he says. The only chink in the security, according to Payton, is that some of the private hangar owners don't bother waiting for the motorized gates to close behind them. They take about thirty seconds to close, long enough for someone hiding nearby to sneak in, especially after dark.

Normally, Payton would have spent at least a couple of nights down in Nashville, "but I had a funny feeling." He struck up a conversation at dinner with some folks from Chicago who mentioned they'd seen news reports about the Barefoot Bandit. "I told them that he was suspected of being in our area up at Monroe, and said, 'You know, I should probably get back there.'" Payton drove back up on Saturday, but everything seemed safely locked down.

Colt had gotten to Bloomington on Sunday the twenty-seventh. His favorite reconnaissance tool, Google Earth, showed a number of places to camp inside the fence of the one-thousand-acre airport. In fact, there's so much wild ground and woods on the property that it supports a growing population of coyotes. For a week, they'd have to share their haunts with Colt.

One stretch of woods at Monroe is cut back into the shape of a person's lower calf, ankle, and foot, with its toes pointed directly at runway 24. It's just one hundred yards off the taxiway, but with the trees sporting their full complement of summer leaves, the wooded patch offered perfect camouflage for someone who wanted to watch all the activities. No one could see him, but Colt had an ideal view of everything, especially the secluded private hangars at the south end. He set up camp.

Over the following nights, Colt crowbarred his way into four of the seven private hangars and comfy'd up his camp with blankets and a couch pillow. He stocked his larder with pilot snacks, including Oreo cookies, peanut butter crackers, power bars, cans of soup, nuts, and even Tyson precooked chicken breasts. He took plenty of water and a good week's worth of food out of the hangars. To help ensure no one saw his head peeking out of the leaves, he even borrowed a camouflage ball cap emblazoned with the Indiana University logo. The cap covered a freshly shorn head—he'd cut his hair and shaved inside one of the hangars, leaving the hair in the sink.

Colt couldn't risk raising a shelter, but he enjoyed perfect weather. He lay back among the trees listening to music on his iPod and flipping through the magazines he'd liberated from a corporate hangar. Sticking with his style, he took a stack of *Forbes*—"The Capitalist Tool"—filled with lists of the world's richest people and most expensive zip codes. He also had time to work on his planes and plans using a yellow pad.

Colt's backpack held everything he felt important enough to carry across the country: personal mementos, a laptop, and a loaded Walther PPK (James Bond's favorite pistol) with its serial number filed off. He also had a very cool little Contour video camera. Designed to shoot high-def footage of extreme sports from the extremist's point of view, the five-ounce camera can be attached to a headlamp strap or the dashboard of a car or airplane. If someone wanted to take a video showing off his skills—say, taking off in a plane—this would be the camera.

Along with his eclectic mix of music, Colt had loaded his iPod with media files. Some were news reports following the career of the Barefoot Bandit. There were also airplane photos and flight training videos, including instructionals on landing several types of planes. One model featured with both a picture and a how-to training video was the Cessna 400 Corvalis, the same model Bill Anders had, which Colt had studied back on Orcas, and that Spider Miller had taken to Georgia.

At noon on Saturday, July 3, Colt's ship finally came in.

SPIDER LANDED HIS YEAR-OLD Corvalis and taxied to his hangar. "I was due for an oil change, so I called the guy at the FBO and asked him if he wanted to knock it out. He said he had time that evening, and towed it across the field to his hangar." The mechanic serviced the plane and started the engine again to check for leaks. Everything looked good, so he taxied it back to Miller's hangar and then brought over the fuel truck to top off the Cessna's tanks. Bingo.

The weather was ideal. The plane was perfect. It was extremely similar to the Cirrus SR22, which Colt had safely landed twice. He knew the Corvalis was equipped with the Garmin G1000 navigation package. And he knew the performance specs: a 310-horsepower turbocharged engine that produced enough thrust to drive it 270 mph—faster than any other plane of its type. If you understood how to lean the fuel mixture, the plane had a range of more than 1,200 miles. As the mechanic pulled away in the fuel truck, Colt even knew it had full tanks without having to risk breaking into the hangar. Everything was falling into place better than he could have dreamed. There was only one potential problem: he'd been unsuccessful getting into this style of plane if its gullwing doors were locked.

The mechanic—who'd been briefed by Bruce Payton about the

Bandit—locked Spider's hangar behind him, but he'd left the Corvalis keys inside the plane and its doors unlocked. Problem solved.

COLT KNEW THAT THE tower crew started work at 6:30 a.m. Dawn began brightening the eastern sky at 5:53 that day, though, so there was plenty of light outside as he raised the big bifold doors of Spider's hangar. He rolled the plane out, then put the hand tug back in the hangar and closed and locked the doors. With any luck, no one would notice the plane was missing for hours, maybe days if he caught a break like he did at Granite Falls and no one paid attention to its emergency beacon.

Colt cranked the engine and taxied to the runway. At exactly 6:01, a security camera captured Cessna Corvalis N660BA taking off into the clear purple sky. It was the Fourth of July, Independence Day.

PART 5

WILD BLUE YONDER

28

———

The transponder on the Millers' Corvalis was set to automatically ping 1200, telling air traffic controllers that it was adhering to visual flight rules (VFR). Under VFR, a pilot takes responsibility for not crashing into mountains, colliding with other planes, or running out of fuel and falling out of the sky. As Colt knew, by simply staying below eighteen thousand feet and avoiding controlled airspace around airports, military installations, or any FAA temporary flight restrictions, small-plane pilots enjoy the full freedom of the American skies. A VFR pilot doesn't need to file a flight plan or even talk to anyone on the radio.

He had a fine plane and he had a plan that made sense, at least to him.

Instead of a short hop, this time Colt planned to leapfrog far ahead of his pursuers. Not that he had any reason to be unnecessarily concerned that they were catching up to him. After all, he had just spent an entire week at an airport within a half mile of where he dumped the last stolen car. This flight would be the big one, bigger headlines, bigger splash. He had a plane that could carry him out of the country to the first stop on a voyage to get to where the good life lives.

Once at his cruising altitude headed south, Colt leaned out the fuel mixture. On paper, the Corvalis could just make it to Cuba. In 1904, Teddy Roosevelt signed an extradition treaty with Cuba that covered fugitives wanted for larceny, which would include Colton's crimes. Complicated relations between the two countries since *la revolución*, however, have made the treaty unworkable and Cuba a reasonable choice for certain fugitives. Flying direct from the United States to Cuba without a flight plan can be dangerous, though, and not just the risk of miscalculating fuel and dropping into the Florida Straits. In 1996, Cuban MiGs shot down two American-flagged Cessnas flown out of Florida by the exile group Brothers to the Rescue. Tensions were higher at the time, but still, attempting to arrive unannounced on Castro's doorstep isn't necessarily a good idea.

Instead, Colt veered east and flew out over the Gulf Stream. Fitting for a story that so far included UFO sites, ancient Indian burial grounds, and Bigfoot hunters, a little over four hours after he took off from Indiana, the Barefoot Bandit entered the Bermuda Triangle.

A half hour later, around 11:15 a.m., several Bahamians noticed the Cessna circling north of Sandy Point, a small village on a beach-fringed spur at the south end of Great Abaco.

The Cessna kept circling in the overcast skies, but no one paid much mind. Private planes often buzz the area, either to take aerial photos of the scenery or to scout for a likely stretch of coast to carve out a development.

Sandy Point's airstrip serves this sparsely populated end of the island, but Colt didn't dare use it. It was daylight, plus he figured there'd be Customs and Immigration officers there to greet planes. He'd have to execute another off-field landing. For the first time in his rough-landing career, finding "flat" wasn't a problem. The southern tip of Great Abaco has miles and miles of pancaked land. Most of it, though, is covered in pine and scrub trees not conducive to safe set downs.

Finally, Colt settled on a section of sugary bog, the margin of a swamp covered in marsh grasses and mangrove sprouts. There's nothing similar to the mangrove in the Pacific Northwest forest. These bushy tropical trees reach into warm, shallow seas, thriving in a saltwater environment that would kill other plants, and forming the basis of an entire ecosystem. The ground here may have appeared solid as Colt extended the flaps and made his approach, but in reality it was a sandy mix of tidal muck.

Normal landing speed on the Corvalis is 70 mph, and once it touches down on a runway, it uses about 1,200 feet to roll to a stop. As soon as Colt's main gear hit the muck, though, it was as if he'd landed in peanut butter. The nose of the plane slammed down onto the front wheel, which burrowed into the soft sand, collapsed, and was torn from the fuselage. An instant later, the nose itself hit, with the propeller whipping into the ground, the blades bending backward like banana peels.

Instead of using four hundred yards, the plane went from flying to a full stop in an eye-bugging 150 feet.

The landing was rough enough to set off the plane's distress beacon, which began signaling that N660BA had gone down hard at 11:44 a.m. The U.S. Coast Guard in Miami picked up the satellite signal and immediately went into search-and-rescue mode.

When Colt gathered himself and lifted the Corvalis's gullwing door, he was 1,050 miles and a world away from where he'd taken off. He could officially check off another item from his prison collage/shopping list: the colorful Caribbean logo.

Even with the adrenaline of surviving another hairy landing, the kid from the misty cool Northwest couldn't help but feel the saunalike assault of the July Bahamas heat, especially back in the mangroves where breath comes in moist bites. The other things that come in bites are the flying teeth, aka no-see-ums or nippers, along with the mosquitoes. In the still air of the marsh, they can be ferocious, especially on cloudy days like the fourth. As Colt climbed out and slid down the wing of the Corvalis, the local bloodsuckers must have rejoiced over the big helping of manna from heaven.

A Bahamian had watched in disbelief as the Corvalis came in lower and lower—apparently under control but far from any sensible landing spot—and then crashed into the swamp. Calls went out to the Royal Bahamian Police Force (RBPF) and Royal Bahamas Defence Force (RBDF), the country's sole military branch.

BACK IN INDIANA, NO one suspected a thing. Even though it was a Sunday and a holiday, Spider Miller went to work. The Fourth of July weekend is a busy time for a beer distributor, especially in a college town like Bloomington. Late that morning, his cell rang, but he let it go to voice mail.

One minute after receiving the distress signal, the U.S. Coast Guard had called Spider's brother, whose contact info was on the Cessna's registration, to check whether it was a false alarm. Don told them he thought the plane was safe in Bloomington, but that Spider was the pilot they should check with.

When Spider retrieved his message, you could have knocked him over with an empty beer can. "It was from the coast guard's Miami station, saying they were receiving an ELT ping that my plane had gone down in the Bahamas." Miller figured there was no sense in calling them back until he could answer their questions, so he jumped into his car and raced to the airport. "I'm thinking, Oh hell, how can this be? I'd never heard of Abaco. I didn't want to believe the plane might be gone, but the ELTs are accurate, they work, so I had myself prepared when I got there."

Spider arrived at his hangar to find it filled with just an echo. He called the coast guard back shortly after noon. The second big surprise was to find out that his $650,000 airplane had been taken by a teenager who'd been on a tear across the country and who authorities suspected had been staking out the airport for a week. To top it off, he learned that his was the fifth aircraft stolen by Colton Harris-Moore, unlicensed pilot.

"Never in my wildest dreams could I have imagined that a kid like him was out there," says Miller.

THE COAST GUARD ALERTED the Bahamians that the plane had been stolen. RBDF soldiers set out for the site by boat, but couldn't get close because it was low tide. Once again a combination of luck and choosing the right spot gave Colt enough time to land and get away before the cops arrived. Part of his luck was the fact that the Bahamians didn't send anyone overland to the site that day.

Colt and the plane sat 2.2 miles from the Great Abaco Highway, the one road that runs through the undeveloped south end of the island. If an officer had gotten within binocular range, he would have been able to see Colt moving, and possibly get men in position to intercept him. As it was, Colt almost stumbled into an RBDF trooper who got close enough to report seeing a white male "with lacerations" who ran off when he was spotted.

Whether he got cut up in the crash or picking his way through the mangroves, Colt was in good enough shape to make his way the eight or so miles to Sandy Point, a fishing village of about four hundred. The owner of a little gas station–convenience store says that sometime after dark, Colt stopped by to fill up. He broke in and left with a Gatorade and two bags of potato chips, though he'd gathered a lot more. The owner guessed that Colt may have been frightened off by someone passing by because he left a bunch of drinks and snacks on the counter. Colt then stole a brown Chevy Tahoe and aimed it north up the highway for the forty-nine-mile drive to Marsh Harbour, the island's single-stoplight main town.

The Bahamians told the coast guard that they were planning a mission to the crash site for early the next morning and requested air support. At 6:11 a.m. on the fifth, a USCG Guardian jet detoured on its way to deliver spare parts to Guantánamo Bay, Cuba, and arrived on scene. The pilots had no trouble spotting the downed plane, and reported, "Does not seem to be in distress." They stayed on-site for three minutes and didn't see anyone in the area.

Later that morning after a four-hour slog, Bahamian police officers got to the plane. As expected, they found no one. Cushions had been taken out of the Cessna and laid on the ground in the shade of the wing. There was also a bucket beside the plane with used towelettes inside.

SPIDER MILLER WAS RELIEVED when he got ahold of the Bahamian police and they told him there was no one at the crash site. "I was happy to hear that he hadn't been hurt and, especially, didn't kill himself in the airplane." Spider's next priority was securing the aircraft. "The first cop I talked with said everything was inside the plane, my four thousand-dollar Bose noise-canceling headsets, oxygen equipment, all the valuables. So I asked him to hold on to that stuff and I'd find someone to go over and collect it from them. When I called the same cop later to say someone was on the way to get my valuables, he said, 'We don't have anything like that.'"

Spider hung up. "That was the second theft committed against me." He says the third was dealing with the insurance company, which didn't want to say the Cessna was totaled. Miller says he wouldn't risk flying his kids in that plane again, so he had to pay the difference in value.

Spider, who has five kids of his own and supports the Boys & Girls Clubs and other youth organizations in the four counties where he does business, saw Colt as "misguided." He and Don grew up as part of a huge family living in a house with only one full bathroom. There were struggles, he says, but it was always a loving and supportive home. "It sounds to me like Colt was dealt a bad hand right from the start."

Even though he'd wind up about $100,000 out-of-pocket, Spider was philosophical about the theft. "I've had people steal from me before, and most of them didn't use a gun. Hedge fund and investment managers, they steal without using guns, and so did this kid. He's just one more in a line of thieves, but I don't mind him because at least he never pretended to be anything but a thief."

BACK IN WASHINGTON, OUR Fourth of July was spent on board a boat with friends, bobbing in Fisherman Bay, Lopez Island, along with what seemed like half the population of the San Juans. We ate and drank too much, laughed more than was reasonable, and whenever there was a lull in the action we fired a pirate cannon off the bow to wake the bay. The Fisherman's Fourth always tops off with the islands' best fireworks show, paid for, in part, by passing the hat—via dinghy—from boat to boat.

I was blissfully disconnected from the news for two days. On the fifth, we did a slow cruise back to Orcas, not getting to the cabin until 9 p.m. Only then did I reluctantly sign on to the Internet. Cue the cartoon reaction, eyes bugging, jaw dropping. It wasn't because Colt had taken a plane—I expected that to happen any day. And it wasn't even that he'd flown a thousand miles and left the country—if at any time he'd turned south and vamoosed to Mexico, we'd have all gone "duh, obvious." My shock came from where he'd chosen to go.

My first trip out of the country was to the Bahamas. It was a flight in an ancient DC-3 "Gooney Bird" with a door that fell open as we took off. In the ensuing thirty years, I'd been back scores of times, flying over on every kind of puddle jumper made, and even flying around the cays in an amphibious ultralight trying to spot mating sharks for a nature documentary. I'd also crossed the Gulf Stream from Florida to the Bahamas in boats as small as a nineteen-footer (at 2 a.m., in search of a bottle of rum) and as big as the cruise ship I worked on for all of a week. Wherever I moved around the world, the Bahamas always remained a second home, especially the Out Islands.

Most people know the Bahamas as just a cruise ship or casino destination because they've only gone to Nassau (New Providence) and Freeport (Grand Bahama). All the others are collectively called the Out Islands, or, as the locals say, the Family Islands. That's where I'd spent almost all my time in the Bahamas, diving, fishing, drinking, and chasing Hemingway's ghost.

Not only did Colt pick the Bahamas, he went to the Out Islands, specifically the Abacos—the place I'd spent more time than any other spot in the archipelago. My Abacos photos and magazine articles are scattered all over the Web. One of my favorite trips ever was a recent visit to Great Abaco for an article about male bonding called "Blood, Sweat and Beers," when my dad, uncle, a cousin, and a friend joined me for a week of marlin fishing, shark diving, rum drinking, and conch fritter feasting.

Now, amazingly, Colt was there. It was already almost tomorrow Bahamas local time, but I picked up the phone. Who can you call at midnight in the Bahamas? A buddy who owns a bar.

The party was in full swing at Nipper's on Great Guana Cay, one of the islands across the Sea of Abaco from Marsh Harbour. Johnny Roberts named his bar for the no-see-ums that bedeviled him and his crew as they hammered together a bare-bones drink shack atop a high bluff overlooking the dramatic blue and white of Guana's Atlantic-side beach. Johnny's joint has since grown into one of the most storied bars in the tropics, famous for its massive Sunday pig-roast parties attended by everyone who can beg, borrow, or steal a boat ride to the cay. Two of the biggest events each year at Nipper's are the concerts put on by another piratical old buddy of mine from back in my days of living on Grand Cayman: the comic Calypsonian, singer of such songs as "Time Flies When You're Having Rum" and "A Thong Gone Wrong," who goes by the name of the Barefoot Man. Barefoot, aka George Nowak, was scheduled to give his Abaco summer concert at Nipper's less than three weeks after Colt landed. When I talked to George, he was already penning the Barefoot Bandit song:

> First he stole my golf cart, then my aeroplane,
> but what really pissed me off, he went and stole my name.

JOHNNY HAD TO SHOUT above the music and laughter. It sounded like a pretty wild Monday, even for Nipper's. He reminded me it was Regatta Time and asked why I wasn't there. The annual Abacos regatta is a giant wind-powered party, with salty crews racing back and forth across the

Sea of Abaco to a different beach bar blowout each day. I told him I was look-ing up flights as we spoke, but it wasn't to get in on the sailing bacchanal.

Johnny had heard the first coconut telegraph beats about Colt, that Nas-sau had sent a team of detectives to Great Abaco that day, but he said no one was sure where the kid was. He told me to call his cousin Tim over in Marsh Harbour in the morning, and he'd have the latest word. Once we narrowed down which cousin—most of the Abaconians are cousins—I hung up.

The U.S. embassy in Nassau and the FBI had already posted a $10,000 reward for Colt's capture. Apparently by taking his road show interna-tional, Colt had finally irked and embarrassed them enough to officially admit they were after him.

The universal reaction to the news that Colt had gone to the Bahamas was "Dumb move." I wasn't so sure. Everyone said he'd be spotted immediately—and not because of his height. They thought a white kid in the Bahamas would stick out like a sugar cube in a cup of coffee. Not so. After the Spanish wiped out the Lucayans who originally inhabited the Bahamas, the Abacos were next settled by British Loyalists who fled the United States at the end of the Revolutionary War. Even today, when countrywide 85 per-cent of the Bahamas is black, half the residents of the Abacos are white.

There's also a population of expats in the Abacos, and about two thousand vacation homes that are mostly American owned. Parts of Great Abaco seem more like a suburb of Fort Lauderdale.

Plus, it was peak tourist season. The Abacos aren't like those Carib-bean destinations that traditionally go nuts only in the winter. Many of its visitors are Floridians who can do easy weekends in the Bahamas all year. Families head over once school lets out for summer, and everyone who comes across is there to be on the water—boating, fishing, diving, and snorkeling, which are all at their peak in June and July.

To make it even easier for Colt to go unnoticed, it was regatta week. Abaco marinas and anchorages were filled with visiting yachties, the Top-Sider shoes and Jimmy Buffett–dreams crowd. They gather every evening for big parties where people start out strangers but become fast friends over their shared love of boats and the sea—and the rum doesn't hurt.

If Colt played it cool and didn't cause trouble, one more laid-back barefoot white guy would blend right into the beach party. He'd want to get a hat and some dark shades in case they put up his picture, but otherwise locals would assume he was just another tourist and stop to give him a ride if they saw him walking along the highway. If he chatted up some regatta folks at a marina or party, Colt would definitely end up invited aboard a boat for the next leg of the race.

When it came to sleeping outside in July, though, I'd much prefer Colt's Turtleback Mountain camp on Orcas to sweating and swatting on an Abaco beach or in its pine forest. But Colt could not have chosen a better place in the Bahamas if he planned on more couch squatting. Great Abaco has hundreds of vacation homes, most concentrated around Marsh Harbour and Treasure Cay, a big resort and real estate development twenty miles farther up the S.C. Bootle Highway.

As for the rest of Colt's MO, there are three airports on Great Abaco. Marsh Harbour and Treasure Cay always have small planes tied down out on the field. A Cessna with a full tank of gas could make it from Abaco to the Yucatán, Cuba, Turks and Caicos, the Dominican Republic, Puerto Rico, or as far south down the Caribbean chain as the Virgin Islands. For boat selection, there are hundreds of all sizes and styles in the Abacos, both in marinas as well as moored at private docks.

Arrayed against him at the moment, there was only a small contingent of RBPF officers in Marsh Harbour. Even though the Bahamian police announced that they were sure they would very quickly round up the young miscreant, it felt to me like Colt had done his homework. Either that or he was just very lucky in that he picked another welcoming, unsuspecting community.

I BOUGHT A TICKET to Marsh Harbour that night, but the more I thought about it the more I worried that I'd wind up on an open-ended stay in the Abacos while Colt went surfing from villa to villa, unseen for months. Or, worse, I'd arrive just as he island-hopped somewhere else. One thing about the Out Islands is that most of them are "you can't get there from here" destinations. Unless you have your own plane or boat—or steal one—getting between Out Islands can take all day or even require an overnight in Nassau.

The next morning I called Tim Roberts at his Concept Boat Rentals office. There was definitely news, and Colt had decidedly not laid low and kept out of trouble. During the night, he'd basically done a Blood, Sweat and

Beers tour, hitting Curly Tails Restaurant and Above & Below Abaco dive shop—both places I'd written about in my story. He'd even attempted to break into the hotel where we stayed. It felt like the *Sports Illustrated* cover curse.

At Curly Tails—named after one of the local types of lizard—owner Alistair McDonald said that Colt broke in at 4:20 a.m. and strolled around the restaurant "as if he owned the place." He calmly probed the dark restaurant with a flashlight until he spotted the three security cameras, and then turned them to the wall. He pulled the network cables out of McDonald's modem and plugged in his laptop to get online. Other than ether, though, he didn't steal a thing.

Colt did a bit more damage at the dive shop. Curly-haired scuba queen Kay Politano said he broke in sometime in the early morning. He neatly sliced three sides of a screen to get to the window, which he jimmied open. He took $156 out of the cash drawer and then pulled four shark T-shirts off their hangers, but threw three of them back. "Only one was missing," said Kay. "I assume he was looking for his size." The shop was filled with expensive scuba gear, but none of that was gone. Her computer hard drive had been pulled out of its slot and the Internet cable disconnected and left unplugged, but nothing else was disturbed. Detectives flown in from Nassau found a handprint on the window. "It was very big, long fingers, and very distinct," said Kay. "It looked like someone had intentionally smacked their hand against the window to leave a calling card."

During the same night, the FedEx building, a bike shop, and the Abaco Cancer Society Thrift Shop were also broken into. A few pieces of clothing were taken from the thrift shop, and a first-aid kit went missing from another business.

"It's a lot of excitement for this little island," said Kay. "Many of the people are expressing frustration, irritation, and anger that he's here doing this." But, she said, there was also a little of that pirate side of the Bahamas showing. "No one is condoning it, but a little twinkle creeps into the eyes of some people as they talk about it."

ONCE AGAIN, COLT ALSO induced a motherly response. The next call I made was to sixty-one-year-old Ruthie Key, who said that Colt had walked, barefoot, into her Bahamas Family Market on Monday, before the police started handing out flyers with his photo.

Along with the Robertses, the Keys settled in the Abacos 230 years ago. The Keys have been boatbuilders and farmers, and Ruthie's brother represents South Abaco as a member of Parliament. Ruthie's late husband, Frank, was from Pittsburgh, and together they ran the friendly store where I always provisioned when boating in the Abacos. After Frank's passing two years ago, Ruthie's kids convinced her to go high-tech, adding computers and offering free Internet at the market. That's what drew Colt.

"He came in and very politely asked to use the Internet," says Ruthie. "I told him I was sorry but the computers were down." Colt noticed that Ruthie's son had a laptop online and told her that if the Internet worked he could use his own computer. "He said he hadn't been in touch with his mom for months, and he also wanted to call his girlfriend. He had a great smile and his eyes . . . very pretty, like to just swallow you up. I said sure, and we set him up at one of the tables."

Colt pulled a laptop and headphones out of his backpack and spent an hour making Internet phone calls. One of Ruthie's granddaughters, a five-year-old, was running around the store. "I said to him, 'I hope she's not disturbing you.' And he said, 'Oh no, she's not bothering me at all, just let her play.' He was kind, and very nice, very nice . . . I never would have suspected him of doing anything wrong. Never. If he told me he was hungry I would have cooked him a meal."

Colt took his time and finished his calls, then bought a deli sandwich, said good-bye, and left. "Then the police came in with a poster and told me to call if I saw this guy," said Ruth. "I looked at the picture and said, 'What?'"

Investigators swarmed in. "I told them I don't really have anything to say, I don't want to get involved." When they left, Ruthie says her main feeling was fear—for Colt. "They're out there with guns, and Lord, if they find him and he tries to protest . . . I'm afraid they're going to shoot him."

BACK IN THE UNITED STATES, Pam the quote machine did not disappoint. She said she was glad Colt was out of the country, "the further the better. I'm glad he's able to enjoy beautiful islands, but they extradite. It doesn't help matters at all." She also wanted a message relayed to Colt, reprimanding him, not for stealing a plane, but for stealing the wrong kind: "Only take twin-engine planes, and carry a parachute. That's the rules."

BY TUESDAY, THE EAST Coast media had descended on Marsh Harbour—"they on our ass," as one Bahamian told me. Another Bahamian friend said he could tell something big was going on because for the first time in recent memory, "the police have actually left their station." With Colt this active, the government decided to reinforce the RBPF with the RBDF. Tommy Turnquest, Bahamas national security minister, who announced, "If he is there to be caught, our police will catch him."

Assistant Commissioner Hulan Hanna of the RBPF said he was locking down Great Abaco. "We have taken steps to neutralize the areas he may try to use to leave the island." Bahamian cops and soldiers flooded in to keep watch on the airports and marinas. Leaflets with Colt's photo papered the island. The game was on.

ON ORCAS, IT FELT like it was going to be all over before I even made it to Seattle to catch a plane east. I was packing when Sandi came home early from work, sick. My selfish first thought was that the last thing I needed was to catch her cold before a long trip. But then her fever soared. I'd never seen her this ill. I changed all my tickets, pushing the trip to Marsh Harbour back a day. I called Tim Roberts again. He said nothing new had happened, but more police were running around. There was also, he said, some local vigilante action, "soon come" style. "A bunch of guys at the bar were talking about getting together to go look for him, maybe snag the reward," he said. "But they were disappointed the FBI was only offering ten thousand dollars," so they ordered another round.

I warned Tim to keep an eye on his boat and said I'd see him on Thursday.

That evening, a bartender said Colt—barefoot and with a cap pulled down on his head—walked into a Marsh Harbour sports bar, ordered a Kalik beer, drank it, and left after five minutes. Another sighting had him stopping by to use a bar's restroom, and one young woman later claimed she had talked with Colt and that he'd told her who he was. None of the sightings was confirmed.

First thing Wednesday morning, my phone rang. It was Tim, but something was wrong. "Bob . . . ," he said in a hoarse whisper, then paused. I immediately thought he was going to tell me that Colt was dead.

After an agonizing few moments of silence, Tim said, "I can't talk louder because there's a TV crew in here sniffing around for information."

My heart started beating again. He said he'd just heard that a boat had disappeared from the marina. Boat theft is not unknown in the Abacos, so that didn't necessarily mean it was Colt. I asked him what kind.

"Forty-five Sea Ray," he whispered.

New and tricked out, a forty-five-foot Sea Ray Sundancer is a $750,000 sex bomb of a boat.

"That's him," I said. "Any idea where it went?" I could hear Tim shuffling the phone around before he said one word into cupped hands: "Preacher's."

I thanked him for the tip and hung up, laughing. Colt was writing his own story and here was some more heavy-handed symbolism. Preacher's wasn't in the Abacos. It was the name of a cave at the north end of Eleuthera, the next island heading southeast down the Bahamas chain. The Lucayans named it Cigatoo, but again the Spanish wiped them out and the island was uninhabited in 1648 when a group of English came journeying south from Bermuda in search of a new homeland that would offer freedom from the Crown's religious mandates. As they sailed toward Cigatoo, they were blown into a treacherous stretch of stony corals, a reef called the Devil's Backbone. They shipwrecked, but were able to make it to the beach.

As the soggy pilgrims waded inland through the seagrapes, they found that Providence had brought them ashore near a large limestone cavern, which provided shelter. It became their holy place. They used Preacher's Cave for religious services and, as the Lucayans before them, as a burial ground.

The pilgrims rechristened Cigatoo "Eleuthera," a derivation of the Greek word for "freedom."

That Colt would choose as part of his great escape to run to an island named "freedom," and then land at the very same spot and in the same manner as the Bahamas' first liberty seekers was storybook imagery.

It was also a very ballsy trip. He had to start a boat and sneak out of a crowded marina that was supposed to be under surveillance. Then he had to navigate the shallows around Marsh Harbour's Eastern Shores before running about twenty miles south through the Sea of Abaco. At Little Harbour, he was forced to leave the protection of the fringing islands, flushed out into the deep blue. As Colt steered the Sea Ray into the open Atlantic, he motored directly past the luxury resort where the dreaded paparazzi— in the form of American network TV crews—were staying.

I spoke with friends who were sailing to Eleuthera that day, and they reported that sea conditions were very rough. Colt had a lot of boat under him, one capable of doing more than thirty knots, but he still had to pound his way across fifty-six miles of open ocean over thirteen thousand feet deep, with big swells rolling in on his port beam the entire trip. It must have been one hell of a ride.

As soon as I got off the phone with Tim, I changed my tickets again, now Orcas/Seattle/Houston/Fort Lauderdale/North Eleuthera, with an overnight in Seattle. Sandi, though, was even sicker. She went to the local doc, and I pushed my trip back another day in case I had to take her to a mainland hospital.

Fortunately, other than the Abacos, the place I'd been to most often in the Bahamas was Eleuthera. I started making calls to local friends, but no one had heard anything about a stolen boat or the Barefoot Bandit. Even police officers I spoke with didn't know anything about it yet. Then reports started coming in of Colt sightings—but these were back in the Abacos. He was seen in the woods, he was seen on the street, he was back hanging in the Marsh Harbour bars.

More media poured into the Abacos and the government sent even more reinforcements. The police patrolled Marsh Harbour with shotguns and German shepherds while the RBDF strode the streets with M4 assault rifles. The assistant police commissioner, Glenn Miller, announced, "We are intensifying our search and we are going to be relentless until we catch him." Each new rumor sent armed troops up and down Great Abaco.

I checked Eleuthera again—still dead quiet. Then even more unconfirmed Colt sightings came in from the Abacos. Picking the wrong island would be very expensive, both time- and money-wise. I reserved a second set of plane tickets, and now held them for Marsh Harbour and Eleuthera.

Sandi started a course of mega-strength antibiotics, but continued to get worse. Neither of us slept that night, and at 3 a.m., I rebooked both sets of tickets, moving them back one more time. Now I was set to leave Orcas Friday afternoon and get to the Bahamas on Saturday evening, July 10.

By late Thursday evening, Sandi's fever finally broke. It felt safe for me to go. But where? All of the media and law enforcement remained on Great Abaco. My gut, though, said Eleuthera.

I TOOK A KENMORE seaplane to Seattle on Friday, and sat in a hotel room until 3:30 a.m., when I went to Sea-Tac for my next flight. As a major handicap for someone who's spent a career traveling, I can't sleep on airplanes. I was bleary-eyed by the time we landed in Fort Lauderdale. I went online at the airport and read the newswires that declared the trail of the Barefoot Bandit had gone "cold." Glenn Miller was now backpedaling on whether Colt was even in his country, saying the only reason his police force suspected he was in the Bahamas was because the U.S. authorities had told them so.

———

Although I did take a twin-engine plane for my flight over the water to the Bahamas, Colt's had more advanced avionics and much more leg room—plus he got to skip dealing with the TSA. He also had a much better view out his windshield. Minutes after takeoff, we left the French-manicured Florida coast and flew across the soft blue line marking the edge of the fabled Gulf Stream. The Stream churns north, forming a fast-moving moat between Florida and the Bahamas, though it's never been an obstacle to pirates, bootleggers, or drug runners, and certainly wasn't a barrier to a boy with a plane.

Ever since Christopher Columbus first got New World sand in his stockings on an Out Island beach, the Bahamas have played host to a long line of outsize characters. For a short eighteenth-century stretch, the Bahamas capital, Nassau, was even declared the pirate republic and run by the likes

of Blackbeard, Calico Jack, and Anne Bonny. During the silliness of Prohibition, Captain Bill "the Real" McCoy ran Irish and Canadian whiskey
from the Bahamas to the States to slake thirsts and stock the speakeasies.
Hemingway pounded typewriter keys, rum, and marlin in Bimini during the
1930s. In the late 1970s and early 1980s, the pirate republic rose once
again, this time fueled by Carlos Lehder's Colombian blow and Medellin
millions. Out Island airstrips transshipped an estimated 80 percent of all the
cocaine inhaled by the United States during those years later caricatured in
Miami Vice. Aviator and recluse Howard Hughes spent his last years holed
up in a Grand Bahama hotel. Gary Hart's Bahamian shenanigans aboard
the aptly named yacht *Monkey Business* blew his presidential chances.
And so on.

There's something about the Bahamas. Now a nineteen-year-old who'd
become the world's most famous airplane pirate and, for the moment, its
most famous living outlaw, was having his moment in the sun.

TOWERING THUNDERHEADS FORCED US to fly a serpentine course toward
Eleuthera. The blooming cumulonimbus clouds rose like slow-motion nuclear explosions in the subtropical summer heat. They have a severe beauty
from a distance, but fliers respect them for the thermal turbulence and
deadly downdrafts. Whenever our pilot couldn't totally avoid the outer
edges of the clouds, the little plane rocked and shuddered.

Coming around one great anvil cloud, a shallow bank topped by the
Berry Islands came into view. And there it was, the vision that has blown
away so many when they first see it: the watercolors of the Bahamas. What
was Colt's reaction, an evergreen kid suddenly engulfed by these shocking
blues? Presumably the same as mine and everyone else's: awestruck. The sea
is so clear that sunlight bounces off the white sand bottom, soaks up a particular tint of turquoise depending on water depth, and then beams it back
into the sky to coat the bottoms of clouds as they float across the flats.

Channels and cuts and currents flowing between the small cays sweep
and swirl the seafloor into fantastical designs, with each change in depth
reflecting a singular blue so that from the air the islands appear set amid
elaborate sand paintings.

Old Bahama boat hands navigate by color, reading the dozens of blues and greens that reveal sandbars, grass beds, and coral reefs. A subtle change in shade can mean the difference between safe passage and shipwreck. Past the Berrys, the water dropped precipitously from Tiffany to ultramarine as we flew out over the fourteen-thousand-foot-deep Great Bahama Canyon, the abyssal valley Colt crossed in the Sea Ray. Then Eleuthera appeared.

Colt joked about having been to the Bahamas when he came back to school tanned from a stretch in juvie. Something put these islands in his mind. For me, it was Hemingway. For Colt, it might have been his James Bond fixation. *Thunderball* and five other Bond films were at least partly filmed in the Bahamas.

Along with a desire to visit tropical islands, both Colt and I grew up wanting adventure. Neither of us was congenitally rich, and apparently neither had the patience to work fifty weeks a year in exchange for two weeks of thrills. My solution was to become a travel writer and photographer. What options did Colt have once he dropped out of school? Pilot? Becoming a private pilot doesn't earn money, it costs money. You need a job to support your flying habit.

Becoming a commercial pilot would have given him both the adventure of flying and a job. A neighbor here on Orcas, Grant, is a great model for someone like Colt. Grant grew up obsessed with planes and flying. So he worked at a gas station every day after school. Every time he got enough cash together, he'd pay for another hour of flight instruction. He slowly earned his way through his ratings and now he's a top pilot for Alaska Airlines. Of course he also had to make his way through college: commercial pilots without bachelor's degrees are almost nonexistent, another big hurdle for Colt.

"This kid could have been Top Gun if he'd gone the right way," says Grant. "Out of the people like me, those totally into flying all their lives and who actually became airline pilots, probably 90 percent would have killed ourselves attempting to do what he did—flying without instruction and landing off-field three times. It's a huge waste of talent."

A WONDERFUL SIDE BENEFIT of what I do is that over the years I've been able to bring family members on some of my travels, particularly my father. Together, we've snorkeled with humpback whales, rappelled into caves filled with the skeletons of human sacrifices, hiked among grizzly bears, and had many other adventures—including several in the Bahamas. Seeing the blue-on-blue water again prompted memories of those trips and even much earlier times, like my dad teaching me to fish and squeezing us into a tiny, inflatable Kmart raft—basically a pool toy because that's all the boat he could afford at the time—for a trip down the Delaware, our first great adventure.

Somewhere down there was a teenage boy who never had that. A kid with a lot of the same interests but no steady male role model to share the fun and teach him the life lessons that go along with learning how to handle boats as well as bullies. What would I have done if I didn't have that man who came home from work every night to do what good fathers do, however imperfectly? My parents didn't have a dime to spare for a lot of years, but they were always there, unconditionally. To grow up without them modeling responsible behavior and the rewards of hard work, I can't imagine how I would have ended up. My own strong tendency toward risk taking got me into enough trouble coming from a good, stable home.

I felt a sudden pang of . . . embarrassment, maybe guilt. My blog that Colt had been reading linked to collections of my stories, including at least a couple of those father-son Bahamas-bonding trips. I wondered if Colt read them and, if so, how they made him feel.

THE PILOT REDUCING POWER to start our descent brought me back to the present. Another threatening cloud dominated the view out my window, dropping a curtain of rain across the north end of Eleuthera and its satellite islands: Spanish Wells, Royal, Russell, and Harbour Island. Suddenly a rainbow arced out of the thunderhead. I took a picture just to prove it wasn't a sleep-deprived hallucination. It had to be a good omen for somebody.

By the time we touched down, the shower had scrubbed the air fresh and moved on, but it was still hot enough—about 90 degrees—that wisps of steam rose saunalike from the tarmac. It was 6:30, p.m., July 10, Bahamas Independence Day.

There's a tiny police substation at the North Eleuthera Airport. Inside the dim room semi-cooled by a rattling air conditioner, a female officer sat behind a desk while a male cop sat opposite, fussing over an imaginary spot on the shiniest shoes I'd ever seen. A wanted poster with Colt's picture hung on the wall. I pointed to it and asked if they had any evidence that he was on the island. I got a couple of noncommittal grunts until I pressed the question. Officer Shiny Shoes looked me up and down, then shared a nod with the other cop. "All inquiries as to current investigations should be made through the public affairs office in Nassau." I asked about the boat at Preacher's. "All inquiries as to . . ."

I walked back outside. Mine had been the last flight in and all the other passengers were gone. Two taxi drivers who hadn't snagged fares sat on a bench solving the world's problems. I went over to get the skinny.

While I was talking to the taxi guys, Kenny Strachan was speaking to God.

"I PRAYED THAT DAY, talkin' to the Lord, and He told me that the Barefoot Bandit was coming here to me," says fifty-three-year-old Strachan. Born in Nassau, Kenny lived in New York for fifteen years, where he learned to install kitchen equipment. He came back to the Bahamas in the late eighties and worked at the Atlantis resort on Paradise Island, but eventually decided to try the slower pace of the Out Islands. In 2005, he moved to Harbour Island, the toniest of the Bahamas, famed for its pink sand beach and the fashion models and celebrities who pose and repose on it.

Harbour Island (shortened to "Briland" by locals) lies just a five-minute taxi-boat ride across a shallow bay from Eleuthera (likewise shortened to "'Lutra"). Kenny worked as head of security for Romora Bay, a marina resort on Briland's harbor side.

Over the previous couple of days, the police had been handing out flyers about Colt all over North Eleuthera. There'd been no recent sightings and there hadn't been any at all on Harbour Island, but on Saturday, a power even higher than the Royal Bahamian Police Force sent a definitive heads-up to Kenny that today was the day.

"When He told me the Bandit was comin', I was axin' the Lord what should I do when he gets here?" God wasn't too specific with His answer, so just to cover his bases, Kenny also texted a message to RBPF detective Sergeant Hart at the Briland station: "When the Barefoot Bandit come, what should I do?"

Hart didn't answer right away, but as Kenny pulled on his black SECURITY T-shirt to start his twelve-hour night shift, he made a fateful decision. "I have three licensed guns and I usually carry a shotgun when I'm on duty."

Kenny packs a gun for its deterrent effect against what he calls the "little lootin'" that goes on. "This island is so calm and so lovely, people leave their doors open . . . and the looters look for that."

There wouldn't be any looting on Briland, Kenny says, if only the Bahamians would stop using the "old England–style, the old Angelo-Saxon–style" of policing where they don't offer rewards. "It's a very small community," he says. "People know who is the culprits, but they just hush hush. If there was a little reward, oh my God, the police start nabbing, back after back."

Kenny says the looters "look to see if you don't have a camera or manpower security. And manpower is best to keep them away."

Strachan's manpower strategy is ninja. "I wear a black hooded jacket and stay in the dark bush, low, like a cat, and you don't see me." The potential thieves never know where Kenny is, and he's also let word spread around that he brings along his little friend when he patrols. "Like hogs in a pen, looters know where it's safe to rub they skins. So when they hear you have guns, they stay away."

There hasn't been a theft at Romora Bay since Kenny took on the job.

Saturday evening, though, Kenny decided to leave the shotgun in his room. "After the Lord showed me His plan that this boy was comin' to me, I said, 'I ain't gonna have no gun when he come.'"

The Bahamian police and FBI were warning everyone that Colt was armed and dangerous, but that didn't worry Kenny. "I wasn't scared," he says with a big gap-toothed smile. He had faith that the Barefoot Bandit was coming, and his plan was still to stop him, but he didn't want to hurt him.

An unmarried father of three ("That's the way it is here in the Bahamas, with a lot of no-wedlock children"), Kenny keeps himself in great shape. Broad-shouldered, six-one, 212 pounds, he cuts an imposing figure in his tight black shirt. "I'm really strong, and if he didn't stop when I asked him to, then my plan was I would toss him and wrassle him."

At 7:38 p.m., Kenny's phone buzzed with an answer from Sergeant Hart: "Bust his ass and hold him until I come."

. . . .

AT THE AIRPORT, I'D gotten the expected stew of rumors and wild speculation from the taxi drivers. The only concrete info was that the big party
tonight was at the Bluff, a small North Eleutheran settlement that hosts
a yearly homecoming that draws Bahamian diaspora living in Nassau,
Miami, and even farther afield for a major fish fry and bashment. This
was one of the years when it fell on Independence Day, which made it even
bigger and better.

A black SUV pulled up and out jumped a petite powerhouse, Petagay
Hollinsed-Hartman. Born in Jamaica, Petagay came to the Bahamas via Key
West when she and her former husband, Mike Hartman, created a ground-
breaking eco resort named Tiamo on Andros Island. Petagay now lived on
Eleuthera, raising her daughter, Bella, and running a small guesthouse, Bella-
Mango, along with the Laughing Lizard Café. The Lizard (motto: "No Hat-
ers") lies in Gregory Town, where Petagay serves fruit smoothies to surfers,
pumpkin soup to locals like rocker Lenny Kravitz, and jerk chicken wraps
to blow-ins such as Robert De Niro.

The Lizard offers wireless Internet, and I'd warned Petagay (who shares
a heaping helping of that islanders' antiauthoritarian streak) that Colt
might stop by to get online. "If he does, I'll make him a panini," she said.

ELEUTHERA IS A GANGLY, 110-mile-long island shaped like a marlin's
skeleton picked clean by sharks. Its bill, severed at Current Cut, points toward Nassau, thirty miles away. The island is so narrow that you can stand
on its limestone spine in many spots and see both the indigo Atlantic and
the aquamarine waters of the shallow Great Bahama Bank.

Gregory Town served as the pineapple capital back when Eleuthera
exported boatloads of the sweet fruit. The village is now the island's laid-
back surf city during the winter swell season when board riders fill up the
guesthouses, spend long days on the break at Surfer's Beach, and then
gather at Elvina's for twice-weekly music sessions where anyone can walk
in and just jam. South of Gregory, Eleuthera is all about quaint towns like
Tarpum Bay and Governor's Harbour, weekly fish fries and sociable bars,
world-class bonefishing, and beach after beach of precious pink and white

sand. There was a lot of Eleuthera for Colt to roam, but the highest concentration of boats was up in the north and it made sense he'd still be near
the top of the island.

I climbed into Petagay's truck and we drove straight out to Preacher's
Cave, a nine-mile run from the airport. It seemed too obvious that Colt
might be sheltering in the cave where he came ashore, but there'd been a lot
of obvious going on lately. It fit the Eleutheran Adventurers' deliverance
story and the Huck Finn archetype, and using the cave wouldn't be a bad
idea as long as he'd already gathered a cache of food and water. There'd be
the chance of a tourist stopping by during daylight, but Colt could hide in
the surrounding woods and move back in at night. The way Preacher's entrance faces the open ocean, he'd even be able to build a fire inside to cook
and keep bugs away without worrying someone might see the glow.

After leaving the paved highway, we bounced down a sandy, rutted track
carved through dense coppice. There wasn't another soul on the road. The
last quarter mile was a narrow, winding path leading into what Bahamians call the backabush. Rainwater filled every pothole and gully. Tropical
rule of thumb says that rain one day brings a bloom of biters in three. According to Petagay, they'd had occasional drenching showers all week,
which meant the mozzies and nippers would be insatiable. I wondered if
Colt had picked up bug juice somewhere along the way.

We parked in a deserted little clearing just as the sun was setting. As we
started walking up the sand trail toward the cave, I suddenly thought of
something. "Do you have your keys?" I asked Petagay. She looked at me
like I was a little crazy, but I convinced her to lock the truck and bring the
key while I grabbed my backpack, which held all my gear and notes. It was
too easy—and fitting to the story—to imagine us coming out of the cave
and finding the truck gone.

Petagay got her Nancy Drew on, checking out footprints. One set leading to the cave was especially large. I noticed a hum that grew louder as we
walked. At first I thought it was the sound of waves, but that didn't make
any sense since we were heading away from the shore. By the time we could
feel the cave's cool exhale, the noise had swelled to the buzz of an electrical
power station. I stopped and looked at Petagay.

"Bees," she said.

A huge hive grew on the upper lip of the cave's mouth. Hundreds of

bees swarmed about twenty feet above us, their drone magnified and ema-
nating from the entrance as a single ominous note. The twilight penetrated
only a few feet past the cave opening, where two rocks poked like fangs
from the ground. Beyond that, a patch of luminous sand pooled beneath a
natural skylight. Beyond that was black.

Petagay pulled a small flashlight out of her shorts and clicked it on. We
stood together at the edge of the darkness, our eyes intently following her
light's sickly yellow glow as it seeped across the rock walls. The weak beam
reached only a short distance, so I slowly moved ahead while Petagay held
the light above my shoulder to show the way.

Bats that cling upside down inside pockmarks in the cave ceiling were
just beginning to stir. We'd gone about sixty feet, past several ancient
Lucayan graves, when Petagay's flashlight died. Ruh-roh.

"Colt?" I called out into the blackness. "Don't shoot . . ." No answer.

Bees, bats, Lucayan and Puritan spirits, yes, but there was none of that
Coltish energy inside Preacher's Cave.

I dug out a headlamp and its cold-blue LEDs blasted any remaining
chills out of the cave. Petagay went back to the entrance looking for signs
anyone had built a fire. I took the light and searched all the way to the back
of the cave, where I found a small opening that looked like it might be a
passageway. I got down on all fours and crawled inside. It didn't go far before
it turned vertical like a chimney. I shined my light up. The cave had saved one
last tingle: a giant spider sprawled across its web a foot above my head. I
thought of young Colton befriending the spider in his Camano backyard.
He could have put a leash on this one and walked it.

Petagay found some wood burned to charcoal, but it looked more than
a couple days old. We left the cave and walked through the lush seagrapes
that enveloped a dune. Over the rise, the trail led to one of the island's
most beautiful reveals: a long coral-sand beach bordering baby blanket–
blue water. We slipped out of our shoes and the sand felt silky cool under-
foot. The light was failing rapidly as it does in the tropics once the sun
sets, but I could still make out the color change that marked the Devil's
Backbone where Colt had grounded the Sea Ray. He'd misjudged the tide.
There hadn't been enough water atop the coral to get the boat across without wrecking its running gear so badly that it would eventually have to be
towed all the way to Fort Lauderdale for repairs.

Like the Eluetheran Adventurers, though, Colt had managed to wade ashore. Of course the colonists didn't have to worry about keeping their laptops and iPods out of the salt water.

We walked back inland, losing the hint of cool ocean breeze and wading back into the humidity. Mosquitoes found us and the sudden screaming trills of cicadas tore through the still air. We had the SUV as a refuge, but Colt left Preacher's on foot. He'd presumably Google Earthed the island and knew he could follow the roads to the North Eleuthera Airport and the pockets of civilization where he could forage for food. His only other options were to stick to the coast and slog along the edge of a mangrove swamp or to try to pick his way through the backabush.

The forest here is a labyrinth of ram's horn, thatch palm, wild dilly, granny bush, and gumbo limbo—nicknamed the "tourist tree" because its peeling bark mimics sunburned skin. Within this confusion of green, brown, and gray sprout shrubs valued by bush medicine practitioners, local alchemists who muddle and mash the leaves of explicitly named plants like "strong back" and "stiff cock" to make therapeutic potions. Radiant tiger lily blooms perch amid the dusty scrub like exotic birds, providing the only splashes of color. If Colt wanted to scout the area by climbing a tree, the tallest were leafy evergreens of the genus *Metopium*. Petagay's husband, Mike, shimmied up one of these to survey their Andros property when he, too, was a Bahamas tenderfoot. They had to airlift him to a Nassau hospital. The tree's common name—which is helpful, but not until you know how to identify it—is poisonwood, and its toxic sap can leave the unwary covered in agonizingly itchy blisters.

We climbed back in the truck. On the road, a car coming the opposite way suddenly zigzagged and then stopped in our lane, its driver hanging out the window shining a flashlight along the shoulder.

"Land crab season," said Petagay. During the summer, these beefy crustaceans climb out of their deep burrows in the sandy forest floor and scuttle en masse to meet and mate in the sea. The next person we saw was a successful hunter pedaling his bike home with a huge crab on the handlebars. With its arms spread wide and claws held high, the crab looked like a roller-coaster rider enjoying a downhill rush. Its amusement would end with a couple days in a pen being fed coconut to purge its system and sweeten its meat before a short visit to a hot kettle.

Petagay suggested we check the area's Haitian settlement, so we bumped along a sad excuse for a dirt road that wound through the bush. A large number of refugees have settled illegally in the Bahamas, many squatting in tin shacks or simple concrete-block homes.

A stereo balanced on the sill of a screenless window poured music into a brown grass yard where five children danced in the dusky light. They waved. Everyone we saw waved. We passed six guys carrying a refrigerator along the road, laughing and joking in Creole. We stopped to ask if they'd seen Colt, but they spoke very little English. We whittled our question down to "Tall white boy?" which got the point across, but they said no.

Next we drove to Jean's Bay dock, where taxi boats connect North Eleuthera with the island of Spanish Wells, a white-Bahamian enclave that's home to the best commercial lobster fishermen in the country. They don't allow alcohol sales on Spanish Wells, so the spot where its residents step ashore on Eleuthera is dominated by a large liquor store painted like a giant Kalik label that's visible from a mile at sea. Wooden garages line the road leading from the dock, most housing vehicles used by Spanish Wells residents during their visits to "mainland" Eleuthera. It'd be the perfect place to commandeer a car, as it might take a week or more before anyone noticed it was missing. All of the padlocks looked intact, though.

We tried calling around the island to see if anyone had heard anything new. Petagay got momentary cell service, then lost it. The islands were having more than their usual hefty share of phone and electrical issues. A pleasure boat off Briland had snagged an underwater cable with its anchor and unplugged almost all the islands' communications for three days. Additional power grid problems also kept cutting electrical as well as cell phone service. Colt, once again, was catching some lucky breaks.

Petagay and I then drove to Three Island Dock—or as most tourists hear the Bahamian pronunciation, "Tree Island Dock." Here, a small limestone peninsula forms a protected lagoon that's home port for a fleet of small taxi boats that connect North Eleuthera to Harbour Island via a $5 two-mile ride. As usual, a couple of boat drivers sat on the cement seawall talking sip-sip (gossip) with the van drivers who link the dock to the rest of Eleuthera.

"Yeah, he messed with my boat Wednesday night," said a burly driver with the sitcom name of Ricky Ricardo. "The tools he used is still in there."

Ricky said three boats had been messed with over the course of two nights. "He really tear up that Bertram there, cut up the wires, fool with the ignition, do something to the engine and the gas . . . The guy couldn't run it for the whole day, had to call out a mechanic."

The Bertram, a twenty-eight-foot classic sportfisher, had a complicated ignition that required both a key and a safety switch, which Colt wasn't able to figure out. Ricky's boat was a twenty-four-foot cuddy cabin set up to ferry a dozen people back and forth to Briland. None of the boats was Colt's preferred style.

"He took one of the key switches and he try to take my batteries. I had the terminals on real tight and he couldn't get them off so he tried to cut the wires. Why he try to take my battery?" Ricardo asked.

I shook my head. Unlike the Abacos, where there are as many boats as cars, Eleuthera has only a couple of marinas and they both lay south, miles away. There were boats around the north end that fit Colt's predilection for speed and style, but they were across the bay at Harbour Island. He'd need a boat just to get over to the better selection. That explained the attempts on the taxi boats. Why, though, try to take a battery?

Ricky Ricardo said he'd actually seen Colton on Wednesday night. "He was walking to the dock, tall guy, short brown hair, no shoes—and that's what I noticed because I only ever know two white guys who walk on the road barefoot."

Ricardo said other boat drivers had also seen the Bandit. "He was sea bathing in the evening, floating in the cove around the corner . . . just seem like a young man, just a tourist." They took notice because the cove is lined with ironshore—limestone bank eroded into chisel-sharp points easily capable of slicing through skin. Only the toughest leather-bottomed bare feet could make it across even a short patch of ironshore without being shredded.

The police eventually showed up with a flyer featuring Colt's picture, and the boat drivers ID'd him.

ACROSS THE PIER FROM the taxi boats lies the tropically painted and grandly named Coakley's International Sporting Lounge. Coakley's consists of a small rum shop with a large covered patio and a pool table that provides the sport. Petagay and I pulled out two of the half dozen bar stools and ordered Kaliks. The name of the local beer comes from the sound of a cowbell, one of the most important instruments, along with whistles and goatskin drums, that create the Bahamas' frenetically loud Junkanoo music.

Denaldo Bain pulled a couple of cold ones from a glass-front fridge that provided the brightest light in the nice, dark bar. Behind Denaldo, shelves held maybe a hundred liquor bottles, mainly rums. A TV suspended in the corner played a Schwarzenegger movie. Jamaican reggae pumping out of the stereo mercifully drowned the one-liners.

I asked Denaldo, who lays down rap songs when he's not tending bar at Coakley's, whether anything strange had happened on his side of the dock in the last few days. He said there'd been a break-in Wednesday night.

"What was taken?"

"Water, Gatorade, snacks . . ."

"Any rum?"

"Nope."

Colt.

"I know he was watching TV, too," said Denaldo. "I came in the morning and the remotes and my chair were moved."

Maybe Colt sat down to check to see if he was still making news. Denaldo pointed out the section of screened wall cut out so the Bandit could climb into the patio. After that, he said, Colt jimmied a deadbolt to get into the rum shop. He said that the same night, someone had also hit the administrative building at the center of the dock.

Denaldo, who lives across the water on Briland, said he'd also spotted Colt. "I saw him when I was closing up Wednesday night about ten o'clock. He was just about to go into the water. He stood up a little when we saw him—tall guy, slim, just shorts, bareback. The water taxi man was saying that the night before, someone trifle with the boats. So we look at this guy and no, no, not him, he wouldn't trifle with the boats, didn't look that way. This is just a tourist, just a tourist having fun. You know: love yourself. When we drove off, he went into the water."

When the police came out to investigate the break-in at Coakley's, they never mentioned the Barefoot Bandit and suspected the burglar was just a local troublemaker.

I ordered another Kalik and asked Denaldo what exactly had been taken. He pointed to cartons of bar snacks on top of the drink fridge. "He got Honey Buns and some of the Planters Go Packs, but his favorite was the Snickers."

Ah, Snickers, the candy bar that fueled fifty burglaries. If he lived through this, I could see Colt's first endorsement deal: "It's tough staking out airports and marinas all night, so when I need an energy boost, I pull out a Snickers."

"How about the drinks?" I asked.

"He took a few bottles of water and a couple Gatorades," said Denaldo. "Oh," he suddenly added, "and a few Heinekens and Kaliks."

Regardless of whether Colt actually took the beers (which I kinda doubt), it was very interesting that he hadn't emptied the place out. Why not fill his entire backpack with Snickers and water? If he'd been willing to carry a boat battery he could certainly handle a dozen bottles of Fierce Grape Gatorade to keep himself hydrated, and more Snickers to keep himself topped up on nougaty goodness. To me, that meant either he already had a campsite or an empty home stocked with food and water . . . or else he was supremely confident in his ability to forage what he needed whenever he needed it.

I looked up at all the candy bars and pastries Colt had left behind. "He's going to come back here," I told Denaldo.

He didn't seem concerned. They'd put up some plywood over the one torn screen, but that left another forty feet of patio screen for Colt to slip through. And he'd already proved that the door lock was no contest. From Colt's experience over the last few days, he must have thought things shut down early on the dock, leaving him plenty of dark hours to come back and raid Coakley's and maybe take another shot at a taxi boat if he hadn't found one elsewhere.

Tonight would be different, though, because of all the parties happening and people moving back and forth among islands. I wondered if Colt knew that.

I finished my beer and looked at the rum display. This would be a fine place to wait for Colt. I've spent many amiable afternoons that stretched into pleasantly lost evenings inside Bahamian rum shops. You order a bottle for your table and the bartender keeps you supplied with Cokes or fruit juice mixers. It's one of the best ways to meet people because, like pubs in Ireland, Caribbean rum shops serve as the social centers of every small village.

Petagay broke my reverie, saying she was starving. I bought her a Honey Bun.

"No thanks," she said. Cell service had popped up momentarily and her phone buzzed in a couple of messages. Two stories were floating around the island. "Some people are saying a boat was stolen today down in Governor's Harbour. Others say a boat is missing from Harbour Island." Denaldo added that he, too, had heard about a boat theft in Governor's.

It was close to 10 p.m. Governor's Harbour was a forty-mile drive south. Harbour Island was a ferry ride across the bay. Both rumors, though, said only that boats were missing. That could mean Colt had found his long-range craft and was already on his way farther down the chain to Cat Island or the Exumas. Both were a day's travel by scheduled flights even though they were only twenty and thirty miles, respectively, from the southern tip of Eleuthera. And there was no way for me to even start a trip tonight. These were also just island rumors. I suddenly felt the sleeplessness of the last few days catching up with me. Even more, I realized I was hungry, too, and yeah, you'd have to be desperate to be in the Bahamas on Independence Day and settle for Honey Buns and Snickers bars. I turned to Petagay. "Let's go to the Bluff."

As I paid our tab, Denaldo remembered one more detail about the burglary.

"Oh yeah . . . he also took the emergency light." He pointed to a spot on the wall where the battery still hung, part of a system designed to pop on whenever the power went out, which was frequently. The lights had been unplugged and taken. The grid had intermittently blinked off Wednesday night, so Colt could have just been ensuring he wasn't suddenly lit up inside Coakley's. But why take the lights?

Another explanation for Colt's machinations aboard the taxi boats suddenly made sense. By MacGyvering together Ricky Ricardo's boat battery and Coakley's fixture, Colt could create a powerful spotlight to illuminate a campsite or cave, or even to use on the front of a boat to help him navigate unfamiliar waters. His portable GPS worked well for charting general courses, but depending on the exact model—as well as meteorological conditions—it might be accurate only to within ten or fifteen yards. Like many, many boaters before him, Colt had already learned a tough lesson on the Devil's Backbone: if you couldn't see the myriad rocks, reefs, and sandbars in the Bahamas' shallows with your own eyes, being off course by just a few feet could mean the difference between smooth sailing and coming to grief hard aground. If he was going to be boating after dark, a light would help him read the water in those shallow areas where just a couple hours of tidal rise separated a safe passage from bellying up to a sandbar.

THE TAXI DRIVERS HAD been right: the Bluff was definitely the place to be that night. We heard the music and smelled the barbecues a block away. People swarmed the waterfront, piling in front of the food and drink stands that lined the settlement's large concrete dock. High-energy calypso pumped from the walls of speakers you find at even the smallest Bahamian public parties. At the booze booth I ordered a rum and Coke in an attempt to maintain the island vibe and stay awake at the same time. Petagay and I then sat on the seawall digging into huge plates of grilled lobster and cracked conch with mounds of peas 'n' rice on the side.

We'd just finished eating when the the Falcons, one of the Bahamas' best party bands, came onstage and kicked into a cover of "Harbour Island Song," which celebrates pink sand on your feet and dancing in the street.

The crowd pressing toward the stage parted for small groups of Bahamian women in impossibly tight jeans who wanted to get their booties bouncing. Then everything suddenly went silent . . . except for the drummer, who kept thumping the bass. Power to the sound system had gone out, cutting all the mics and guitars. I took the opportunity to sidle up to an RBPF chief inspector who stood out from the crowd in his bright tunic, red-sashed cap, and swagger stick. I started to say hello but double-taked because hidden behind the six-foot-three well-fed inspector was a scrawny patrolman about a foot shorter whose cartoonishly large round motorcycle helmet made him look like Marvin the Martian.

I nodded to Marvin, who stood stiffly at attention, ignoring me. I looked up at the chief inspector, wished him a happy Independence Day, then said, "I hear the Barefoot Bandit may be in the area."

He looked me up and down, then finally said, "We have that information," and he made it clear that was all I was going to get.

"EVERYTHING FOR US AT that point was just information, information, information," says another chief inspector, Roston Moss. "There was only suspicion, no proof that this individual had landed on Eleuthera."

At forty-two, Moss is already a twenty-five-year veteran of the Royal Bahamian Police Force. He's spent most of his career in Nassau, home to the Bahamas' meanest streets. At the end of February 2010, however, he was reassigned to Harbour Island. Normally, Briland, like Orcas, has a sergeant as its top cop, but there'd been a recent surge in crime, primarily what Kenny Strachan calls "looting." In just the week before Moss arrived, the tiny island suffered eight burglaries. The night after he got there, robbers broke into an American tourist's hotel room and hit him with a cutlass (the pirate-era name still used in the Bahamas for a machete). Since Harbour Island is the Bahamas' prime destination for the rich and famous, it was extremely important to the country's overall tourist industry to quell the crime wave and ensure it maintained its pastel-colored, celebriquaint reputation. So Nassau sent the big man—Chief Inspector Moss stands six feet two inches, 295 pounds—to take over the station.

To assist him, Moss had eight regular officers and five reserve officers. They provided twenty-four-hour policing for the 1.3-square-mile island (compared to forty-square-mile Camano and fifty-seven-square-mile Orcas, both of which have fewer cops). As soon as he took charge, Moss also created a citizens advisory board to enhance the local crime watch.

Moss followed the events on Great Abaco after the stolen plane landed and knew about the boat found off Preacher's. It wasn't until Thursday, though, after the incidents and sightings at Three Island Dock, that he felt there was enough evidence the Barefoot Bandit was in his area to plan a search.

"On Friday, the ninth, at eight a.m., myself and seven officers started the manhunt in North Eleuthera," says Moss. He split his men into two teams. Four drove around the top of the main island while Moss and three others searched by sea in a "go-fast boat," scouting the beaches and rocky shorelines of Spanish Wells, Russell Island, Current Island, and Harbour Island.

"We were looking for footprints, a tent, a boat out of place . . . ," says Moss. "But there was no sign of him." Moss called off the search at 7 p.m. Friday, and resumed it Saturday morning, Independence Day. At five that afternoon, after again finding nothing suspicious, Moss stopped by the homecoming party at the Bluff to grab something to eat before heading back across to Briland.

AFTER NEARLY TEN MINUTES of solo boom, boom, booming, the Falcons' drummer was drenched with sweat and looked about to pass out. I felt the same way. The cell towers were dead again. The only rumor we could scare up from anyone at the Bluff was another sketchy report about "the Bandit." In the Bahamas, where so many people are often barefoot, almost everyone dropped that part of his nickname. The Bandit had maybe been spotted and maybe jumped off a boat and swam away. Didn't sound likely.

A sudden screech of feedback and an electrician jumping three feet into the air after sticking something somewhere it shouldn't have gone told me that the music wasn't coming back for a while. Worse, the line at the drink booth was now twenty minutes deep.

Decision time. Whereas I'd made pretty good gut calls up to this point, I now made one of the worst.

I could take a chance and go over to Briland, maybe wind up having to spend the night on the beach if I couldn't scare up a hotel room. We could go back to Coakley's and wait until it closed and hope Colt showed up. I was going on thirty hours with no sleep, though, and if he did show, either my snoring would scare him away or I'd wake up with a bare foot drawn on my forehead. Option three won: go crash on Petagay's couch.

We had people all over Eleuthera and the surrounding islands keyed up to call us if anything broke. Besides, what were the chances something big would happen in the next few hours? My gut told me he was still around and wasn't planning on going anywhere tonight.

I hate being half right.

. . . .

WE SWUNG BY THE airport on the way home. The police substation was empty, closed down. There was no security at all besides a chest-high chain-link fence along the runway. Commuter planes sat close to the tiny, dark terminal. Private planes—at least a dozen, including seven that Colt could fly—were farther down the tarmac. No lights, no police, no guards, and the world's most successful plane thief somewhere within a few miles.

One of the planes on the field was a Cessna 400 that looked ready to leap into the air if you just tickled its tail. Suddenly I felt a strange urge to hop the fence, jump in, and take off.

At Petagay's, I lay sweating beneath a ceiling fan with Bella's dog, Jazzy, beating her tail against the couch as I fell asleep petting her.

BACK AT THE BLUFF, they finally fixed the sound system and Homecoming cranked up again. Ferry boats carried so many Brilanders over to Three Island Dock to go to the party that the couple of taxi vans still working couldn't keep up with the flow. A crowd gathered near Coakley's waiting their turn. One of the dock staff from Romora Bay Resort, nineteen-year-old Mauris Jonassaint, stood at the end of the dock talking to a friend while they waited for a ride. Suddenly they heard a boat engine coming toward them. The water was pitch-black except for the reflection of lights from Harbour Island, two miles away. Mauris says he figured it was a boat coming to pick someone up, but he could tell it was moving way too fast through the shallows.

A small white hull appeared out of the darkness headed right for the dock. Everyone started waving it off, shouting, "Whoa! Slow down!" When the driver got close enough to see that there was a crowd of people there, he immediately spun the boat around and started back for open water. "But he didn't slow down," says Mauris. "Just went back out at full speed. Mauris and the others watched, dumbfounded, as the tall white guy, in a light T-shirt and camouflage shorts, drove the little boat aground on a submerged rock within sight of the pier.

Colt had busted into a vacation home at Whale Point, a finger of North Eleuthera that points at Harbour Island from across an 850-foot-wide inlet. He broke in looking for one thing: a key to the shiny new thirteen-foot Boston Whaler Super Sport sitting on a trailer outside. He found it inside the garage, then muscled the half ton of boat and motor into the water and started its forty-horsepower Mercury outboard. The unsinkable $10,000 Whaler, designed for use as a yacht tender or as an all-purpose sport boat, wasn't big enough to get Colt farther down the Bahamas chain, but it was plenty of boat for buzzing between the islands at the top of Eleuthera.

After running aground, Colt was able to rock the Whaler free and then drove off a ways. Then he did something that set the course for his foreseeable future: he decided to turn around and come back.

Colt motored up and stopped the boat about twenty feet away from the pier, then shut off his engine. Mauris says Colt was laughing. "I asked him what he was doing."

Colt looked up at Mauris and said, "Did you hear about the plane I crashed?"

"That was you do that?"

"Yeah," admitted Colt.

"What's your name?" asked Mauris.

"Colton Harris."

Mauris says Colt was very friendly, and as they started talking, he sat back and put his bare feet up on the gunwale. Mauris asked why he'd come to the Bahamas. Colt told him that he couldn't get any farther. "He said he didn't have enough fuel to go to Cuba."

Colt answered every question Mauris and his friend asked. He told them he was from Camano Island and still planned on getting to Cuba. "I asked him how he's getting there and he said, 'Plane.' My buddy was playing with him and said he wanted to go. But Bandit said, 'No, I fly alone.'"

Mauris told Colt that there were plenty of planes at the airport for him to choose from, but apparently the Bandit had already checked out the flying stock. He shook his head, saying, "I don't drive old planes."

While they were chatting, the current carried the little boat toward the dock. Mauris and his friend knew about the $10,000 FBI reward and watched as the boat came closer and closer. When he was just about within jumping range, though, Colt calmly reached over and started the engine.

"He moved out to about twenty feet away and shut it back down . . . and he was laughing."

Mauris asked Colt if he was hungry. "He said, 'No, I'm fine.' And we asked him if he wanted some liquor, and he said, 'I don't drink and drive.'"

The Bahamian then mimed a toke and asked if Colt was interested in a little weed, but Colt just laughed and said no. As the Whaler again drifted in close to the dock, Mauris asked, "Why don't you come up here and talk?" Colt nodded to the large group of men standing off a little ways. "You see all those guys? You think I'm crazy?" Then he slowly motored the boat back out of reach and stopped again.

"He was just chillin'," says Mauris, who nonetheless remembered the "armed and dangerous" part of the police warning.

"Do you have a weapon?" he asked.

Colt smiled. "Maybe I do, maybe I don't."

"I was like, yeah, he's packin'. So there's this big steel pole I was standing next to and I moved a little behind it."

Mauris says the conversation had gone on for more than half an hour when Colt started to get agitated. "I ask him if he miss his mom, and he's like, 'Yeah,' so I said, 'Then why don't you go back home?'"

"Too many cops," said Colt, who then asked, "So where are your cops?"

"We don't have that much cops," answered Mauris.

"Well, call them," said Colt. "I'm bored . . . I want to get chased."

Naturally, Mauris first thought Colt must be joking. "But then he started to get mad, saying, 'Call the cops, call the cops! I want to get chased! For real, call them! Call them!'"

Mauris tried to calm Colt down. "I'm like, 'There ain't no cops, man.'"

AND THERE WEREN'T. No one had called them despite everyone on the dock figuring out that it was the famous Barefoot Bandit bobbing in front of them. Some of the other men tried to engage Colt in conversation, but he would talk only to Mauris and his pal.

After Colt got mad, Mauris slid a bit farther behind the steel pole and signaled to his buddy, who pulled out a cell phone. He didn't dial the RBPF, though, he called friends who had a boat, whispering to them to hurry up and get there, that they had the Bandit "right here at the dock."

Colt spotted the guy making the call. "Why is that guy on the phone?"

Mauris told him not to worry about it. Colt gave him a big smile and said, "I'm gone!"

He started up the outboard and began to pull away, turning back to yell to Mauris, "Read about me on the Internet!"

MAURIS SAYS THE WHALER blasted away in the direction of Harbour Island, aiming for the lights of a resort a third of a mile north of Romora Bay. "He went toward Valentines, so I told our friends in the boat to head that way and listen for the motor because he was running really hard and was the only boat moving out there."

A taxi boat with a 115 Yamaha got within sight of Colt, but his little forty-horse Whaler could run over 30 mph and turn on a dime. A second boat joined the pursuit, but neither could corner the nimble Whaler out in open water as Colt ran circles around them in the darkness.

On the other side of the bay, Kenny Strachan was manning the shadows of Romora Bay Resort, lurking for looters. About twenty boats resided in the marina that night—big live-aboard yachts along with smaller speed-boats in the twenty-five- to thirty-two-foot range that the yacht owners used for fishing and diving excursions. A few people were on board, asleep, but most guests were down in Dunmore Town celebrating the holiday at Gusty's, Vic-Hum, and Daddy D's, leaving Romora and its docks deserted.

Shortly after 11:30, Kenny heard a commotion out on the black bay. "Engines were roaring and I could hear guys yelling, 'See him? See him?'"

At 11:43, Kenny was heading toward the marina just as Colt came flying in. "He drive that boat under the dock, right under the marina office and jumped off," says Kenny.

The docks at Romora stand high off the water, designed for big boats. Only one spot, a floating dinghy dock just below the office, sits low enough to disembark from a small tender. Colt drove directly there, climbed out, and tied the Whaler to a cleat, leaving the engine idling. He strapped on his backpack, grabbed his Walther PPK, and ran up the ramp to the main dock.

At the top of the ramp, Colt bolted through the office breezeway and turned left, running full speed down one hundred yards of dock before coming to dead wet end with nothing ahead of him but bay. He realized his mistake, spun around, and raced back, finally hurrying off the dock and onto the hotel grounds, where Kenny Strachan had positioned himself at the bottom of a stairway.

As Colt, who was obviously in some kind of distress, ran toward him, Kenny shouted, "What happened?"

"They're trying to kill me!" Colt yelled.

That's when Kenny saw a flash of silver in Colt's hand, the pistol, and realized that God had kept His word and brought the Barefoot Bandit to him.

" 'Oh, that's Bandit!' I said to myself." Kenny had purposely left his guns at home, but the $150-a-week security guard hadn't received a divine strategy for how to handle the situation in case the Bandit brought his. "I was excited, but I didn't want to get shot," he says.

Colt kept running and Kenny kept pace alongside. "I didn't want to show him my fear and give myself away. I wanted him to think I was on his side." So Kenny played along, telling Colt, "I ain't gonna let nobody kill you."

Colt wasn't buying it. "He looking at me tensified and kept exactly the same distance between us, eight feet, and wouldn't let me get closer," says Kenny. "I kept running beside him, asking, 'Who tryin' kill you?' and saying, 'Let me help you!' When I moved a little closer, though, he put his finger on the trigger . . . He didn't want to shoot me, he wasn't evil, but I know he was thinking it was going to get physical and I was bigger than him."

Kenny quickly weighed his options and his chances and made the wise decision. "Can't run down a man with a gun, gotta let him go," he says.

Colt ran off the Romora grounds heading east. Kenny grabbed his phone and dialed Sergeant Hart to tell him the Bandit was loose on Briland. "Hart told me to go get my shotgun."

Kenny also had the presence of mind to do something that severely limited Colt's chances of escape. He ran back down to the dinghy dock, turned off the Whaler's engine, and pocketed the key.

LANDLINES WERE STILL DOWN throughout the island, and cell service was spotty, so Sergeant Hart sent a runner to wake Chief Inspector Moss. Hart then grabbed his weapon and rushed down to Romora. Kenny met him at the edge of the resort and was just pointing out which way Colt had fled when they heard a scream. The men ran east and found a woman standing in the street crying. She'd come outside because of the shouting, and suddenly Colt appeared, gun in hand. He looked at her, she screamed, and Colt dashed off into the bushes next to her property. As Hart and Strachan ran up, the woman was trembling. She pointed to the trees. "I just saw him! Right through there!"

Kenny says they clearly saw the path where Colt parted the scrub. "If the police had a good canine or good experience, they would have got him right there in the bush . . . But they didn't go in."

Instead of rushing into the black woods, Hart began to gather as much manpower as possible. "He called up some other neighborhood crime fighters," says Kenny. "They all have licensed guns, and he directed us to spread out and try to keep Bandit trapped in the woods."

Hiding in the bushes, Colt was in his element, but also in his nightmare. He'd told his mom that a doctor said he had PTSD. "And Colt thinks it's from the cops chasing him in the dark," says Pam. "He said, 'Every time I see a little light in the dark, I go insane.' "

Now Colt was crouched amid strange scrubby trees on an unfamiliar island three thousand miles from home with a rapidly growing group of armed men probing the woods with flashlights. He was also already bleeding. Instead of the soft moss and cedar branchlets of the Northwest, the ground here was sharp limestone rock, and the forest was filled with tearing thorns and scaly, tripping roots.

Colt had gotten his chase. Now he could see the lights and hear the voices and crackle of walkie-talkies as the men tried to pen him in. But he wasn't ready to give up by a long shot.

The two-hundred-square-yard section of Briland backabush where Colt hid was connected to other patches of woods he could sneak through to reach any of nearly one hundred nearby homes. He could also stay under cover all the way across the island, which is only five hundred yards from bay to beach in this area. Or he could pull a Colt and try something no one would ever expect.

CHIEF INSPECTOR MOSS WOKE to the banging on his door and got the news about Colt. He knew he'd need more manpower to have any chance of corralling the outlaw who'd escaped so many police operations over the last two years. Neither his landline nor cell phone was working, so Moss pulled on a pair of jean shorts, threw his bulletproof vest over a muscle tee, grabbed his 9mm, and ran out of the house in his slippers.

Like everyone else on Briland, the police generally drive around in golf carts. Moss, though, had brought in an actual patrol car after taking over. He raced to Pink Sands, the island's most famous resort, which had an Internet connection that didn't rely on the phone lines. Moss booted up Vonage and called Nassau headquarters and Governor's Harbour. The same VoIP technology Colt had been using to communicate during his time on the lam was now used to call in reinforcements to catch him.

Calls were relayed via radio to officers spread across Eleuthera, still out policing the late-night festivities. Eight of them hightailed it to Three Island Dock and commandeered a boat to carry them over to Briland.

By 1 a.m., Moss had sixteen men. He broke them into two teams. With no night-vision equipment and no dogs, his strategy was simply to contain Colt until sunrise, when he'd be easy to spot in the low scrub. Moss led Team One, which included unarmed members of the local Crime Watch. Their job was to seal off the island so Colt couldn't escape. Team Two—all cops packing Uzi submachine guns, shotguns, and their 9mm sidearms—was ordered to continue patrolling the edges of the woods near Romora to keep Colt bottled up.

Dawn would break in five hours.

Moss and his team drove to the island's other marinas, telling them "to remain on red alert" so Colt couldn't grab another boat. They handed out more wanted flyers and gathered drinking water and bug juice for everyone involved in the operation.

"It seemed like half the island was up and around by now," says Moss. Many came up to the chief inspector asking to be deputized. He told them to just keep their eyes open but not to put themselves in danger since this was an armed fugitive.

Word had gotten downtown, and all the guests had returned to Romora Bay. One of the boats in the marina, a ninety-two-footer named *Picasso*, lay berthed adjacent to the dock office. The captain of the $4 million aluminum yacht checked the footage from its surveillance cameras and found images of Colt running back and forth.

Kenny Strachan went back to his post, patrolling the resort, now with his shotgun strapped across his back. Time dragged on, with no sightings and no action for more than two and a half hours. It was the dead of a dark, moonless night. Everyone was tired and bleary-eyed. Talk among the cops dropped to occasional whispers, then to nothing. Kenny walked out onto the dock and sat down.

At 2:45 a.m., Chief Inspector Moss got a report of a possible escape boat on Pink Sand Beach. He and his team drove across the island to check it out. As soon as they left, Colt made his move.

Kenny and another guy were on the dock near the marina office, discussing whether Colt might be able to sneak back and take one of Romora's boats . . .

"Just then a white guy come up and say he heard a boat startin'," says Kenny. "We listen and suddenly hear boat engines bog down and go WHOOOOO like when you go full throttle. We start yellin', 'Dat's him! Dat's him!' "

COLT HAD MANAGED TO creep from the woods east of Romora Bay and through the cordon of Team Two cops. He crossed the resort grounds and then made it out onto the dock. At the farthest corner of the marina lay the *Lady BJ*. The owners of this seventy-six-foot yacht—a Miami real estate investor and his family—were fast asleep belowdecks with the generator thrumming and air conditioners blowing. They never heard Colt climb down off the dock onto the thirty-two-foot Intrepid they'd towed over from Key Largo as their sport boat. The keys were on board, and Colt fired up the pair of 275-horsepower Mercury outboards.

Colt pulled out of the slip and pushed the throttles forward. With a full tank of gas aboard what the Bahamians would definitely call a "go-fast boat," Colt had the range to get to Nassau or Cat Island or Rum Cay or Long Island, or to lose himself amid the hundreds of Exuma Cays—all before daylight. If he could just get out of the bay.

Colt opened her up and headed south toward the deep cut between Harbour Island and Whale Point that led to open water.

. . . .

SERGEANT HART AND THE cops of Team Two ran down to the dock with guns at the ready, but Colt's boat had already disappeared into the darkness. The only chance to catch him was to find a boat of their own. Hart asked the *Picasso*'s owners if the RBPF could borrow their sport boat and their captain, New Orleans native Ron Billiot. The owners said yes. The *Picasso*'s go-fast was the owners' son Jordan's *Dr. J*, a twenty-seven-foot Boston Whaler Outrage powered by twin 250s. With one or two people aboard, this boat could top 50 mph, just like Colt's Intrepid. However, Sergeant Hart, three RBPF officers heavy with body armor and weapons, Jordan, and another visiting boater also got aboard. Billiot fired up the engines, tossed off the lines, and headed out into the dark bay. They were already about four minutes behind Colt, and all the extra weight meant there'd be no way the Whaler would ever catch the Intrepid in a chase. All they could hope for was a lucky break.

A FEW MINUTES AFTER the *Dr. J* took off, Moss arrived at the dock and commandeered another civilian boat. This one, though, wouldn't crank, so they tried another. That started, and with Moss, five cops, and the captain aboard, it too roared off into the pitch-black night.

It was the first time the chief inspector had been out on a boat after dark in this area. Fortunately, he wasn't driving, because the deceptively calm bay hides a nasty surprise for anyone who is unfamiliar with the local waters or is in too much of a rush to check the charts.

COLT, NEVER ONE TO be afraid of going full speed at night when the adrenaline surfing comes in even bigger waves, blasted south along Harbour Island. The few lights burning on shore and the slightly blacker black of the land were all he could see. However, all he had to do was make it to the end of the island, just 1.1 miles from Romora, and he'd be able to pick out the smudge on the horizon that marked the inlet leading to open water and continued freedom.

Colt had not only gotten his chase, he'd toyed with the locals, dodged the cops, and then ninja'd himself right under their noses for yet another spectacular escape. He had an excellent boat and plenty of good-life islands within reach. Colt had broken through to unlock whole new levels of the game.

Then, suddenly, everything went to shit. Three-quarters of a mile south of the marina, the Intrepid abruptly slowed as if the seawater had turned to Jell-O. The engines growled and the propellers churned. Colt pulled back the throttles. He'd hit a sandbar.

TWO THINGS CONSPIRED to finally end the Barefoot Bandit's long run. First was the sandy shoal that stretches more than halfway across the bay between Briland and North Eleuthera. To get to the Whale Point cut, boaters have to first steer toward the Eleutheran shoreline to skirt the bar. It's marked on charts and obvious on satellite photos. It's also easy to spot during the day when the shallows glow a brilliant aquamarine compared to the deeper blue surrounding waters. At night, though, it's invisible.

The other thing that got him was also invisible that night. One of Colt's first fascinations and one of his very first words—the moon—betrayed him. Hitting its darkest phase that morning, the new moon brought dramatic tides. It'd sucked water off the sandbar until it sat dead low tide at 2:22 a.m., less than an hour before Colt showed up. A few hours and another eighteen inches of incoming tide later, and he would have skimmed right across.

Same thing if he'd been aboard the little Whaler he left tied at the dock.

ABOARD THE DR. J, Ron Billiot knew all about the sandbar. He slowed as he neared the shallows, and they flicked on the spotlights. A light-colored hull popped out of the darkness. Dr. J idled closer and the men aboard her could see Colt at the controls of the Intrepid's center console, one hand on the throttles, one on the wheel. The police began shouting at him: "Stop!" "It's over!" "You're caught!" "Put your hands up!"

Colt's hand came up; it was holding a pistol, though, and he fired.

The officers, each with an Uzi or shotgun aimed at Colt, saw the muzzle flash but didn't return fire. They yelled at him to drop his weapon.

Colt hollered back, telling them to get the lights off him. Then he screamed, "Don't come any closer! I'm not going back to jail! Don't come any closer or I'll kill myself!"

The two boats were only about fifty feet apart when the cops saw Colt lift the pistol to his head, shouting, "Go away! I'll kill myself!"

The cops weren't going away, though, and unlike at Granite Falls, they weren't backing off. After a few tense moments, Colt pulled the gun away from his head. But he wasn't giving up. Colt turned back to the boat's controls and pushed the throttles forward. The Intrepid dug down in the stern, the props chewing into the bottom, but slowly it began to make headway. Colt had bogged down at the shallowest part of the bar, and now his boat's powerful engines were plowing through the sand, taking him toward deeper water.

Aboard the *Dr. J*, Billiot told Sergeant Hart that if the Intrepid got just a little farther it'd be off the sandbar and they'd never be able to catch it. The Barefoot Bandit would get away again.

BACK AT ROMORA BAY, Kenny Strachan stood on the dock staring out at the black water when he heard what sounded to him like a war. "Bloom-bloom-bloom-bloom-bloom! On and on and on. I thought, Oh my God, they killed him!"

THE FIRST SHOTGUN BLAST hit the portside outboard engine. Other officers fired their Uzis, the 9mm bullets spraying the starboard engine. At least two rounds went toward the center console where Colt was standing. One passed through the stainless-steel piping in the middle of his seat, then tore through the cushion, and cracked the windshield. A second bullet punched into the steel pipe behind the seat and ricocheted inside until it was spent. Another round went well high and ripped into an aluminum outrigger ten feet above the waterline.

Bullets and shotgun pellets filled the air. Rounds careened off the outboards' engine blocks and exploded back out, showering the boat with shrapnel. The police officers finally ceased fire after pumping at least twenty rounds into the Intrepid.

Acrid smoke filled the still night air. The only sound was the soft rumble of the *Dr. J*'s engines.

"Stop shooting! I can't hear! I can't hear!" Colt rose from the deck of the Intrepid screaming and waving his arms.

The police shouted for him to put up his hands, but Colt was still thinking. He opened his backpack and reached inside. Hart told Billiot to move in closer and the cops lined up with guns ready, yelling, "Drop your weapon! Show us your hands!" Instead, Colt pulled out his laptop and threw it over the side, followed by his GPS and iPod. Finally, he tossed his pistol and backpack into the sea.

When the *Dr. J* came alongside, the cops ordered Colt down on the deck. Once they saw that he didn't have any more weapons, they jumped across and handcuffed him. At that point, officers say, a calmness came over Colt. All he said was "You should have killed me."

MOSS'S BOAT ARRIVED AND officers jumped into the waist-deep water to try to find the gear Colt had thrown overboard. His backpack floated, and they picked that up, but now with three boats churning the shallows there was an underwater sandstorm and they couldn't see anything on the bottom. Both captains marked the spot on their GPS. The cops transferred Colt to the *Dr. J* and a tow line was rigged for the Intrepid since both of its engines had been destroyed. At 3:15 a.m., they started back toward Romora Bay.

After the guns had gone silent, Kenny held his breath, fearing the worst. A few minutes later, his cell phone rang. "They say, 'Kenny, we got him.' And my God! I'm so glad they didn't kill him."

Moss received a radio call that a large crowd had gathered—or at least large for three in morning on Briland. About forty people were milling around the marina. "I didn't know if they wanted to just observe or if they wanted to harm the suspect," he says. "So we wanted to clear the path." Those allowed to remain were guests off the boats in the marina, Kenny, and the police and Crime Watch folks.

When the *Dr. J* arrived and they lifted Colt out of the boat, the onlookers crowded around with cell phone cameras while police ordered, "Stand back! Stand back!" Moss hadn't been able to get ahold of his police car by radio, so they'd backed a red golf cart down to the dock. As the cops steered Colt toward it, the crowd pushed in.

"Some Americans was yelling, 'Shame on you!'" says Kenny. "And Bahamians was sayin', 'Don't come here, this no place for you to be! You come to Briland and get caught!' Everyone was trying to get his picture, but he kept his face down and wouldn't talk to anyone. I felt so sorry for him because he was not that kind of hard-core criminal like they thought he was." Kenny helped them load Colt onto the cart and rode along to the edge of the property.

They took Colt to the Briland police station and handcuffed him to a chair. Moss sent word to Nassau that they'd successfully captured the Barefoot Bandit. He pressed his superiors to come get Colt as soon as possible because he didn't have the resources on Harbour Island to handle crowd control and any "media frenzy" that might occur. "We just wanted him off the island," says Moss. A nurse came to check out the scratches on Colt's legs and feet while investigators gathered around. They hoped that, like many fugitives, Colt might be so relieved it was all over and that he'd survived, that he'd have loose lips.

Colt remained eerily calm and cool, though. He spoke politely to the officers but was careful not to implicate himself. "He was very evasive," says Moss. The cops offered him food and drink: "No, I'm good," he said. They brought out a photo of Spider Miller's Cessna 400 nose down in the Great Abaco muck and asked Colt about it. "I never saw that plane before in my life," he said. The officers laughed and began bantering, trying to get Colt to respond to some good cop–good cop.

"How you crashed if you a good pilot?" one of them laughed.

"You missed the runway, eh? You overshoot?"

One of the cops was a licensed pilot who tried flattery. "He didn't crash . . . He did a good job. He meant to put it there. That plane didn't break up, it didn't explode . . . I couldn't even do better myself with plenty years of experience."

The other cops added the chorus, saying it'd been an excellent job. One said, "He land in the mud . . . That mud saved his neck."

Colt laughed along with the police, but got testy when he noticed an officer was filming the interview on a cell phone. "Get that camera out of my face," he said.

"Where you get that gun?" an officer asked him.

"I don't remember," said Colt.

IN A SEPARATE ROOM, detectives opened Colt's backpack and laid out the contents. Along with a black nylon shaving kit, there were Ziplocs that had protected his important papers. These were the things he'd carried with him thousands of miles across the country, through all the campsites and chases and midnight boat crossings.

Inside one plastic bag was a series of drawings. Colt had been designing his fleet of future aircraft. One depicted an ultramodern helicopter with an enclosed tail rotor. Another showed a single-propeller plane on floats—larger than a Beaver and with similar lines to a Pilatus, it looked like a melding of the two planes in Chuck Stewart's hangar, where Colt had spent so much time. Another craft was a twin-tailed wonder, a civilian spacecraft. The drawings showed a definite design flair. And all of the aircraft were marked with the name of Colt's dream company: Phoenix Aerospace.

In the other Ziploc was Colt's fifth-grade class picture from Elger Bay Elementary School along with his fifth-grade headshot. The only other paper he carried all this way was the certificate from the Boy Scouts of America awarding him the rank of Wolf Scout.

The Bahamian police claim that when they captured him, Colt had less than $40 in cash and no credit cards on him. By my accounting, though, Colt could have been carrying well over $20,000, most likely in a Ziploc. The money has never been reported found.

SHORTLY AFTER DAYBREAK, CHIEF Inspector Moss grabbed his snorkel gear and went back out to the sandbar. Now high tide, he estimated it was about ten feet deep at the spot where Colt had gotten stuck—way more depth than the Intrepid needed to cross safely. Moss quickly found a black zippered case that held an Apple laptop. Then he spotted a handheld GPS, and Colt's iPod with earbuds still attached. It took him fifteen minutes to locate the pistol, a black-and-chrome .38 caliber Walther PPK with the serial number filed off.

The Walther looks cool and, of course, has the "Bond, James Bond" cachet, but it definitely would not be the first choice for an experienced gunslinger headed to the Bahamas. Colt had spent the last week in the sand and muck and moist salty air. A Walther PPK, if not kept fastidiously clean in that kind of harsh environment, is prone to extractor failures.

Colt fired one round as the police approached. In a semiauto like the Walther, the force from one shot ejects the spent shell casing while a spring in the clip automatically loads the next round. Simply pull the trigger again and another round will fire.

When Colt fired his first shot, though, the shell casing never ejected, and the next round didn't chamber. He could have pulled the trigger again, whether aiming into the sky, at the police, or at his own head, but until he manually cleared that spent shell, the gun wouldn't have fired.

There were two live rounds left in the clip, both hollow points.

KENNY WENT OVER TO the Briland police station later that morning to give his statement. He sat down in a chair next to Colt, who, he said, looked a little worse for wear from his Bahamian visit. "Oh, he had skin look like checkers from mosquitoes! He had a lot of bits in him!" As Kenny sat there, a nurse came to check on Colt again. "The nurse was asking him if he was all right, if he feel any pain, and he said, 'No pain, I'm okay.' He was extremely mannerly, respectful, humble. He didn't give no aggressive answers like I seen some criminals when I was livin' in New York." Kenny laughs. "But he wasn't giving too much information!"

Colt did eventually loosen up enough to tell the Bahamian police what his future plans were—no crime in just thinking about it. Like he'd told Mauris, Colt said his next stop was Cuba, where the American authorities wouldn't be able to follow him. Once he lost them, he said he planned to move on to the Turks and Caicos Islands because his research showed they had very few cops.

It wasn't a bad plan, but it had some problems. A number of U.S. citizens have gone to Cuba to stay out of the reach of American courts. However, they tend to bring very large amounts of cash with them to smooth their way, like Robert Vesco, or else they're high-profile asylum seekers, like Black Panthers Huey Newton and Eldridge Cleaver.

Colt may have been packing some new Spanish vocabulary words, but he didn't mention any plans to officially seek asylum. His $20,000-plus— if he had it—would have gone a long way in a country where doctors earn less than $50 a month. Even if he made it to the island without getting shot down or blown out of the water, though, the odds of a six-foot-five gringo fading anonymously into the Cuban countryside were slim. The Cuban people are very open and friendly, though, so if he arrived with enough greenbacks that he didn't have to steal to feed himself, and kept a big smile on his face, Colt might have been okay.

It would have been bad timing, though, to make the Turks and Caicos a long-term stop on his Caribbean tour. The British had recently kicked out a crooked premier there who'd been putting the banana back in the concept of a banana republic. The Brits reinstituted direct rule from Westminster and had launched a law-and-order campaign to keep the islands safe for tax evaders and tourists, the two legs of the Turks and Caicos economy.

Colt would have most likely had a similar experience in the Turks as he'd had in the Bahamas. If he'd been able to stay at large for a couple more months, he'd be heading into the Caribbean's September swelter season when the air becomes a sopping, oppressive stew. A week in that late-summer tropical humidity—caked with salt sweat and covered in no-see-um bites, with fine sand invading every orifice—is enough to force a nun into taking a bird bath in a baptismal font. If Colt couldn't find an air-conditioned hideaway, he'd be begging to get back to the cool Northwest.

A TEAM OF OFFICERS arrived from Nassau and took charge of Colt. They wrapped a heavy chain around his ankles and closed it tight with padlocks. And Colt finally got the bulletproof vest Pam wanted him to wear. Then they hustled him—still barefoot—onto a ferry boat and to the North Eleuthera Airport where an RBPF plane waited.

OVER AT PETAGAY'S, THE instant the service came back on, our phones lit up with the news Colt had been caught. On the Romora dock, I met

Kenny, Mauris, and police officers who were on the boat that caught him. Going through the events of the entire night moment by moment with them, there was only one spot of disagreement: how Colt got out to the Intrepid. Both Kenny and an American boater who claims he saw Colt as he motored away say that he waded in from the shore and swam beneath the dock out to the boat. Chief Inspector Moss, though, noted that Colt's T-shirt and shorts were "perfectly dry" when they captured him, meaning he must have simply—and once again, audaciously—ninja'd his way past all the cops and down 275 yards of dock to where the Intrepid was tied up.

At the Intrepid that morning, one of the policemen was watching the owner tie the boat alongside its mothership, *Lady BJ*. The owner told the cop he wished they'd shot "the little shit" instead of his outboards.

I asked the officer if Colt had ever threatened to shoot back at them.

"At one point, yeah," he said. "I guess when we opened fire he sorta changed his mind."

When I looked closely at the Intrepid, I spotted drops of blood on the rod holder and the driver's seat. Kenny, standing next to me, said that Colt had not been hit by any bullets or pellets. "He was all torn apart with trees and briars from coming through the bush and running on the rocks with his bare feet."

It was, once again, almost inconceivable that Colt wasn't seriously injured or dead. Black night, jerking spotlights, the chase boat rocking as police jostled into firing position, Colt's boat lurching along the sandbar, Colt actually firing a shot, then refusing to drop his gun . . . then somehow not getting hit by a stray, a ricochet, or one of the shots that went straight toward the spot where he'd been standing.

"You can see on the boat that they did fire a shot to hit him!" Kenny said. "But God put it so it was not for him."

The RBPF say they didn't shoot at Colt. When I press Chief Inspector Moss, he admits that Colt gave his men more than enough excuse to fire at him instead of the boat engines. Moss credits the "experience, professionalism, maturity, and discipline" of the officers on the boat as to why Colt came out of it alive . . . along with "divine intervention."

Kenny agrees with the last part. "The Lord put it so Bandit come runnin' to me," he says. "He needed to get a blessing to make sure he don't die that night."

29

Escorted by Bahamian police with assault rifles, Colt deplaned in Nassau. They marched him barefoot across the tarmac for the first of many perp walks. The asphalt was hot enough to feel through my shoes, but it didn't seem to bother Colt. He maintained his head-down posture, though it wasn't in disgrace, just disdain for "the paparazzi."

Catching a fugitive that the FBI, Homeland Security, Canadian Mounties, and a host of local departments hadn't been able to get their cuffs on was a heroic moment for the oft-maligned RBPF, and they wanted to make the most of it. The fourth time they paraded the shackled Barefoot Bandit for the cameras within twelve hours, Colt appealed to his guards, "Come on, let's make this one fast."

I expected Colt to be shipped back to the United States as fast as possible after the Bahamian police got to show him off. There was an impressive list of crimes the Bahamians could nail him with: at least five burglaries, three boat thefts, a car theft, and, most serious, possession of a loaded gun during a crime. But no way they would. The Bahamian authorities were in a tough spot, politically. There's only one prison in the country, the notorious Fox Hill, which doesn't make it into tourist brochures and is rarely mentioned by locals without a shudder. Past inmates talk of its maximum-security block as an overcrowded, HIV- and TB-infested, shit-and-sweat-stinking hellhole lorded over by abusive guards. Along with U.S. State Department and Amnesty International condemnations, almost all Bahamian citizens themselves feel the conditions at the jail are deplorable.

Recent reports say that all convicted prisoners are initially sent to the (mad) Max unit as a means of "breaking them in" to prison life. With all the press attention focused on Colt, sticking him in Fox Hill would turn the Bahamians' moment of glory into an embarrassing exposé. While many arrestees go to Fox Hill just to await trial, Colt was instead held at the RBPF's Central Detectives Unit, a menacing enough government-issue stained-concrete building.

Colt tried to phone his mom, but couldn't get through. So he made a tearful call to his aunt Sandy.

BAHAMIAN LAW ENFORCEMENT BRASS HELD a press conference about Colt that Sunday . . . then realized that not all the international media had arrived in Nassau yet, so they scheduled a repeat for Monday.

At the E Street Barracks, Commissioner of Police Ellison Greenslade announced that the investigation was progressing, that the firearm charges against Colt were "very serious," and that they looked forward to proffering charges very soon. I kept waiting for the punch line: ". . . but, we're going to turn him over to our good friends in the U.S.A. tomorrow." But it never came.

"He has committed criminal offenses in the Bahamas," said Greenslade. "Our laws are very clear . . . A number of people have made legitimate claims to the police department and we will bring charges where they are necessary to the satisfaction of those victims."

The commissioner himself said he'd already interviewed his famous prisoner. He was clearly smitten. He smiled when asked about the Bandit. "Colton is obviously a very intelligent young man . . . level of diction, semantics . . . He gives a good account of himself. He's quite a stand-up guy, quite a mature young man."

Greenslade said that Colt understood his rights and was being afforded due process. Also that he was very calm, he "understood the realities of the situation he was in," and had given them no problems since the capture.

On Monday, the U.S. federal authorities started making noises that inferred it could be a long time—months—before the fugitive was repatriated.

Colt dominated the local Bahamian news just as he'd become a front-page and top-of-the-newscast story across the United States. Everyone was fascinated with the kid determined to fly no matter what. A seventy-two-year-old Bahamian who pumped me for every detail taught me a local expression I'd never heard before: after each plane crash or SWAT chase I recounted, he exclaimed, "Mutha Blue!"

ON TUESDAY, A SUNNY, hot, and humid afternoon, the entire press corps gathered outside the Bahamas' courts complex. A line of metal barricades held back a large, mostly local crowd of the curious that included a few very vocal Bahamian Colt supporters. In front of the barriers posed the RBPF's top officers, all spit-shined and smiling. RBDF soldiers and police tactical units patrolled the area along with a couple of oversize guys packing serious weaponry and scary eyes, which were all you could see because their heads were covered with black balaclavas—Colt would finally get to meet some real ninjas.

The police orchestrated everything so that the media could capture another all-important perp walk. I got a quizzical look from the RBPF press officer when I repeatedly told her I didn't care about seeing the show, but that I'd really like to get inside the courtroom. She finally waved me across the barricade.

There are a couple old-school English-style courts in Nassau, impressive buildings, and I'd expected Colt to appear in one of them. Instead, we were led upstairs into a tiny, dimly lit workaday courtroom used for minor cases. It was hard to tell what this meant until a woman, one of about eight Bahamians in the small gallery, leaned over and whispered to me that she recognized the man sitting at the prosecution table as an immigration officer. Aha. Colt definitely wasn't going to Fox Hill.

Suddenly we heard a muffled commotion outside. The crowd began yelling and cheering as Colt—in chains and surrounded by a cordon of cops—was baby-stepped down the street. He bent low at the waist to avoid the eyes of all the cameras, but some bystanders mistook it for shame and a few began shouting encouragement: "Hold ya' head up, boy!" "You a hero, dog!" "Tell it to the world!"

Finally, he was led into the courtroom. In deference to the formality of the court, Colt wasn't barefoot. Not that he wore dress shoes—they'd given him a pair of bobo-white sneakers but had confiscated the laces. The huge tongues flopped out absurdly. Colt had on a bulletproof vest over a white T-shirt and black baggies. With no cameras allowed in the courtroom, he walked upright, though he kept his eyes down as an officer escorted him to the defendant's dock about ten feet from where I sat.

After staring at Colt's goofy self-portrait for the last ten months trying to decipher what was behind that strange expression, I was a little surprised that he was actually a good-looking kid. Even after the circus outside under the hot sun, he also appeared remarkably calm and cool.

All rose as Chief Magistrate Roger Gomez entered and took his place on the bench below a small Bahamian coat of arms, with its conch shell, blazing sun, leaping marlin, and pink flamingo.

Gomez, a large man with a bright streak of gray like a paint splash in his black hair, began speaking very softly. Everyone in the gallery leaned forward, straining to catch the words.

"Colton Harris-Moore, please stand." Colt stood up straight, taller than anyone else in the room. He looked directly at the judge.

"Colton Harris-Moore, you are charged contrary to section 19-1 and 2 of the immigration act . . . You were found in Harbor Island, Eleuthera, in the Commonwealth of the Bahamas, having landed from a destination outside of the Bahamas without legally going through immigration. Do you understand the charge?"

"Yes, Judge," Colt replied in a deep voice.

"How do you plead to the charge—"

Before the judge could finish his sentence, Colt jumped in and said, "Guilty."

The judge calmly finished, ". . . guilty or not guilty?"

"Guilty," Colt repeated.

The immigration officer testified that he'd checked the files and there was no official record of Colton Harris-Moore arriving in the Bahamas and presenting his passport.

Colt's attorney was Monique Gomez, the judge's niece, who'd been retained by the same person back in Washington State who offered Colt

$50,000 to turn himself in when he began his summer road trip. Colton, she told the judge, admitted that he "swam to the Bahamas" sometime in June, but neglected to bring along a passport. She said that he wished to save the court the trouble of a trial and thus was pleading guilty.

The judge shuffled some papers and seemed a bit reticent to speak. Finally Colt was asked to stand again. He stood and looked down at his marshmallow-like shoes and shuffled his feet awkwardly.

"Colton Harris-Moore," began Chief Magistrate Gomez, "having pleaded guilty to the charge of illegal landing, and in consideration of you saving the court's time by pleading guilty to the charge, we impose a fine of three hundred dollars or three months in prison . . . and immediate deportation is recommended."

The clerk immediately said, "All rise," and the judge bolted out a side door.

THAT WAS IT. COURT dismissed. Everyone began to shuffle past, but I stayed put, watching the side of Colt's face, hoping for a look at his eyes to get a read of what he was thinking and feeling. He hadn't turned toward the gallery throughout the entire proceedings. A detective walked up and reached for Colt's hands to redo his cuffs. At that point, Colt took a quick sideways glance around the room. I was staring intently, looking for fear, relief, sadness, despair . . . The last thing I expected to see was recognition. Colt looked at me and suddenly broke into a huge smile.

I involuntarily broke into one of my own.

I DIDN'T KNOW WHAT Colt saw other than an unexpected familiar face. Later I'd wonder if he recognized me just from photos on the Internet or if he'd gotten close enough to see me back home in the Northwest. At this moment in the courtroom, though, all I saw was a big, genuine smile from a kid in bad circumstances.

Colt looked down as the detective pulled his arms around and re-cuffed one of his wrists. Then Colt looked up at me again, smiling and giving a nod that seemed to acknowledge, maybe appreciate, that I'd come this far.

Colt glanced down again, then looked back with one more grin, this one accompanied by a sly little head shake that unmistakably said, "What a ride, eh?"

————

That third smile was noticed by the detective clamping on Colt's cuffs. He glared at me, then barked at Colt, asking twice, "Him man your friend?" I couldn't hear what Colt answered, but I started out the door before I found myself with my own immigration problem. A TV producer in the room had also noticed, and when it was reported, some folks put that together with the coincidence of my Bahamas background and blog posts in order to speculate that I'd been doing some travel consulting for Colt. Obviously not true.

I tried to linger in the courthouse hallway to get close enough to talk to Colt, but the larger of the two ninjas persuaded me to move along. I did manage to hold against the tide near the outside door, though, and asked Colt if he was okay. He'd already gone into his anti-paparazzi bow, but lifted his face and said, "Yeah." A few steps past me, he entered the gauntlet, with reporters shouting questions, including repeatedly asking if he had any messages for his mother. Colt told them to "go to hell."

The RBPF then marched Colt on what must be a world-record perp walk from the court building, through a shopping center, then up the street to a police station. The American authorities announced again that it might take a long time to get Colt back to the States. But as expected, he was in Miami later that afternoon.

The Bahamian government had played it smart. Their police force received well-deserved praise and worldwide recognition for capturing Colt without anyone getting hurt. The decision to not charge him caused some political blowback, however, with the leader of the opposition calling it "a national disgrace," and some editorial commenters saying it proved there was a double standard, that a Bahamian citizen could not have fired a shot from a stolen boat and received only a small fine. A fine that, by the way, was also paid for by the mysterious Washington benefactor who'd offered the $50,000.

PART 6

GAME OVER

30

C olt's next flight was aboard the U.S. Marshall's *Con Air*. The Feds transported him back to Washington State and placed him in solitary confinement at the SeaTac Federal Detention Center. After waiving his Sixth Amendment right to a speedy trial, Colt's attorneys John Henry Browne and Emma Scanlon began an attempt to herd cats in the form of a dozen prosecutors representing a multitude of victims and politically beholden to the affected communities. Browne's strategy was to create a "global" plea deal for Colt that wrapped all the federal and state charges into one package.

Meanwhile, it was an election year. In Island County, Mark Brown ran unopposed and won his second term as sheriff—though there was at least one write-in vote for Colton Harris-Moore. Since 2008, budget problems have forced the Island County sheriff's office to ax a quarter of its deputies. At the same time, the money crunch also hurt the county's ability to do anything with at-risk youth other than lock them up. According to prosecutor Greg Banks, new evidence-based interdiction programs had been enjoying "great success at reducing the amount of juvenile crime and incarceration" in the county. However, he says, the best of these programs were being cut due to budget.

Down on Camano, Colt's mom, Pam Kohler, remained in the public eye by calling local reporters and radio programs and pumping out quotes. After the tsunami hit Japan in March 2011, she went on a radio show to say that Colt could fly over relief supplies. On Seattle's *Ron and Don Show*, she complained that someone had stolen her IF YOU GO PAST THIS

SIGN YOU WILL BE SHOT sign. Ron, speaking for all the listeners howling at their radios, said to her, "These kids that steal things, I can't stand them."

THROUGH HIS ATTORNEYS AND in messages passed to friends on the outside, Colt repeatedly said he felt bad for his victims, and even that he regretted hurting or killing the planes. Colt's victims responded to this in various ways. The owners of the three planes Colt "killed" each had significant out-of-pocket financial losses after insurance settlements. Seattle radio personality Bob Rivers, however, says he isn't holding a grudge.

"I was irresponsible in my youth, and honestly didn't get my shit together until I was thirty-three, so I can empathize with a young guy who made bad decisions," said Rivers. "He also had a tough upbringing. On the other hand, in my charity work I've seen kids whose disadvantages make Colton's childhood look like a cakewalk—and some of them his age are studying to be doctors. I'm glad Colton was caught, and he needs to pay his dues, but I hope he finds a way to have a good future."

In Indiana, Spider Miller, whose plane Colt took to the Bahamas, said sending Colt to jail for a long time wouldn't do Colt or the victims any good. He wished the kid could instead be sentenced to something more constructive, "like having to wash a lot of airplanes."

Out in Idaho, though, former attorney Pat Gardiner thought whatever prison sentence they gave Colt wouldn't be long enough. When asked by prosecutors to submit a victim impact statement, Gardiner wrote that "Colton Harris-Moore represents a severe danger to the public and will most likely revert to his old ways as soon as he's released."

One person who knows Colt well, and passionately felt he deserved a break, is Bev Davis. Bev's faith in Colt was sorely tested during those strange episodes at the trailer back when he was fourteen, and then again later when she learned he'd been carrying a gun while on the lam. She feared Colt's run would end tragically. "I'm astounded, given his life, that he didn't lash out and really hurt someone—or commit suicide. That showed real strength of character."

When Colt was captured, Bev again reached out a caring hand, and he responded. They began communicating regularly by phone and email. "I'm amazed at the change in him," she says. "At how much more mature he is than when I last saw him. He truly understands the impact of his actions, and he's sincerely sorry for the damage he's caused, especially to the people of Orcas and Camano Islands."

Bev says that Colt has adapted to prison life fairly well. "But that's not a big surprise, since he's already had a lot of practice at dysfunction, discomfort, pain, and fear in his young life. He's an extraordinary person, and I know in my heart that when he gets out he will be okay and he'll lead a productive life—like the one he would have had if his circumstances had been different." Bev says that she's only one of many who are willing to help Colt transition back into society. Already, friends have pledged to pay for special counseling while he's in prison, and for college when he gets out.

Colt says that when he's released, he wants to study aeronautical engineering, and hopes to someday launch that aircraft design company.

COLT'S GLOBAL PLEA PROVED unworkable, so the charges were split into two batches. On Friday, June 17, 2011, he pleaded guilty to seven federal charges including bank burglary for the Islanders Bank attempt on Orcas; two counts of interstate transport of a stolen aircraft for the Idaho and Indiana plane thefts; foreign transport of a stolen firearm for carrying a .32 pistol across the Canadian border; interstate transport of a stolen vessel for his Columbia River crossing; and piloting an aircraft without a valid airman's certificate for the Anacortes-to-Orcas Island flight during the Winter Olympics.

As part of the same plea, Colt admitted responsibility for more than twenty-five other crimes committed outside Washington State during his cross-country run, from stealing eyeglasses to Escalades, pistols to pleasure boats, to "threatening to inflict physical harm" on Kelly Kneifl in his South Dakota basement. The sentencing recommendation calls for sixty-three to seventy-eight months in prison plus additional time on probation. The plea also stated that the monetary loss attributable to just these federal and state crimes was "not less than $1,409,438." Of that, Colt agreed to pay $959,438 in restitution to the victims.

As for how a high school dropout could ever begin to pay that kind of restitution in just a single lifetime, a full quarter of the document's twenty-eight pages dealt solely with Colt's ability to tell or sell his story. U.S. Attorney

Jenny Durkin said that the agreement ensured that Colt would never personally make a dime off his crimes. Even once he's paid back the victims in full, Colt agrees to forfeit to the government any money he earns from anything related to his crimes or tagged "Barefoot Bandit," whether movies, books, commercial endorsements, video games, Happy Meal toys, or toe rings. With so many kids looking at Colt as a hero, the prosecutors wanted to send a clear "crime doesn't pay" message to all of his fans, followers, and potential imitators.

All during his run, even as he became more and more famous and appeared to court the media attention, Colt steadfastly maintained that he would never tell his story. He finally agreed to sell his life rights only once the reality of restitution set in. Normally, crime victims receive piddly payments stretched over many years. Signing away his story rights, difficult as it was for Colt, enables his victims to recoup their losses quickly if a movie gets made. It was also a valuable bargaining chip in the overall plea deal, and could allow him to walk out of jail debt-free as opposed to having his paychecks docked for the rest of his life. As to signing away the money itself, Colt says that was the easy part because he never wanted himself or anyone in his family to make anything off his story.

Shortly after the federal plea was filed, Colt entered into a film contract with 20th Century Fox, which had already optioned this book. If cameras start rolling, more than $1 million will go to Colt's victims. Even with the movie deal, though, there are parts of his story that Colt refuses to tell. While he admits that he occasionally met and even stayed with friends at times during his run, Colt is never going to name them.

TALK OF THE MOVIE deal again brought up the phenomena of Colt's large number of fans. Throughout his run, many commentators seemed to take the idea of people rooting for the outlaw Colt as a sign of the apocalypse. Colt himself said he didn't understand and recoils at the attention— seeing no disconnect between feeling that way and the facts of him signing notes "The Barefoot Bandit," drawing thirty-nine footprints on the floor of a burglarized grocery store, repeatedly committing high-profile airplane thefts, and telling friends and even new acquaintances to watch for him on the news. The only real surprise, however, is that anyone, including Colt, could claim they're shocked that he attracted so much notice.

The Great Recession was as fertile a ground for Colton Harris-Moore to emerge as an outlaw hero as the Great Depression was for John Dillinger. The Internet and social networks simply ensured that Colt became a world-famous outlaw at warp speed compared to all those who'd gone before him.

Even though Dillinger and his gang went on a tear across the country that left a dozen dead—including cops and bystanders—people rallied to him just as they would seventy-five years later to Colt, who was much, much safer to root for because he hadn't physically hurt anyone. In *Dillinger's Wild Ride*, Elliot Gorn quotes people of the gunslinger's day venting in ways remarkably similar to Colt's Facebook defenders about what they saw as a corrupt system rigged against the common man. "If folks had jobs and could feed themselves, if government protected citizens from the banks that preyed on them . . . they wouldn't make heroes of men like Dillinger."

According to professor Graham Seal, author of *The Outlaw Legend* and one of the world's foremost authorities on outlaws both historical and in folklore, to break into the pantheon of great outlaw heroes, the person must go beyond common criminality. "He needs a few actual or mythical characteristics, such as the ability to elude capture . . . and he needs a bit of style." Colt had all that, plus a sense of humor, which always helps.

Americans like to believe that our national character still includes a little bit of the frontier outlaw. And compared to most outlaws, Colt was easy to get behind. He was a clean-cut rural kid who was nonconfrontational and hadn't killed anyone yet. The most repeated plea on his Facebook pages was "Don't hurt anyone!"

In all outlaw stories, though, the victims are forgotten. They get in the way of the fun, and the outlaw's fans prefer they'd just exist in the background with their hands in the air. Stopping to look at them slows down the tale and risks impugning the character of the sympathetic bandit. In Colt's case, some of his supporters caricatured and dehumanized the victims simply as "rich people" and thus somehow deserving of having their stuff and their security stolen. The fact that Colt also stole from middle-class folks and those running mom-and-pop businesses was an inconvenience best ignored.

The last refuge was the "So what? They're insured," rationalization, obviously made by those who'd never had to deal with an "insured" loss.

ON DECEMBER 16, 2011, Colt stepped into an Island County courtroom to face sentencing for thirty-two Washington State charges. Judge Vicki Churchill, the same judge who sentenced Colt in 2007, presided. Colt's attorneys filed a mitigation package that presented a narrative of Colt's early years. It was the most damning report yet of his mother's "toxic presence that shaped his childhood." Much of it was in Colt's own words: "My mom is also a heavy alcoholic . . . No question that her entire life, house, family and friend relationships have been ravaged by her alcoholism." Colt talked about Gordy Moore, too, recalling an argument in the trailer about child support payments, when Gordy "literally picked my mom up and threw her across the room," the event that Colt says Pam claims is when she broke her back.

A large part of the defense's argument for granting Colt leniency was based on the assertion by the psychiatrist Dr. Richard Adler: that Colt suffers from Fetal Alcohol Spectrum Disorders. The diagnosis was based on numerous neuropsychological tests and on the testimony of Pam Kohler's brother, Ed Coaker. Coaker said of Pam, "When Pam drinks one beer she gets mean, and when she drinks two beers she wants to fight. But, Pam drinks twenty beers . . . she would drink until she couldn't hardly walk." Coaker admitted to drinking with Pam while she was carrying Colt and claimed "her pregnancy didn't affect her drinking whatsoever."

The other revelation from Ed Coaker was his claim that Pam had met at least two of the men who shared the trailer with her and Colt, including Bill Kohler, through prison pen-pal programs.

The mitigation report also took the state CPS system and Stanwood-Camano school district to task for letting Colt "fall through the cracks." Dr. Adler notes that "All of the CPS investigations were closed in short order, ironically due to mother's lack of cooperation."

Colt says he loves his mother and wants her to be happy. Her alcoholism, though, "is the number one, and as far as I am concerned, the only problem my mom has that prevented a friendship with me." As of press time, Colt has been in Seattle for seventeen months, but has not yet seen Pam.

. . . .

ON THE WASHINGTON STATE side of things, Greg Banks from Island County and Randy Gaylord from San Juan County told the judge that they'd taken Colt's rough childhood and his nonviolence into account in recommending that she give him the high end of the sentencing range: nine years and eight months.

After the prosecution and defense had finished their presentations, Judge Churchill recessed for twenty minutes then came back into court and made a remarkable speech:

> I think this case is a tragedy in many ways, but it's also a triumph of the human spirit. I sympathize with the defendant due to the terrible upbringing he had. As one investigator indicated, "it was a mind-numbing absence of hope." It was a tragedy he had to steal food . . . to endure the taunts and jeers of classmates . . . that he had an alcoholic and abusive mother . . . We can all shake our heads and wonder how did this all happen, and more importantly, how can we keep it from happening to another child?

Judge Churchill said that in reviewing Colton's upbringing and the psychological reports of his mental health issues, "I was struck that I could have been reading the history of a mass murderer . . . I could have been reading about a drug-addicted, alcoholic, abusive young man who followed in the path of his mother. Yet I was not reading that story. That is the triumph of Colton Harris-Moore. He has survived."

Sitting in the courtroom, it felt like the judge was about to let Colt walk out a free man or maybe give him a medal. But there came a "nevertheless . . ." Judge Churchill said she was elected to uphold the law, was bound by the state's sentencing reform act, and needed to protect the public. She acknowledged that "Mr. Harris-Moore has an extensive criminal history, and a high offender score." She said, though, that because she felt he was remorseful, contrite, and because he was paying full restitution—"something that is unique in cases like this"—she would give Colt the minimum sentence allowed within the standard range: seven years and three months. She ended with, "I wish him well."

Colt, who was ready to accept the max, was happy and relieved with the judgment. Churchill tacked on the $292,167 in restitution owed to the San Juan and Island County victims, and Colt was taken away.

Colt's federal and state sentences will run concurrent, but the state clock does not begin counting down until he turns twenty-one on March 22, 2012. With time off for good behavior, he could be stepping out of a Washington State prison just after his twenty-sixth birthday.

SANDI, MURPHY, AND I remain perched on Raven Ridge, our mossy little patch of Northwest paradise. I think of Colt every night as I go around and check the cabin doors. It's not a happy chore. Ironically, Colt says he chose to come to Orcas Island mainly for the same reason we did: because it's such a peaceful, beautiful place. Colt even says he spent most of his time here in Deer Harbor, but says that while he did see me a number of times, he was not the one we heard under the cabin. Murphy, for one, is not convinced.

After piecing together what I know of Colt's entire life, though, there's no anger, just frustration and sadness. I feel both for the victims that are still affected, and also for Colt due to the past events that were out of his control coupled with his own bad choices that will result in him spending at least six and a half years behind bars. But I also have hope for his future. I realize now that Colt's big smiles in the Bahamas were also a sign of his remarkable resiliency.

Colt appears to have sloughed off his negative identity as an alienated bad boy and now sees himself as a student. It's certainly better that his energies are going toward planning for college instead of plotting helicopter attacks on Costco.

Colt reached out through a friend to say that although he doesn't like the idea of the book and movie about him because he thinks it will make it harder to eventually melt into anonymity and live that "normal" life he so craves, he doesn't hold it against me. He also said that he hopes we can go kayaking or hiking on Turtleback Mountain together when he gets out.

I look forward to that. I'm just glad he didn't ask me to go flying.

Acknowledgments

Other than the parts of this story that I personally witnessed, this book is based on reporting in the form of hundreds of interviews and reviewing reams of legal documents. It would be a much poorer telling if I did not have the generous help and cooperation of so many sources whose personal stories brought this tale to life. A number of people I spoke with requested anonymity and thus unfortunately can't be thanked here by name. Some were afraid of losing their jobs; others were concerned for their personal safety. I also disguised the names of several crime victims who requested I do so for privacy reasons. In every use of an anonymous source, I checked details against police and court records as well as secondary sources wherever possible.

To set the scene on Camano Island and to recreate Colt's early life, I relied on interviews with: Bev and Geof Davis; Bill, Doreen, and Megan Wagner; Pam Kohler; Jack "Skeeter Daddle" Archibald and his wife, author Karen Prasse; Josh Flickner; Joel Bradfield; Bonnie Bryand and her son, Kory; Harley Davidson Ironwing; Anne Pitser; Jim Pettyjohn; Helen Owens; Kara Weber; Shannon Kirby; Maxine Kostelyk; Christa Postma; Carol Star; Josh Richardson; Mike Bulmer; Patty Morgan; Brandi Blackford; Leslie Hawthorne; Glen Kramer; and Jacquie Staggs.

Early on in my research, I got a call from what I thought was the ghost of Walter Brennan. It turned out to be a man named Pete Poeschel. Pete's call led to a mysterious mainland meeting where he introduced me to an important source. Thanks, Pete, you've got a good heart and a great laugh. Thanks, too, to Donna Poeschel.

I received terrific support from my friends and neighbors on beautiful Orcas Island. The one upside to having the crime wave hit here is that I got to meet even more of the nice folks who call Orcas home. Special thanks to those who contributed their personal stories and expertise: Bob Rivers; Kyle Ater and Cedra Gutschmidt; Belinda Landon and Marion Rathbone; Teri Williams and Jay Fowler; Jack Cadden; Jeremy Trumble; Ryan Carpenter; Cory Wiscomb and his 2010 senior class at Orcas High—Go Vikings!; flyboys Bill Anders, Eric Gourley, Grant Schumaker, and Geoff Schussler; flygirl Bea Von Tobel; John Gorton; Jason Linnes; Jay Longfellow; Rosemary Hennessy and Fred Vinson; Maggie Vinson; Henry and Donna McNeil; Mike and Matt Stohlmeir; Dick Greaves; Babs Briggs; Colleen Armstrong; Kevin and Carol McCoy; Mark Morris and the Orcas Craic'ers; Scott Lancaster; and Suzanne Lyons. Over on Lopez Island, thanks to Kim and Michelle Smith, and Stephanie Dallas and Krista Mann.

Current and former law enforcement officers and prosecutors from more than a dozen local, state, federal, and international departments and agencies contributed to this book—some willingly and graciously, others through the Freedom of Information Act. Thanks to Island County Sheriff's Office detective Ed Wallace, former ICSO lieutenant Chris Ellis, and Island County prosecutor Greg Banks. In San Juan County, thanks to former sheriff Bill Cumming, current sheriff Rob Nou, county prosecutor Randy Gaylord, and public records officer Stan Matthews. Ray Clever, Stu Smith, and Frank Friel are ex-cops with more stories between them than the Library of Congress, and each served as a great resource. Thanks also to Hancock County, Illinois, sheriff John Jefferson; Warrenton, Oregon, police chief Mathew Workman; Clackamas County, Oregon, detective Jim Slovnik; the Royal Bahamian Police Force's chief inspector Roston Moss and sergeant Chrislyn Skippings; and FBI special agent Linwood Smith.

On the other side of the law-and-order ledger: Thanks to defense attorney John Henry Brown, private eye Shauna Snyder, defense attorney Rachel Miyoshi, and attorney Jim Johansen.

I was able to detail Colt's cross-country run only with the help of: Kelly Kneifl, Jim McLaughlin, Brad Hernke, Pat Gardiner, Homer Woolslayer, Larry Johnson, Shane Vande Vort, Graham Goad, Alan Daniels, Gary Taylor, Mike Vadeboncoeur, Rachel Tiede, John "Spider" Miller, Mary Beaird, Tom Francis, Steve Black, Michael Isaacs, Bruce Payton, Gary Carlson, Ray Jilek, Rich Rasmussen, and Mike Rocha.

Out of my many, many trips to the Bahamas over the last thirty years, following Colt there was one of the strangest. All t'anks to Petagay Hartman for playing Nancy Drew to my Scooby Doo, and for providing a soft couch and fresh mangoes. Thanks also to Kenny Strachan, Mauris Jonassaint, Denaldo Bain, Tim Roberts, Johnny Roberts and Nippers, George "Barefoot Man" Nowak, Kay Politano, Ruthie Key, Alistair Macdonald, and Ricky Ricardo.

A select group of world-class experts generously offered their time and vast knowledge to educate me on a range of topics from childhood development to the juvenile justice system to the psychological underpinnings of our fascination with outlaws. Thanks to judge Bobbe Bridge, who's doing amazing, important work at her Center for Children and Youth Justice; Dr. Delton Young; Dr. Eric Trupin; Dr. Edwin Camiel; Sandi Burt; Dr. Rayner Hernit; and professor Graham Seal.

Amid the often competitive and insecure world of journalism, I warmly appreciate the professional courtesy of CBS producer Paul LaRosa for some significant shares, and the *Seattle Times*' Jennifer Sullivan for a timely phone number.

Author and friend Nikki Jefford was an immense help on this book. While serving as research assistant, she made hundreds of calls to charm interviews and documents out of sources all across the country. Several times she and Seb also talked me into eating food that for some strange reason didn't include meat.

Author and old friend Janet Bohac waded through a very early, very long draft of the manuscript and kindly didn't tell me I should go back to feeding sharks. Her check marks and "You're losing me!" notes were a great help in refining the story's pacing.

Aloha and thanks to Bill and Rita Quinlan. Thank you Lance Black, Matt Reilly, and Rich Green.

A major thank-you to the whole team at *Outside*, especially Mary Turner and Chris Keyes, who were adventurous enough to recognize the importance of this story way before it made headlines.

In the dizzying atmosphere of today's publishing industry, I'm very fortunate to have Joe Veltre as my literary agent. Joe shaped my book proposal and then helped me make a very tough decision during negotiations by asking the immortal question: "What would Colt do?"

I'm supremely grateful to Elisabeth Dyssegaard, who not only championed *The Barefoot Bandit* for Hyperion Books but also personally and patiently worked with me, providing invaluable help in taming a wordy, digressive monster of a manuscript. Thanks also to Hyperion's Ellen Archer, Kristin Kiser, Megan Vidulich, Amy Vreeland, Karen Minster, Bryan Christian, Jon Bernstein, Sarah Rucker, and Sam O'Brien.

Finally, eternal thanks and love to my family and friends who saw very little of me for nineteen months but were always ready when I needed a laugh, a drink, a patient ear to rant in, or a companion to go hike the woods. My parents, Bob and Carol Friel, have always been there for me with love and support. Thanks also to Carol and Gary and their wonderful kids, aka my niece and nephew: Meghan, a talented writer and ardent conservationist, and Brendan, a future PGA tour winner/astronaut/meteorologist. A big thank you treat goes to Murphy who dragged me away from the computer and out of the cabin at least once every day, rain or shine. And last, and most, thank you, Sandi, for everything.